Ways of Reading

Third Edition

Praise for the second edition:

> 'Thorough, clear, thought-provoking and stimulating, *Ways of Reading* is the best available introduction to literary studies and the issues connected with reading.'
>
> Jean Jacques Weber, *University Centre Luxembourg*

> '*Ways of Reading* is a valuable and immensely usable book . . . Its range of text samples is admirably wide-ranging and eclectic.'
>
> John McRae, *Language and Literature*

Ways of Reading is a well-established core textbook that provides the reader with the tools to analyse and interpret the meanings of literary and non-literary texts.

Six sections, split into self-contained units with their own activities and notes for further reading, cover:

- basic techniques and problem-solving
- language variation
- attributing meaning
- poetic uses of language
- narrative
- media texts.

This third edition has been substantially revised and redesigned throughout with many fresh examples and exercises. References have been updated, the overall organization of the book has changed and new material has been added to include information on electronic sources and the Internet, plus a completely new unit: Ways of Reading drama analyses plays as a dramatic performance and a dramatic text.

Martin Montgomery is Director of the Scottish Centre for Journalism Studies; **Nigel Fabb** is Professor of Literary Linguistics; and **Tom Furniss** is Senior Lecturer in English Studies, all at the University of Strathclyde. **Alan Durant** is Professor of Communication at Middlesex University, London; and **Sara Mills** is Professor in the Department of English Studies at Sheffield Hallam University. The authors have written and edited numerous books on linguistics, communication studies, study skills, literary theory and cultural studies.

Ways of Reading

Third Edition

Advanced reading skills for students of English literature

Martin Montgomery, Alan Durant, Nigel Fabb, Tom Furniss and Sara Mills

Routledge
Taylor & Francis Group

LONDON AND NEW YORK

First published 1992
by Routledge
Reprinted 2001, 2002, 2003, 2005, 2006
Third edition published 2007
by Routledge
2 Park Square, Milton Park, Abingdon,
Oxon OX14 4RN

Simultaneously published in the USA
and Canada
by Routledge
270 Madison Ave, New York, NY 10016

*Routledge is an imprint of the Taylor &
Francis Group, an informa business*

© 2007 Martin Montgomery, Alan Durant,
Nigel Fabb, Tom Furniss and Sara Mills

Typeset in Times and Futura by
Florence Production Ltd, Stoodleigh, Devon
Printed and bound in Great Britain by
TJ International, Padstow, Cornwall

*British Library Cataloguing in Publication
Data*
A catalogue record for this book is available
from the British Library

*Library of Congress Cataloging in Publication
Data*
A catalogue record for this book has been
applied for

ISBN10: 0–415–34633–9 (hbk)
ISBN10: 0–415–34634–7 (pbk)
ISBN10: 0–203–59711–7 (ebk)

ISBN13: 978–0–415–34633–7 (hbk)
ISBN13: 978–0–415–34634–4 (pbk)
ISBN13: 978–0–203–59711–8 (ebk)

Contents

Section 1 Basic techniques and problem-solving

Section 2 Language variation

Section 3 Attributing meaning

Notes on contributors

Alan Durant is Professor of Communication, Middlesex University, London. His books include *How to Write Essays and Dissertations: A Guide for English Literature Students* (co-written with Nigel Fabb, Pearson, 2006), *Literary Studies in Action* (co-written with Nigel Fabb, Routledge, 1990), *How to Write Essays, Dissertations and Theses in Literary Studies* (co-written with Nigel Fabb, Longman, 1993), *Ezra Pound: Identity in Crisis* (Harvester/Barnes & Noble, 1981) and *Conditions of Music* (Macmillan/SUNY, 1984). With Nigel Fabb and others he edited *The Linguistics of Writing: Arguments between Language and Literature* (Manchester University Press/Routledge, 1987).

Nigel Fabb is Professor of Literary Linguistics in the Department of English Studies at the University of Strathclyde, Glasgow, where he was recently Head of Department. He is an editor of the *Journal of Linguistics*, and the author of five books, including *Linguistics and Literature: Language in the Verbal Arts of the World* (Blackwell, 1997).

Tom Furniss is Senior Lecturer in English Studies at the University of Strathclyde, Glasgow. His books include *Reading Poetry: An Introduction* (2nd edn), co-written with Michael Bath (Longman, 2007).

Sara Mills is Professor in the Department of English Studies at Sheffield Hallam University. Her books include *Feminist Stylistics* (Routledge, 1995), *Discourse* (Routledge, 1997) and *Gender and Politeness* (Cambridge University Press, 2003).

Martin Montgomery is Reader in Literary Linguistics at the University of Strathclyde, Glasgow, where he was head of English Studies. He is now Director of the Scottish Centre for Journalism Studies. He is the author of *An Introduction to Language and Society* (Routledge, 1995) and is a contributor to several books and journals.

Preface to third edition

This third edition of *Ways of Reading* has been substantially revised in the light of developments in the field, in the light of our own experience using the book and in the light of feedback from others, both colleagues and students. References have been updated and fresh examples introduced, a new unit has been added and the overall organization of the book has changed.

The central emphasis of the original book – on reading as an active and reflective process – remains. We continue to treat reading as much more than the simple decipherment of words on the page. Instead, *Ways of Reading* is designed to encourage a critical and analytic engagement with text, one in which readers pose questions and attend to details of form and structure in pursuit of understanding. To enable or facilitate this process we have assembled a set of tools for thinking and reading. Many of these 'tools for reading' amount to particular skills of analysis; and this helps to explain the structure of units, each of which moves from exposition of an approach to its application. In this way, the book is not only reader-centred but also student-centred, treating knowledge as a set of procedures for inquiring about and exploring text as much as a set of pre-constituted facts.

The units are grouped into six sections. Section 1 introduces basic techniques and problem-solving. Section 2 presents the dimensions along which language may vary, and gives attention to issues of historical change, gender and social position. Section 3 explores questions of meaning, including modes of indirection such as irony and allusion. It also explores the respective roles of the author and the reader in the process of creating and constraining meaning. Section 4 focuses on the sound patterning and grammar of poetic texts, including ways in which such texts may both achieve an extra layer of patterning and break with normal patterns of linguistic construction. Section 5 is concerned broadly with aspects of narrative – what makes a story and how stories are told. Section 6 addresses the question of translation between one medium and another, from prose fiction to film, and from the page to performance.

Acknowledgements

The book originated in a course in English Studies developed and taught primarily by the then staff of the Programme in Literary Linguistics, University of Strathclyde, Glasgow. The original planning team for the course also included Gillian Skirrow and Derek Attridge, and *Ways of Reading* owes much to their inspiration. The title itself derives in part from John Berger's book, *Ways of Seeing*; but there was also a course of the same name (though different in aims, scope and constituency) taught by Deirdre Burton and Tom Davis in the English Department at the University of Birmingham.

In writing the book, the authors benefited a great deal both from the responses of students in workshops and also from postgraduates who assisted in the teaching of many of the units – Shân Wareing, Christine Christie, Lena Garry, Linda Jackson, Vassiliki Kolocotroni, Lindsay Hewitt, Luma Al Balaa and others. In addition, we would like to thank Gill Morris and Keith Knightenhelser. Special thanks go to Judit Friedrich and Professor Michael Toolan, who read and commented upon the complete typescript of the book. Its faults, of course, remain our own.

The publishers and the authors would like to thank the following for permission to reproduce copyright material: Tom Philips, *A Humument: A Treated Victorian Novel* [1980], 4th edn (2005), p. 14. Copyright © DACS 2006. Reproduced with permission. Philip Larkin's 'High windows' 1974. Reproduced by kind permission of Faber & Faber. 'High windows' from *Collected Poems* by Philip Larkin. Copyright © 1988, 2003 by the Estate of Philip Larkin. Reprinted by permission of Farrar, Straus & Giroux, LLC. 'An Introduction', by Kamala Das, *Collected Poems*, volume 1, 1984, reproduced by kind permission of Kamala Surayya. 'Vlamertinghe: Passing the Chateau, July 1917', by Edmund Blunden is reproduced by permission of PFD (www.pfd.co.uk) on behalf of the estate of Mrs Claire Blunden. Excerpt from 'Heartsearch' column of the *New Statesman* (May 1987). This is taken from an article that first appeared in the *New Statesman*. Excerpt from H.G. Wells's *The War of the Worlds* (1898) reproduced with permission of A.P. Watt Ltd on behalf of the literary executors of the estate of H.G. Wells. Four seventeenth and eighteenth century Japanese Haiku from the *Penguin Book of Japanese Verse*, translated by Geoffrey Bownas and Anthony Thwaite, and published in 1964. Reproduced by kind permission of Geoffrey Bownas and Anthony Thwaite. 'You Fit into Me' from *Power Politics* by Margaret Atwood. Copyright © 1971, 1996 by Margaret Atwood. Reprinted by permission of House of Anansi Press, Toronto.

Figure 12.5: René Magritte, Belgian, 1898-1967, *Time Transfixed*, 1938, oil on canvas, 147 × 98.7 cm, Joseph Winterbotham Collection, 1970. 426, The Art Institute of Chicago. © ADAGP, Paris and DACS, London 2006. Photography © The Art Institute of Chicago. L'ART, 1910 By Ezra Pound, from PERSONAE, copyright © 1926 by Ezra Pound. Reprinted by permission of New Directions Publishing Corps and Faber & Faber. Adrian Henri's 'On the Late Late Massachers Stillbirths and Deformed Children a Smoother Lovelier Skin Job' Copyright © 1986 Adrian Henri. Reproduced by permission of the estate of Adrian Henri c/o Rogers, Coleridge & White Ltd, 20 Powis Mews, London W11 1JN. 'I am a young girl' from *The Penguin Book of Women Poets* written anonymously, in France during the thirteenth century, trans and eds Carol Cosman *et al*. Reproduced by kind permission of Carol Cosman. *If*. Words and music by Neil Hannon. © copyright 1996 Damaged Pop Music Limited. BMG Music Publishing Limited. Used by permission of Music Sales Limited. All rights reserved. International copyright secured. Horoscope for Libra and Aquarius from the *Observer* Magazine (2005). Reproduced by kind permission of Neil Spencer. Martin Luther King, speech delivered 28 August 1963, at the Lincoln Memorial, Washington DC, USA. Reprinted by arrangement with the Estate of Martin Luther King Jr, c/o Writers House as agent for the proprietor New York, NY. Copyright 1963 Martin Luther King Jr, copyright renewed 1991 Coretta Scott King. E.J. Scovell 'The Paschal Moon' from *Selected Poems*, 1991, Carcanet Press Ltd. Reproduced with permission. 'A Very Short Story' from *The First Forty-Nine Stories by Ernest Hemingway*, published by Jonathan Cape, reprinted by permission of The Random House Group Ltd. 'A Very Short Story,' reprinted with permission of Scribner, an imprint of Simon & Schuster Adult Publishing Group, from *The Short Stories of Ernest Hemingway*. Copyright 1925 Charles Scribner's Sons. Copyright renewed 1953 by Ernest Hemingway. From *Trainspotting* by Irwine Welsh, published by Secker & Warburg/Vintage. Reprinted by permission of The Random House Group Ltd. *Cloud Nine* by Caryl Churchill, copyright © 1979, 1980, 1983, 1984, 1985 by Caryl Churchill. Reprinted by permission of the publisher: www.nickhernbooks.co.uk. 'Message Clear' by Edwin Morgan, reproduced by kind permission of Carcanet Press Ltd.

Introduction

Debates about the nature and purpose of English Studies have been common-place since the 1960s and have led to important advances in our ways of understanding the subject. These debates have often been conducted in terms of theoretical critique and analysis; but, alongside such critique, and in the wake of it, there is an important need for materials that can help translate theoretical and analytic insights into practical methods of study, especially for students in the earlier stages of their work. *Ways of Reading* is designed to provide such materials.

Our perspective in *Ways of Reading* is one that places less emphasis on Literature as such and greater emphasis on exploring relationships between literary and other types of text. Examples in this book will be taken from the fields of journalism and advertising, film and television, as well as from the field of Literature as traditionally defined. *Ways of Reading*, then, explores non-literary as well as literary texts, at the same time and in relation to each other. In this respect, our use of the term 'text' may be sometimes puzzling. For one thing, we use it not in the familiar sense of 'set text' – one of the canon of great books. Instead we use it more abstractly to refer to the trace or record of a communicative event, an event that may be performed in words but that may equally take place in images or in a combination of words and images. Therefore, not only do examples discussed in this book come from everyday life as well as from literature, some of them also include a significant visual component.

Important changes of critical emphasis follow from broadening the range of texts that we examine. Although the texts that we use for illustration and discussion tend broadly to be playful or persuasive in character, we do not focus particularly on questions of relative value, or on issues of tradition or influence. We focus instead on what might be called the rhetorical organiza-tion of texts – or how they work to create meanings and produce recognizable effects by means of identifiable techniques, each of which can be described, analysed and studied. The ability to identify and recognize modes of patterning and rhetorical organization in text is part and parcel for us of ways of reading.

To this end, the book is composed in terms of discrete units, each of which aims at establishing a technique of analysis and interpretation that should prove useful in reading texts, whether they are literary or non-literary, verbal or visual. Each unit not only introduces a concept or technique relevant to critical reading; it is also designed to give crucial practice in its use, by culminating in a concrete activity. These activities at the end of each unit are thus as important as the exposition itself, providing simultaneously a test of the concept's usefulness, and also scope for the reader to extend for him- or herself, in a practical fashion, competence in its application.

Although the units are devoted to discrete topics, they may also be seen as working collectively to furnish tools for use in interpretation. As such, they provide a compendium of critical and analytic strategies to enable critical reading. Critical reading, as we envisage it, examines how texts make sense, what kinds of sense they make, and why they make sense in one way rather another. This is important because – we believe – the rhetoric of texts contributes to the creation and circulation of meanings in society, to the point that we understand the world and our place within it through the texts that we make and interpret. Hence our concern in *Ways of Reading* to relate readings of the text to readings of the world around the reader.

The book is loosely organized into six main sections. Section 1 considers basic techniques and problem-solving, and deals with fundamental starting points for studying text. Section 2 presents a broad picture of the dimensions along which language may vary, including attention to issues of historical change, gender and social position. The units that comprise this second section thus help us to see the range of variation that provides the linguistic backdrop for the particular features and strategies of a specific text. Section 3 considers modes of textual practice, including figurative language, crucial to the production of meaning whether directly or indirectly, by metaphor and irony, or by juxtaposition and allusion. It also explores the respective roles of the author and the reader in the process of creating and constraining meaning. Section 4 focuses on the sound patterning and grammar of poetic texts, including ways in which such texts may both achieve an extra layer of patterning and break with normal patterns of linguistic construction. Section 5 is concerned broadly with aspects of narrative – what makes a story and how stories are told. Section 6 addresses the question of translation and shift between one medium and another, from prose fiction to film, and from the page to performance.

The book is thus structured in terms of certain kinds of progression – from smaller features of texts (e.g. rhyme) to larger features (e.g. story structure); from poetry to prose; or from text to performance. However, we would not wish to make too much of these kinds of progression. Instead, each unit may be seen as adding to a network of concepts; and, because each unit opens out upon others in different parts of the book, the reader will find cross-references from one unit to another. At the same time, because many of the units can work in a relatively self-standing fashion, it is possible to study or consult them individually without necessarily referring to other parts of the book. In sum, *Ways of Reading* can be used as a class-book; for individual study (working through it topic by topic); or for reference (by consulting the glossary, index or table of contents). In this respect we hope that the book will itself be put to use productively in different ways that nonetheless contribute to its underlying aim: to develop an awareness of reading as a broader process, where reading the word is a part of reading the world.

Section 1

Basic techniques and problem-solving

Asking questions as a way into reading

You open a book which begins:

PROLOGUE

The Storming of Seringapatam (1799)

Extracted from a Family Paper

I address these lines – written in India – to my relatives in England.

My object is to explain the motive which has induced me to refuse the right hand of friendship to my cousin, John Herncastle. The reserve which I have hitherto maintained in this matter has been misinterpreted by members of my family whose good opinion I cannot consent to forfeit. I request them to suspend their decision until they have read my narrative. And I declare, on my word of honour, that what I am now about to write is, strictly and literally, the truth.

How does your **reading** proceed? Clearly you try to comprehend, in the sense of identifying meanings for individual words and working out relationships between them, drawing on your implicit knowledge of English **grammar** (see **Unit 3, Analysing units of structure**). If you are unfamiliar with words or idioms, you guess at their meaning, using clues presented in the context (as possibly with 'the right hand of friendship'). On the assumption that they will become relevant later, you make a mental note of **discourse** entities such as 'my relatives in England' and 'John Herncastle', as well as possible links between them. You begin to infer a context for the text, for instance by making decisions about what kind of **speech event** is involved: who is making the utterance, to whom, when and where? (In this case, an unnamed writer in India is addressing relatives in England – relatives who are therefore presumably also related to a certain John Herncastle – in order to correct an impression we are invited to believe the writer feels they have formed of the writer's 'reserve' in a matter that has not, at this stage, been explained.) A world created by the text begins to build up, even though you are obliged to leave gaps: who *is* the writer who remains for the time being just 'I'? Who *are* the relatives? What has gone on before?

As you follow such interpretive strategies, which apply to all discourse (not just to literary works), you are likely to speculate about what kind of text this is: how it fits into whatever you take to be its discourse-type, or genre (see **Unit 4, Recognizing genre**). As it happens, the author's Preface at the beginning of the particular book you have picked up opens with the words, 'In some of my former novels . . .', so you may surmise that the text that follows is a novel, as its title also suggests: *The Moonstone: A Romance*, by Wilkie Collins, published in 1868. Your possible assumption that you are reading a slightly formal letter must now be embedded in a more complex model: that of a fictional letter within a **narrative**, functioning (so we are told by the subtitle) as the 'Prologue' to a story that will include 'the Storming of Seringapatam' – about which you expect at some stage to be informed. Because of the fictional context, you also have to adjust any straightforward reading you may have made of the assertion that what you will be told will be 'strictly and literally, the truth'; that assertion may apply within the fictional world but is unlikely to hold beyond it.

1.1 Comprehension and interpretive variation

The ways of reading indicated here are without doubt kinds of comprehension. But they show comprehension to consist not just of passive assimilation but of active engagement in **inference** and problem-solving. You infer information you feel the writer has invited you to grasp by presenting you with specific evidence and clues; and you make further inferences, for instance about how the text may be significant to you, or about its plausibility – inferences that form the basis of a personal response for which the **author** will inevitably be far less responsible.

Conceived in this way, comprehension will not follow exactly the same track for each **reader**. What is in question is not the retrieval of an absolute, fixed or 'true' meaning that can be read off and checked for accuracy, or some timeless relation of the text to the world. Rather, we ascribe meanings to texts on the basis of interaction between what we might call textual and contextual material: between kinds of organization or patterning we perceive in a text's formal structures (so especially its language structures) and various kinds of background, social knowledge, belief and attitude that we bring to the text.

Such background material inevitably reflects who we are. Factors such as the place and period in which we are reading, our gender, ethnicity, age and social class will encourage us towards certain interpretations but at the same

time obscure or even close off others. This doesn't, however, make interpretation merely relative or even pointless. Precisely because readers from
different historical periods, places and social experiences produce different but
overlapping readings of the same words on the page – including for texts that
engage with fundamental human concerns – debates about texts can play an
important role in social discussion of beliefs and values.

How we read a given text also depends to some extent on our particular
interest in reading it. Are we studying that text and trying to respond in a way
that fulfils the requirement of a given course? Reading it simply for pleasure?
Skimming it for information? Ways of reading on a train or in bed are likely
to differ considerably from reading in a seminar room. Such dimensions of
reading suggest – as others introduced later in the book will also do – that we
bring an implicit (often unacknowledged) agenda to any act of reading. It
doesn't then necessarily follow that one kind of reading is fuller, more advanced
or more worthwhile than another. Ideally, different kinds of reading inform
each other, and act as useful reference points for and counterbalances to one
another. Together, they make up the reading component of your overall
literacy, or relationship to your surrounding textual environment.

1.2 Types of meaning

Faced with variability within reading, many people maintain that they would
prefer one single route that all textual investigation could follow: a search for
'meaning' that would follow some pre-given sequence of procedures or tests.
The points made above, however, suggest that meaning cannot be uniform or
singular in this way. Looking for the meaning or meanings of a text involves
exploring many different sorts of question – or alternatively blocking off those
different sorts of question in order to settle on a possibly more comfortable
but significantly reduced, single interpretation.

There is a more positive way of looking at variability of meaning,
however, that doesn't see it as merely loss of truth or clarity. Diversity within
reading can be productive as a catalyst to reflection on how language works,
what meaning is and how reading contributes to the creation of beliefs and
social values.

Before moving on to consider specific local questions that can kick-start
your reading of any given text, we list here the main alternative kinds of general
meaning that compete for attention and interact as you read.

1.2.1 The intended meaning?

One of the commonest ways of looking for the meaning of a text is to wonder
what the author meant by it. To speculate about authorial intention, such as
Shakespeare's intention in writing *Hamlet*, involves trying to extrapolate from

what the text says, second-guessing a set of social circumstances very different from your own. In effect, you try to reconstruct the likely meanings or effects that any given sentence, image or reference might have had: these might be the ones the author intended. In doing this, you make a huge imaginative leap: you try to gauge an author's beliefs, emotions, knowledge and attitudes, and to guess what the author 'had in mind' at the time of writing.

There are obvious difficulties with deciding on a text's meaning like this. A **persona**, or invented voice, might have been deliberately adopted, separating what the speaker or **narrator** of a text says from the writer's own feelings. In plays, novels and narrative poems, characters speak as constructs created by the author, not necessarily as mouthpieces for the author's own thoughts. Even the speaker of a first person **lyric poem** (the poetic 'I') must be regarded as an invented speaker, not a clear window into the writer's self.

Besides, there is no infallible way in which an intention can be verified. That is largely why the critics W.K. Wimsatt and M.C. Beardsley (1946) dismissed the quest to discover what the author 'had in mind' as an **intentional fallacy**: an unwarranted shift from what the words of a text appear to mean to what we imagine the author meant by using them. In addition to difficulties presented by reading a text produced in a different place or period, language can occasionally escape the speaker's intentions, producing meanings that were not anticipated. Sometimes slippages or failures of meaning may undermine any seemingly intended or coherent meaning completely (see **Unit 14, Authorship and intention**).

1.2.2 The text's own meaning?

If you look for this kind of meaning (which some critics have called 'objective' interpretation), then specific features of the text will be the key to your interpretation. How the text is organized (what words and structures it uses, how images and ideas are patterned) will direct you towards a specific meaning. What is important in this framework is to observe details of language and **form**. You examine choices of expression and the use of stylistic devices, such as parallel structures or **figurative language**, and contrast the ways the text is presented with other, alternative ways it might have been presented (which would have produced different meanings).

If pursued in isolation, however, this search for a meaning that should be predictable simply from the text's own organization runs into difficulties. The fact that texts are interpreted differently in different historical periods, and by differing social groups or **readerships**, challenges the notion of an 'objective' meaning determined by the text alone – unless only you are right and all those other readers were somehow simply mistaken. Interpretive variation suggests that the social circumstances in which a text is produced and interpreted, and the expectations readers bring to it, can significantly affect what it will be taken to mean.

1.2.3 An individual meaning?

Perhaps the meaning of a text is whatever your personal response to it is: what the text means to you. Texts are suggestive, and they connect with individual experiences, memories and personal associations for words and images. What you might value, therefore, is your own direct engagement with the text, reworking it into a form linked to your own life experiences.

Many critics, however, including Wimsatt and Beardsley (1949), have argued that this sort of reading involves an **affective fallacy**: an over-attention to personal response at the expense of what the words of the text actually say. Concern with personal resonances of a text can displace attention from the text's own structures and rhetorical organization. It is also possible that many of the memories or associations triggered as you read may be either stock responses or idiosyncratic reactions that go off at purely personal tangents, having little to do with the text that prompted them.

1.2.4 General processes of making meaning?

Meanings are undoubtedly produced by creative acts of reading that you perform on a text. So, perhaps, instead of investigation of textual details that guide a particular interpretation, emphasis should be placed on the mechanisms or procedures by which texts come to have whatever meanings are attributed to them. If so, looking for meaning should involve exploring the interpretive conventions and social institutions of reading, such as identifying and contrasting themes or treating particular elements of a text as central symbols, rather than reporting local outcomes of particular acts of reading. Readings that are produced would be valuable to the extent that they offer illustration of general reading processes; and meanings you articulate would be finally only as interesting as the processes by means of which they were arrived at.

Reading texts in this way, however, could easily become highly repetitive. Almost any text would be equally useful or interesting; and, while reading clearly does involve general processes, readers bring different expectations and ideologies to bear, with the result that readings cannot be analysed exhaustively in terms of general codes. Nor is interest in reading texts normally reducible to how interpretation takes place in the mind. It is often prompted by concern with the experiences or topics being represented.

1.2.5 Meaning and a text's reception?

People don't all think as you do, and they certainly haven't always thought the same as you in the past. So, perhaps, what a text means, since readers bring their own beliefs, attitudes and expectations into how they read, is all the various things it has meant to different readerships in the past, together with the different meanings it has for different communities of readers today.

Readings of texts are diverse, but they are not random; they fall into categories or groups, with the shared or overlapping meanings of these groups changing over time and differing between places in describable ways. Understanding the meaning of a text might therefore mean not only accounting for individual personal response, but also charting such responses within larger, social and historical patterns of reception.

In advertising and market research, readers (for instance, of newspapers or magazines) are classified on the basis of variables such as class, age, gender and income (as As, Bs, ABs, C1s, C2s, etc.). In literary criticism, readers have more often been distinguished on the basis of their imagined relative taste (as elite and mass audiences, or readers with highbrow or popular taste, for example). Readerships, however, might be identified on the basis of other considerations, including the function reading a given text serves (e.g. as a marker of social accomplishment, for study, as distraction from pain or work, or out of cultural curiosity). What potentially makes patterning within the responses of actual readers or audiences interesting is how different groups of readers appropriate core features of or statements in a discourse into their own preoccupations or ways of thinking and living.

1.2.6 Critical social meanings?

Critical social meanings are formed when a collision or contradiction occurs between one reader's response and a meaning commonly accepted by a significant group of other people. As an individual reader, you are always a specific social subject, with an age, gender, ethnicity, class and educational background. Your responses and interpretations are to some extent guided by these aspects of your location. If you express a critical or polemical view of a given text's significance and influence, you are reading in an actively socially engaged, rather than detached, disinterested or simply curious way. Support for critical readings, like that for established readings they challenge, lies in combined forms of analysis: analysis of a prevailing culture's established imagery (how particular topics such as race, sexuality, work, religious belief, social conflict or money are conventionally represented); and analysis of how images of any of these topics relate to your own sense of how such topics should be represented.

1.3 How to get started in ways of reading

In practice, the different senses of the 'meaning' of a text are not always easily separable from one another; but, historically, different aspects of a text's meanings have been emphasized in different schools of criticism and embedded in different kinds of reading strategy. Listing the principal directions of analysis here is useful if it helps to overcome a tendency to assume that looking for or finding one kind of meaning exhausts the interpretive possibilities.

Often when you start reading, questions about a text and a sense of its potential for meaning will come flooding in. Your own responses begin to form, and are traceable back – if you stop to do so – to particular textual features, echoes of other texts, and parallels and contrasts with your own beliefs and experiences. But not always. Sometimes you may feel stuck or uncertain how to start, as if the text is somehow blocking your usual strategies. When that happens a checklist of conventional entry points may be a welcome aid. With such occasions in mind, we offer the following list of question prompts, before going on in subsequent units to investigate specific topics in more detail. Each question should lead into a practical line of enquiry for you to follow; use the contents page and index to find the relevant units in which we explore each topic further.

1.3.1 Textual questions

- Is the piece of text you are looking at the whole of that text?
- Does the text exist in only one version or in many different versions? If in many versions, are there likely to be significant differences between them (e.g. as regards spelling, layout, typeface or even **content**)?
- Has the text been cut, edited or expurgated?
- Has the text been annotated, possibly for a new readership or new market? If so, who provided the annotations, and do the annotations direct you towards one particular way of looking at the text?

1.3.2 Contextual questions

- When, where and in what circumstances was the text written or produced?
- Do aspects of the text (such as elements of its narrative, setting or themes) have obvious connections, especially parallels or contrasts, with the society contemporaneous with the text being produced?
- Who was the text originally aimed at? Are you part of that anticipated readership or audience?
- Was the author or producer of the text male or female? Professional or amateur? A native speaker of English or a non-native speaker?
- How old was he or she when the text was produced?
- How does the particular text you are looking at fit into what you know of the rest of the text-producer's output?

1.3.3 Questions regarding the 'speech situation'

- Who is supposed to be speaking the words of the text?
- From whose point of view is the text being told?
- Who is the text addressed to?

1.3.4 Referential questions

- Does the text contain quotations from other texts?
- Does the text refer to particular social attitudes, facts or beliefs about the world, or to particular historical or geographical knowledge?
- Does the text contain references to other literary, media, mythological or religious texts, figures or events? If so, do you know – and how much does it matter whether you know – what these references refer to?

1.3.5 Language questions

- Is the text in its original language or a translation?
- Is it likely that all the words in the text, especially words used to describe key topics or narrate key moments, still have the same meaning they did when the text was produced?
- Are the sentences generally of the same length and complexity? If not, is the inequality patterned or distributed in any way that might be significant?
- What sort of vocabulary do the words of the text generally come from (elevated or colloquial; technical or non-technical; standard or regional; Latinate or Germanic; etc.)?
- Were all the words and structures still current at the time the text was written or is it possible that some (e.g. 'thou') are archaisms?
- As regards all of the above, is the text consistent, or are there contrasts or shifts within the text? (For example, do different characters or speakers use language in significantly different ways?)

1.3.6 Questions of convention

- Should the way you read the text be guided by specific conventions to do with the sort of text it is (e.g. satire, pantomime, sitcom)?
- How realistic do you expect the text to be? How, for instance, does the text achieve its appearance of being real or true, if it has one (by checkable details and evidence; on the basis of an underlying truthfulness despite surface implausibility; etc.)?

1.3.7 Symbolic questions

- Do names in the text refer to particular, unique individuals or do they seem representative, standing for general characters or character-types?
- Is it likely that places (mountains, sea . . .), weather (storms, sunset . . .) or events (marriage, travel . . .) have extra, symbolic meanings?
- Is the text concerned with a specific set of events or does it seek to represent one set of concerns in the form of a story about another, as a kind of allegory?
- How far could the text's title be a key to its meaning?

1.3.8 Questions of emotional effect and identification

- Do you see significant aspects of yourself in any of the characters or events depicted?
- Do any of the problems, dilemmas or issues represented in the text resonate especially with your own experience, as a member of a given social group or class?
- Does the text present anything that you consider to be a conventional fantasy scenario or wish fulfilment?
- Do any sections or aspects of the text repel, offend or embarrass you?

1.3.9 Questions of representation

- Do you think the text is typical – for its time, place and context of presentation or publication – in terms of its **representation** of its selected themes?
- Does the text present images of race, women, industry, money, crime, health, personal success or fulfilment (or other socially core themes)? If so, do these images seem to you unfair, biased or problematic?
- Does the text omit any major aspects of the topics it deals with, in ways that may restrict or limit the viewpoint it offers?
- Does the text treat topics in ways that are new to you and instructive?

1.4 Starting your reading with questions

If, when you first engage with a given text, you instantly see interesting features or details and have interpretive hunches to follow, then it is best not to interrupt your reading to work through a checklist of questions of the kind given above. Better, in such circumstances, to use such a list after you have made notes or drafted an essay on the strength of your own first insights. At that later stage in your thinking, you may be able to fill out ideas (and build the evidence you present to support them) by comparing the viewpoint you have already developed with other perspectives implicit in the checklist.

The questions listed are only starting points. They should lead into active modes of enquiry, rather than being taken as a complete agenda for reading if you simply answer them. (This applies especially if you pick out individual questions from the list and focus on those exclusively.) One practical way of using the questions is to skim quickly through them after reading the text, deciding without further reference to the text what you might say about each (in many cases this may be nothing at all – see below). As you work through the questions, your attention is likely to be drawn back to details you may not have consciously noticed, some of which may now seem relevant information or evidence and may stimulate directions for further enquiry. Answers to questions you ask yourself – even provisional or negative answers – carry with them informal kinds of reasoning or explanation that you can now bring into conscious thought. (Generally, asking questions will show that you already have richer intuitions about a text than you thought, simply by being a language user and because you have been exposed to many texts previously.) When you have skimmed through all the questions, go back to whichever ones either fit your prescribed task or prompted your most engaged answers; follow those up, including by reference to later units in this book.

Finally, how do you deal with having no information or answer at all in relation to a given question? First, you should not see this as a serious or permanent setback; seeing a question in need of an answer positively identifies something specific to look into. Often being aware of how an answer might – or would not – contribute to an interpretation can guide insightful reading even without that answer ever being found. For many questions we ask about texts no unique, correct answer could exist; only the answers of others who have asked and investigated such questions before. That is partly why it is empowering to develop ways of reading for which you try to articulate your own analysis and evidence.

ACTIVITY 1.1 ━━━━━━━━━━━━━━━━━━━━━━━━━━━━━━━━━━

1   Make a list of questions you feel it would be useful to ask about the following text. Alongside each question, note the specific piece(s) of information it would be helpful to know.

2   Arrange your questions under the various headings listed above ('Textual questions', 'Contextual questions', etc.). Don't worry about answers to the questions, or even about where such answers might be found. Focus instead on what *kinds of question* you feel are worth pursuing.

Tranquerah Road

1
Poor relative, yet well-connected,
same line, same age as Heeren Street
(more or less, who knows?),
the long road comes and goes –
dream, nightmare, retrospect –
through my former house,
self-conscious, nondescript.

2
There was a remnant of a Portuguese settlement,
Kampong Serani, near the market,
where Max Gomes lived, my classmate.

At the end of the road, near *Limbongan*,
the Tranquerah English School,
our *alma mater*, heart of oak.

By a backlane the Methodist Girls' School,
where my sister studied
See me, mother,
Can you see me?
The Lord's Prayer, Psalm 23.

The Japanese came,
and we sang the *Kimigayo*,
learnt some *Nihon Seishin*.

Till their *Greater East Asia Co-Prosperity Sphere*
collapsed, and we had to change
our tune again – God Save the King.
Meliora hic sequamur.

The King died when I was in school,
and then, of course, God Save the Queen.

While *Merdeka* inspired –
for who are so free
as the sons of the brave? –
and so *Negara-ku*
at mammoth rallies
I salute them all
who made it possible,
for better, for worse.

3
A sudden trill,
mosquito whine
like enemy aeroplane
in a blanket stillness,
the heave and fall of snoring sea,
swish and rustle of coconut,
kapok, tamarind, fern-potted,
where *pontianak* perch
by the midnight road.

Wind lifts its haunches off the sea,
shakes dripping mane,

then gallops muffle-hoofed,
a flash of whiteness in sparse bamboo
in a Malay cemetery.

Yet I shall fear no evil
for Thou art with me
though the wind is a horse
is a *jinn* raving free
Thy rod and Thy staff
they comfort me
and fear is only in the mind
as Mother said
why want to be afraid
just say *Omitohood Omitohood Omitohood*
                                    Amen.

3   When you have completed your list, read the information about the poem
    given on p. 339. This information is drawn from notes provided to accom-
    pany the poem in the author's *Selected Poems*. Consider how far the
    pieces of information provided answer the questions you have asked.

4   How would having access, when you *started* reading, to the information
    you have now been given affect the kind of interpretation you would be
    likely to produce?

5   Now examine questions that remain *unanswered* by the information
    provided on p. 339. Some of these questions may just require specific
    pieces of information not provided in the notes; but many will involve
    the word 'why?'. Consider whether there is a difference between ques-
    tions asking 'why?' and your other questions. If so, how would you
    describe that difference?

6   Finally, consider how far texts in general rely on background informa-
    tion that will be available to differing extents to readers with different
    cultural background knowledge and experience, in the way that this poem
    appears to?

Reading

Fabb, N. and Durant, A. (2005) *How to Write Essays and Dissertations: A Guide for English Literature Students*, Harlow: Pearson.

Furniss, T.E. and Bath, M. (2006) *Reading Poetry: An Introduction*, 2nd edn, London: Longman, Chapter 1.

Lodge, D. (1992) *The Art of Fiction*, Harmondsworth: Penguin, esp. Chapter 1 ('Beginning').

Wimsatt, W.K. and Beardsley, M.C. (1946) 'The Intentional Fallacy', in D. Lodge (ed.) (1972) *20th Century Criticism*, Harlow: Longman, pp. 334–44.

Wimsatt, W.K. and Beardsley, M.C. (1949) 'The Affective Fallacy', in D. Lodge (ed.) (1972) *20th Century Criticism*, Harlow: Longman, pp. 345–58.

Unit 2

Using information sources

2.1 Information and reading

To read a text we must decode what the text literally says but at the same time we must bring our knowledge to the text to determine what the text actually means (to us). The knowledge that we bring can be of history, of the everyday world, of geography, of zoology or botany, of literature, of science and so on – any kind of knowledge can in principle be relevant in making sense of a literary text. When we read Herman Melville's 1851 novel *Moby Dick*, the text (in a parody of the use of information sources) gives us some of the knowledge about whales and the whaling industry that we might need; but there might be other facts about nineteenth-century America that the text does not tell us and that would nevertheless be useful knowledge in making sense of the text. In 1851 Melville might have assumed that his reader would know enough about the Bible to recognize it as the origin of the first sentence of his first chapter, 'Call me Ishmael.' Today many readers will need to consult an information source to tell them this – either the footnotes of a critical edition of the novel, or perhaps a **concordance** to the Bible. Information sources are searchable collections of fragments of knowledge. They can be useful for our reading when they help us decode the text (to find the meaning of a particular word, for example) but their primary importance is that they can help us bring contextualizing knowledge to the text, particularly when we are separated from texts by history or geography and hence have drifted away from the knowledge that might have been assumed for the original readers of those texts.

2.2 Examples of the use of information sources

Information sources come in many forms and include footnotes to a poem, a dictionary of symbols in the library, the *Encyclopaedia Britannica*, the Modern

Language Association bibliography on CD-ROM, or the Internet. Information sources have many uses in literary study, and this chapter illustrates some of them. We begin by looking at some sample problems that can be solved by consulting information sources.

(1) An old English folk poem begins 'A frog he would a-wooing go'. One question you might ask about this is: why a frog? A useful type of reference book if you are concerned with the meanings of objects is a dictionary of symbols. For example, if you look up 'frog' in de Vries' *Dictionary of Symbols and Imagery*, you are given the following meanings:

> a frog is amphibious and therefore often ambivalent in meaning; its natural enemy is the serpent; it has a number of favourable meanings – it symbolises fertility and lasciviousness, creation, the highest form of evolution (hence princes turn into frogs), wisdom, and poetic inspiration; it also has unfavourable meanings – in religious terms it is considered unclean, and it is said to have a powerful voice but no strength.

This dictionary also tells us that 'Frogs are great wooers': there are several songs about frogs who go 'a-wooing' a mouse; perhaps a spinning song as the mouse itself is referred to as 'spinning' several times. So we have a possible answer: frogs are symbols of fertility and lasciviousness, hence wooers. The other meanings do not seem to be relevant here (e.g. creation, wisdom, uncleanness). Similar results can be found by using a search engine (such as Google™) on the Internet, but you would need to search for 'frog as symbol' (just searching for 'frog' or for 'frog wooing' will not be productive). The next question we could ask is: why does he woo a mouse? By looking for 'frog as symbol' we have begun to explain the text and opened up another question to ask about the text, both of which are potentially productive; but at the same time we need to acknowledge the risks of doing this: frogs have many other meanings attached to them, and furthermore the meaning of 'fertility' turns out to be attached to many animals (including a mouse). Thus there is some looseness about this first stage of interpretation, which we might want to pin down by trying to find out whether frogs were associated with fertility in the specific English folk tradition from which this poem probably emerged; a possible reference here might be the *Oxford Dictionary of English Folklore*. It is often worth using a dictionary of symbolism to investigate the symbolic implications of natural things that are mentioned in texts: body parts, animals and plants, planets and stars, weather, geographical phenomena, etc.

(2) A sonnet by Christina Rossetti (1881) begins with the following lines:

> 'I, if I perish, perish' – Esther spake:
> And bride of life or death she made her fair.

In order to understand the poem, the reader needs to know that Esther is a historical character and to realize who she is. Some editions of the poem will explain this in a footnote, but, if there is no footnote, what do you do? Many information sources are useful for finding out about names. A classical dictionary lists all the names from Greek and Roman mythology; a Bible concordance lists all the names from the Bible; and many names are also listed in general reference works, such as *Brewer's Dictionary of Phrase and Fable*. You need to guess which reference source will be useful, or alternatively decide how to search for it on the Internet. As it happens, *Brewer's* has nothing about Esther, but a Bible concordance will (i.e. it is a name from the Bible). (Similarly if you search for the combination of the two words 'Esther' and 'Bible' on a search engine, you will find her.) If you look up 'Esther' in a Bible concordance you see all the lines listed that include this name, with references to the parts of the Bible where the lines are found; in fact they all occur in the Book of Esther, and you could look at this part of the Bible in order to find out about the character. You might also notice that one line listed in the concordance under 'Esther' is 'and Esther spake yet again', which is echoed in Rossetti's poem in the words 'Esther spake'. So you have found a biblical **allusion** (see **Unit 13**) in the language as well as finding out who the character is.

(3)   Shakespeare's play *The Tempest*, written in 1611–12, has among its themes those of sea travel, bad weather, the wrecking of ships (and loss of travellers) and the discovery of strange things in distant places. If you want to place these themes in their historical context, you could use annals, which are lists of events, organized by date. For example, if you look up 1611 in *The Teach Yourself Encyclopaedia of Dates and Events*, you find that in this year the Dutch began trading with Japan, the British explorer Hudson was lost in Hudson Bay in North America, and there were publications of a scientific explanation of the rainbow, a book of maps of Britain and an autobiographical travel book by Thomas Coryate. These facts may or may not be significant; the point is that it is very easy to find them using this information source (you would have to decide whether to investigate any that seem to be particularly relevant).

Because information sources are random collections of fragmentary knowledge, the risk in consulting an information source (that you are wasting your time) is balanced by the possible rewards (that you might find a richly rewarding clue for very little effort). Information sources can generally act as ways of generating ideas and getting you unstuck if you do not know how to begin to work with a text.

2.3 Adapting an information source to your needs: the *OED*

In this section we look at some of the uses of the *Oxford English Dictionary*, the largest dictionary of English vocabulary, first published by Oxford University Press in 1888 as *A New English Dictionary on Historical Principles*. The full version of the *Oxford English Dictionary*, or ***OED***, now exists as a second edition in a number of forms: as a collection of twenty volumes published in 1989, as a single volume with tiny print (and a magnifying glass), or as a CD-ROM. The dictionary is also available online.

The *OED* is a list of English words that, in certain respects, is very complete; it is most complete for Southern British English, but for other dialects there are similar dictionaries. For each word, a number of meanings (all those the word has had in its history) are distinguished, and quotations are given showing the word in use, including the earliest known use. Dictionaries are usually used as guides to the current usage (meaning, spelling or pronunciation) of difficult words, but the *OED* can be adapted to many other uses. We can illustrate this by looking at the first stanza of Percy Bysshe Shelley's 'To a Skylark' (1820):

> Hail to thee, blithe Spirit!
> Bird thou never wert,
> That from heaven, or near it,
> Pourest thy full heart
> In profuse strains of unpremeditated art.

If you look up 'blithe' in the *OED* you will find two appropriate meanings:

> *Meaning 2*: exhibiting gladness ... In ballads frequently coupled with 'gay'. Rare in modern English prose or speech; the last quotation with this meaning is 1807.

> *Meaning 3*: Of men, their heart, spirit etc.: joyous ... Rare in English prose or colloquial use since 16th century but frequent in poetry.

This dictionary entry acts as more than just a definition of the word; it tells us a number of interesting things relating to the poem. First, the word is used primarily in poetry – though in Shelley's poem it might have seemed a little old-fashioned (since 1807 is the date of the last citation for meaning 2). Second, the word is typically used in ballads; a significant fact when we consider that Romantic poets like Shelley were influenced by folk poetry of this kind. Third, it is explicitly associated with the word 'spirit' in the entry under meaning 3; the only quotation given that supports this association is in fact one from 1871, but nevertheless there may have been a traditional co-occurrence of these two words that Shelley drew upon. (It is also worth remembering that the *OED*, like any information source, provides only fragments and clues: there might be earlier or later uses of words that are not recorded in the dictionary.)

We could do the same with most of the words in this stanza; we might, for example, wonder how 'hail' was generally used (what does it tell us about the spirit?), what meanings 'spirit' had, how necessarily religious the word 'heaven' was at this time, what the significance of combining 'unpremeditated' with 'art' was, and so on. It often happens that we may have one reason for looking a word up, but will find something unexpected in the process (e.g. with 'blithe' I expected the term to have been old-fashioned, but I did not expect the link with ballads or with 'spirit').

The *OED*, like other dictionaries, can also be used as a 'brainstorming' aid when starting out on a research project. For example, if you were interested in the notion of 'spirit' in Romantic poetry, it would be a good and easy start to look up 'spirit' in the *OED* to see who used the word, what its history up to that time had been, how religious or otherwise its meanings were, and so on. By doing this you are adapting the *OED* to a new goal: you are using it as an admittedly partial guide to culture, as embodied in language use.

Other information sources can also be adapted in a similar way. A concordance, for example, can be used as a specialized dictionary of quotations (all from the same author), or an indication of the words that an author tends to combine together (a Shelley concordance would tell us instantly whether Shelley uses 'blithe spirit' elsewhere), or an indication of the meaning that a particular word has for an author. Often you need to interpret the facts that the information source presents to you, and use them as a guide to further research.

2.4 Digital texts

Another way of working with words is by using an electronic version of a text, in combination with a text editor that can search for words or phrases. Electronic versions of many texts (primarily those out of copyright, which means texts published before the twentieth century) can be found on the Internet, where some universities host large collections of electronic texts. (Look for a text on the Internet by using a search engine to search for the first few words of the text as a quotation.) Electronic versions of better-known texts can also be bought on CD-ROM. You could, for example, download all of Jane Austen's novel *Persuasion* or John Milton's epic poem *Paradise Lost*. Once you have an electronic version of the text, you can use a word processor or text editor to search for all the examples of a particular word, such as the word 'persuasion' in the novel *Persuasion*; this would be a good way to start understanding why the novel is named as it is. Some text editors (such as Peter Kehler's 'Alpha' for Macintosh, also available on the Internet) will extract out all the uses and give surrounding textual context (like an instant concordance), or you can just use the search function with a word processor. You might, for example, have an electronic version of *Paradise Lost*, and ask which lines contain the word 'fruit' (the last word in the first line, and potentially a key word in the poem). The Alpha text editor pulls out ninety-three such lines as a separate file. Given this easily obtained collection of lines, various possibilities are open to you. You might notice that in nine of the lines 'fruit' is combined with 'flower' (a conventional combination?), that the phrase 'fruit of thy womb' is used (thus connecting the fruit with both sex and procreation), or that the word 'fruit' is used much more intensively in some parts of the text than in others (for example, after the first line it is not used again until line 1944, but then is used often between lines 7360 and 7991). Because your version of the text is 'digital information', it can be reinterpreted and manipulated in various ways; you can, for example, paste the list of line numbers (for 'fruit') into a spreadsheet and draw a graph to show the frequency of use at various points in the text.

2.5 The Internet as a source of information

The Internet offers files about authors, recordings of authors speaking, files that contain whole novels or poems that you can copy, pictures of original printings of texts, critical essays and other scholarly information, and of course files that just give any kind of relevant general knowledge. Library catalogues and the sites of bookshops and publishers can help fill out information about a particular book. Contents of journals, abstracts of articles, and lists of articles cited can be found at particular sites. The cost of this richness of information is that you have to know how to find the files you need. One approach to this is to consult a source (printed or on the Internet) that lists the addresses of files that are relevant to your interests; your library might have some suggestions of places to start. The second approach is to embrace the randomness of the Internet by using a search engine such as Google. You might, for example, ask the search engine to find files with the phrase 'Call me Ishmael' in them (the first sentence in *Moby Dick*). For the second edition of this book, such a search showed up 451 files containing this phrase; now for the third edition six years later, when I conduct such a search I find 26,500 files: this is an indication of how the Internet has grown, a fact both exciting and problematic, making more information available but also hiding the relevant information under a pile of junk.

One of the mantras or mottos of the Internet is that 'information wants to be free'. This has several meanings. First, it applies the **pathetic fallacy** to information itself; like the Romantics who attributed human desires and feelings to the landscape, contemporary 'Internet Romantics' treat information as though it is a living entity; like many kinds of non-literal thinking (or metaphor), this can be a useful way of thinking about information. Second, it suggests that information should be free of charge or payment, and thus is part of a struggle over who controls what information and how they will make it available; in practice, publishers and other controllers of information can charge such high fees for access that many libraries, and hence users, are unable to afford them. Hence it is worth knowing about projects that, often government- or university-funded, make useful information freely available, such as MIT's open courseware project (which aims to make all teaching materials used at MIT freely available), or the University of Toronto's 'representative poetry on-line'. Third, and most profoundly, it suggests that information wants to be free of restraints and control, both in being able to 'go' anywhere (or more specifically be accessed from anywhere), and in being free from editors or censors. The 'Wikipedia' project, which is an encyclopedia to which anyone can contribute, is an example of this notion in action. The notion that information wants to be free raises questions about intellectual property rights (the ownership of what a person invents), and about the truthfulness or accuracy of information; particularly on the Internet, there is often no guarantee that information is provided lawfully or accurately. In contrast, one of the guarantees that is (implicitly) given when information is bought is that this information will be correct.

2.6 The reliability of information sources

All information sources should be used with caution, because the information available is always partial and always selective. The information that goes into information sources has to be selected by someone, and hence the information is filtered through someone's value judgements and can be altered through someone's error. Thus the basic flaws of information sources are: they are partial, they are partisan, and they may misinform. When using the Internet, you should try to use sites that are most likely to be reliable, such as sites associated with government sources (often with .gov in the address) or with universities (often with .edu or .ac in the address).

The partisan aspects of information sources make them interesting; information sources are themselves cultural artefacts that are worth study in their own right. In Samuel Johnson's *A Dictionary of the English Language* (1755), the choice of words to include, the definitions of words and the choice of quotations to illustrate them carry value judgements that may be used as a guide to issues in the language and society of the period. The same applies to all dictionaries and other information sources – all are to some extent partisan, though few make this explicit. One information source that does make its partisan nature explicit is Kramarae and Treichler's *A Feminist Dictionary* (1996), where quotations are used as the major form of information about words, and are selected to question the conventional meanings of words as well as to inform about them.

2.7 Avoiding plagiarism

If in your essay you use ideas, phrases or other information taken from a book or the Internet, you should always say that you are doing so, and give a reference back to the original source. This means that, when you are gathering this information, you should always label the information with its source. If the source is printed material, you should keep detailed information on the author or editor, date, title and publisher or journal (the kind of information that you might include in a bibliography); at a minimum you must indicate in your notes and carry over into your essay the fact that the information comes from someone other than you. The same applies to material you find on the Internet, where you should in addition copy the website address (and ideally the date when you consulted it as well, as sites change). Be sure to include proper acknowledgement in your essay; if you don't have notes on the actual source, you should still say that the words or ideas are someone else's even if you can't remember who they are. This means that when you write your essay there is no danger of your accidentally inserting material that is not yours into your essay as though you wrote those words or had those ideas or knew those things yourself. (If you do so, you are plagiarizing, whether accidentally or deliberately.) Be particularly careful when making notes or working with Internet material that, if you copy and paste any material into your notes, you always put quotation marks around it to show that you are quoting.

--- **ACTIVITY 2.1**

In this activity we ask you to test your ability to find various kinds of material or information on the Internet. Include in your answer for each task the URL (Internet address, usually beginning http:// and ending .htm or .html) of the page on which you found the material or information.

1   Graham Swift's *Waterland* is a novel whose lead character is a history teacher (with a particular interest in teaching about the French Revolution). The final sentence of the novel is 'On the bank in the thickening dusk, in the will-o'-the-wisp dusk, abandoned but vigilant, a motor-cycle.' Is there an allusion or quotation in this sentence?

2   Find information about a shipwreck that might have influenced Shakespeare in his 'shipwreck play' *The Tempest* (1611–12). Do this specifically by looking for shipwrecks in the years leading up to the date of the play.

3   Find an audio file of Tennyson reading from his own poem, 'Charge of the Light Brigade'.

4   John Keats's poem 'On first looking into Chapman's Homer' was written in 1816. Among the discoveries mentioned in his poem is the discovery of a 'new planet': 'Then felt I like some watcher of the skies / When a new planet swims into his ken.' Find out which planet this was likely to have been by looking for information about the discovery of the various planets.

5   Daniel Defoe's novel *Robinson Crusoe* has as one of its key incidents a discovery of a footprint in the sand. One way of exploring the significance of this is to ask whether the 'foot' is an important part of the body in the novel. Find an electronic version of the whole novel (ideally all in one file, rather than in separate chapters) and search for all examples of the word 'foot' in the novel. Cite three uses of the word 'foot' that might be useful in exploring the symbolism of feet in the novel.

Reading

Baker, N.L. and Huling, N. (2001) *A Research Guide for Undergraduate Students*, 5th edn, New York: MLA Publications.

Durant, A. and Fabb, N. (1990) *Literary Studies in Action*, London: Routledge, Chapter 4.

Harner, J.L. (2002) *Literary Research Guide: An Annotated Listing of Reference Sources in English Literary Studies*, 4th edn, New York: MLA Publications.

Kirkham, S. (1989) *How to Find Information in the Humanities*, London: Library Association.

Williams, R. (1988) *Keywords: A Vocabulary of Culture and Society*, London: Collins.

Unit 3

Analysing units of structure

When we talk about texts, we use categories. It would be almost impossible not to. Such categories include not only text types, or genres (see **Unit 4, Recognizing genre**), such as sonnet, thriller or tragedy, but also smaller-scale elements of composition that make up those text types: **verse**, rhyme, sentence, character, etc. Is there a list of correct and incorrect categories that we should use? And are textual categories just a part of **metalanguage**, or how people talk *about* the language of texts, or do they actively guide understanding or even shape composition?

Texts, we might say, have a sort of 'mechanics'. They are constructed for a purpose, with anticipated meanings and effects likely to be prompted by the chosen combination of signs. Intuitive judgements about the elements that combine to form an overall text can be a starting point for interpretation, and so contribute to the active process of understanding as making meaning outlined in **Unit 1, Asking questions as a way into reading**. For example, an arrangement of textual components that has interesting regularities, or forms a pattern, can point towards a text's meaning and significance. To understand how a text works, we are accordingly helped by finding out about its units of structure and how they combine. The field of **stylistics** – whether discourse stylistics generally, or literary stylistics – is based on this insight: that interpretations are guided to a significant extent by perceptions of structure that can be described, even if they are not always immediately evident to the reader.

Consider the twelve-bar blues as an illustration. The blues form consists, with some variation, of the following units (among others): three groupings of words, as lines, with the second line a repeat of the first, and with each line harmonically accompanied by particular chords in a given sequence of bars. In this description, lines, chords and bars are important units of structure for the twelve-bar blues. Here is a verse from a twelve-bar blues in the key of C:

chords:	C	/	F	/	C	/ C7 /
line 1:	Early one mornin',	/	on my way to the penal	/	farm	
bars:	[1]	/	[2]	/	[3]	/ [4] /

chords:	F	/	F	/	C	/ C7 /
line 2:	Early one mornin',	/	on my way to the penal / farm			
bars:	[5]	/	[6]	/	[7]	/ [8] /

chords:	G7	/	F7	/	C	/ G7 /
line 3:	Baby, all locked up	/	and ain't doin' nothin'	/	wrong.	
bars:	[9]	/	[10]	/	[11]	/ [12] /

(Francis Blockwall, c.1910–20)

We cannot, of course, be certain that the labelling offered here is a 'correct' description of the units; the singer and subsequent performers may not themselves use such terms and many admirers of the blues might not recognize them or feel that these units are significant in their listening. Nor can we be certain that the list is exhaustive or comprehensive. How many times, for example, is the chord strummed each bar and what is the unit for that? We cannot presume, either, that the grouping of elements, as units, matches real distinctions rather than simply reflecting categories we have chosen to impose. On the other hand, without some notion of units of structure (lines, chords, bars), it would be impossible to describe what distinguishes the blues from other forms that prompt fairly consistent judgements that, whatever they are, they are not blues.

3.1 'Form' and 'structure'

Units of structure are also called formal elements, and sometimes formal properties. The terms 'structure' and 'form', each of which has a long history and has given rise to critical movements (**formalism** and **structuralism**), are used here simply to describe the arrangement of elements in a text. It should be noted, however, that these terms are used widely in discussion of aesthetic objects and texts with varying meanings and implications.

3.1.1 'Form' as coherence and unity

One sense of 'form', which has a long history in philosophy since Plato, considers it as an underlying essence or ideal of something that exists beyond its physical manifestation. 'Form' in this sense is something inherent, beyond analysis. The poet Samuel Taylor Coleridge (1772–1834) developed the term **organic form** to capture the idea that aesthetic form occurs or grows of itself, naturally, rather than being a human or social construct. In **New Criticism** (an American literary theory at its height between the 1930s and the 1960s), the idea of organic form in literature takes on an added dimension: poetic 'form' is said to involve a complex balancing of potentially conflicting elements (hence the emphasis placed in New Criticism on **irony**, **paradox** and **ambiguity**). What unites this sense of form with the Platonic sense is that, in each case, formal elements are seen as in some sense inseparable from the text as a whole. By contrast, when we refer to formal elements in this unit, we are working with a different assumption: that it is possible to isolate and examine individual formal elements.

3.1.2 'Structure'

The term 'structure' is also commonly used in discussion of how formal elements in a text are arranged. Structure refers to the 'insides' of a text: its network or system of underlying relations, which can be discovered by analysis. But here again it is worth remembering that there is another common use of the term 'structure', which refers to the text itself (a use analogous to calling a house or a bridge a structure).

3.2 Grammars of language

The most basic way we can represent the structure of a written (or spoken) text is by means of a set of organizing principles called a grammar. To under-stand how units of structure function in a particular text we need first to consider the grammar of a language more generally.

3.2.1 The descriptive grammar of a language

The descriptive grammar of a language is a theory of how words can be thought of as different kinds of unit, how those units fit together into larger units (called phrases), and how these larger units combine into sentences. The grammar of English (like all other human languages) turns out to be quite complicated, and parts of it are even now, despite generations of research, not well under-stood. It is nevertheless possible, by looking at the most basic elements of the system – words and the different parts of speech they can be grouped into – to see the scope and power of even incomplete grammatical description.

If we were to build a grammatical description of our own, we might begin with a basic rule that says that a sentence is made up of a sequence of units called 'words'. This seems adequate for the following sentence:

(1)   someone lived in a pretty little town

But if we reorder these words, our basic grammatical rule turns out to be only partly reliable:

(2)   someone pretty lived in a little town

(3)   someone lived a in pretty little town

We recognize that sentence (2) is an acceptable sentence, while sentence (3) is not. Our theory of units, as it stands, cannot explain why (3) is not an acceptable sentence. So, in order to understand why changing the order of words gives these different results, we need to distinguish between different *kinds* of words, on the basis of their different functions in sentences. In other words, we need to divide the basic unit 'word' into a number of sub-units, such as 'noun', '**verb**', 'adjective', 'article' and so on. These different sub-units, or types of words, are called **parts of speech**.

Using available distinctions between parts of speech, we might now analyse our original sentence as follows:

(4)   someone lived in   a   pretty   little   town
      (noun)   (verb)(preposition) (article) (adjective) (adjective) (noun)

In sentence (3) above, the problem seems to lie in the sequence 'a in pretty'. Using analysis by part of speech, this sequence takes the following form: article–preposition–adjective. Since this sequence does not make sense in the above example, we might add a provisional descriptive rule to our grammar: that a preposition does not come between an article and an adjective.

Rules are only useful, however, if they apply in most cases. So we should now try out our rule using other words in the article–preposition–adjective positions. The sequence 'the of happy', for example, also turns out to be a combination that is never found in a normal-sounding English sentence. In fact, we have found a general grammatical rule in English and can safely predict that prepositions will never appear in between an article and an adjective.

Table 3.1 Parts of speech

Name of unit	Examples
Verb	go, went, seemed, give, have, be, am, eat, broken
Noun	thing, book, theory, beauty, universe, destruction
Adjective	happy, destructive, beautiful, seeming, broken
Adverb	fast, quickly, seemingly, probably, unfortunately
Preposition	in, on, beside, up, after, towards, at, underneath
Article	the, a
Demonstrative	this, that, those, these
Modal	should, could, need, must, might, can, shall, would
Degree word	how, very, rather, quite
Quantifier	some, every, all

Not all grammatical rules are as straightforward or as general in their application as this one. But the process of discovering them would be essentially the same. By analysing sequences, formulating provisional rules, testing them out with different combinations of words, and modifying the rules where necessary, we could build up our own descriptive grammar of English. In doing so, we would learn important things about the structure and possibilities of the language.

The system of units called 'parts of speech' has been studied since classical times. Some fairly generally accepted names for different parts of speech, together with examples, are set out in Table 3.1 (note that this list of parts of speech is not exhaustive).

3.3 Literary applications of grammatical description

Analysing a text into **constituent elements** becomes useful when it illuminates how that text is working. Rather like an action replay, descriptive analysis can examine in slow motion and close detail a process that in composition or in spontaneous reading occurs without conscious attention.

3.3.1 Descriptive analysis

Perhaps the most basic usefulness of analysis employing units of structure in literary texts is that it enables us to describe potentially significant patterns, such as repetition. Take the first stanza of William Blake's 'London' (1794), for example:

> I wander thro' each charter'd street,
> Near where the charter'd Thames does flow,
> And mark in every face I meet
> Marks of weakness, marks of woe.

This textual fragment could be described in terms of a range of different units: stanza, sentence, line, phrase, word, parts of speech, etc. The notion of repetition would almost certainly be involved in a description involving any of these units. Consider here, though, a description based simply on observed repetition and using analysis by part of speech. An account of the poem might want to discuss not only the repetition of 'charter'd' in the first and second lines of the stanza, but also the repetition of 'mark' in the third and fourth lines. It is more accurate, however – and so potentially more useful – to note that 'mark' in line three is being used as a verb, meaning to see or to notice, while in line four it is used (in the plural) as a noun. We might then use that distinction to ask why these 'marks' in the fourth line are being linked, through the verbal echo, with the speaker's act of seeing, or 'marking', them in the previous line.

3.3.2 Parallelism

By identifying units in a text that are repeated, or repeated with local variation, we can make visible the structure of certain kinds of **parallelism** (see **Unit 18, Parallelism**), for example the repetition of grammatical structures. Consider Blake's 'London' again. The whole of this poem is highly structured by verbal and grammatical parallelism, a characteristic illustrated in the fourth line of the verse quoted above: 'marks of weakness, marks of woe'.

3.3.3 Descriptions of style

The example drawn from Blake focuses on specific, local effects. By analysing larger stretches of text (or a number of whole texts), however, it is also possible to identify characteristic linguistic choices made by individual writers. A writer, for example, may show a predisposition towards – or a reluctance to use – adverbs, complex sentences or relative **clauses**. By detailed analysis of recurrent structures (or noting structures that do not occur but that are known to occur frequently in the given type of discourse generally) it is possible for editors to ascribe a text of unknown origin to a particular author. This process of attribution of authorship is greatly helped by computer analysis of a large number of texts, or **corpus** (as discussed in **Unit 2, Using information sources**). It is also possible to begin to describe exactly why the **styles** of different authors can feel different when you read them, almost irrespective of what they are writing about. The perceptible differences between the writings of Ernest Hemingway, Virginia Woolf and Henry James, for example, can be accounted for in grammatical terms.

3.3.4 Deviation

A grammar of a language is the set of rules for combining units (parts of speech) into sequences. But it is always possible to break the rules in order to achieve a specific effect (see **Unit 19, Deviation**). Rule-breaking texts can be analysed by looking at which rules have been broken and considering what effects are created by each transgression.

Consider, for example, the first line of a poem by e e cummings (1940):

anyone lived in a pretty how town

This line seems odd. But we can begin to explain its oddity by showing which grammatical rules it deviates from. The sequence 'a pretty how town' is odd because 'how' is a degree word (see Table 3.1 on p. 32), which appears in a place where we would expect not a degree word but an adjective (e.g. nice, awful). In fact, the sequence article–adjective–degree word–noun is not a possible sequence in English. (A parallel example would be 'the stone very houses'.)

Another problem with the line is 'anyone'. 'Anyone' is an indefinite pronoun, and as such potentially fits into the place it appears in. The pronouns 'it' or 'someone', for example, would be perfectly acceptable before the verb 'lived'. But users of English instinctively realize that 'anyone' does not make sense in the sequence of words that cummings has used.

How can analysis in terms of units of structure help with reading in this case? The reader might simply abandon the poem as nonsensical. Alternatively, however, he or she might try other ways of reading it. It might help, for example, to rearrange the words in order to 'make sense' of them, as if other, related strings of words are being echoed or evoked:

how anyone lived in a pretty town

In this new sequence, 'anyone' does make sense in the position preceding the verb 'lived'; and we seem to have the beginnings of an interpretation, which would go something like 'how anyone lived in a pretty town like that is a mystery to me'. However, if we try to match this interpretation with the rest of the poem, we find it doesn't seem to work – nothing similar or evidently compatible seems to happen elsewhere – and so this beginning of a reading probably needs to be abandoned. There is, however, another way we might use analysis of units of structure to deal with this grammatical problem. If we look at other uses of 'anyone' in the poem, we may discover a pattern. Consider:

anyone's any was all to her (line 16)

one day anyone died i guess (line 25)

Neither of these lines makes grammatical sense. But we can see that 'anyone' appears consistently in a position in sequences where we would normally expect expressions that refer to particular, definite entities (e.g. proper names; noun phrases, such as 'the woman'; or pronouns, such as 'he' or 'she'):

one day (Bill/Alice/the woman/he/she) died i guess

Close reading of the poem following this insight suggests that 'anyone' could be a man who lived in a pretty town and married a woman referred to as 'no-one', and that they were eventually buried side by side. Whatever the merits of this reading, we have begun to make sense of the poem by exploring how it may work through a kind of grammatical substitution: indefinite pronouns used as if they are definite pronouns referring to particular people.

The next step would be to ask why the poem would be written like that, and what effects it has as a result. The paraphrase given above suggests that, if we substitute definite nouns in place of 'anyone' and 'no-one', the poem becomes quite banal. One general effect of using 'anyone' and 'no-one', therefore, might be that of making the poem ambiguous or more thought-provoking. The two figures and their experience are given more general significance (they stand for every man and every woman) by being kept anonymous and emptied of individual significance (they are both anyone and no one).

3.4 Extending the notion of grammar

Our suggestion so far is that the grammar underlying a text governs how it is constructed. We have also suggested that a text's grammatical organization constrains and guides how it will be interpreted. If both of these claims are sound, then notions of grammar are essential in bringing to conscious attention organizing principles that, in our everyday practice of reading texts, may be simply acted on spontaneously and taken for granted.

In addition to being useful in analysing written texts, a grammatical approach can be applied quite generally to systems of signs. Think of any grammatical sequence as a series of slots that can be filled by different items; we can then extend the notion of grammar to domains besides language, for instance by viewing how we dress as possible combinations of what might be thought of as clothing units. If we extend the notion of grammar in this way, the body is divided into zones, each of which is thought of as a 'slot' within the clothing system: head, upper torso, legs, feet, etc. Each of these areas may be covered with an item of clothing, chosen from a set of available alternatives. The 'fillers' for the slots are individual items of clothing (e.g. for the feet: boots, shoes, sandals, nothing at all). Specific fillers can be used in some slots but not others; and predictable effects are generated by patterns of their combination. By examining combinations of selected items, specific styles can be described in terms of their consistency in selection. Deviations from conventional clothing 'statements' can also be described (e.g. wearing Wellington boots and a headscarf with a suit), in ways that parallel the treatment of the e e cummings poem above.

Consider the same general approach applied to narrative film. The film as a whole has a number of slots: its credit sequence (and possibly pre-credit sequence); the main body of its narrative (including sub-units such as establishing **shots**, dialogue, car chase sequence, etc.); and end credits. Each of these slots can be handled in different ways by a director, by selecting different options or by omitting optional elements. Car chases, for instance (where they are included in a film 'statement'), can end in the death of the person chased, loss of the person being followed, collision involving the car chasing, etc. An overall filmic style is produced by manipulating possibilities within each slot –

and so also implicitly alluding to how slots are typically filled and combined in other texts (See **Unit 13, Intertextuality and allusion**).

Study of the units of structure (slots and fillers) of a wide range of cultural texts, institutions and ideas (from literature and photography through to what people eat) forms a central part of the theoretical movement known as structuralism, which developed in the late 1950s (see Culler, 2002). The grammar of narrative, which allows us to describe the range of possible slots and fillers for any narrative, has received particular attention (see **Unit 20, Narrative**).

3.5 Constitutive rather than regulatory rules

The rules of what might be called the 'cultural grammars' proposed by structuralism are often described as 'constitutive'. This means that, as grammatical rules, they are not regulating an already existing system (as rules do that tell you what you must and must not do while driving); instead, they define what can count as allowable within a conventional system that only comes into being at all because of the existence of those rules. It is only by invoking particular conventions or rules of a game of chess or football, or social behaviour such as greeting or eating in a restaurant, that you are able to recognize the activity as whatever you know it to be. The same applies to social institutions such as weddings, birthday parties, money or law.

Structuralism's descriptions gained much of their power and interest from the possibility they offered of isolating and describing basic structures of how conventional social codes operate. That power of description was often linked to two further claims. The first is the suggestion, made by many thinkers, that the formulation of grammatical rules in terms of layers of often **binary oppositions**, or oppositions involving a contrast between only two alternative terms, has deep origins in human psychology. The second claim is that the means for describing such systems – considered to be available in linguistic techniques for analysing the grammar of language – would be similar across a very wide range of sign systems.

3.6 Possibilities for analysis

How useful, in our everyday practice of reading, is analysis in terms of units of structure likely to be? Arguably the value of such analysis ranges from better understanding of how a given form comes to have a particular meaning to general ideas about how to create new forms that build on but extend existing ones.

In many areas of analysis, little work has been done on naming and justifying use of relevant units or working out their possible combinations. It may often be the case, therefore, that when you analyse a text you must invent your own units and your own rules of combination, and justify them in terms of new ideas and insights they make possible. There are only the beginnings, for example, of a grammar of contemporary popular music. In creating such a grammar, we would need units such as intro, verse, hook, riff, chorus, bridge, fade and mix. This unit has suggested that, even though such a grammar might require new units and rules of combination, the procedure for developing it would follow broadly the same operations (including tests of replacement and movement to identify units and how they function) that have long been used in descriptions of English grammar.

ACTIVITY 3.1 ▬▬▬▬▬▬▬▬▬▬▬▬▬▬▬▬▬▬▬▬

The fifteen sentences below make up a plot summary of Charles Dickens's novel *Oliver Twist* (1837–8), but they have been jumbled up to form a different order. Each sentence describes an event in the novel (so the unit of structure here is 'sentence' and/or 'event'). To contrast that level with a different level of analysis, the words of sentence (1) within the jumbled sequence of sentences have themselves been scrambled. (The original ordering is given on p. 340.)

1   Construct a possible English sentence out of the jumbled words of sentence (1) below. Use all the words and do not use any word twice. Keep a note of how you rearrange the scrambled sentence. (Your note may show that you can do this on a more systematic basis than trial-and-error.)

    (1)   escape and tries Nancy's cry to following hue the death Sikes

2   Now work out a plausible sequence for all fifteen jumbled events. Again, keep a note of the kinds of evidence – especially particular linking words or expressions, or possible and impossible/implausible sequences of events – that you use to help you decide in favour of one particular order rather than another. (It may help to photocopy the page and actually cut the copy into strips, with one event on each, so that you can physically reorder them.)

3   When you have found and noted what you take to be the most plausible sequence, rearrange the fifteen events into a *new, different order*, this time an order that tells the story in a different way. In carrying out this second reordering, only take into account what happens, not the particular wording of each event as given above. In your rewritten novel sequence, you can refer to a single event more than once (for example, if you want to insert events into the description of a particular event in order to create a flashback).

4   Finally, consider how different your new narrative structure is from the one created by the summary you assembled earlier. What are its differences at other levels of structure for which relevant units of analysis might also be developed: point of view; suspense; chronology; genre?

(1)   [*Write your rearranged version of sentence (1) here.*]

(2)   Keen to take advantage of these offers, the gang of thieves kidnap Oliver from Mr Brownlow.

(3)   The thieves try to convert Oliver into a thief.

(4)   Nancy discovers that Monks knows about Oliver's true parentage; having developed redeeming traits, she informs Rose of the danger Oliver is in.

(5)   With Sikes dead, the rest of the gang are captured; Fagin is executed.

(6)   Oliver accompanies Sikes on a burglary, but receives a gunshot wound.

(7)   Nancy's efforts are discovered by the gang, and she is brutally murdered by Bill Sikes.

(8)   Oliver runs away and is looked after by benevolent Mr Brownlow.

(9)   The thieves become especially interested in Oliver, because they receive offers concerning him from a sinister person named Monks.

(10)   Found and threatened with exposure, Monks confesses that he is Oliver's half-brother, and has pursued his ruin in order to acquire the whole of his father's property.

(11)   Oliver falls into the hands of a gang of thieves, including Bill Sikes, Nancy and the Artful Dodger, and headed by a rogue called Fagin.

(12)   Suffering pain from the gunshot wound, Oliver is captured by Mrs Maylie and her protégée Rose, who brings him up for a time.

(13)   Monks emigrates and dies in prison; Oliver rejoins Mr Brownlow and is adopted by him.

(14)   He accidentally hangs himself in the process.

(15)   Oliver Twist, a pauper of unknown parentage, runs away to London.

Reading

Aitchison, J. (2003) *Teach Yourself Linguistics*, Teach Yourself Series, London: Hodder.

Culler, J. (2002) *Structuralist Poetics: Structuralism, Linguistics and the Study of Literature*, London: Routledge, Chapter 1.

Fabb, N. (2005) *Sentence Structure*, 2nd edn, London: Routledge.

Leech, G. (1969) *A Linguistic Guide to English Poetry*, London: Longman.

Leech, G. and Short, M.H. (1981) *Style in Fiction*, London: Longman, Chapter 1.

Unit 4

Recognizing genre

In its most general sense, 'genre' simply means a sort, or type, of text: thriller, horror movie, musical, autobiography, tragedy, etc. The word comes from the Latin word 'genus', meaning 'kind' or 'type' of anything, not just literary or artistic works. ('Genus', in fact, is still used to describe a technical sense of type, in the classification of species; and 'generic' is sometimes used to mean 'broad' or 'with the properties of a whole type or class'.) There is an obvious convenience in being able to label texts. We can fit any given text into a class that offers a convenient shorthand in which to describe what it is like: it resembles others that people already know. The notion is useful when applied not only to literary works but also to non-literary discourse, distinguishing the typical features of, say, a shopping list from those of food labelling, a menu or a recipe.

For all its convenience, however, the notion of genre presents difficulties. Is there a fixed number of sorts of text? If so, when and how was this decided, and on what basis? And who will decide for still evolving types, such as emergent styles in popular music, texting or multimedia? A more theoretical question also arises: whether genre is a prescriptive category – grouping features to be incorporated into writing or production of a given type – or whether it is descriptive, generalizing on the basis of agreement among language users.

4.1 Sorting texts into types

Each of the main criteria involved in distinguishing members of one genre from members of another has its own history and implications, and typically they work in combination with one another. It is, however, worth listing them individually before considering complications in how they work.

41

4.1.1 Classification on the basis of formal arrangement

One basis for classifying texts is their formal properties (see **Unit 3, Analysing units of structure**). Sonnets, for instance, have fourteen lines and follow distinctive stanzaic and rhyme patterns. At the same time, sonnets are a type of poetry, which in turn exists within a conventional three-way distinction between poetry, drama and fiction – a classification derived historically from Aristotle's distinction between lyric, epic or narrative, and drama.

Aristotle's distinctions were primarily, though not exclusively, based on formal properties. Poetry typically involves **rhythm** and other kinds of sound patterning; fiction does not, at least not necessarily; but it does involve narrative. Drama involves characters speaking and acting in relation to each other. In *Poetics* (fourth century BC), Aristotle further emphasized one particular, distinguishing aspect of form: who speaks. Lyrics are uttered in the first person; in epic or narrative, the narrator speaks in the first person, then lets characters speak for themselves; in drama, the characters do all the talking.

Although common ever since Aristotle, genre classification on the basis of formal differences can be difficult to sustain. What about verse drama? Or narrative poetry (as in ballads)? Or dramatic monologue (in which a single character or persona speaks, but without any given dramatic context or action)? And the difficulties multiply as soon as multimodal kinds of discourse or other media are taken into account that bring together conventions drawn from more than one **medium** (say words and pictures).

4.1.2 Classification on the basis of theme or topic

Sometimes subject matter is the basis for genre classification. Texts show thematic affinities by treating the same or similar topics, often topics or subject matter that may be especially important for the society in which the texts circulate (e.g. war, love and marriage, royal succession, independence struggles).

The pastoral, for instance, is concerned with country life; crime fiction is about crime; biography relates events in a life; and science fiction explores possible future or alternative worlds; but in principle it is possible to treat any of these topics following formal conventions of any of the different kinds listed above, or in different moods that will create different kinds of effect on the reader or viewer.

4.1.3 Classification on the basis of mood or anticipated response

What a text is about can overlap with an attitude or emotion conventionally adopted towards that subject matter. **Pastoral** often implies not just concern with country life, but also a reflective or nostalgic mode. **Elegies** – although first defined on the basis of the metre they used – became primarily concerned with lamenting deaths (and often take the form of pastoral elegies, delivered in the personae of shepherds). War poetry has a complex history both of jingo-istic and anti-war traditions, though both strands tend to explore ideas of patriotism, moral values and loyalty.

A more complex case is that of **tragedy**. Classical tragedy combines conventions about the **protagonist** (the 'tragic hero', who has a character with a crucial flaw) and conventions about the nature of the **plot** (in which the main character typically suffers and dies). At the same time, tragedy is also defined (at least in Aristotle's account in *Poetics*) by its characteristic mode of audi-ence response: what Aristotle called **catharsis**, or a purging or purification by means of feelings of pity and fear aroused in the audience by the dramatic spectacle. Later developments of tragedy – associated particularly with Seneca (first century AD) in classical Rome, then during the European Renaissance and into the modern period – vary in each of these main respects, while retaining some quality that is still thought to be distinctive of tragedy. Whereas classical tragedy involved kings and princes, for instance, modern tragedy commonly involves relatively anonymous, often socially alienated protagonists; and modern tragedies tend to involve little or no significant action, in con-trast with the major political events and destinies of nations that formed the usual concern of classical tragedy (see Williams, 1966). Given the scale of such changes within the genre, it is arguable that what most allows a modern audi-ence to consider a new text to be a tragedy is less its formal properties or subject matter than the mood it creates or audience reaction it evokes.

4.1.4 Classification on the basis of occasion

Literary forms may now seem specialized kinds of discourse, isolated from the rest of society and mainly discussed in literature classes, but for most of its history literature has not been marked off within specified boundaries in this way. Rather, its involvement in public life, including in various kinds of social ritual, meant that many different texts had their origins in composition for or performance on specific kinds of social occasion.

Drama in classical times, for instance, was a ritual involving important cultural customs and had significant social implications for members of the audience. Many later dramatic genres also developed in particular histor-ical contexts and for special kinds of occasion: **chronicle plays** dealing with English history flourished in the sixteenth century in a period of patriotic fervour following the defeat of the Spanish Armada in 1588; and in the late sixteenth and early seventeenth centuries **masques** were a form of court entertainment combining poetic drama, music, dancing and elaborate costumes and staging, and involved participation by the aristocratic members of the audi-ence in the performance (for further discussion, see **Unit 25, Ways of reading drama**).

Poetic genres have developed in analogous ways. An **epithalamium** is a poem written for – and proclaimed at – a public occasion, in celebration of a victorious person (e.g. an athlete or a general). The genre of elegy evolved during the seventeenth century into its modern role as a consolatory lament for the death of a particular person. **Ballads** began as poems to be danced to, but evolved into two divergent traditions: continuing folk ballads in the oral tradition, and urban **broadside ballads** circulated as single sheets or chapbooks that typically contained popular songs, jests, romantic tales and sensational topical stories.

4.1.5 Classification on the basis of mode of address

Even when dissociated from specific social occasions or performance rituals, texts are still in some cases labelled on the basis of how they **address** their readers or audience. Some texts involve **direct address** to a reader or audience (e.g. public speeches, letters and e-mails, news anchoring); others have a specific **addressee** named in the text but are written so as to be overheard (e.g. odes, dialogue in most stage drama). Sometimes within a single form there is variation between **modes of address**. Essays addressed to 'Dear Reader' are interpolated into narratives in some eighteenth-century novels, stepping outside the frame of the imagined world and narrative style of the rest of the text.

4.2 Recognizing or deciding what genre a text is in

Criteria for distinguishing different genres, we have said, tend to work together rather than independently of one another. Deciding what genre a text is in therefore involves weighing up a number of interlocking considerations. This can make it difficult to judge whether a text fits a category simply by ticking off features in a list of required attributes.

Consider the **sonnet**, which is often viewed as an exemplary case of a highly codified form. Sonnets consist of fourteen lines grouped as an octave (eight-line stanza) and a sestet (six-line stanza), with ten **syllables** in each line, a prescribed **rhyme scheme**, and a change of direction or reversal in the poem's argument between the two stanzas at a point called the volta. This attractively simple picture has nevertheless to be refined, because of the existence of two main traditions: the Italian (or Petrarchan) style, with its highly patterned, closed and interlaced rhyme scheme (abba, abba, cde, cde); and the English (or Shakespearean) style, with a different rhyme scheme (abab, cdcd, efef, gg) that reshapes the poem as a douzain (twelve lines, consisting of three open-rhyme quatrains) plus a final rhyming couplet that in effect shifts the volta to near the end. This still simplified account then needs to be refined further, to acknowledge that each of these traditions allows for variation. The description also needs to incorporate thematic criteria: specialized conventions relating to love, heroic and sacred sonnets, as well as (later in development of the form) to nature sonnets and political and moral sonnets. Even this enriched account of rules governing the sonnet still needs to be refined further before it could function as a complete list of necessary and sufficient conditions of being a sonnet.

Refined, though, in what direction? What is inevitably missing from this account, focusing as it does on formal and thematic conventions, is relevant history, in this case the composition of sonnets almost continuously from the thirteenth century through to the twenty-first century, with complex interaction between sonnet traditions in different languages and different periods.

To view the sonnet form in a way that incorporates social dimensions involves thinking not only of formal rules but also about cultural interaction and influence, with forms evolving through innovations that are based on established conventions but do not respect pre-set boundaries. When Milton writes broadly Petrarchan sonnets with the volta apparently out of place, or when Blake writes a sonnet that doesn't rhyme, or when John Updike writes a sonnet in which none of the lines after the first even have words, they are not so much failing to follow rules as pushing back boundaries (for discussion of these and other examples, see Fuller, 1972). It is readers, and subsequent writers, who decide whether such experiments are still sonnets – and when a new genre or sub-genre has been created that merits a category of its own.

4.2.1 Genre as an expression of conventional agreement

An alternative to thinking of genre as a list of essential properties is to start instead with the idea that genres may be focused in especially influential texts that serve as exemplary cases. Sophocles's *Oedipus Rex* (*c.*400 BC) is often appealed to as an exemplary tragedy, for example: a sort of benchmark, with other texts defined as tragedies to the extent that they are similar to it. This view of genre, where a prototype is taken to exist and where other texts are judged to be more or less close to the prototype, enables texts to be assigned to genres even when they do not have all the apparently necessary features. It then becomes possible for a text to be a novel even if it has no discernible narrative (as many experimental novels don't), so long as the text works with or exploits our expectation that it should have.

Even notions of the typical or 'prototypical' are not fixed, however. Generic conventions come to us as a historical legacy, shaped and reshaped by the changing production and circulation of texts, as well as by changing attitudes to them. What constitutes a typical novel in the early twenty-first century – even allowing for huge variation within the novel form – is not the same as what constituted a typical novel during the eighteenth or nineteenth centuries. It is this difference in the genre prototype that makes possible the paradoxical observation that some novelists may be said to be writing highly successful nineteenth-century novels even now, at the beginning of the twenty-first century.

4.3 Functions of genre

So far we have looked at different ways of understanding what genre is. But why should it matter whether we assign texts to types or classes, and who in fact does? To understand what functions genre serves, we need to explore how distinctions created by notions of genre fit into the larger, aesthetic and social frameworks that govern how texts are created, how they circulate and how they are evaluated (see **Unit 13, Intertextuality and allusion**).

The various functions that are attributed to genre, as we shall see even in the brief descriptions that follow, are problematic, resting on a major fault line within literary history. In some periods and places, it is thought a valuable achievement to produce a good 'generic text': a pastoral ode that respects the conventions, a formulaic but clever detective thriller, or a good pop song recounting a failed relationship completely irrespective of the song-writer's actual circumstances, for example. In other periods and places, the aspiration to write within a genre is dismissed as vacuous and imitative, lacking in imagination and individual creativity. This unresolved issue of the nature and scope of literary creativity is reflected in the various functions genre is thought to serve.

4.3.1 Genre as a framework for a text's intelligibility

The main psychological function of genre is to act as a sort of **schema**, or structured set of assumptions within our tacit knowledge, that we draw on to guide reading, rather like a series of signposts or instructions. Expectations in reading are structured at many different levels, from the sorts of local inference we make in order to fill in gaps between obviously related but not continuous details through to vague assumptions about overall point or significance. Genre dictates procedures for reading at each level, signalling the general trajectory that a text is likely to be following, the amount of detail we expect it to go into at any given stage or on any topic, and the degree of **realism** or truthfulness it is likely to show.

4.3.2 Genre as reflecting the nature of human experience

Relating this cognitive role of genre to speculation about basic human categories of thought, some critics have suggested connections between specific genres and fundamental kinds of human experience. The distinction between tragedy and **comedy** is often made along these lines. One notable scheme in this area is that of **archetypal genres** developed by the literary critic Northrop Frye (1912–91). For Frye, four selected genres (comedy, romance, tragedy and satire) correspond emotionally to the four seasons, which are linked in turn to perceived stages of human life and a rich cultural reservoir of myth.

One problem with such a view of genre, however, is that it is likely to have little to say about the emotional functions of less traditional or less high-cultural genres: the dance mix, the performance pop-video, the Bollywood masala movie or the blog. Archetypal classifications take for granted a distinction – in itself 'generic' – between serious or profound forms that somehow correspond to essential human experience and other, non-serious forms that are presumably less worthwhile or significant.

4.3.3 Genre as a promotional device

By comparison with the previous two functions, most other functions suggested for genre are concerned more with the social circulation of texts than with cognitive processes involved in interpreting them. Sometimes genre provides structure, for instance, in classification systems used to identify a textual product range or locate texts in a given market. In this context, genre signals an appeal to different audience tastes and wishes (for news, for the problem-solving pleasure of detective fiction, for a story to make you cry, etc.). Genres allow audiences to predict and plan kinds of experience for themselves, and to repeat, with local variation, kinds of pleasure or entertainment they have previously enjoyed. TV scheduling displays this type of thinking (indeed, the vocabulary of media scheduling consists largely of such classification). Genre categories then feed back to 'content providers', or text producers, who can work to genre expectations in order to fill a given market niche and respond to known audience tastes.

4.3.4 Genre as a way of controlling markets and audiences

This view of the usefulness of genre categories overlaps with the last; but it extends it, with the idea that genres do not so much reflect audience wishes as create them. Genres in this view are part of a process of controlling the production of entertainment and directing culture markets, by actively repeating the formula of whatever has already been successful. Saturating media space with texts created according to proven formulae allows confident investment in production; but to many people this use of genre as a set of planning categories represents a kind of conspiracy, bringing about a detrimental standardization of cultural products into predictable forms. (The financing of Hollywood films, with notable exceptions, is often argued to follow this pattern.)

4.4 Exploited genres

Once genres are established in our patterns of expectation, they lend themselves to quotation and creative adaptation, and can be mixed, merged and manipulated. Such secondary use of genre categories takes a number of forms, but the two most common are **collage** and **pastiche**.

4.4.1 Collage and pastiche

In collage, different genres (or features of different genres) are placed alongside one another and thus are implicitly joined together. Such collage can be used, as it commonly is in modernist texts, to set up a dialectic, or process of contrastive judgement that results from the juxtaposition of different voices or quoted texts. (See **Unit 12, Juxtaposition**.)

Pastiche (along with other sub-genres, such as burlesque, mock-epic and mock-heroic) is similar, insofar as it undermines or offsets a seemingly authentic speaking voice by bringing different styles together. But it does so by clearly signalling the element of imitation – especially incongruous imitation – generally by merging conventions from one genre with subject matter from another.

Both kinds of genre mixing or genre layering are common techniques in satire, whether in print, film, or radio and television comedy sketches. In the case of collage, something in the text – or in our expectations – signals that we are to respond to one of the genres in the compound as more powerful or convincing than the other(s). That genre undermines or displaces those other genres or genre features, and so implies an often critical comparison anchored in the values carried by the dominant genre. In pastiche, tension between the subject matter and the generic conventions followed indicates the satire, which can be directed either towards the form adopted or the topic (for discussion of techniques in satire, see Simpson, 2003).

Ironies created in this way are not always controllable, however. Genre combinations sometimes escape from authorial control, and can leave the text an open-ended dialogue between voices it has juxtaposed, with no stabilizing, dominant voice to confer a fixed point or meaning (see **Unit 11, Irony** and **Unit 14, Authorship and intention**).

4.4.2 Postmodernism and genre

When generic compounding and formulaic imitation bring a text's genre directly into the foreground, and make irony or implied comment on the genre a dominant or continuous aspect of the text, they create one major dimension of **postmodernism**.

Roughly, postmodernism is a response to a set of cultural conditions believed to characterize the contemporary period. As viewed in postmodernism, our exposure to language and media so saturates social experience that any act of communication inevitably involves a high degree of self-awareness of the genres in which communication takes place. In most situations, self-consciousness about the means rather than the content of communication – about the range of conventional forms available for representing things – is played down. What makes a text postmodern is that, rather than just trying to communicate its contents to you, it draws attention to the modes of writing and reading that are in play, often undermining them by doing so. This kind of postmodernist effect is seen mainly in texts that use the sorts of collage and pastiche technique outline above; but such effects can be found in texts written or produced before the rise of postmodernism, too, by looking for traces of juxtaposed styles, moments of uncertain **register**, or incongruities between topic and adopted form. (A Romantic poem, for instance, might be approached not as an expression, in apparent good faith, of its author's spirit but as a text pondering its own creation as an example of the Romantic poetic genre.) In most postmodernist readings, the notion of genre is foregrounded; and many contemporary thinkers suggest that you can only read a text in a culturally postmodern framework by reading its complex relationships to a history of other texts (see **Unit 13, Intertextuality and allusion**).

_____**ACTIVITY 4.1**

This activity explores the ability of readers and viewers to recognize text types almost instantly and fairly precisely. (You can check the general claim that readers and viewers can do this by surfing channels on a TV or scanning radio frequencies.)

Four brief extracts are given below. Each is from the beginning (or very near the beginning) of the work it comes from. All four extracts are from works that in a broad sense are in the 'novel' genre; but arguably they are placed differently in relation to that genre.

1   Make a list of qualities or attributes of each text that support the idea that it is broadly in the novel genre. Compare what happens when you do this by invoking a list of 'essential features of a novel' and when you start with a looser, prototypical idea of what a novel is or with a particular novel you are familiar with, using that novel as an exemplary case. (See discussion in this unit for details of these approaches.)

2   Now identify any qualities or attributes of each text that suggest it may be problematic in relation to the novel genre. Take care only to identify features that would affect inclusion in or exclusion from the genre; this will oblige you to distinguish attributes you take to be criteria for the novel genre from more general description of the extract.

3   Finally, consider how exposure to further cues in a text may prompt revision to an initial genre categorization. Even without knowing or trying to research answers, decide what you would now look for in the continuation of each extract in order to test the genre judgements you have made so far.

Text A

A   In the beginnings of the last chapter, I informed you exactly *when* I was born; – but I did not inform you *how*. No; that particular was reserved entirely for a chapter by itself; – besides, Sir, as you and I are in a manner perfect strangers to each other, it would not have been proper to have let you into too many circumstances relating to myself all at once. – You must have a little patience. I have undertaken, you see, to write not only my life, but my opinions also; hoping and expecting that your knowledge of my character, and of what kind of a mortal I am, by the one, would give you a better relish for the other: As you proceed further with me, the slight acquaintance which is now beginning betwixt us, will grow into familiarity; and that, unless one of us is in fault, will terminate in friendship.

(Laurence Sterne, *The Life and Opinions of Tristram Shandy* (1759–67), Volume 1, Chapter 6)

Text B

B   Of late years an abundant shower of curates has fallen upon the north of England: they lie very thick on the hills; every parish has one or more of them; they are young enough to be very active, and ought to be doing a great deal of good. But not of late years are we about to speak; we are going back to the beginning of this century: late years – present years are dusty, sunburnt, hot, arid; we will evade the noon, forget it in siesta, pass the midday in slumber, and dream of dawn.

If you think, from this prelude, that anything like a romance is preparing for you, reader, you never were more mistaken. Do you anticipate sentiment, and poetry, and reverie? Do you expect passion, and stimulus, and melodrama? Calm your expectations; reduce them to a lowly standard. Something real, cool and solid lies before you; something unromantic as Monday morning, when all who have work wake with the consciousness that they must rise and betake themselves thereto.

(Charlotte Bronte, *Shirley* (1849), Chapter 1)

Text C

C   My father has asked me to be the fourth corner at the Joy Luck Club. I am to replace my mother, whose seat at the mah jong table has been empty since she died two months ago. My father thinks she was killed by her own thoughts.

'She had a new idea inside her head,' said my father. 'But before it could come out of her mouth, the thought grew too big and burst. It must have been a very bad idea.'

The doctor said she died of a cerebral aneurysm. And her friends at the Joy Luck Club said she died just like a rabbit: quickly and with unfinished business left behind. My mother was supposed to host the next meeting of the Joy Luck Club.

The week before she died, she called me, full of pride, full of life: 'Auntie Lin cooked red bean soup for Joy Luck. I'm going to cook black sesame-seed soup.'

'Don't show off,' I said.

(Amy Tan, *The Joy Luck Club* (1989), Chapter 1: 'Jing-Mei Woo, The Joy Luck Club')

Text D

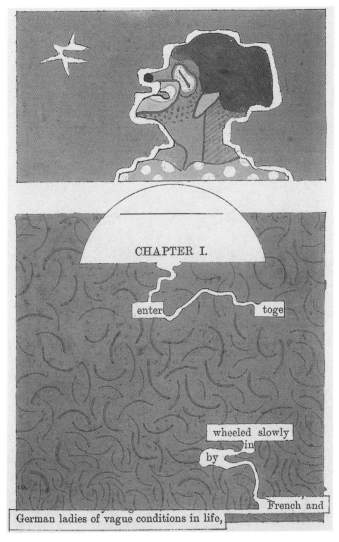

CHAPTER I.

enter   toge

wheeled slowly in by

French and

German ladies of vague conditions in life,

(Tom Phillips, *A Humument: A Treated Victorian Novel* [1980], 4th edn (2005))

Reading

Aristotle (*c.*400 BC), *Poetics* (many editions available, e.g. in (1996) trans. Malcolm Heath, Harmondsworth: Penguin).

Duff, D. (ed.) (2000) *Modern Genre Theory*, London: Longman.

Frye, N. (1957) *Anatomy of Criticism*, Princeton, NJ: Princeton University Press, esp. pp. 158–239.

Fuller, J. (1972) *The Sonnet*, London: Methuen.

Watt, I. (1972) *The Rise of the Novel*, Harmondsworth: Penguin.

Williams, R. (1966) *Modern Tragedy*, London: Chatto & Windus.

Section 2

Language variation

Unit 5

Language and time

All languages change over the course of time. Within a language group, these changes may develop to the extent that the language use of a particular community is significantly different from that of other users. This language use may then be described as a **dialect** (if those changes are at the level of small differences in grammar and vocabulary), and as a separate language (if those grammatical and lexical differences are significant). The fact of language change is relevant to the study of texts in several ways. A text may be a force for language change or it may attempt to retain older usages for particular effects. A text may become difficult to understand because of language change; it may contain words and phrases that are associated with earlier periods of the language's history, that have now become archaisms, and that rely on an understanding of what the state of the language was at any given time. A modern text may also deliberately use archaisms for particular effects.

5.1 Theories of language change

There are various different accounts of why and how language changes over time.

5.1.1 Formalist theories: change as an autonomous process

Many linguists have described language change as being caused by and working according to structural pressures that are internal to the language itself. For example, between 1500 and 1700 many of the vowel sounds of English changed into other vowel sounds in a process called the **Great Vowel Shift**. The modern English word 'make', for example, was pronounced in the sixteenth century with a different vowel, a little like the one you get in the modern English word 'mack' if you stretch the vowel out. In pronouncing these words, the tongue is higher and therefore nearer to the roof of the mouth in 'make' than it is in 'mack', so we can say that the vowel was 'raised' from its sixteenth-century pronunciation to its modern pronunciation. Many linguists, from nineteenth-century philologists to contemporary generative linguists, have investigated how these changes relate to each other and to the larger structures of the language. For example, one might classify vowels as 'high', 'mid' and 'low' on the basis of the height of the tongue when it makes them, and we could then say that, in the above example, a low vowel becomes a mid vowel. This change seems to have 'pushed' the old mid vowel to become a modern high vowel (modern 'meat' changed from a sixteenth-century word sounding like 'mate') and the older high vowel to have become a modern low vowel (modern 'ride' was once pronounced like 'reed'). What interests linguists, then, is that there seems to have been a system of interrelated changes that can be understood in relation to one another. Such linguists give a **formalist** account of these changes in language (that is, an explanation in terms of the form or units of structure of the language) (see **Unit 3, Analysing units of structure**).

5.1.2 A functionalist account: change as a politically motivated process

There is another view of language change and how to study and explain it that suggests that changes in language result from social activity, in particular from political struggle. Dick Leith (1983) accounts for the Great Vowel Shift by suggesting that the migration of workers into London in the period produced a clash of dialects that induced Londoners to distinguish their speech from the immigrants by changing their vowel system. Culpeper (1997) argues that the development of Standard English, through the use of the East Midlands dialect in the fifteenth century, can also be accounted for by examining social factors; the East Midlands dialect was used by William Caxton when he set up his printing press in London in 1476, and this dialect had become a lingua franca among merchants and government officials in the London area. This particular **functionalist theory** therefore claims that language change is socially motivated, rather than being solely motivated by the formal system of the language itself. A functionalist way of looking at language therefore analyses language change from the perspective of the social values carried by certain usages at specific points in time.

It is possible to combine functionalist and formalist accounts; for example, the Great Vowel Shift may have been triggered and supported in general terms by a struggle for linguistic identity, but the details of the shift – for example, which vowels changed and how they changed – might best be explained in formalist terms. Political, economic and social change can result in words being pronounced in new ways and given new meanings, and can lead to new words being invented. Also, it should be remembered that rarely, if ever, do words have one single fixed meaning or pronunciation. According to some

Marxist accounts of language, the pronunciation and meaning of words can be a 'site of struggle' when two or more social groups or interests have a political stake in enforcing one meaning of a word or phrase (see **Unit 9, Language and society**). For example, the local government tax levied on property in Britain in the 1980s was termed 'the community charge' by the Conservative government that introduced it, and 'the poll tax' by those opposed to its introduction. The latter term was coined because it has political implications in English history. The *OED* tells us that 'poll' used to mean 'head' (the current usage associated with voting comes from the poll as a counting of heads); one reason for reviving the archaism 'poll tax' is because it is levied on all 'heads' – i.e. on everyone of a voting age. But the term poll tax is also a specific allusion to the Peasants' Revolt of 1381, which, *Brewer's Dictionary of Phrase and Fable* notes, was 'immediately occasioned by an unpopular poll-tax at a time when there was a growing spirit of social revolt' in England. Thus, the revival of the term poll tax was a politically motivated gesture that seemed to make an analogy between 1381 and the situation at the time of the introduction of the property tax. (Ironically enough, the *OED* informs us that an archaic meaning of poll was 'to plunder by . . . excessive taxation; to pillage, rob, fleece'.) The success of the opposition to the new tax can be judged in part by how widely and by whom the alternative name 'poll tax' was used during the controversy. Now, however, the Labour government has introduced the more neutral 'council tax'.

5.2 Change and linguistic media

The main linguistic media – the media in which verbal language is used – are speech and writing (see **Unit 22, Speech and narration**), together with various other technologically enabled forms (language can be broadcast, recorded, telephoned, e-mailed, texted, etc.).

5.2.1 Writing

Before the seventeenth century, written texts varied enormously in terms of spelling and punctuation. This arose partly from the lack of a central standardization of spelling, partly from the variability and rapid changes in pronunciation, and partly from typesetting practices such as the symbolic use of capital letters to indicate importance and the insertion of letters to fill out a line. From the seventeenth century onwards, however, printed texts began to look more like modern English texts because standards were instituted that still hold. One of the results of this is that, while spellings have stabilized, pronunciations have continued to change, so that spellings that once corresponded to pronunciation no longer do so. This is one of the many reasons for the difficulties that all English speakers encounter when writing, since, when

English spelling was formalized, it resulted in a rift between the way words were spelt and pronounced in the seventeenth century and the way the pronunciation of words changed over time.

5.2.2 Speech

It has only recently become possible to record speech as sound; our evidence for how English was spoken in the past is generally in the form of: (a) the reports of contemporary linguists; (b) transcripts of speech, as in trial transcripts; (c) representations of speech in literature and drama; (d) indirect evidence from sound patterns in literature (e.g. rhymes); and (e) indirect evidence from informal writing such as diaries and letters.

Speech seems to change more rapidly than writing, partly because it is not codified in the same way, and partly because it is open to much wider cultural variation. Youth subcultures generate a large number of new terms and phrases to mark membership of groups, and more importantly to mark non-membership. Such subculture words and phrases filter into mainstream spoken English or into the written standard only very occasionally. Consider, for example, the word 'wicked' as meaning something exceptionally good, which appeared in mainstream pop music via African American youth subculture groups several years ago; today, however, the term no longer appears in the mainstream, except parodically. American Valley girl expressions such as 'Whatever', as a response that displays a bored, cool indifference, were initially restricted to youth subcultures; but they are now used in the mainstream (but no longer among youth subcultures). In the 1960s' subcultures, one of the key distinctions was that between 'heads' (those who took drugs and shared a set of radical beliefs about the world) and 'straights' (those who did neither of these). Today, these terms seem archaic and, indeed, 'straight' has now changed its reference to mean 'heterosexual'.

5.2.3 Twentieth-century technologies and linguistic change

New technologies have brought new ways of using English. This is most obvious with specialized languages such as those used for short-wave radio or for telegrams. It is also true, however, of linguistic practices developed for talking on the telephone or on the radio: so-called 'BBC English' was a pronunciation standard developed for radio and television.

Electronic mail has resulted in a number of changes mainly centring on questions of register. Because e-mail messages are generally short and sent immediately, a style of writing has developed that is more informal than letters or memos and that does not include formulae such as 'Dear Sir/Madam', 'Yours faithfully' and so on. Grammatical and typographical errors are often left uncorrected in e-mail messages. E-mail style has more in common with informal notes left for friends or family, and this informality seems to be used even when the person you are addressing is not known to you. This new informality very much accords with recent work by Norman Fairclough, which suggests that within British English in general the use of more informal and seemingly more personalized forms of expression is becoming more widespread (Fairclough, 1992). However, other commentators have begun to complain about the supposedly detrimental effects on language usage of 'e-mail English'.

Text messaging, because of the technical limitations on expression, has generated a particular style where it is permissible to leave out words and to use shortened forms. A host of shorthand symbols, such as 'gr8' for 'great', have been developed by users to enable them to send short messages without having to use many keys.

5.3 Some types of language change

5.3.1 Sound

We have seen that many of the English vowel sounds (particularly long vowels) changed as a result of the Great Vowel Shift. But the relics of older pronunciations are still preserved in the spellings of English words that were codified before the Shift was completed. For example, the related words 'meet' and 'met' are spelt with the same vowel letter (because they were originally pronounced with the same vowel sound), but are now pronounced with different vowel sounds. A more extreme example would be the word 'knight', whose spelling reflects a very different pronunciation from the current one; if we go back five hundred years we have evidence that the 'k' was pronounced, that the vowel was pronounced more like the vowel in 'neat', and that the 'gh' was pronounced like the 'ch' of 'Bach'.

5.3.2 The arrangement and interrelationships of words (syntax)

In the early form of English known as Anglo-Saxon or Old English (spoken in much of Britain, in various dialects, from about AD 400 into the early Middle Ages), word order was fairly flexible, since the relations between words was signalled by word-endings. Some aspects of this flexibility survived into the modern English of the seventeenth century – such as allowing particular parts of sentences (such as the verb or an object) to be moved to the front of sentences. But the fact that this flexibility seems to have survived only in literary texts (it is difficult to find examples of this in non-literary documentary evidence such as letters and diaries) provides one example of the way that literature uses archaism to create literary effects. Vestiges of this flexibility in word order can be found in Wordsworth's writing in the eighteenth century. The first stanza of 'The Last of the Flock' (1798) is given an archaic feel by repeatedly placing elements (italicized in the extract) before the verb, which would normally follow it:

> *In distant countries* I have been,
> And yet I have not often seen
> A healthy man, a man full grown,
> Weep in the public roads alone.
> But such a one, *on English ground*,
> *And in the broad high-way*, I met;
> *Along the broad high-way* he came,
> His cheeks *with tears* were wet.

In the first line, for example, a more usual sequence in modern English would be:

I   have been in distant countries
(subject) (verb)   (adjunct)

Although adjuncts (in this case a prepositional phrase) are more movable than other elements, it is unusual for them to be consistently placed before the verb as they are here. This can also be thought of as a literary deviation (see **Unit 19, Deviation**) from more usual syntactical sequences.

5.3.3 Pronouns

The history of the distinction between the second person pronouns 'thou' and 'you' is a revealing example of how language change relates to social change. The *OED* tells us that early forms of 'thou' (plus 'thee', 'thine' and 'thy') and 'you' (plus 'ye', 'your' and 'yours') were both used in ordinary speech in Old English, where the distinction was primarily a grammatical one. In Middle English 'you' began to be used as a mark of respect when addressing a superior and (later) an equal, while 'thou' was retained for addressing an inferior. This distinction between 'thou' and 'you' was related to the rigid stratification of society in the Middle Ages. It allowed an aristocratic speaker to distinguish between an equal (referred to as 'you') and someone inferior in social standing (referred to as 'thou'), or to signal intimacy. The lower orders, on the other hand, were required to address aristocrats as 'you' as a mark of deference. In the fifteenth century, the rising merchant classes began using 'thou' to the lower orders. Increasing social mobility and competition between this merchant class and the aristocracy meant that by Shakespeare's time there was widespread confusion about who should use the term 'thou' to whom. The seventeenth-century radical Quaker movement seized on the confusion about 'thou' and 'you' by using 'thou' to everyone, as a political act of levelling. The distinction eventually collapsed, and only 'you' survived. 'Thou' only appears now in archaizing registers, including those of poetry and religion, where it functions, curiously enough, as a marker of respect rather than of inferiority.

The *King James Authorized Version of the Bible* (1611) perhaps influenced this change in the function of 'thou' by having biblical characters address God as 'thou'.

A second distinction between 'thou' and 'you' was one of register (see **Unit 7, Language and context: register**), since 'thou' was a familiar form of address, whereas 'you' was more formal. Shakespeare's texts often seem to mix 'you' and 'thou' indiscriminately, but the distinction is important in the following exchange between Hamlet and his mother:

> *Queen.* Hamlet, thou hast thy father much offended.
> *Hamlet.* Mother, you have my father much offended.
> *Queen.* Come, come, you answer with an idle tongue.
> *Hamlet.* Go, go, you question with a wicked tongue.
>
> (*Hamlet*, c.1600, III, iv, 10–13)

The queen's initial use of 'thou' to Hamlet and his 'you' in return are quite standard choices for parent-to-offspring and offspring-to-parent, respectively. It is the queen's follow-up 'you' that is significant; annoyed by Hamlet's caustic rejoinder, she switches icily to a distancing 'you'.

5.3.4 Lexis or vocabulary (words and their meanings)

The vocabulary of a language can change (1) through the introduction of new terms on the model of older forms (for example, 'personal stereo' describes a new machine by using a combination of already existing words; 'air rage' describes a form of violent behaviour on aeroplanes on the model of word-combinations such as 'road rage'), or (2) through adopting foreign language forms, such as 'pizza' or 'segue'. Vocabulary changes often result from pressures of social change or because of new technological inventions. Thus, in Britain at the moment, many American vocabulary items are being adopted (such as the use of the verb 'to progress something' and nouns such as 'ball-park figure' and 'raincheck') because of the social, economic and political influence of America on Britain. The vocabulary of computers has been very productive in introducing new terms into mainstream usage (e.g. 'log in/out', 'interface', 'to access').

5.4 Archaism

A linguistic **archaism** is the use of a particular pronunciation, word or way of combining words that is no longer in current usage. The term comes from the New Latin word *archaismus*, meaning to model one's style upon that of ancient writers (*Collins' English Dictionary*). Thus, an archaism is an anachronistic use of a word or phrase. Certain registers are characterized in part by their use of archaism, particularly registers associated with institutions, such as the Church or the legal system.

The Bible exists in a number of different English translations. Until recently, the King James Authorized Version (1611) was the most widely used translation. Many Christian groups and churches have now adopted more recent translations such as *The New English Bible* (1961), partly because it seems more 'up to date' and accessible. A measure of the difference between them can be seen by comparing the language of equivalent passages (I Corinthians 15, 53):

> *King James Version*: For this corruptible must put on incorruption, and this mortall must put on immortalitie.

> *New English Bible*: This perishable being must be clothed with the imperishable, and what is mortal must be clothed with immortality.

Although the new version is easier to understand, the old version is still preferred by some Christians, in part because its archaic language seems more mysterious and appropriate to religious experience. Perhaps it is precisely because it is different from everyday language and more difficult to understand that this type of language is deemed more appropriate.

English legal texts are also characterized by archaism. If we take the English Copyright (Amendment) Act 1983 as an example, we find archaisms such as 'be it enacted', 'shall have effect' and 'cinematograph film'. The extensive use of archaism in legal texts arises partly from the fact that the law was the last institution to stop using the French and Latin of the Norman occupation (French was still used in the law into the eighteenth century). It is, however, also due to the fact that legal language has to be seen to be distinct from ordinary usage; lawyers would argue that it needs to be more precise and less open to ambiguity, but it might also be due to the fact that one of the jobs of the legal profession is to be the paid interpreters of this archaic language. (For a more extended discussion of the legal register, see **Unit 7, Language and context: register**.)

There is a long tradition of poetic texts using archaism. Edmund Spenser, writing in the late sixteenth century, developed a vocabulary for poems like *The Faerie Queene* by copying archaic words from Chaucer (writing 200 years earlier). Spenser's language was itself imitated by later writers – especially by Romantic poets such as Keats in the early nineteenth century. Because of this, most attempts to define a poetic register would probably include some archaism as a component feature. Here, for example, is a line from Walter Scott's 'The song of the Reim-kennar' (1822): 'Enough of woe hast thou wrought on the ocean'. Archaisms here include the syntax (word order) – a modern English word order would probably be 'You have brought enough' – and words such as 'thou', 'hast' and 'wrought'. A more recent poem that exploits archaism is W.H. Auden's 'The Wanderer' (1930), which is explicitly modelled on an Anglo-Saxon poem of the same name and uses Anglo-Saxon word-formation patterns, such as 'place-keepers' or 'stone-haunting', and alliterative patterns common in Anglo-Saxon poetry. The first line of the poem is: '*D*oom is *d*ark and *d*eeper than any sea-*d*ingle', which uses a repeated 'd' sound on stressed syllables (see **Unit 16, Rhyme and sound patterning**). In using such archaisms, the poem may seem to explore meanings and values that give the impression of transcending time and place.

It should be added, however, that there is a problem with the identification of archaism, since 'archaisms' are sometimes not archaic in the register in which they are used. For example, 'thee' and 'thou' are not archaic forms in a certain type of poetic register; they are archaic only in relation to our contemporary day-to-day speech. Thus the use of an archaism can be interpreted as either conforming to a register or looking back to the past (or both). One of the questions you should ask, therefore, in reading a text that seems to be using archaisms, is whether they are archaic relative to our current usage, or whether they would have been archaisms in literature at the time the text was written. Only by using a dictionary such as the *OED*, which is a historical dictionary, giving the meanings of words over time, will you be able to find out whether certain words were current or archaic at the time of writing.

5.5 Feminist changes to language

Recent writers on the relation between language and political and social power, such as Michel Foucault (1978), stress the fact that language is both an instrument of social constraint and a means of resisting that constraint.

This is most clearly seen in recent feminist theory, where language is identified as one of the means through which patriarchal values are both maintained and resisted (for a fuller discussion of this, see **Unit 8, Language and gender**). Feminists such as Dale Spender (1980) draw our attention to the fact that there are many elements in language that are sexist and offend women, for example the use of 'girl' to refer to adult females. However, because there have been many campaigns by feminists against sexist language, sexism has now changed and has become much more indirect. For example, on Radio 1 DJ Chris Moyles uses many phrases that are openly sexist to his female co-presenter and to female callers to the programme, but the BBC argues that he is using these terms in a parodic and humorous way. This masking of sexism by irony and humour makes sexism much more difficult to identify and take issue with.

Jane Mills's *Womanwords* (1989) is a dictionary that demonstrates the way that words associated with women often have a revealing history of meanings. For example, the word 'glamour' once meant 'magical strength', and was used to refer to both men and women; however, when the word began to be used for women alone it took on sexual and trivializing connotations, as in 'glamour girl'. A similar trajectory can be noted for words like 'witch', which was once used for both men and women but started to acquire negative connotations once its usage was restricted to referring to women. It would be hard to identify a particular individual or group responsible for such changes; rather, we interpret them as occasioned by the ideological and discursive structures that make up what feminists generally call 'patriarchy' (i.e. the economic, social and political norms within a society whose end result is that women are treated as if inferior to men).

To counter this verbal discrimination against women, some feminists have attempted to reform the language in a variety of ways. For example, feminists argue that offensive or discriminatory terms should be replaced by more neutral terms: 'chairperson' instead of 'chairman'; 'humankind' instead of 'mankind'; 'staff' instead of 'manpower' and so on. Pauwels (1998) has demonstrated just how successful this type of language reform has been and it is to be noted that many of the trivializing and discriminatory terms that feminists campaigned against in the 1980s now have an archaic feel to them or are no longer used (consider, for example, words like 'usherette' and 'aviatrix'). However, as Deborah Cameron (1985) has noted, although it is possible to make changes in language on a small scale, getting the changes adopted more generally is not so easy. This is partly because the changes have to go through what she calls 'the **gatekeepers of language**' – i.e. institutions such as the media, education, the government, lexicographers and so on, which tend to be resistant to the type of changes feminists wish to introduce. Changes that feminists wish to make may also be labelled mere 'political correctness' by their detractors (Dunant, 1994). However, as Cameron makes clear, one of the effects of this debate about the negative connotations of gendered terms is that, within the public sphere at least, sexist terms are now largely unacceptable. In addition, those who wish to continue to use terms such as 'chairman' for women will be viewed as making clear statements about their beliefs:

> By coining alternatives to traditional usage, the radicals have effectively politicised all the terms. They have made it impossible for anyone to speak or write without appearing to take up a political position for which they can then be held accountable.
>
> (Cameron, 1994, p. 31)

The more general point that emerges from this is that, for the most part, changes in language occur outside the conscious control of particular individuals or groups. Even when 'the gatekeepers of language' attempt to resist or introduce change there is no guarantee that they will be successful: British and American history furnishes many examples of failed attempts to reform the language according to some arbitrarily imposed standard (see Cameron, 1995). However, as Pauwels (1998) has shown, the concerted efforts by anti-racist, feminist and gay and lesbian activists have demonstrated that pressure groups can effect change in language, though this change is often resisted and derided by other groups in society.

ACTIVITY 5.1

This activity uses two poems (Lord Byron's 'If that high world' (1814), and Philip Larkin's 'High windows' (1974)) in order to make some provisional observations about differences in language and poetic conventions between 1814 and 1974.

1   On the evidence of Byron's poem (below), list the language-related conventions that appear to have held for poetry in around 1814 (e.g. use of archaism, choice of words, order of words, metre, rhyme, visual layout of the lines).

2   On the evidence of Larkin's poem (below), list language-related conventions that appear to have held for poetry in 1974.

3   Using the evidence you have gathered, make a list of the changes in poetic language between the two poems and a list of what does not seem to have changed.

4   Prevailing conventions constrain what we say, but they also enable us to say things in particular ways. Compare the two sets of conventions, and try to classify them for each poet into limiting and enabling conventions; in each case justify your decision (e.g. if you think Byron's use of rhyme is enabling while Larkin's use of rhyme is limiting, explain why).

If that high world

I
If that high world, which lies beyond
Our own, surviving Love endears;
If there the cherished heart be fond,
The eye the same, except in tears –
How welcome those untrodden spheres!
How sweet this very hour to die!
To soar from earth and find all fears
Lost in thy light – Eternity!

II
It must be so: 'tis not for self
That we so tremble on the brink;

And striving to o'erleap the gulf,
Yet cling to Being's severing link.
Oh! in that future let us think
To hold, each heart, the heart that shares;
With them the immortal waters to drink,
And soul in soul, grow deathless theirs!
(Lord Byron, 1814)

High windows

When I see a couple of kids
And guess he's fucking her and she's
Taking pills or wearing a diaphragm,
I know this is paradise

Everyone old has dreamed of all their lives –
Bonds and gestures pushed to one side
Like an outdated combine harvester,
And everyone young going down the long slide

To happiness, endlessly. I wonder if
Anyone looked at me, forty years back,
And thought, *That'll be the life;*
No God anymore, or sweating in the dark

About hell and that, or having to hide
What you think of the priest. He
And his lot will all go down the long slide
Like free bloody birds. And immediately

Rather than words comes the thought of high windows:
The sun-comprehending glass,
And beyond it, the deep blue air, that shows
Nothing, and is nowhere, and is endless.
(Philip Larkin, 1974)

Reading

Barber, C. (1976) *Early Modern English*, London: André Deutsch.
Cameron, D. (1985) *Feminism and Linguistic Theory*, London: Macmillan, pp. 79–90.
Fairclough, N. (1992) *Discourse and Social Change*, London: Polity Press.
Leith, D. (1983) *A Social History of English*, London: Routledge & Kegan Paul, pp. 32–57.
Pauwels, A. (1998) *Women Changing Language*, London: Longman.

Unit 6

Language
and place

Texts can create a sense of place in two main ways. First, they can describe places, incorporating many different sorts of detail. Where this occurs in fiction, the effect is what we think of as 'setting'. Second, place can be represented in how characters (or a narrator or poetic persona) are made to speak. This second way of representing place relies on connections we typically make between distinctive properties of voices and places with which they are conventionally associated. The two means of representing place work together to express complex beliefs, desires and fears about how human life fits into the natural and social environment. Evaluative contrasts within a text, between the country and the city, are an especially common device in creating a celebratory or critical sense of place; but there are also whole literary genres, such as the pastoral, which have established changing but recognizable conventions for achieving this (see **Unit 4, Recognizing genre**).

6.1 Describing places

Consider description first. In each of Thomas Hardy's novels, the author precisely describes aspects of 'Wessex', Hardy's fictional name for the Southwest of England. In *The Mayor of Casterbridge* (1886), for example, the arrival in Casterbridge of Henchard's wife Susan, while searching for Henchard, provides an early opportunity for description of the town. Casterbridge, Hardy writes, is a place 'at that time, recent as it was, untouched by the faintest sprinkle of modernism'; and he continues:

> It was compact as a box of dominoes. It had no suburbs – in the ordinary sense. Country and town met at a mathematical line.
>
> To birds of the more soaring kind Casterbridge must have appeared on this fine evening as a mosaic-work of subdued reds, browns, greys, and

crystals, held together by a rectangular frame of deep green. To the level eye of humanity it stood as an indistinct mass behind a dense stockade of limes and chestnuts, set in the midst of miles of rotund down and concave field. The mass became gradually dissected by the vision into towers, gables, chimneys, and casements, the highest glazings shining bleared and bloodshot with the coppery fire they caught from the belt of sunlit cloud in the west.

From the centre of each side of this tree-bound square ran avenues east, west, and south into the wide expanse of corn-land and coomb to the distance of a mile or so. It was by one of these avenues that the pedestrians were about to enter.

Note in this passage different kinds of detail that build Hardy's description: presentation of two viewpoints (eye level and bird's eye view); mapping of directions and layout ('east, west, and south'); the topography of the land ('rotund down and concave field'); and references to specific plants ('limes and chestnuts') and to colours ('reds, browns, greys, and crystals'), as well as close attention to architectural detail ('towers, gables, chimneys, and casements'). Note also, however, a further dimension of the fictional sense of place – contrasts and boundaries that potentially contribute to the novel's moral and political themes: the boundary here, for example, between country and city (the two meet in Casterbridge, 'at a mathematical line') and social changes that affect places over time (Casterbridge even at that recent time was, 'untouched by the faintest sprinkle of modernism') – themes we now expect to find explored in the narrative. As in much fictional writing, Hardy's description of Casterbridge here provides the novel not only with a specific geographical background or setting but also with important thematic or symbolic underpinning.

6.2 How characters (and the narrator) speak

In tandem with description of this kind, a sense of place can also be conveyed by how characters (and the narrator, where there is one) are made to speak. Such representation in a written text calls on the association we make between recognizable differences in grammar, vocabulary and pronunciation and how we suppose people speak in different places.

Creating a sense of place by incorporating particular, regional speech mannerisms can be more problematic than description of place, however. Written representations of dialect or **accent** draw on conventional – sometimes stereotypical – images and connotations for varieties of language, since it is such images and connotations that can be relied on to prompt a response. However, while such images permit vivid associations of voice with place, in doing so they trade on received ideas and contrasts, for instance the notion that some regional voices are more naive, stranger, rougher, more erotic or more authoritative than others.

6.3 Language variation

To investigate how we read such conventional 'imagery' of different textual voices, we must first consider how variation in language correlates with place. We can then explore more precisely how such variation is manipulated in literary, non-literary and media texts as a significant resource.

6.3.1 Variation within as well as between languages

The many languages of the world are related to each other in families (Indo-European, Dravidian, etc.). This family structure of languages involves overlapping and historically connected varieties, which in many cases have loaned each other words, sounds and structures. Even within what is called a single language, however, there is typically variation from region to region, as well as between classes, ethnic groups and genders.

6.3.2 Dialect and accent

Variation within a given language can involve differences in the sound system, when speakers from a particular region (or social group) consistently pronounce words in different ways from other groups. Examples of this type of variation are the words 'rather' and 'farmer', which are pronounced differently in different parts of Britain. 'Tomato' and 'dynasty' differ between British and American English; and 'nothing' and 'hotel' differ between British English and Indian English.

Alongside differences in pronunciation, there can also be consistent differences in other aspects of the language. Different words are used in different places to refer to equivalent things or ideas. The word 'throat', for example, varies with 'gullet', 'thropple' and 'quilter' in different parts of Britain. A 'faucet' is what American English speakers call a 'tap'; 'pants' are 'trousers'; and 'suspenders' are equivalent to 'braces'. A 'cot' in India is an adult 'bed', not, as in British English, a child's bed. In South Africa, a 'robot' is a traffic light as well as an automaton. 'Outwith' in Scotland means the same as 'outside' or 'beyond' in England. **Dialect maps** of such variation can be drawn to show the traditional geographical distribution of different words representing the same (or closely similar) meanings.

Differences also occur in grammar. Scottish English, 'the potatoes need peeled', matches Southern English English 'the potatoes need to be peeled'. Yorkshire 'thou knowest' parallels Southern English English 'you know'. American English 'they did it Monday' parallels British English 'they did it on

Monday'. British English 'I didn't like it either' matches Indian English 'I didn't like it also'.

When variations according to place are found exclusively in pronunciation, we speak of different accents; when variation according to region occurs simultaneously at the level of sound, vocabulary and grammar, we speak of different dialects. It is possible, therefore, to speak of a Yorkshire accent if we are referring only to pronunciation, or of a Yorkshire dialect if we are referring to all the ways language in Yorkshire varies in relation to other regions. Similarly, we can speak of a 'West of Scotland' accent or dialect, and of a 'South East of England' accent or dialect.

The issue is complicated, however, by the fact that language also varies according to class (and, to a lesser degree, according to age, subculture and profession). Because these variations affect vocabulary and grammar as well as pronunciation, it is also possible to speak of class dialects and social dialects, as well as accents (see **Unit 9, Language and society**). The relation between regional dialects and social dialects is variable. Sometimes they reinforce one another; sometimes one will override the other. For example, the language of the upper classes in Scotland is likely to have more in common with that of the equivalent social group in England than with that of working-class speakers in Scotland.

6.3.3 Attitudes towards variation

What makes accent and dialect important – both in social interaction and as regards ways of reading – is that people feel very strongly, and also quite differently, about different varieties. Attitudes are often based on stereotypical contrasts between the localities with which the varieties are historically associated, for instance the contrast between rural and industrial. Such attitudes also rely on our ability to 'place' a language variety; when this is not possible, and judgement is made simply on the basis of the sound itself rather than on the basis of attached social knowledge, stereotypical views tend to evaporate. Conventional attitudes towards different language varieties also rely on an assumed fixed point of 'standard' pronunciation or grammar. The 'standard' variety is the one that is given most prestige. Pronunciation or grammar that is thought to stray from it is implicitly compared with it, and as a result perceived as 'non-standard'.

One limitation of stereotypical views about accent and dialect is that, although they are apparently attuned to the idea of variation, they tend to be insensitive towards actual variations: do all working class people really sound the same? Or all Americans? Or all Scots? Or all Nigerians? Or all English people? The further from a person's own experience someone else's variety is, the less precise intuitions about it – and about the contrasts it enters into with other varieties – are likely to be. (This insight is easily tested by considering how much accent differentiation you can confidently match with social distinctions in television programmes or films produced in some part of the English-speaking world relatively distant from where you live.)

6.3.4 The repertoire of varieties available to individual speakers

The fact that language varies according to the regional and social identity of the user does not, however, result in each speaker being consistent in how he or she speaks or writes. In different situations, or when communicating about different topics, a speaker will automatically modify his or her language. Speakers shift – in response to subtle changes in situation and relationship – between different parts of the linguistic **repertoire** available to them. Variations that arise according to situation of use, rather than according to the identity of the user, are known as registers (see **Unit 7: Language and context: register**). Speakers who are able to use more than one dialect can manipulate those dialects as if they were registers, changing between them to achieve specific effects in any given situation (e.g. of appropriacy or marked inappropriacy). This type of shifting is especially common between a regional and a 'standard' variety. (For a literary example of this, see the discussion of *Lady Chatterley's Lover* in **Unit 9, Language and society**.)

6.4 Varieties of English

Marked contrasts in attitude towards varieties of English are partly a consequence of the history of the language. Virtually all languages involve hierarchies between regional varieties, but the detail differs from language to language. Variation is created by, and then remains left over from, historical, social and political changes in the society; and different amounts of prestige (as well as unequal distribution of social benefits that accompany such prestige) attach to the respective varieties.

6.4.1 History: British Isles

Throughout their history, the British Isles have been host to many different languages, including Gaelic, Welsh, Anglo-Saxon, Latin, Norman French, Punjabi, Chinese and so on. The number of languages in regular use (as well as the number of users of each language) has been reduced at different times by military conquest and by legal and educational suppression, as well as by the emerging prestige of one language or variety as compared with others.

During the sixteenth and seventeenth centuries, English spelling was regularized and aspects of the grammar were codified, bringing the issue of language standardization openly into critical debate. The continuing complexity of relations between varieties of English in modern times bears the marks of this history, even though present users of the language are generally familiar only with contrasts between current varieties, not with the history that brought them into being or determined their relative status (for further discussion, see Crystal, 2005).

6.4.2 History and geography: the English-speaking world

In the English-using world beyond Britain, variation within American English, Indian English, Nigerian English and Jamaican English – to take only a few instances – correlates not only with regional differences (and, in cases of bilingualism, with the first languages of the speakers); it also relates to social and educational inequalities between metropolitan and outlying regions, and between industrialized urban classes and rural classes. In many of these societies, the presence of English at all results from an imperial history that imposed English on the indigenous population. However, processes of decolonization have led to language changes that give new prestige to regional varieties, and in doing so encourage new, national standard varieties (such as American English or Indian English) that are nevertheless divergent from British English.

The legitimacy of these emergent 'standard' varieties is not universally recognized. In many countries, in fact, continuing tensions surround the use of English, which is widely viewed as being at a crossroads. The language has residual (and controversial) status as a left-over, imposed language favoured by those associated with the earlier colonial period, and at the same time has actively expanding prestige, as an increasingly global language of access to business and to information and communication technologies. Within many countries, nevertheless, and despite continuing conflicts over linguistic and cultural values, English functions as a crucial marker of class and as an agent of social mobility.

6.4.3 Received pronunciation

In terms of pronunciation, the major phase of standardization in English comes much later than it does in spelling, grammar or punctuation. It is only during the nineteenth century – mainly through the influence of English public school education, and the role of an army-officer corps – that one accent emerges as a non-regional prestige form: **Received Pronunciation**. This accent, which is itself undergoing changes (taking on increasingly negative connotations in the changing social and class structure of British society), is most closely connected with the dialect of English spoken in south-east England ('Educated Southern British English'), itself undergoing changes in contact with another, emergent variety: so-called **Estuary English**. Standardization in speech has in this respect followed the pattern established by earlier standardization of the written system, influenced as that was by the location of the royal court, and of the main political, legal and commercial institutions.

6.5 Language variety in literary texts

Historically, the language in which literary texts might be written in Britain has been a troubled question. Quite apart from the issue of Welsh and Gaelic, it is worth noting that, before the sixteenth century, Latin and French were serious competitors to English. In the sixteenth century itself, English was not always thought good enough for literary work (though writing in it did take place).

During the period of the late Elizabethans and early Jacobeans, the attitude that English might not be good enough for literary work gradually changed, partly in celebration of existing writing in English, partly because of attitudes towards Latin during the Reformation. Little more than a century later, however, English was widely believed to have produced an especially eminent literature. Many of the arguments about which language to write in, in many parts of the world today, have in this way (despite their otherwise major differences) an analogue in the circumstances of English in Britain during the later medieval and early Renaissance period.

6.5.1 Dialect representation

In the history of literary writing in English, there have been clear but shifting constraints on which variety or varieties might be used and how. A criterion of **decorum** was often invoked as a standard of appropriate style within a given genre, so excluding a wide range of voices from serious literary writing. Because of conventions of this kind, dialect speakers were represented in many works only as comic characters, with jokes (including many jokes specifically about dialect) made at their expense.

In tracing this history, it is important to remember that accent and dialect are primarily associated with speech rather than writing, and that representation of speech in writing does not reproduce how people actually speak. Rather, it draws on conventions that produce an illusion of speech (see **Unit 26, Literature in performance**). Representation of dialect speech in writing draws on a further set of specialized (but never formalized) conventions, including non-standard spellings, which are meant to signal that a character's speech is different from that of other characters in the text.

Conventions surrounding dialect representation are more than a matter of how particular sounds should be represented, however. Differences between 'standard' and 'non-standard' voices set up a **hierarchy of voices** within a literary work. In nineteenth-century novels, for instance, the narrator and central characters tend to use Standard English, while regional or working-class characters – often minor characters in narrative and thematic terms – may speak with an accent or in a dialect. This raises the question of how far non-standard speech is used to reproduce the way people actually spoke in the place where the novel is set, and how far such use aims simply to signify contrasts of class or moral authority.

Consider *The Mayor of Casterbridge* again. Hardy's Wessex novels are peopled with minor rural characters who speak in West Country dialect. Within this setting, however, Hardy typically explores the fate and fortune of middle-class characters, whose speech is more standard than that of the rural characters. In the following scene from *The Mayor of Casterbridge*, which centres on the rise and fall of a character called Michael Henchard (from destitute rural worker to mayor of Casterbridge, then back to destitution), Henchard chastises one of the workers on his farm for being late in the mornings:

> Then Henchard ... declared with an oath that this was the last time; that if he were behind once more, by God, he would come and drag him out o' bed.
>
> 'There is sommit wrong in my make, your worshipful!' said Abel, '... I never enjoy my bed at all, for no sooner do I lie down than I be asleep, and afore I be awake I be up. I've fretted my gizzard green about it, maister, but what can I do? ...'
>
> 'I don't want to hear it!' roared Henchard. 'To-morrow the waggons must start at four, and if you're not here, stand clear. I'll mortify thy flesh for thee!'

The worker's dialect is rendered here through non-standard spelling ('maister'), non-standard grammar ('no sooner do I lie down than I be asleep') and dialect phrases ('I've fretted my gizzard'). More interestingly, though, in his anger Henchard 'lapses' into dialect (and/or biblical language) in a way that reminds us of his origins ('thee' and 'thy' remain in use in dialects long after their disappearance from Standard English). The narrative voice reinforces this, by introducing Henchard's first comments in Standard English using **indirect speech** ('Henchard declared with an oath that this was the last time') and then switching into **free indirect speech** in order to let Henchard's own, non-standard speech come through: 'by God, he would come and drag him out o' bed'. (For discussion of 'indirect' and 'free indirect speech' see **Unit 22, Speech and narration**.)

6.5.2 Modernist polyphony

One distinctive feature of twentieth-century modernist writing is that a wider range of voices is sometimes presented than was usual (or even possible) in earlier literary works in English. In many cases, this introduction of a wider range of voices takes the form of variety switching (as in James Joyce's *Ulysses* (1922)), or juxtaposition (as in T.S. Eliot's *The Waste Land* (1922)). But a fundamental question about dialect representation then arises: Do such texts introduce representation (or mimicry) of regional and class voices as a fundamentally new kind of polyphony, in which voices have become equal? Or is there still a hierarchy of voices in terms of relative seriousness and authority, with the extra voices included merely so that they can be finally subordinated to, or refined into, a reaffirmed, authoritative standard voice of the narrator or poetic persona? (The second of these alternatives is directly arguable in relation to T.S. Eliot's *The Waste Land*; for a discussion of this issue in *Ulysses*, see **Unit 7, Language and context: register** and **Unit 12, Juxtaposition**.)

In such experimental writing it is significant that regional varieties are used as much to create a visible (or 'visible-audible'), schematic contrast between Standard and non-Standard English as for their own qualities. Arguably only in forms of dialect writing linked to an expressed sense of regional identity (as in much Scottish writing since the early twentieth century) does dialect function less to contrast with the established standard than to affirm a distinct regional idiom.

How dialect will be used in literary works in future is far from certain. In contemporary Britain, people have many quite different experiences of place, partly because of the regional, class and ethnic diversity of the population; so this seems likely to give rise to continuing experimentation with juxtaposition and mixing of language varieties. Also, since people move from place to place and take their dialect with them, interaction between the regional and social dimensions of dialect seems likely to result in changing and unpredictable connections between voice, region and sense of identity.

6.6 Post-colonial writing in English

In many **Anglophone** post-colonial societies (such as India, Pakistan, Anglophone Africa, the Philippines, Malaysia, the Caribbean and many other places) the idea of using English at all in creative writing remains contentious. Some influential writers (such as the Kenyan novelist and dramatist Ngugi wa Thiong'o (b. 1938)) have argued that using the former colonial language merely reinforces the power of emerging neo-colonial elites at the expense of developing a self-confident and emancipated local or national literature. Other writers have argued that the linking function of a language like English enables different communities (including different African communities) to become more aware of each other. In this view, using English in literary and other contexts may open up new possibilities for redefining relations between communities in a way that would be impossible if they remained separated by walls of linguistic difference.

In some post-colonial writing in English, dialect is viewed as a kind of **anti-language**, or mode of expression deliberately adopted to mark it off from dominant traditions of writing that are being rejected. In other cases, the argument for using dialect is made in terms of authenticity, and an aspiration to give a true representation of the writer's identity (see **Unit 14, Authorship and**

intention). Dialect contrasts – as well as individual varieties – vary from place to place, however; and the new forms of dialect spelling and code-switching to be found in such writing are likely to be read differently as they circulate beyond the region or country in which the variety being represented is actually used.

6.7 Dialect and accent in media

Film and television have largely inherited, and helped maintain, the legacy of associating character stereotypes with particular accents or dialects. The simple fact of mass exposure in media, however, can alter the standing of entire dialects and accents. Soundtracks of Hollywood films in the 1930s, for instance, were sometimes thought incomprehensible in Britain – a fact hardly believable now. US radio announcers imitated British accents until around 1930, before the conventions were established of what has come to be called the **Network Standard** variety of American English. It was only later, most obviously in popular music and popular culture, that the trend of transatlantic influence was reversed.

In Britain, exposure to regional, class and ethnic dialects and accents on radio and television has increased massively over the last two decades, a social change that has already had a significant effect on accent connotations and stereotypes. Over time, such increased exposure will almost certainly contribute to language change. It remains unclear, however, how current media adoption of a wide range of varieties of English will affect future systems of accent and dialect significance. Rather than abolishing the kinds of hierarchy among varieties illustrated above, changing media use of accents and dialects may only alter the underlying system of relative prestige and connotation. New and different meanings may be conferred within a system of contrasts that has only been locally adjusted to match changing patterns and conflicts in social identity and aspiration.

ACTIVITY 6.1 ▬▬▬▬▬▬▬▬▬▬▬▬▬▬▬▬▬▬▬▬▬▬▬▬▬▬

Each of the two passages below is concerned with finding a language to convey a specific 'Indianness' of Indian life. One describes a scene or 'setting'; the other presents thoughts on how an Indian use of English may represent – or misrepresent – a specific notion of 'Indian identity'.

> *Text A*
>
> The painted streets alive with hum of noon,
> The traders cross-legged 'mid their spice and grain,

The buyers with their money in the cloth,
The war of words to cheapen this or that,
The shout to clear the road, the huge stone wheels,
The strong slow oxen and their rustling loads,
The singing bearers with the palanquins,
The broad-necked hamals sweating in the sun,
The housewives bearing water from the well
With balanced chatties, and athwart their hips
The black-eyed babies; the fly-swarmed sweetmeat shops,
The weaver at his loom, the cotton-bow
Twanging, the millstones grinding meal, the dogs
Prowling for orts, the skilful armourer
With tong and hammer linking shirts of mail,
The blacksmith with a mattock and a spear
Reddening together in his coals, the school
Where round their Guru, in a grave half-moon,
The Sakya children sang the mantras through,
And learned the greater and the lesser gods.

    (from Sir Edwin Arnold, *The Light of Asia*, 1879)

Text B

        I am Indian, very brown, born in
Malabar, I speak three languages, write in
Two, dream in one. Don't write in English, they said,
English is not your mother-tongue. Why not leave
Me alone, critics, friends, visiting cousins,
Every one of You? Why not let me speak in
Any language I like? The language I speak
Becomes mine, its distortions, its queernesses
All mine, mine alone. It is half English, half
Indian, funny perhaps, but it is honest,
It is as human as I am human, don't
You see? It voices my joys, my longings, my
Hopes, and it is as useful to me as cawing
Is to crows, or roaring to the lions, it
Is human speech, the speech of the mind that is
Here and not there, a mind that sees and hears and
Is aware. Not the deaf, blind speech
Of trees in storm or of monsoon clouds or of rain or the
Incoherent mutterings of the blazing
Funeral pyre.

    (from Kamala Das, 'An Introduction',
        Collected Poems, 1984)

1   For each passage, make a list of words and/or grammatical constructions that are not part of your own dialect. In the case of individual words, do you know what these words mean or refer to? How far do such words appear to be associated with a particular place or way of life?

2   Which of the two passages contains *more* locally specific vocabulary?

3   Do the two passages give equal attention to the problem of finding appropriate language in which to represent a sense of place or a sense of belonging to a place? If not, which focuses on this issue more?

4   In the light of your answers to Questions 1 and 2, does your answer to Question 3 surprise you? If so, why? If not, why not?

5   Sir Edwin Arnold was a (male) nineteenth-century British Orientalist scholar, as well as a poet; Kamala Das is a contemporary (female) Indian writer. How far do you think the different historical, geographical and cultural locations of the two writers may affect how they try to represent their relationship to India?

Reading

Crystal, D. (2005) *The Stories of English*, Harmondsworth: Penguin.
Gifford, T. (1999) *The Pastoral*, New Critical Idiom Series, London: Routledge.
Kachru, B. (ed.) (1982) *The Other Tongue: English Across Cultures*, Oxford: Pergamon.
McCrum, R., Cran, W. and McNeil, R. (2002) *The Story of English*, London: Faber.
Williams, R. (1985) *The Country and the City*, London: The Hogarth Press.

Unit 7

Language and context: register

The term 'register' is used by linguists and literary critics to describe the fact that the kind of language we use is affected by the context in which we use it, to such an extent that certain kinds of language usage become conventionally associated with particular situations. Our tacit knowledge of such conventions of usage enables us to judge whether what someone says or writes is 'appropriate' to its context. This is highlighted by our reactions when a text deviates from its appropriate register – as happens towards the end of the following announcement by a guard on a train:

> May I have your attention please, ladies and gentlemen. The train is now approaching Lancaster. Passengers for the Liverpool boat train should alight here and cross to platform one. Delays are being experienced on this train and passengers intending to use this service should consult the notice board on platform one *to find out what the score is.*

The comic effect of this arises basically through a sudden (and presumably unintentional) switch of register (in the last italicized phrase). For the most part the announcement is typical of the formal language that British travellers have come to associate with train announcements, though we may feel that it is a little too 'high-flown' for what is after all only information about trains and platforms. The unintended humour arises when the announcer juxtaposes the formal opening of the announcement with the much less formal conclusion ('to find out what the score is') and thereby comically undercuts what has gone before. (See **Unit 12, Juxtaposition**.)

The most obvious way in which a text 'registers' the effect of its context is in the selection of vocabulary. Our experience of language in context allows us to recognize that vocabulary items such as 'alight' and 'consult' are characteristic of the professional idiom that the railway company has selected for communicating to the public, and we are equally sensitive to the fact that 'to find out what the score is' does not belong to that idiom. But differences in register involve differences in grammar as well as in vocabulary. For example, in the phrase 'Delays are being experienced', the use of the impersonal passive construction contributes as much as the vocabulary choice to the formality of the announcement's register.

Each of us experiences a variety of language situations every day and from moment to moment: speaking in a tutorial, talking on the phone to a bank manager, chatting to friends in a coffee bar, writing a letter. In response to these contexts, each of us switches from one register to another without effort and we are able to recognize when others do the same. By the same token, as we have seen in the railway announcement example, we are all sensitive to deviation in register.

7.1 Contexts that affect register

It is possible to isolate three different aspects of any context or situation that will affect the register of a text:

1   the medium of communication (e.g. whether the language is spoken or written);
2   the social relationships of participants in the situation (which determines the tone);
3   the purpose for which, or the field in which, the language is being employed.

7.1.1 Medium

The register of a text is partly constituted by the medium that is adopted for communication. The medium of a text is the substance from which the text is made, or through which it is transmitted, or in which it is stored. For register, the most prominent difference in medium is between speech and writing (see **Unit 22, Speech and narration**). Speech is usually made up on the spot and interpreted as it is heard. Writing, on the other hand, may involve long periods of composition and revision and the resultant text may be read and reread at leisure in circumstances quite remote – both in time and place – from that in which it was written. Written texts, therefore, tend to be more formal than spoken texts, which, by contrast, tend to be looser and more provisional in their structure and to feel less formal. In addition, speech and writing may also be shaped according to whether they pass though other media: a telephone conversation is not the same as a face-to-face chat; e-mail and texting have recognizably different register features from letters or newspapers. In public settings, spoken texts may be carefully prepared in advance and may take on the formal characteristics of the written mode. Our rail announcement begins in this fashion before slipping into something much closer to everyday speech.

7.1.2 Tone (or tenor)

A second aspect of the context that affects register relates to the social roles that are prescribed for, or adopted by, participants in the communication situation. Differences in the text will result from whether the relationships between participants are informal or formal, familiar or polite, personal or impersonal. Thus, the tone of the text can indicate the attitude or position adopted by the writer or speaker towards the reader or listener. In the rail announcement, for example, 'ladies and gentlemen' (which constitutes a marker of social distance signalling politeness), the intricate syntax (which, together with words such as 'attention', 'approaching' and 'alight', signals formality), and the passive voice (which avoids reference to human agency – as in 'Delays are being experienced') are all features of the impersonal register. The suggestion that passengers should 'find out what the score is', on the other hand, assumes a much more informal and familiar relation between speaker and addressee – one that seems to clash with the context that has been previously set up.

7.1.3 Field and role

A third aspect of the context that affects register is the role of the communication. Language can be used for a variety of different purposes (to convey information, to express feelings, to cajole, to seduce, to pray, to produce **aesthetic** effects, to intimidate, etc.), each of which will leave its mark on what is said and the way it is said. In addition, most human activities employ their own characteristic registers because they employ 'field-specific' vocabularies (or **semantic fields**). Fields in this sense include those occupied by the legal profession, the scientific community, the culinary arts, religious institutions, academic disciplines, advertising, football commentary (and the list could be extended almost indefinitely). All these fields involve the use of terms that are particular to them, the use of which thereby invokes particular situations. In Britain, for example, rail companies no longer address their passengers as 'passengers' (people travelling in a train, etc.) but as 'customers' (people who buy something). This involves an odd switch in field (and hence in register) from public transport to the general field of shopping that subtly changes the relationship between the rail company and the people who travel on its trains.

7.2 The social distribution of registers

It is important to remember that each of us is able to control the appropriate register for a wide variety of contexts and that we each have, in addition, a passive familiarity with a range of others (e.g. of advertising, of income tax returns, of legal documents) that we are rarely called upon actively to use. But the range of registers we feel comfortable with (both actively and passively) may be affected by a number of factors, including our age, social background, education, gender, race and work status. Register positions, or can be used to position, the participants of a dialogue differently according to who those participants are. Thus the conventional distinction between register and dialect as that between *language according to use* and *language according to user* (see **Unit 6, Language and place**) seems to break down when considering how the relative social roles in any communication situation govern, or are governed by, the register adopted. The registers we become familiar with and learn how to manipulate in higher education, for example, might well be alienating to those who have not had access to them. (In fact, one of the purposes of any degree course is to familiarize the student with the special register of the discipline being studied. In the study of literature, students are generally required to write essays in a formal and sometimes impersonal register that includes the use of a specialized critical vocabulary and excludes words and phrases that they might be accustomed to using in other contexts.)

Although linguistic usages usually change with time, some historical periods, societies or professions try to preserve the 'purity' of particular registers and maintain rigorous hierarchical distinctions between them. In the early twenty-first century it is possible to see how institutions such as the Church and the law have been relatively successful in maintaining their field-specific registers virtually unchanged across the centuries. Consider, for example, the following extract from a legal notice printed in the *Glasgow Herald*:

> Notice is Hereby Given, That ... the sheriff at Campbeltown, by Interlocutor dated 30th December, 1986, ordered all parties desirous to lodge Answers in the hands of the Sheriff Clerk at Castlehill, Campbeltown within 8 days after intimation, advertisement or service, and in the meantime, until the prayer of the Petition had been granted or refused, nominated Alistair White to be Provisional Liquidator of the said Company on his finding caution before extract.

From this example, we can see that the legal register is relatively opaque to the non-specialist. It is possible to offer different reasons why this should be so: one response might be to say that the legal profession maintains its register in order to intimidate the general public and force us to employ lawyers and solicitors to represent us in legal matters; another response might argue that such intricate and highly specific language is necessary in order to prevent potentially costly or crucial ambiguities. (See the discussion of archaism in **Unit 5, Language and time**.)

Leaving these questions aside, however, a brief analysis of some of the features of the legal register that are displayed in this text can serve as a model for the way we might analyse any register:

- *Vocabulary*: The most obvious feature of this text is its field-specific words and phrases, as seen in 'Provisional Liquidator' and 'finding caution before extract'. There are also archaisms ('desirous'), and highly Latinate vocabulary ('Interlocutor', 'intimation', 'Petition', 'nominated', 'Provisional', 'caution', 'extract').
- *Syntax* (sentence structure): Syntax makes an equal contribution to this register (and to its opacity): remarkably, the complete notice is made up of a single complex sentence with an array of subordinate clauses whose interrelations with each other are acutely difficult to follow.
- *Typography* (the appearance of the printing): Archaic typography is also a feature of this register, since it makes extensive use of capitalization for words that are no longer capitalized in modern English.

Institutions that seek to preserve their particular registers in this way and to isolate them from the linguistic changes taking place in the society surrounding them may be said to employ 'conservative' registers. Compared with these, areas such as advertising, journalism, pop music, TV and texting have more 'open' or 'liberal' registers that change frequently, sometimes invent new words and phrases, and often borrow from each other and from the 'conservative' registers that surround them.

7.3 Literature and register

There are two ways in which register impacts upon literature. First, the fact that literature – especially novels and plays – typically attempts to represent recognizable social worlds in convincing ways means that literary texts may draw on, or quote, any of the non-literary registers that exist in the social world at the time of writing or in the period in which the text is set. Second, literature has its own register, or registers, that have been built up and transformed through history. Consequently, the reader of any literary text needs to be alert to the various non-literary registers that it is 'voicing' and to the way that it is engaging with the various possible literary registers that are available from the history of literature.

7.3.1 The novel and non-literary registers

In essays such as 'Discourse in the Novel' (written in 1934–5, first published in Russia in 1973), the Russian critic Mikhail Bakhtin argues that the novel as a genre is typified by what he calls **dialogism** – that is, a novel, any novel, is comprised of a multiplicity of different, and potentially conflicting, voices. At its most obvious level, this refers to the fact that novels typically include the voice(s) of the narrator(s), together with the voices of its characters. All these voices will necessarily be marked by register. Who or what or where is the narrator supposed to be? Is he or she supposed to be speaking or writing? Is his or her narration 'literary' or not? How are the characters located in terms of class or employment? What **speech situations** are they placed within? Do they write letters, and if so to whom? At a second level, though, Bakhtin is suggesting that novels are typically composed out of a wide range of language types – i.e. the palette of the novelist is precisely the whole range of possible registers. In fact, Bakhtin's list of the kinds of 'voices' that may be woven into a novel is a list of registers:

(1) Direct authorial literary-artistic narration (in all its diverse variants);
(2) Stylization of the various forms of oral everyday narration (*skaz*);
(3) Stylization of the various forms of semiliterary (written) everyday narration (the letter, the diary, etc.);
(4) Various forms of literary but extra-artistic authorial speech (moral, philosophical or scientific statements, oratory, ethnographic descriptions, memoranda and so forth);
(5) The stylistically individualized speech of characters.

(in Leitch, 2001, p. 1192)

Bakhtin then suggests that the discursive material available to the novel constitutes what is in effect an almost inexhaustible range of registers:

The internal stratification of any single national language into social dialects, characteristic group behavior, professional jargons, generic languages, languages of generations and age groups, tendentious languages, languages of the authorities, of various circles and of passing fashions, languages that serve the specific sociopolitical purposes of the day, even of the hour . . . this internal stratification present in every language at any given moment of its historical existence is the indispensable prerequisite for the novel as a genre.

(in Leitch, 2001, p. 1192)

In order to test out what Bakhtin is saying we can look at Daniel Defoe's *Robinson Crusoe* (1719), which is often regarded as one of the first novels in English. Although it is a first person narrative, and although for a great deal of the novel the narrator is alone upon a deserted island, *Robinson Crusoe* is a good example of the dialogic nature of the novel genre. This is so because the narrator's monologue is actually composed of a polyphony of various 'voices' or registers that were in circulation in early eighteenth-century Britain. Crusoe's narration contains features of the Puritan spiritual autobiography of the period, along with features of another related contemporary genre – the private journal. Yet close analysis reveals that the registers of other contemporary discourses also inhabit Crusoe's private inner voice. One of these is the register of seafaring and navigation – an important and prominent discourse at a historical moment when England's imperial project was carried out via sea voyaging. Other prominent registers include the languages of building, agriculture and husbandry as Crusoe begins to exploit the natural resources of his island. At the most general level, Crusoe's response to his situation wavers between the register of Protestant self-examination, with its notions of sin, providence, divine retribution and salvation, and the twin registers of early capitalism (business and trade, profit and loss) and economic individualism (an emphasis on individual effort, rational calculation, trial and error, cause and effect). This means that Crusoe's monologue is internally riven by two of the dominant registers in English culture of the period. The two come together in the following passage in which Crusoe sets out a balance sheet of his condition on the island:

> I now began to consider seriously my condition, and the circumstances I was reduced to, and I drew up the state of my affairs in writing ... and as my reason began now to master my despondency ... I stated it very impartially, like debtor and creditor, the comforts I enjoyed against the miseries I suffered, thus:

Evil	Good
I am cast upon a horrible desolate island, void of all hope of recovery.	*But I am alive, and not drowned as all my ship's company was.*
I am singled out and separated, as it were, from all the world to be miserable.	*But I am singled out too from all the ship's crew to be spared from death; and He that miraculously saved me from death, can deliver me from this condition.*

In this passage, the register of the content is partly that of Protestant faith ('He that miraculously saved me from death, can deliver me from this condition'), but its form – the balance sheet of 'debtor and creditor' – draws on the register of economic individualism. While these two registers and impulses sometimes went hand in hand in early eighteenth-century England, and sometimes do in *Robinson Crusoe*, Defoe's weaving of these two registers into Crusoe's narration sometimes shows them to be mutually incompatible views of the world.

In *Robinson Crusoe* the various registers that resonate in Crusoe's narration are generally motivated. In other words, there tend to be realistic reasons for the presence of these registers: Crusoe uses the registers of seafaring and navigation when describing his experiences at sea, for example. Even the mixing of religious and rational/economic registers is motivated in that these are the voices of Crusoe's inner conflict and derive from the historical moment in which Defoe was writing. This use of motivated registers is generally characteristic of the novel from the early eighteenth century through to the early twentieth century, especially in the 'realist' novels of the nineteenth century. The experimentation that characterizes the modernist literature of the early twentieth century, however, includes an experimentation with register mixing that largely abandons realistic motivation.

James Joyce's *Ulysses* (1922) epitomizes **modernism**'s use of unmotivated register mixing; its pages often seem like a ragbag of odds and ends taken from a huge variety of different and usually incongruous registers. However, although, as we might expect, this mixing of registers is often used for comic effect, it also seems to have more far-reaching implications. In the following paragraph, for example, one of the central characters of the novel, Leopold Bloom, has invited the other main male character, Stephen Dedalus, back to his house for tea after a bizarre night on the town; it is late, and Bloom has to move carefully in order not to wake his wife sleeping upstairs. The places where the register changes have been numbered:

[1] What did Bloom do?
[2] He . . . drew two spoonseat deal chairs to the hearthstone, one for Stephen with its back to the area window, the other for himself when necessary, [3] knelt on one knee, composed in the grate a pyre [4] of crosslaid resintipped sticks and various coloured papers and irregular polygons [5] of best Abram coal at twentyone shillings a ton from the yard of Messrs Flower and M'Donald of 14 D'Olier street, [6] kindled it at three projecting points of paper with one ignited lucifer match, [7] thereby releasing the potential energy contained in the fuel by allowing its carbon and hydrogen elements to enter into free union with the oxygen of the air.
[8] Of what similar apparitions did Stephen think? . . .

In order to identify the various registers here, we need to identify the context in which each one would usually occur. Tentative names for these registers are given in Table 7.1, together with the textual features that provide evidence for such decisions.

According to the analysis in Table 7.1, this short passage from *Ulysses* contains six different registers. Part of its comic effect depends upon our sensitivity to a number of clashes between language and context – for example, the incongruity of describing the act of lighting a fire in a terraced house in Dublin in the early part of the twentieth century in various registers (the religious, the technical, the scientific) that seem too 'elevated' or too precise for this humble action. Note, however, that each of these registers would be appropriate for describing the lighting of a fire in a different context (e.g. in a religious ceremony or in a scientific experiment). A second context to be considered is that of the novel genre itself: in a realist novel (see **Unit 23, Narrative realism**) we would expect the scene to be narrated in register 2 rather than in registers 3–6.

Table 7.1 Identifying registers in an extract from *Ulysses*

Portion of text	Provisional name	Usual context	Textual evidence
1	catechism	Christian teaching	question and answer
2	descriptive prose	realist novel	use of simple past tense ('He . . . drew')
3	religious	description of ceremony	'knelt', 'pyre'
4	technical description	report	'irregular polygons'
5	language of commerce	advertisement	'best Abram coal'
6	technical description, as 4	report	'ignited lucifer match'
7	scientific description	textbook or journal	'potential energy', 'carbon and hydrogen'
8	catechism, as 1	Christian teaching	question and answer

Furthermore, we do not expect a novel to be narrated in a series of questions and answers (as this whole chapter is) – this procedure is, in fact, more appropriate to religious instruction by catechism in the Christian Church.

The mixing of registers in this passage not only produces comic effects but also raises a series of unsettling speculations. The description of this commonplace action in the religious register seems to invite us to recall the spiritual significance of fire, while the scientific register forces us to remember that fire is a process of chemical transformation. Thus we could argue that these incongruous registers defamiliarize a process that has become so familiar that we hardly think about it any more. Conversely, it could be argued that the 'conservative' registers of the Church and science are being undermined insofar as they are shown to employ 'pretentious' terminology to describe the most commonplace of events (the interweaving of the commercial register perhaps adds to this by undercutting the religious and technical registers that precede it). The passage is unsettling, however, in that it gives us no clues about which of these readings is 'correct'. Hence it becomes impossible to decide whether the 'elevated' registers are meant to have more authority than the 'low' register of commerce or vice versa. This is partly because the text seems to abdicate the authority that realist texts usually maintain through a clearly defined narrative voice. The register of narrative prose (2) is simply one register among others in this passage, without any special authority; and, although the narrative is presented through a technique reminiscent of the Christian catechism, the mixing of registers undercuts the potential authority of both question and answer. *Ulysses*, then, by undermining or rejecting the register thought appropriate for narrating novels, can be interpreted either as attempting to rejuvenate the novel genre or as challenging the genre's claims to be a special or elevated discourse.

7.3.2 Literary registers

One of the ongoing debates in literary criticism and literary theory is whether literature has its own register or registers. For a large part of the history of thinking about literature, the answer to this would have been 'yes'. The assumption that literature had its own peculiar registers was based on the notion of 'decorum' – the idea that there was an appropriate language for each kind of subject matter and genre. Just as we expect that a funeral sermon, say, will be conducted in an appropriate language, so too did literary critics from classical Greece through to the eighteenth century assume that the subject matter of a literary text ought to dictate the register. In fact, this was partly a matter of genre: each genre – epic, tragedy, comedy, pastoral and so on – was linked to a particular register. But the notion of appropriateness was also shaped by social, political and cultural factors. In the eighteenth century – an age characterized by reason, politeness and social distinctions – literature was governed, for the most part, by notions of decorum: its language is educated, polite, upper middle class. Its assumptions about what kind of language is appropriate to literature are best summed up by Alexander Pope in 1711: 'Expression is the dress of thought, and still / Appears more decent, as more suitable' (*An Essay on Criticism*, II, 318–19).

At the end of the eighteenth century, however, when ideas of democracy and revolution began to challenge the stabilities of the neoclassical period, there was a parallel revolution in the register thought appropriate to literature. In the 'Preface to *Lyrical Ballads*' (1800), Wordsworth explains that *Lyrical Ballads* 'was published as an experiment . . . to ascertain, how far . . . a selection of the real language of men in a state of vivid sensation' might be a suitable language for poetry, and he indicates that the language 'of low and rustic life' – suitably adopted and 'purified' – was chosen because 'such men . . . convey their feelings and notions in simple and unelaborated expressions'. Wordsworth thus attempts to change the register considered appropriate to poetry and so participates in a struggle over literature's role in society (raising questions such as whether it should be the preserve of an elite or be as widely available and accessible as possible).

At the same time, however, in some of his other poems – such as 'Tintern Abbey' (1798) and *The Prelude* (1805) – Wordsworth developed a recognizably 'Wordsworthian' register that is part of a larger 'Romantic' register that came to characterize poetry from the late eighteenth to the early twentieth century and that is still the register of poetry for many readers. When Keats's speaker addresses a Grecian urn (or a figure on its design) as 'Thou still unravished bride of quietness', we know we are in the presence of poetry – or at least of 'Romantic' poetry. However, just as modernist writers experimented boldly with the registers of the novel, they also attempted to transform the existing poetic register – or perhaps to destroy the very notion that there was a special register for poetry. The opening lines of T.S. Eliot's 'The Love Song of J. Alfred Prufrock' (1915) provide a shock that is largely produced by the way the third line jars with our preconceptions about the poetic register:

> Let us go then, you and I,
> When the evening is spread out against the sky
> Like a patient etherised upon a table.

While the first two lines are in a recognizably poetic register that correlates with the idea of a love song, the third line provides a simile for the evening sky that comes from a wholly different and incongruous register (a medical register or, more precisely, that of surgical theatres).

Following in Eliot's wake, the history of twentieth-century poetry – and of poetic theory – can be seen as a history of attempts to escape from the (Romantic) poetic register. Yet, as St John Butler demonstrates, the fact that a text (any text) is set out on the page as poetry is itself a signal of poetic register regardless of what the words themselves consist of. When we see this typographic generic signal (poetic layout) we tend to read what we are presented with as poetry; and, if the content (the subject matter and the vocabulary) seems radically non-poetic, then this produces a register clash between form and content. Rather than abandoning or refusing to recognize the poetic register, then, such poems depend on our notion of the poetic register for their effect. Thus, as St John Butler puts it, 'Those who would maintain that there is no such thing as poetic register need to answer the question: what is it that such poems as these are reacting against?' (1999, p. 194).

We should be wary, however, of assuming that register mixing and clashing is somehow unique to modernist poetry and the poetry that followed it. In fact, it could be argued that the practice of recycling and mixing registers is central to the literary process and its effects in general. One simple but revealing example of this is that parody is a genre that depends upon the notion that certain kinds of language are conventionally associated with particular genres and themes. Pope, who was cited above as arguing that poetic language should be 'suitable', can also exploit the possibilities set up by this notion in order to produce comic irony. In his *The Rape of the Lock* (1712/1714), the humorous effect depends precisely upon the reader's familiarity with the register used in epic poetry and consequent ability to recognize the mismatch between Pope's use of this 'high' register and the 'low' subject matter of the poem. In just the same way, novels such as *Ulysses* or poems such as 'The Love

Song of J. Alfred Prufrock' depend upon the notion of appropriateness built into the fact of register in order to achieve their effects – whether this be to challenge established ideas about literature, or make a joke, or both.

We might summarize this discussion by making a number of general observations about the way literature draws upon the possibilities opened up by register:

1   Literature – because it uses language – draws on and is continuously open to all the non-literary registers that surround it.

2   Through unusual juxtaposition, parody, irony and so on, literature can draw attention to the notion of register by foregrounding the features of particular registers and can show how arbitrary and often absurd certain registers can be.

3   By being so open to the registers that surround it, literature seems to challenge the strict distinctions maintained by conservative registers and seems ultimately to question the idea that literature itself is a privileged or special discourse.

4   At the same time, there are special literary registers that have been created and transformed by writers throughout the history of literature. As our reading experience develops, we become sensitized to these registers and are able to recognize when a text deviates from its established register (sometimes by 'quoting' registers from the past). Even when a poem is written in a non-poetic register, its impact depends on the reader's inner sense of the poetic register it is deviating from.

5   At different historical moments, literary and poetic registers may be conservative or open. Nonetheless, literary and poetic registers are continually renewed or changed, often by borrowing from other registers or by recycling the registers of previous literature. One of the skills that readers need to develop is the ability to recognize the registers of a wide range of different periods and genres: Renaissance courtly love poetry; Restoration drama; eighteenth-century satire; Romantic lyric poetry; the realist novel; modernist poetry; and so on.

ACTIVITY 7.1

This activity focuses on Edmund Blunden's 'Vlamertinghe: Passing the Chateau, July 1917' (1928). Vlamertinghe is a village in Belgium, near Passchendaele, where some of the heaviest fighting of the First World War took place in 1917.

'And all her silken flanks with garlands drest' –
But we are coming to the sacrifice.
Must those have flowers who are not yet gone West?

May those have flowers who live with death and lice?
This must be the floweriest place
That earth allows; the queenly face
Of the proud mansion borrows grace for grace
Spite of those brute guns lowing at the skies.

Bold great daisies, golden lights,
Bubbling roses' pinks and whites –
Such a gay carpet! poppies by the million;
Such damask! such vermilion!
But if you ask me, mate, the choice of colour
Is scarcely right; this red should have been much duller.

1   Read the poem carefully and then try to identify the poem's register or
     registers by marking where you feel the register changes. To do this, you
     might ask the following questions of each phrase or line of the poem:
     does this sound like: (a) poetry or some non-poetic use of language? (b)
     written or spoken? (c) the language of 1917 or from an earlier period?
     (d) the kind of thing a soldier might say to another soldier in the First
     World War or something else (if so, what is that something else?).

2   What features of the language have influenced your answers to Question
     1 – is it a matter of vocabulary and/or of syntax?

3   Try to identify the poem's register or registers by writing a 'register label'
     alongside the relevant words, phrases, lines or sections of the poem. For
     example, if you think that parts of the poem, or even the whole poem,
     is in 'poetic' register, then write that label alongside the relevant lines.

4   Register variation is one of the best ways of spotting poetic allusion (see
     Unit 13, Intertextuality and allusion); are there any lines or phrases in
     this poem that you think might be an allusion to another poem? Try out
     your hunches by doing an Internet search on these phrases (e.g. by using
     Google).

5   You should now have discovered that Blunden's poem makes three allu-
     sions to one of the most famous poems in the English language. Do you
     think that the language of the rest of Blunden's poem is: (a) trying to
     imitate the register of that poem, or (b) commenting on that register in
     some way, or (c) developing a different register?

6   Are there any other registers in the poem that come from the poem's
     context rather than from the individual speaker? If so, identify the rele-
     vant words or phrases and try to decide what register they come from.

7   Which of the registers in the poem is the voice of the speaker? On the basis of your answer to this, how would you identify the poem's speaker in terms of class, education or rank in the army?

Reading

Bakhtin, Mikhail (1981) 'Discourse in the Novel', trans. Caryl Emerson and Michael Holquist, in Vincent B. Leitch (ed.) (2001) *The Norton Anthology of Theory and Criticism*, London and New York: Norton.

Furniss, T.E. and Bath, M. (1996) *Reading Poetry: An Introduction*, London: Longman, pp. 3–24.

Halliday, M.A.K. (1978) *Language as Social Semiotic: The Social Interpretation of Language and Meaning*, London: Arnold.

Leech, G. (1969) *A Linguistic Guide to English Poetry*, London: Longman, pp. 9–12, 49–51.

Simpson, Paul (1997) *Language Through Literature: An Introduction*, London: Routledge.

St John Butler, Lance (1999) *Registering the Difference: Reading Literature Through Register*, Manchester: Manchester University Press; New York: St Martin's Press.

Unit 8

Language
and gender

Language plays a crucial role in signalling the way that we think about others and in displaying to others the way that we think about ourselves. Our relationships with others are largely managed through language, and we can thus signify to others how we see ourselves as gendered, classed and raced individuals through our choice of language items and styles of language. Since the 1970s, language has been of interest to feminist linguists because the use of certain types of language can signify particular attitudes towards women and men. Language seems to encode systematically a view of women as aberrant from a male norm. However, more recently feminist linguists have stressed the fact that, despite this embeddedness of certain stances towards women within the language, words do not 'contain' meaning in any simple way. Instead, meanings are worked out contextually and can be contested. Thus, while it is clear that sexist attitudes are still expressed, they no longer have such a normative feel to them and they take their meanings within the context of contesting discourses, such as feminism, which have suggested alternative forms of expression. Those who wish to express sexist attitudes may also be driven to be more indirect, to use irony or presuppositions rather than to be direct. First, let us consider the way that the language encodes women as a marked case and males as the norm.

8.1 Male as the norm

In many languages, reference to human beings is often made as if all humans were male (Pauwels, 1998). This happens partly through the operation of the noun 'man', when it is used generically to stand for the species, but also through the use of 'he' as a **generic pronoun** (generic means general rather than specific – the generic 'he' is therefore supposed to include females as well as males). However, as Rosalind Coward and Maria Black (1981) have pointed out, if generic 'man' is genuinely inclusive then both of the following sentences should sound equally odd:

(1)   Man's vital interests are food, shelter, and access to females.

(2)   Man, unlike other mammals, has difficulties in giving birth.

In practice, however, sentences like (1) are more likely to be produced and accepted unreflectingly than sentences like (2). Even when operating generically, therefore, words such as 'he' and 'man' carry their masculine connotations with them. This tendency also operates at more restricted levels of reference, when generic 'he' is not intended to refer to the human species as a whole but to some non-gender specific group within it, as, for example, in the following:

(3)   When the police officer has completed his investigation, he files a report.

(4)   The modern reader may at first feel baffled by the overpunctuation, as it will feel to him that there are too many commas.

The conventions of usage of the generic pronoun say that we should understand the use of 'he' and 'his' in (3) as referring to all police officers (that is, including female officers). Similarly, in (4) the conventions of usage suggest that both male and female readers are being included in the reference. However, research has revealed that readers of sentences containing generic pronouns often do not read them as having general reference, but in fact read them as referring strictly to males. Kidd (1971), for instance, has demonstrated that, when students are asked to visualize the referent of a generic pronoun, they almost invariably draw a male referent, even when the intended referent seems at first sight to be general.

A similar process may be seen at work in the following caption from an advertisement for Lufthansa airlines: 'What does today's business traveller expect of his airline?' Most people would read 'his' as having generic reference here, since it follows a **generic noun** 'business traveller'. But the picture that accompanies this advertisement makes it clear that the reference is only to males, since it shows a plane full of male business travellers relaxing on board an aeroplane, the only female on board being the steward who is serving them drinks. Thus, so-called generic nouns and pronouns are quite commonly not truly generic in practice: apparently non-gender specific, they often turn out to be referring actually to males. As a consequence of this, feminists such as Spender (1980) have argued that general categories of persons and indeed of the human species are often constructed through the language in male-oriented or androcentric terms. This process serves to make women less visible in social and cultural activity; the use, for instance, of the generic 'he' in example (3), or in the advertisement, serves to erase the fact that there are women who work as police officers, or who travel on business.

In some ways generic nouns (such as 'business travellers') that masquerade as non-gender specific terms are more insidious than the generic pronoun, 'he'. This is partly because there are so many of them, and partly because – unlike 'he' – they do not give any explicit signals that they might be excluding women. Because of this they become powerful ways of carving up social reality in implicitly masculine ways without announcing that they are doing so. Cameron (1985), for instance, shows that even expressions such as 'astronaut', 'firefighter', 'lecturer', 'shop assistant', 'scientist' and so on disguise a tendency to refer only to men – despite their apparently neutral generic potential. Cameron cites two newspaper reports:

(5)   The lack of vitality is aggravated by the fact that there are so few able-bodied young adults about. They have all gone off to work or look for work, leaving behind the old, the disabled, the women and the children. (*The Sunday Times*)

(6)   A coloured South African who was subjected to racial abuse by his neighbours went berserk with a machete and killed his next-door neighbour's wife, Birmingham Crown Court heard yesterday. (*The Guardian*)

In example (5), the generic expression is 'able-bodied young adults', yet it is clear from the rest of the sentence that what is really meant is 'able-bodied young men', since women and children are subsequently excluded from its reference. In the second example (6), the generic expression is 'next-door neighbour' since this word ostensibly means both male and female neighbours, and yet it is clear that, when it is used to refer to women, it needs to be modified to 'neighbour's wife'. Thus, neighbour, rather than being a generic in this context, is in fact only referring to male neighbours.

It can clearly be seen that generic nouns often refer solely to men in the fact that women doing a job that is conventionally seen as stereotypically male are sometimes described as 'lady doctor', 'female engineer', 'woman pilot', etc. However, as more and more women take up jobs that have been conventionally seen as male, the most salient feature of their work will not continue to be their gender and true generics such as 'fire-fighter' will be used to refer to both females and males.

Apart from the discrimination entailed within generic nouns and pronouns, they can also be ambiguous in their reference, as, for example, in the following sentence:

(7)   The more education an individual attains the better his occupation is likely to be.

It is unclear here whether the 'individual' is supposed to be a man or whether this is indeed a generic use (this is not cleared up by 'his' – which may also be generic). Because the reference of generic nouns and pronouns is ambiguous and because they serve to make women seem invisible, feminists such as Dale Spender (1980), Casey Miller and Kate Swift (1979) have objected to their use. As Pauwels (1998) has noted, feminists have been active in campaigning against their use in official documents so that in the public sphere, at least, their use is much less common, and feminists have developed alternative terms that are more acceptable to women. Because of the development of guidelines on language usage, it has also become more acceptable to object to sexist usage.

Feminists have suggested a number of ways around the problem of the generic pronoun and generic reference: some writers have begun to avoid using generic 'he' entirely, by using the passivized form, as in the following:

(8)   When a police officer has finished an investigation, a report should be filed.

Or the 'he' can be avoided by using the plural 'they':

(9)   When police officers have finished their investigation, they should file a report.

In these sentences, it is clear that the reference is truly generic. But it is also possible to signal more positively that there may be female as well as male police officers:

(10) When the police officer has finished the investigation, he or she should file a report.

Some writers even use 'she' throughout their work to draw attention to the problems with generic 'he' usage, or they use a plural 'they' after a singular subject:

(11) When the police officer has finished the investigation, they should file a report.

These forms are often contested, particularly examples (10) and (11), and even though usage has changed greatly in the last five years, since nearly all publishers, educational institutions and organizations have issued their staff with guidelines on language use to cover reference to gender and race, the subject of the use of generics is still contested and debated.

8.2 Female as downgraded or derogated

There is a range of words that are used solely for males or females and are therefore **gender-specific**. Many of these words have a slightly archaic feel about them now – this is an indicator of the way language has been changing rapidly in this area in recent years (see **Unit 5, Language and time**). So, for example, the word 'poetess' is only used for women, and the word 'courtier' is usually only used for men. Many female actors, particularly those who are at the top of the profession, do not use the word 'actress' to describe themselves, preferring to use the generic 'actor'; this indicates the extent to which 'actress' is seen to be a demeaning word that describes someone who is not serious about her profession.

Analysis reveals that there are significant patterns in the use of gender-specific language, in that pairs of gender-specific nouns are not always symmetrical; instead, they tend to downgrade (or derogate) women by treating them as if they were only sexual objects rather than full human beings. This emerges in the following sets of pairs:

    master/mistress
    courtier/courtesan
    host/hostess

Most of the terms on the male side have positive or neutral connotations and seem to refer solely to an occupation, whereas the female equivalents often have negative sexual connotations. There is a further asymmetry in the way that women are often referred to as 'girls'. In the following advertisement from *The Guardian*, 'girl' is used as if it were the female equivalent of 'man', whereas 'girl' generally refers to female children rather than adults:

    EFL TEACHERS: required first week in February. Girl with driving
    licence for Italy; man with experience and girl with degree in
    German for Germany.

This usage is also common in sports commentaries, where adult women athletes are often described as 'girls' (or as 'ladies'). However, it should be remembered that 'girl' is not intrinsically sexist, since it may be used playfully by women to refer to themselves; thus, the context will determine whether the terms are used to express sexism.

Women and men are also named in different ways. Women's marital status is signalled by the use of the terms Mrs and Miss, for which there are no current male equivalents (Mr does not indicate whether a man is married or single). To resist this, the term Ms was introduced in the 1980s so that women would be able to have an equivalent title to males. Its use has become much more general in recent years, despite a great deal of opposition. Some women still feel wary about using it since it is associated with feminism or is assumed to refer to women who are divorced or separated. Nevertheless, a surprisingly large number of companies and institutions now offer Ms as an option for women to refer to themselves on forms and documents. However, this radical initiative to invent a new term to refer to women has resulted in there now being three terms rather than two, all of them posing problems for women when they are asked for their name.

Analysis also reveals a covert asymmetry in the way that women are referred to in tabloid newspapers, where they are frequently identified by their marital or family status (wife, mother, grandmother) rather than by their profession. This is clear in a headline from the *Daily Star*: 'MAD GUNMAN HUNT AS WIFE IS SHOT'. It is also quite common in tabloid newspapers for women to be described in terms of their physical appearance (hair colour, body shape and so on), whereas men are usually described with reference to their jobs and age.

Stereotypes about males and females inform the type of language that is used. These stereotypes of masculinity and femininity can influence the way that scientific reports are written, for example in assertions made about the activity of eggs and sperm (Martin, 1997) or when describing animals in nature programmes (Crowther and Leith, 1995). Martin describes the way that scientific reports tend to draw on stereotypical notions of male and female activity and passivity when analysing sperm and eggs; she claims that:

> The egg is seen as large and passive. It does not move or journey, but passively 'is transported', 'is swept' or even 'drifts' along the fallopian tube. In utter contrast, sperm are small, 'streamlined' and invariably active. They 'deliver' their genes to the egg, 'activate the developmental program of the egg' and have a velocity which is often remarked upon. Their tails are strong and efficiently powered.
>
> (1997, p. 87)

Despite the fact that both egg and sperm play an active role in conception and both move, scientists still tend to represent conception in terms that accord with the notion of the female element being passive. In a similar way, Crowther and Leith have found that, in nature programmes on television, in descriptions of the way that lions organize themselves in social groups, terms such as 'harems' have been used to describe a situation where the female lions in a pride allow one male lion to mate with them, excluding all others. In this way, the stereotypes of female passivity associated with the term harem are carried over to the way lion communities are described.

8.3 The potential for reform

Some feminists, such as Dale Spender (1980), see such asymmetries in language as demeaning to women and urge that language should be reformed accordingly. For many feminists it is important to suggest alternative terms to use, thus 'chairperson' should be used instead of 'chairman' and 'manager' should be use for both males and females. Others, such as Deborah Cameron (1985), have suggested that sexism cannot be eradicated simply by changing language items, since this only changes the surface manifestation of beliefs about women. (See also **Unit 5, Language and time**.)

8.4 Women's speech

Much early feminist research in sociolinguistics was concerned with investigating whether women speak differently from men. Robin Lakoff (1975), for example, claimed that women use different words from men (e.g. 'pretty' and 'cute') and different sentence structures (e.g. tag questions: 'This is hard to understand, isn't it?'). She characterizes women's language as being prone to hesitation, and as being repetitive and disjointed. This sociolinguistic work has now been questioned, since it is clear that women are not a unified grouping: there are many hierarchies within the grouping 'women', such as differences of class, race, economic power, education and so on, with the consequence that groups of women speakers differ from other female speakers, and also each woman varies the way she talks depending on the context (Bergvall *et al.*, 1996; Holmes and Meyerhoff, 2003). Within the business environment, women managers may choose to take on more masculine, assertive styles of speech. The speech patterns of the former UK Prime Minister, Margaret Thatcher, or the US Secretary of State, Condoleezza Rice, bear greater similarities to the speech of males in similar positions of power than they do, say, to working-class women's speech. It is for this reason that it is now extremely difficult to assert that women speak in a different way from men.

However, there are certain elements of speech that we can classify as stereotypically 'feminine': that is, those elements that seem to signify lack of confidence or assertiveness. These may be drawn on by both women and men in certain situations. O'Barr and Atkins (1982) have shown that within a courtroom setting both men and women from low-income groups are likely to adopt what they term 'powerless speech', that is, speech that bears a strong resemblance to Lakoff's definition of women's speech: hesitant, repetitive, disjointed and so on. Thus it is probable that, when discussing 'women's speech', theorists have been describing 'powerless speech' (see also **Unit 9, Language and society**). However, this assumes that assertive language is necessarily better than non-assertive language. This seemingly powerless language may be ineffective in a courtroom setting (and that itself is debatable) but appropriate in a more intimate situation, such as when friends engage in 'troubles talk'.

8.5 The female sentence: a woman's writing?

Work on female speech has been echoed by work on women's writing, since many theorists claim that women's writing is qualitatively different from men's writing. For example, Virginia Woolf proposed that Dorothy Richardson's writing had developed a new way of using language, which Woolf termed 'a woman's sentence'. Woolf did not describe in detail what this 'psychological sentence of the feminine gender' consisted of, but, if we compare the following two extracts by Anita Brookner and Malcolm Lowry, it seems quite easy to argue that Brookner is using a 'feminine' style, while Lowry is using a 'masculine' style:

> From the window all that could be seen was a receding area of grey. It was to be supposed that beyond the grey garden, which seemed to sprout nothing but the stiffish leaves of some unfamiliar plant, lay the vast grey lake, spreading like an anaesthetic towards the invisible further shore, and beyond that, in imagination only, yet verified by the brochure, the peak of the Dent d'Oche, on which snow might already be slightly and silently falling.
>
> (Anita Brookner, *Hôtel du Lac*, 1984)

> Two mountain chains traverse the republic roughly from north to south, forming between them a number of valleys and plateaux. Overlooking one of these valleys, which is dominated by two volcanoes, lies, six thousand feet above sea-level, the town of Quauhnahuac. It is situated well south of the Tropic of Cancer, to be exact on the nineteenth parallel, in about the same latitude as the Revillagigedo Islands to the west in the Pacific, or very much farther west, the southernmost tip of Hawaii – and as the port of Tzucox to the east on the S. Atlantic seaboard of Yucatan near the border of British Honduras, or very much farther east, the town of Juggernaut, in India, on the Bay of Bengal.
>
> (Malcolm Lowry, *Under the Volcano*, 1967)

The Brookner passage describes the landscape from a particular point of view, that is, as seen from a character's perspective rather than from an omniscient narrator's standpoint. This personalized account consists of descriptions of colours, and the effect these colours have on the character. There seems to be a certain vagueness about the description; instead of facts, this account is concerned with what 'was supposed to be', what 'seemed' and what 'might be' happening. This modification or tentativeness is conventionally said to characterize a feminine style. In contrast, the Lowry passage seems far more distanced; the narrator dispenses facts, using a scientific objective passive voice ('it is situated . . .' and 'the town . . . is dominated'). The information emanates thus not from an identifiable character but from a seemingly objective, omniscient narrator. In fact, the style used is reminiscent of the **register** (see **Unit 7**) of guidebooks or of geographical descriptions.

For many readers, these two passages may seem to characterize a feminine and masculine style respectively – one a personalized style, describing in detail relationships and the actions of characters, and the other more concerned with factual descriptions of the world. This accords with assertions made by Deborah Tannen that women tend to adopt certain strategies in speech that she calls rapport talk (talk that is concerned with maintaining relationships), while men adopt those strategies that she terms report talk (talk concerned with giving information and establishing hierarchies) (Tannen, 1991). However, it is clear that these distinctions, although fairly easy to make, are based on stereotypical notions of gender difference (women are supposed to be vague and concerned with relationships, whereas men are supposed to be precise and interested in facts). Not all male writers write like Lowry, and not all women writers write as Brookner does here. Iris Murdoch, for example, often writes in a manner more akin to Lowry's writing, and frequently uses a male narrator. Also, it should be noted that much of the imprecision of the Brookner passage arises from the fact that she is focusing on the impressions of a character who is unfamiliar with the landscape (the character has a 'brochure' of the area).

Thus, the idea that there is a masculine style and a feminine style appears to be based more on stereotypical notions of sexual difference than on any inevitable textual difference in the way men and women write. Although the way a person uses language (in writing as in speech) will be influenced by conventional stereotypes about gender, and although readers often apply those same stereotypes when reading literature, it is important to remember that these stereotypes are neither natural nor inevitable. If women do sometimes use language differently, this is related to the way that women are derogated in language and the way that social pressures may encourage them to adopt certain speech styles. It may also be the case that women may choose to adopt feminine styles because that may be strategically more effective in a particular context. At the same time, however, women writers (like their male counterparts) may adopt different linguistic styles for particular artistic and political ends. Feminist critics and writers often employ language in ways that challenge the gender biases embedded in language and resist the derogation and disempowering of women. On the other hand, early twentieth-century writers, such as Woolf, Richardson and Rosamond Lehmann, can be seen as adopting a 'feminine' style precisely in order to subvert or question the assumptions of 'masculine' objectivity. Thus, it is important to be able to recognize masculine and feminine elements within language but to be aware that these may have different objectives and interpretations depending on the context.

ACTIVITY 8.1 ─────────────

1   Read the text below from the 'Heartsearch' column of the *New Statesman* (May, 1987) and underline the words that reveal or hint at the sex of the writer.

2   Put a circle round all uses of generic nouns (e.g. terms like 'scientist', which seems to refer to all scientists, regardless of whether they are male or female).

3   Are there any differences between the ways that male and female writers use generic nouns in these advertisements?

4   What other linguistic differences are there that relate either to the sex of the writer or the sex of the person being sought?

5   Are there any possible confusions with generic uses here?

> CAMBRIDGE GRADUATE: vaguely academic; likes films, opera, Europe, old things. Lithe, fit, 6', sporty. Still attractive despite thinning hair.

> INCURABLE ROMANTIC, charming, uncomplicated, attractive woman, not slim, not young, feminine, wide interests, seeks personable caring, retired male, sixty plus, middle brow for commitment.

> GOOD-LOOKING German writer, early 30s, wishes to indulge in voyeuristic fantasy with young couple or single FORUM minded female.

> LADY, ATTRACTIVE, intelligent, independent mind and means, seeks similar man 40–50. Devon Cornwall only.

> Rich 1948 Claret with firm strong body sensuous flavour and adventurous bouquet, handsomely bottled, seeks younger crisp and frisky Chablis, equally well-packaged, for mulled fun, including weekends and holidays abroad with a view to durable casting. Photo appreciated.

> SENSITIVE HIPPY, 24, seeks sincere and caring female for loving relationship.

Reading

Bergvall, V., Bing, J. and Fried, A. (eds) (1996) *Rethinking Language and Gender Research: Theory and Practice*, London: Longman.

Cameron, D. (1985) *Feminism and Linguistic Theory*, London: Macmillan.

Holmes, J. and Meyerhoff, M. (eds) (2003) *Handbook of Language and Gender*, Oxford, Blackwell.

Mills, S. (1996) *Feminist Stylistics*, London: Routledge.

Pauwels, A. (1998) *Women Changing Language*, London, Longman.

Unit 9

Language and society

A language is constituted of a vocabulary, whose words are all made from a specific set of sounds, and whose words are combined in specific ways into sentences. A language such as 'English' can be thought of as a group of related dialects, which have many elements in common, but differ to some extent in vocabulary and rules of combination. Dialects usually also differ from each other within a language by being associated with different accents (different ways of pronuncing the words). Which dialects and accents a person is able to use fluently, and when they use those dialects and accents, relate both to geography and social class. As we will see in this chapter, where alternatives are possible in language, the choice of one alternative over another has social implications, relating to ideology, power and social status. These alternatives involve not just choice of dialect or accent, but also choice of word, choice of interactional style and choice of sentence structure.

9.1 Vocabulary in social history

Our experience of the world is shaped for us by our language. Partly this is a question of vocabulary. The emergence of particular vocabulary items in a language helps to bring aspects of reality into focus for its speakers, and a shift between vocabulary items or expressions may reflect or produce a redefinition of that reality. The history of a society, and the struggles within that society, can be manifested in the vocabulary spoken by that society. Raymond Williams showed this in his book *Keywords* (1988), which traces the history of certain words, and shows how these histories are also social histories (see also **Unit 5, Language and time**). For example, the word 'family' has often been at the centre of political debates; while it is often used as though it is unproblematic, this is not reflected in its complex history. It first entered English from Latin

104

in the late fourteenth century, at which time it tended to refer to a household (incorporating not only blood-relations but also servants living together under one roof). It was then extended to include the notion of a house formed by descent from a common ancestor. The specialization of the term to refer to a small kin-group living in a single house is a fairly late development in the history of the word in English (between the seventeenth and nineteenth centuries), and may be related to the growing importance of the family as an economic unit in developing capitalism. One of the reasons why words change their meanings through history is because they reflect both the transformations of social structures and the fact that society is not a single entity but differentiated along lines of class, race and gender. The use of the term 'the family' in recent political debate emphasizes the heterosexual, parenting couple as a self-contained economic unit living in its own home independent of state and social support (the 'nuclear family') – a sense which tends to exclude single parents, unmarried parents and so on. The fact that such a definition does not accord with the way many people live in English-speaking societies in the twenty-first century goes some way to demonstrating the ideological work to which language can be recruited in an attempt to promote or legitimate particular versions of reality. It seems as if language cannot escape becoming the site of social and political contestation. It gives us categories for organizing experience and understanding the world that may seem neutral and unbiased but are inevitably partial and particular.

9.2 Language and social relations

At the same time as language constructs a social reality for us, it also constructs and shapes our social relationships. When we speak or write, we speak or write *about something* but we also speak or write *to someone*. Consequently, every time we speak or write we articulate our social identity in relation to the social identity of the hearer or reader: as Valentin N. Voloshinov (1973) pointed out, every utterance is a bridge between self and other. One way in which this works is through the choice of address terms, or more generally in the way that the text codifies the position of its addressee (see **Unit 15, Positioning the reader or spectator**). The incumbent of the White House is not addressed in press conferences as 'Bill' or 'Ronald' or 'George', but as 'Mr President', or 'Sir', or even 'Mr President, Sir'. Similarly, exchanges in the Westminster Houses of Parliament have elaborate codes of address in which speakers in the lower house refer to each other as 'the Right Honourable Lady' or 'my Right Honourable Friend' and to members of the upper house as 'my noble Lords'. Such formulations, involving titles and honorifics, encode social distance, formality and status in graduated ways. Title (Mr President) is more formal than Title + Last Name (President Bush) – which in turn is more formal than

First Name (George). Collectively, such formulations constitute a system of modes of address. Selecting from within the system is a way of defining (and redefining) the nature of the relationship between speaker and hearer, addressor and addressee. In addition to direct address, of course, the audience is also addressed by implication. In effect, texts project or invoke 'a position' – a framework of beliefs and common understanding – from which they make sense.

Both types of address – direct and indirect – work hand in hand. Consider, for instance, Henry Fielding's novel, *Tom Jones* (1749), which frequently uses direct address to define and redefine the relationship of the narrator to the reader:

> We are now, reader, arrived at the last stage of our long journey. As we have therefore travelled together through so many pages, let us behave to one another like fellow-travellers in a stage coach, who have passed several days in the company of each other; and who . . . mount, for the last time, into their vehicle with chearfulness and good-humour . . .
>
> And now, my friend, I take this opportunity (as I shall have no other) of heartily wishing thee well. If I have been an entertaining companion to thee, I promise thee it is what I have desired.
>
> (Book XVIII, chapter 1)

Notice that 'the reader' is not only addressed as such but is also being constituted, both directly and indirectly, in quite specific terms as singular ('thee'), as equivalent to a companion or friend, as capable of being 'chearful' and 'good-humoured' and so on. Indeed, the positive, ideal traits of sociability, benign good-humour, tolerance and conviviality that are so much espoused in the narrative world of the novel are also projected outwards onto its implied addressee.

The mode of address in *Tom Jones* is worlds apart from the less formal, offhand, but strictly impersonal opening of Forster's *Howards End* (1910):

> One may as well begin with Helen's letters to her sister.

Thus, every text, spoken or written, through its modes of address organizes social relationships. This is achieved partly through address terms (gentle reader, Mr President, etc.). We should note also that language organizes social relations by means of its capacity to perform actions in words in relation to the addressee. Through words we can question, command, state, challenge, promise, insult, offer, invite, request and so on. Many of our most important institutions depend upon using words to perform quite specific actions, whether it be in the context of a marriage ceremony, Parliamentary debate, a job interview or union negotiations.

9.3 Transitivity, and the notions of overt and covert agency

A speaker can align themselves with a social position by their choice of words, but also by the way in which they combine the words into sentences. A sentence represents an **eventuality**. 'Eventuality' is a cover term for an event, or an action, or a state of affairs, and all sentences represent one of these three types of occurrence or situation. An event is something that happens. An action is something that is caused to happen: it involves an agent, a sentient individual, usually a person, who makes something happen. A state of affairs just *is*; it has no agent. The important point for our purposes is that the actual eventuality that is being reported can be reshaped in the reporting, such that, for example, an action can be made to seem more like an event. Consider, for example, in Table 9.1, a two-page spread of headlines from a right-wing British newspaper.

Each of these headlines is a sentence that represents an eventuality. All six eventualities are actions (as is clear when the articles are read: they all involve events initiated by agents). But the headlines present these as actions to different degrees: some are presented much more clearly as actions than others. The clearest examples of actions are (c) and (e), where there are explicit agents. It may be significant that these are also the two eventualities where the non-liberal editorial stance of the newspaper is most disapproving; perhaps agency is emphasized when the action is considered bad. In contrast, the police disappear as agents from (a), which might even be read as representing a state of affairs, and the warner (the agent of warning) disappears from (f).

Table 9.1

	The headline	The eventuality (extracted from news story)
(a)	Five held in hunt for animal rights extremists who desecrated grave	Police have arrested . . .
(b)	Greek and Latin become easier to pass	An exam board is to reduce vocabulary requirements . . .
(c)	Liberals delay appointing new bishops	Liberal bishops decided not to appoint . . .
(d)	*Who* guitarist's lover found dead from 'overdose'	She was found by a family member . . .
(e)	Parents of sick children dupe nurseries	Working parents are leaving sick children with nurseries . . .
(f)	Health warning over long working hours	The chief executive of a charity has said that . . .

The distinction between eventualities represented as actions and eventualities represented as events or states of affairs is a rather crude one. A more complex and multi-dimensional differentiation uses the notion of **transitivity**. The core notion of transitivity involves an action where an agent does something to someone or something else (called the **patient** of the action). In traditional grammar, a transitive sentence is a sentence with both a subject and an object, such as 'Mary ate the cheese', where 'Mary' is both the subject of the sentence and also the agent of the action, and 'the cheese' is both the object of the sentence and also the patient of the action. Core transitive sentences of this kind can be thought of as 'high in transitivity', where transitivity is a gradient characteristic (it can be greater or lesser) of a sentence. Some of the elements of a sentence that make it highly transitive are these:

1   The subject of the sentence (the phrase before the verb) expresses the agent of the action, and there is an object of the sentence (the phrase after the verb), which expresses the patient of the action. Passive sentences such as headline (d) above get a low transitivity score on this criterion, because they do not have objects (the patient of the action is expressed as the subject of the sentence).

2   The action takes place at a moment in time and is not currently ongoing, but has finished. On this criterion headline (e) is low in transitivity, though it is high in transitivity on criterion (1).

3   The action is done on purpose. Purposiveness is an important component of being an agent in any case, and the more clear that the action is purposeful, the higher its transitivity. Headline (b) scores low for transitivity in this regard, though it can be argued that the transitivity of the actual eventuality that it reports has been reduced in reporting it.

4   The patient is an individuated entity that is totally affected by the action. Thus, for example, headline (a) scores high on transitivity because five distinct people are individuated and affected by the action; in contrast, headline (c) scores low on this type of transitivity because no specific person is affected by the action.

These kinds of criterion enable us to assess the level of transitivity on various different scores. We can then interpret the results. For example, the fact that headline (a), about the arrests, is low in transitivity criterion (1) and high in (2), (3) and (4) makes even more salient the fact that the agency of the police has been concealed; it is as though they do not act as individual agents (but perhaps as representatives of the social order). In complete contrast, headline (c), about the delay in appointing gay bishops, is high on criterion (1) but low in (2), (3) and (4). Here, despite the generally low transitivity of the eventuality (the action of delaying an action), the salience of the actors makes an interesting contrast to the absence of the police from the other headline; here, perhaps, the salience of the bishops as actors suggests that they do not represent the social order, the order to which the readers of the paper belong.

The theoretical approach of 'Critical Discourse Analysis' or CDA explores the extent to which it is possible to make political sense of how eventualities are portrayed, particularly in the media. Such an analysis could, for example, be undertaken for the reporting over the period 25 to 26 March 1999 at the beginning of NATO's air campaign to prevent the violent expulsion by Serbs of Albanians from their homes in Kosovo. Here is a set of headlines all representing essentially the same eventuality (or sequence of eventualities):

(g)   The onslaught begins
(h)   Serbs remain defiant as the missile attacks go on
(j)   NATO vows to bomb Serbs until resistance is destroyed
(k)   'No sanctuary' warns NATO as Serbs are bombarded again
(m)   Belgrade rocked by bombs as British jets join NATO
(n)   Air strikes begin as Blair says 'we must end vile oppression'
(o)   Onslaught
(p)   Firestorm!
(q)   Nowhere to hide
(r)   Justice
(s)   Clobba slobba.

Bombing is in itself an eventuality that should be capable of being represented with high levels of transitivity: it has to be a deliberate action on the part of an agent, which affects a patient, taking place at a point in time and then stopping (for individuated events of bombing, though less so for a campaign). However, none of the headlines represents it as highly transitive. Headline (j) comes the closest to having an agent subject of the verb 'bomb', but in fact this sentence is about vowing to bomb, not directly about bombing; that is, the verb 'bomb' here does not have an overt subject. Similarly, (m) implies that British jets are dropping the bombs mentioned in the first part of the headline, but does not explicitly say so; instead the eventuality 'Belgrade rocked by bombs' is a passive sentence, relatively low in transitivity (even the choice of 'rocked' instead of 'damaged' de-emphasizes the effect on the patient). In other headlines, (n), (g), (o) and (p), the eventuality of bombing is named, but there is no mention either of the agent (the bombers) or the patient (the Serbs of Belgrade). It is also noticeable that the eventualities tend to be represented as nouns not as verbs: 'attack', 'onslaught' and 'air strikes' are all noun phrases that are inherently less transitive than equivalent verbs because they lack subjects and tend not to be located as clearly in time. Thus these headlines all function in a similar way by reporting the eventualities in ways that de-emphasize transitivity, reporting an event in ways that make it seem as if we (the readers of the newspapers) – or our representatives – are not trying to kill them (the Serbs of Belgrade).

9.4 Language and social structure in the novel

The novel is a literary genre that is more overtly 'social' than poetry (or even drama). This is partly to do with its form, because it includes a range of different voices rather than the single consciousness often present in poetry. The social status of the novel is also partly to do with the themes it was used to treat in the nineteenth century, typically the tensions between different classes. Also it is partly to do with its origins as a means of representing the rising middle classes in the eighteenth century.

The nineteenth-century 'realist' novel in Britain often dramatizes the (usually fraught) relations between three classes – the upper class, the middle class and the working class. These distinctions and struggles are typically registered through a sociology of language as well as in themes, characters and plots. Charles Dickens's *Great Expectations* (1860–1), for example, explores these issues through having a character (the narrator Pip) cross the boundaries of social class. Pip is brought up in a working-class household by his sister and her husband Joe Gargery, a blacksmith with whom he develops strong ties in the first third of the novel. Through the support of a mysterious benefactor, however, Pip becomes a 'gentleman', takes rooms in London, and begins to regard his humble past as an embarrassment. Thus when he receives word that Joe intends to visit him in London, Pip anticipates meeting his old friend 'with considerable disturbance, some mortification, and a keen sense of incongruity':

> As the time approached I should have liked to run away, but . . . presently I heard Joe on the staircase. I knew it was Joe, by his clumsy manner of coming up-stairs – his state boots being always too big for him – and by the time it took him to read the names on the other floors in the course of his ascent. When at last he stopped outside our door, I could hear his finger tracing over the painted letters of my name . . . Finally he gave a faint single rap, and Pepper . . . announced 'Mr Gargery!' I thought he never would have done wiping his feet . . . but at last he came in.
>
> 'Joe, how are you, Joe?'
>
> 'Pip, how AIR you, Pip?'
>
> . . .
>
> 'I am glad to see you, Joe. Give me your hat.'
>
> But Joe . . . wouldn't hear of parting with that piece of property, and persisted in standing talking over it in a most uncomfortable way.
>
> 'Which you have that growed,' said Joe, 'and that swelled, and that gentle-folked'; Joe considered a little before he discovered this word; 'as to be sure you are a honour to your king and country.'
>
> 'And you, Joe, look wonderfully well.'

(Chapter 27)

Dickens uses a number of devices here to indicate the social distance that has arisen between these characters. He registers Joe's uneasiness through the way he wipes his feet and holds his hat, and also registers Pip's equally revealing attention to these details; but the social difference between Pip and Joe is also indicated by their language: not only their different kinds of language but also their different relations to language. Joe's difficulty with the written language is foregrounded through Pip's acute consciousness of his ponderous attempts to read the names on the doors, but more to the point here is the way Joe speaks. While Pip conceals his unease behind the register (see **Unit 7**) of polite affability, Joe precisely reveals his sense of awkwardness in echoing Pip. In attempting to imitate his young friend's speech, Joe hypercorrects his own accent by revealingly overdoing the 'proper' pronunciation of 'are' (as 'AIR'). Joe quickly 'forgets himself' by 'lapsing' into his normal accent in what we may take as a flood of genuine feeling and admiration. Pip, by contrast, continues in a polite register, which signals his inability to respond to his old friend and maintains the social stratification through language that this passage dramatizes.

In the twentieth-century novel, such sociolinguistic stratifications are often challenged or undermined. D.H. Lawrence's fiction typically attempts to reverse the kind of hierarchy set up in the Dickens passage above. This can be seen in several places in *Lady Chatterley's Lover* (1928), including the following exchange between Lady Chatterley and her lover (who is a gamekeeper on her estate):

'Tha mun come one naight ter th'cottage, afore tha goos; sholl ter?' he asked, lifting his eyebrows as he looked at her, his hands dangling between his knees.
   'Sholl ter?' she echoed, teasing.
   He smiled.
   'Ay, sholl ter?' he repeated.
   'Ay!' she said, imitating the dialect sound.
   . . .
   ''Appen Sunday,' she said.
   ''Appen a' Sunday! Ay!'
   He laughed at her quickly.
   'Nay, tha canna,' he protested.
   'Why canna I?' she said.
   He laughed. Her attempts at the dialect were so ludicrous, somehow.
(Chapter 12)

On one level, this presents a tender scene between the two lovers in which the social difference in their ways of speaking becomes material for a lovers' game. At the same time, however, the social significance of this difference cannot be overlooked. At several points in the novel, Mellors, the gamekeeper, uses the fact that he can move at will between one way of speaking and the other as a weapon in a class war against the upper-class family that employs him. Lady Chatterley's attempt to imitate the dialect of a 'lower' social class (which reverses the situation in *Great Expectations* examined above) can be read as a bid to escape from the restrictions of her own class. This is reinforced by the fact that the gamekeeper's dialect is treated throughout the novel as if it were the authentic expression of desire in contrast to the coldly mental, sexless language of the upper classes. In this respect, Lady Chatterley's imitation of her gamekeeper's dialect – which is an amusing failure in Mellors's eyes – becomes symptomatic of a wider failure in the novel's terms to achieve an authentic modality for the enactment of desire across the divide of social class. (For a fuller discussion of accent and dialect, see **Unit 6, Language and place**.)

ACTIVITY 9.1 ▬▬▬▬▬▬▬▬▬▬▬▬▬▬▬▬▬▬▬▬▬▬▬▬▬

1   Read the following passage from Elizabeth Gaskell's *North and South* (1854–5). The central character, Margaret Hale, has recently moved from the south of England to Manchester (one of the main centres of industrial development in the nineteenth century) and is discussing an impending strike at a local mill with a poverty-stricken leader of the union, Nicholas Higgins ('to clem' is a dialect term for 'to starve'):

> 'Why do you strike?' asked Margaret. 'Striking is leaving off work till you get your own rate of wages, is it not? You must not wonder at my ignorance; where I come from I never heard of a strike.'
>
>   . . .
>
> 'Why yo' see, there's five or six masters who have set themselves again paying the wages they've been paying these two years past, and flourishing upon, and getting richer upon. And now they come to us, and say we're to take less. And we won't. We'll just clem to death first; and see who'll work for 'em then.'
>
>   . . .
>
> 'And so you plan dying, in order to be revenged upon them!'
> 'No,' said he, 'I dunnot. I just look forward to the chance of dying at my post sooner than yield. That's what folk call fine and honourable in a soldier, and why not in a poor weaver-chap?'
> 'But,' said Margaret, 'a soldier dies in the cause of the Nation – in the cause of others.'
> '. . . Dun yo' think it's for mysel' I'm striking work at this time? It's just as much in the cause of others as yon soldier . . . I take up

John Boucher's cause, as lives next door but one, wi' a sickly wife, and eight childer, . . . I take up th' cause o' justice. . . .'

. . .

'But,' said Margaret, . . . 'the state of trade may be such as not to enable them to give you the same remuneration.'

'State o' trade! That's just a piece o' masters' humbug. It's rate o' wages I was talking of. Th' masters keep th' state o' trade in their own hands; and just walk it forward like a black bug-a-boo, to frighten naughty children with into being good.'

(from Chapter 17, 'What is a Strike?')

2   Make a list of all the words and phrases that Higgins uses to describe: (a) the mill owners; (b) the workers; (c) himself; (d) the mill owners' actions; (e) the workers' actions; and (f) his own actions. From this evidence, try to describe Higgins's view of the strike (for example, by considering who does what to whom).

3   Make a list of all the words and phrases that Margaret uses to describe: (a) the mill owners' possible actions; (b) Higgins's description of his own role; and (c) the actions of workers in a strike. From this evidence, try to describe Margaret's view of the strike.

4   What is the difference between Margaret's suggestion that 'the state of trade' might not allow the owners to give the workers the same 'remuneration', and Higgins's response that he is not talking about the state of trade but 'rate o' wages'? How, in Higgins's view, do the owners use the term 'state of trade'?

5   What is the effect of the fact that Higgins speaks in a working-class northern dialect, while Margaret speaks in Standard English? Does it make his view of the strike more credible? less credible? more authentic? less authoritative?

Reading

Burton, D. (1982) 'Through Glass Darkly: Through Dark Glasses', in R. Carter (ed.) *Language and Literature: An Introductory Reader in Stylistics*, London: George Allen & Unwin, pp. 195–214.

Fabb, N. (1997) *Linguistics and Literature*, Oxford: Blackwell, pp. 173–92 on transitivity.

Fairclough, N. (1992) *Discourse and Social Change*, London: Polity Press.

Montgomery, M. (1995) *An Introduction to Language and Society*, 2nd edn, London: Routledge.

Simpson, P. (1993) *Language, Ideology and Point of View*, London: Routledge.

Williams, R. (1988) *Keywords: A Vocabulary of Culture and Society*, London: Collins.

Section 3

Attributing meaning

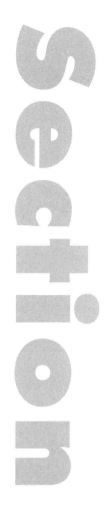

Unit 10

Metaphor and figurative language

The recognition and analysis of figurative language, or figures of speech, depend upon a general distinction between literal and figurative uses of language. It should be stressed that the notion of literal meaning does not depend on the idea that each word has only one meaning. In fact, the word 'literal' itself has several meanings. The *Shorter Oxford English Dictionary* tells us that the term derives its original meaning from the Old French or Latin for 'letter', and one of its primary meanings is 'Of or pertaining to letters of the alphabet' or 'expressed by letters'. In this sense, all writing is literal. A related meaning appears in the theological notion of interpreting the Christian scriptures according to the letter – that is, 'taking the words of a text, etc., in their natural and customary meaning, and using the ordinary rules of grammar'. In this sense, literal is distinguished from the mystical or allegorical interpretation of scripture. This meaning and distinction is related to the way we will be using the term here: literal is 'applied to taking words in their etymological or primary sense, or in the sense expressed by the actual wording of a passage, without recourse to any metaphorical or suggested meaning'. But what we are not concerned with here, however, is the recent tendency to use the term 'literally' as an intensifier. As *Collins' English Dictionary* notes, this usage either adds nothing to the meaning (as in 'the house was literally only five minutes away') or results in absurdity (as in 'the news was literally an eye-opener to me'). Such usages should be avoided altogether in literary criticism.

Literal, then, tends to be defined in opposition to 'metaphorical' or 'figurative'. The term 'figurative' also has several meanings. One of its meanings is related to the representation of figures in visual art: 'Pertaining to, or of the nature of, pictorial or plastic representation'. An alternative meaning relates to language use: 'Of speech: based on figures or metaphors; metaphorical, not literal' (*Shorter OED*). In literary criticism, figurative language is a general term for a variety of non-literal uses of language. Although 'metaphorical' is also used as a general term in this way, 'metaphor' is also a name for a particular type of figurative language (as we will see below). Thus it is better to use 'figurative' as the umbrella term and to restrict 'metaphorical' to its specific meaning. (As the use of 'umbrella' in the previous sentence indicates, figurative language appears in all discourses or language uses – including student textbooks.) Figurative use of language, then, can be defined as the use of words or phrases whose literal meaning (1) does not make sense, or (2) cannot be true, or (3) should not be taken as true, but which implies a non-literal meaning that does make sense or that could be true. Thus it is not literally true to say that 'figurative language is an *umbrella* term' (a piece of language cannot be an umbrella, since an umbrella is a device that we take cover under to keep out the rain), but the phrase does make sense – as we will see below.

10.1 Types of figurative language: metaphor, simile, metonymy, synecdoche, allegory, apostrophe

The analysis of figurative language has a long history that goes back at least as far as the analysis of **rhetoric** in ancient Greece and Rome. Classical rhetoric, which was largely concerned with the art of persuasion, identified a large number of different kinds of figurative language, each with its own name. In literary studies today, critics and theorists tend to focus on just a handful of figurative devices: metaphor, simile, metonymy, synecdoche, irony, allegory, apostrophe and a few others. We will be analysing irony in the following unit. In the present unit, we will concentrate on the others in this list.

10.1.1 Metaphor

The word **metaphor** comes from a Greek word *metaphora*, 'to transfer' or 'carry over'. Metaphor occurs when a word or phrase in one semantic field is transferred into another semantic field in order to talk about one thing as if it were another quite different thing. For example, in a phrase like 'to live a quiet life was the summit of his ambition', the term 'summit' has been transferred from the semantic field to do with mountains into a sentence concerning a man's life aspirations. The highest point of the man's ambition is talked about as if it were the top of a mountain. Metaphors work on the basis that there is some similarity between the two ideas that have been brought together, as can be seen in the similarity between 'highest point' and 'summit' (the highest part of a mountain). To interpret the metaphor, we look for the element of similarity between the non-literal word or phrase (here 'summit') and the implied idea (highest point) and transfer it into the new context. We also register the implications of the dissimilarity between the two ideas. In the metaphor we are looking at, there may be an ironic criticism in the perceived disparity between the ambition involved in climbing a mountain and the implied lack of ambition in the desire to lead a quiet life.

All metaphors work like this, and can be analysed in the way described. When Paul Simon sings 'I am a rock' we are unlikely to think that he is made of stone or wonder how a rock can sing. Rather, we select those aspects of a rock that might characterize how the singer may feel or want to represent himself and then transfer them to the new context. The metaphor that results vividly describes psychological or emotional experience by transferring our associations of rock – such as hardness, isolation or imperviousness – to the singer. At the same time, the obvious differences between a human being and a rock may suggest to us that the singer's emotional condition is not to be envied or admired. In the same way, in the statement 'by the year 2010 manufacturing will be dominated by industries now at an embryonic stage', the word 'embryonic' does not initially appear to fit in a discussion of industry and manufacturing (because literally it is a term for the offspring of an animal before birth or emergence from an egg). To make sense of 'embryonic' in this unusual context, we select those parts of its meaning that allow us to interpret the word in a discussion about industry. 'At an embryonic stage' becomes a metaphorical way of saying that the industries of the future are at a rudimentary level of development. The idea of natural gestation is also transferred into the new context, however, and we are therefore invited to see the development of industry as in some way a natural process; this, perhaps, offers us a reassuring sense that the new industries are to be welcomed. In this way, metaphor can significantly affect how we perceive or respond to what is being described.

10.1.2 Simile

Simile is a subdivision of metaphor in that, as its name suggests, it draws attention to a similarity between two terms through words such as 'like' and 'as'. Simile does not, strictly speaking, always entail figurative language, since both terms of a simile can often be understood literally. The simile 'the sky is like a polished mirror', for example, invites the listener or reader to imagine how the sky might actually appear like a polished mirror. The difference between simile and metaphor in this respect can be demonstrated by turning the simile into a metaphor. If we say 'the sky is a polished mirror' this formulation can no longer be understood literally: we know that the sky is not really a polished mirror, though it might look like one, and therefore 'polished mirror' has to be read metaphorically. But simile is included in figurative language because there are many similes that cannot be taken literally. In his 'To a Skylark' (1820), for example, Shelley describes the skylark through an extraordinary catalogue of similes, including the claim that the bird is 'Like a cloud of fire' (8) – a simile that cannot be understood literally.

10.1.3 Metonymy

Metonymy (Greek for 'a change of name') is distinguished from metaphor in that, whereas metaphor works through similarity, metonymy works through other kinds of association (cause–effect, attribute, containment, etc.). The sentence 'Moscow made a short statement' makes sense only if we understand it figuratively, taking 'Moscow' to stand for the Russian government. This figure is possible not because of any obvious similarity between the government and the city, but because they are associated with each other (the government is based in the city). Metonymies can be formed through many different kinds of associative link. Typical dress, for example, can be used metonymically to stand for those who wear it: if someone says 'a lot of big wigs came to the party', we understand 'big wigs' to refer to 'important people' (a metonymy that probably derives from the fashion among the upper classes in earlier centuries in Europe of wearing elaborate wigs in public – a practice still followed by judges and barristers in court).

10.1.4 Synecdoche

Synecdoche (Greek for 'taking together') is a sub-branch of metonymy. It occurs when the association between the figurative and literal senses is that of a part to the whole to which it belongs. 'Farm hands' is a common synecdoche for workers on a farm; 'a new motor' comes to mean 'a new car' by using one part of the car, its engine, to stand for the whole. (Note that the 'big wig' is not a part of the person to which it belongs, and so would not be called synecdoche.)

10.1.5 Allegory

The term **allegory** comes from the Greek for 'speaking otherwise'. An allegory 'is a narrative fiction in which the agents and actions, and sometimes the setting as well, are contrived to make coherent sense on the "literal," or primary, level of signification, and at the same time to signify a second, correlated order of agents, concepts, and events' (Abrams, 1993). Allegory, then, differs from the other kinds of figurative language we are looking at, since an allegorical story makes sense at the literal level as well as indicating that it needs to be understood at a second allegorical level.

10.1.6 Apostrophe

Apostrophe has been described (by Abrams, 1993) as a rhetorical figure rather than as a figure of speech. Whereas figures of speech involve describing things in terms of other things, a rhetorical figure is a modification of normal usage in order to achieve a rhetorical effect. Apostrophe is one of the most important rhetorical figures in poetry. One of the first things to do in understanding a poem is to work out its speech situation – i.e. who is speaking to whom. An apostrophe is a special variant on the poetic speech situation in that it involves the speaker addressing either someone who is not there, or even dead, or something that is normally thought of as unable to understand language or reply (e.g. an animal or an object). Thus, in 'To a Skylark', Shelley apostrophizes the skylark: 'Hail to thee, blithe spirit'; in 'Ode on a Grecian Urn' (1820) Keats apostrophizes a Greek urn and the figures in its design. One of the consequences of apostrophe is that it personifies the thing that is addressed and thus works, in a way, like personifying metaphor (see below). Apostrophe also typically (but not always) involves the use of an archaic second person pronoun and its associated verb form:

> Hail to *thee*, blithe spirit!
> Bird *thou* never *wert*,
> That from heaven, or near it,
> *Pourest thy* full heart
> In profuse strains of unpremeditated art.

One of the consequences of this archaism is that it elevates the thing being apostrophized, partly because of the association of this pronoun and verb form with the Bible and with the mode of addressing God in Christian prayer: 'Our Father which *art* in Heaven, Hallowed be *thy* name'.

10.2 Analysing metaphors

Metaphor is by far the most important and interesting of the various kinds of figurative language, especially to students of literature. A great deal of scholarly and theoretical analysis has been devoted to metaphor (some of which is mentioned in the further reading for this unit). Thus the bulk of the rest of this unit will be devoted to examining various aspects of metaphor and to presenting ways of reading metaphor.

10.2.1 Metaphor and inferencing

One account of the way we understand figurative language is that we do it through the same kind of **inferencing** process that we employ when trying to identify authorial intention (see **Unit 14, Authorship and intention**). Inferencing is a process of assigning a meaning to uses of language by making educated guesses based on evidence from the text and other sources. Deciphering figurative language involves 'reading between the lines' to discover what the author is 'really' saying.

Most users of the language will be able to make sense of the statement that figurative language is an 'umbrella term'. But how do we do this? Most of the time we make sense of figurative uses of language without paying attention to how we do so. Often, we are able to do this because we have heard or read the figurative usage before. However, although there must be a moment when we hear a figure for the first time, we seem able for the most part to understand new figures without conscious effort. Yet, as with most things that we do unconsciously or without effort, when we try to analyse what we do it suddenly seems difficult or strange. Nonetheless, it is important and useful to analyse the process that we follow in understanding a metaphor.

In the case of 'figurative language is an *umbrella* term', we can break down the process of understanding into several stages. First, we notice that the literal meaning cannot be true. Second, we assume that the phrase must have a potentially true meaning and that we are required to invent or infer a non-literal meaning that is plausible for the sentence. Third, we set about trying to infer that plausible non-literal meaning. (Plausibility depends on a number of factors: the meaning must be capable of being true, it must fit with the rest of the text, and it must have some relation to what is actually said – the non-literal meaning must have some relation to the literal meaning.) In the case we are looking at, we ask what aspects of 'umbrella' might apply in the context: what features or uses of an umbrella might be relevant in the phrase we are trying to understand? Keeping out the rain does not seem relevant to what is being said about the term 'figurative language'. What is possibly relevant is the idea that an umbrella (especially a large one) can cover more than one person. The notion of covering more than one thing appears to fit, since we also said earlier that figurative language is 'a general term for a range of different non-literal uses of language'.

All speakers of the same language should decode the same literal meaning from the same text, but they might differ in the non-literal meaning that they infer from a text. This has several consequences for non-literal meanings. First, a range of non-literal meanings might all be plausible for the same text; some-times these meanings are compatible with one another, and sometimes they are not. Sometimes the non-literal meaning is very easy to derive and some-times quite difficult, perhaps because it is only weakly evidenced by the text or because the text can be interpreted in more than one non-literal way. Metaphor – and figurative language more generally – thus generates a degree of indeterminacy in a text, which might be an important part of that text's aesthetic effect. The attempt to interpret figurative language, then, is simply a particular case of the general problem of trying to determine authorial inten-tion through inferencing: it leads not to certainty but to various degrees of uncertainty.

10.2.2 Metaphors as different parts of speech

The process of inferencing just described can be aided by the recognition that metaphors may be formed by different parts of speech and that the inferred meaning of a metaphor needs to be the same part(s) of speech as the meta-phorical word or phrase itself. This is because metaphor generally works through a process of substitution, or of comparison, of like with like. In the example 'figurative language is an *umbrella* term', 'umbrella' could be said to be substituting for other possible words that would make better literal sense: 'general', 'all-encompassing' and so on. This substitutive relation is emphasized by the fact that 'umbrella', 'general' and 'all-encompassing' would all function in the sentence as adjectives (that is, they modify the noun 'term'). 'Umbrella', of course, is normally a noun, as in the following sentence: 'We need to develop a nuclear *umbrella* to defend the world against asteroid collision.' In this case, the metaphorical 'umbrella' could be substituted by a noun phrase such as 'defensive system'.

In the phrase addressed to Spring in Blake's 'To Spring' (1783), 'let our winds / Kiss thy perfumed garments' (9–10), the metaphor is made up of three different parts of speech. In the context, the verb phrase 'kiss thy perfumed garments' seems to mean something like 'blow lightly over the fragrant flowers (of spring)'. Within this metaphor, 'kiss' (verb) could be replaced by 'blow lightly' (verb phrase), 'perfumed' (adjective) could be replaced by 'fragranced' (or some similarly plausible adjective for the smell of flowers), and 'garments' (noun) could be replaced by 'flowers' (noun).

10.2.3 Tenor, vehicle, ground

The recognition that metaphor involves the substitution of equivalent parts of speech is an important step in the analysis of metaphors. It helps us to understand the inferencing process described above, and it also helps us to understand and use an influential method of analysing metaphors developed by the literary critic and philosopher I.A. Richards. Richards's analysis of metaphor involves identifying the different components of metaphor – which he called tenor, vehicle and ground. (Sharp readers – to use a metaphor – will notice that both 'vehicle' and 'ground' are themselves metaphors.) The word or phrase in a sentence that cannot be taken literally in the context is called the vehicle. The meaning that is implied, or referred to, by the vehicle is called the tenor. To work out the ground of the metaphor we need to identify what vehicle and tenor have in common (their 'common ground') and filter out those aspects of the vehicle that do not relate to the tenor. In the case of 'Figurative language is an *umbrella* term', the ground that links vehicle ('umbrella') and tenor ('general') are that both cover more than one thing. The ground of the metaphor is thus something like 'cover all'.

10.2.4 Explicit and implicit metaphors

Another distinction that helps us to understand and analyse metaphors is that between explicit and implicit metaphors. In an explicit metaphor, both vehicle and tenor are specified and present in the text. For example, in the statement 'the M1 motorway is the artery of England', the tenor is 'M1 motorway', the vehicle is 'artery', and the ground is the similarity between motorway and an artery. In an implicit metaphor, by contrast, while the vehicle is present in the text, the tenor has to be inferred (following processes described above). Thus in 'figurative language is an *umbrella* term', the vehicle is 'umbrella' while the tenor (general, all-encompassing) is merely implied and has to be inferred.

10.2.5 Classifying metaphors: concretive, animistic, humanizing

Another important strategy for analysing and understanding a metaphor is to compare vehicle and tenor in order to identify what kind of transference of meaning or connotations goes on between them (see Leech, 1969). A concretive metaphor uses a concrete term to talk about an abstract thing. Common examples include 'the burden of responsibility' and 'every cloud has a silver lining'. Religious discourse often uses concretive metaphors to make abstract ideas more vivid: heaven is frequently referred to as if it were a place or a building – 'In my Father's house there are many mansions.' An animistic metaphor uses a term usually associated with animate things (living creatures) to talk about an inanimate thing. Common examples include the 'leg of a table' and 'stinging rain'. A humanizing metaphor or anthropomorphic metaphor (sometimes called **personification**) uses a term usually associated with human beings to talk about a non-human thing. Common examples include the 'hands' of a clock and the kettle's 'sad song'. Humanizing metaphor is connected with the **pathetic fallacy** (the idea that the world reflects or participates in one's emotions): 'the kettle's sad song' might thus be used as a way of indicating a character's mood by implicitly describing how he or she perceives the kettle's sound.

These are not the only kinds of transfers that can be used to form metaphors. Consider the phrase 'the nightclubs are full of sharks'. Given that it is unlikely that this will be true, we infer that the statement means that the men (and/or women) in the nightclubs behave in predatory ways like sharks. In other words, human beings are metaphorically described as a kind of animal. In the statement 'the dog flew at the intruder's throat', the dog's action is described as if it were the action of a bird (hence we get an animal–animal transference). In general, though, metaphors tend to represent abstract things – ideas, emotions, thoughts, feelings, etc. – in physical ways (as objects) or to represent things or events in the world in ways that reveal how we think or feel about them. In these ways, metaphors (and figures in general) make thoughts and feelings more vivid or more tangible – they give a 'figure' to thoughts and feelings or transfer connotations to ideas that allow us to see those ideas in new ways. This is why metaphors in particular can be found in abundance in poetry and other forms of literature.

10.2.6 Extended metaphor

When a piece of language uses several vehicles from the same area of thought (or semantic field) it is called an extended metaphor. Extended metaphor is a common literary device, especially in poetry. In the last two stanzas of her poem 'The Unequal Fetters' (1713), Anne Finch develops an extended metaphor to suggest that marriage ('Hymen') is a set of 'unequal fetters' (chains or bonds) for men and women and that, as a consequence, she intends to avoid it:

> Free as Nature's first intention
> Was to make us, I'll be found
> Nor by subtle Man's invention
> Yield to be in fetters bound
> By one that walks a freer round.
>
> Marriage does but slightly tie men
> Whilst close prisoners we remain
> They the larger slaves of Hymen
> Still are begging love again
> At the full length of all their chain.

10.2.7 Mixed metaphor

Books on 'good style' used to condemn the use of mixed metaphor (the combination of two or more metaphors whose vehicles come from different and incongruous areas or semantic fields) because they can have unintentionally ludicrous effects. For precisely this reason, corny jokes often exploit mixed metaphor. However, Abrams (1993) claims that mixed metaphor can have interesting effects in literature (he refers to the 'To be or not to be' speech from *Hamlet*, III, i, 56–9). Mixed metaphor also has powerful effects in the opening lines of the following sonnet, 'To the Pupils of the Hindu College', by Henry L. Derozio (1809–31):

> Expanding like the petals of young flowers
> I watch the gentle opening of your minds,
> And the sweet loosening of the spell that binds
> Your intellectual energies and powers
> That stretch (like young birds in soft summer hours)
> Their wings to try their strength.

Here, the effect of education on the pupils' minds is figured as an expanding of flower petals, as an opening (a dead metaphor), as the release from a spell, and as the stretching of fledglings' wings in order to get ready for first flight. Yet this is not such an incongruent mixing of metaphors as that in Hamlet's speech. While these metaphors figure the pupils' minds as flowers, as a box or room to be opened, as someone under a spell, and as young birds, all these metaphors have a 'common ground' that could be labelled as growth, release, flight or escape.

10.2.8 Vital metaphors and dead metaphors

New metaphors are constantly being developed whenever a new area of experience or thought needs new descriptive terms. Gradually, however, metaphors become over-familiar and cease to be recognized as metaphors at all. When this happens, they lose their power to confront us with their effects as metaphors. Everyday language is full of such terms. A speaker of English would not normally be conscious of producing two (very different) metaphors in claiming that 'things are looking up for the team since the landslide victory last week'. Yet both 'things are looking up' and 'landslide' have to be understood as metaphors since they cannot be taken literally in the context. Words and phrases that are metaphorical, but cease to be regarded as metaphors, are called dead metaphors (notice, incidentally, that the phrase 'dead metaphor' is itself a dead metaphor).

Dead metaphors tend to reproduce commonplace thoughts and do not require much imagination to be understood. By contrast, vitally new metaphors force us out of established ways of thinking. As Wallace Stevens puts it, 'Reality is a cliché from which we escape by metaphor'. An original metaphor that draws attention to itself as a metaphor can make demands on our powers of creative interpretation. Each time such challenging metaphors are produced, the way language maps the world is altered. Domains that the language usually keeps separate are momentarily fused, and new meanings are brought into existence.

10.3 Reading metaphor in literature

It is sometimes suggested that literature can be distinguished from non-literary discourse because literature uses language metaphorically, while non-literary discourse uses it literally. Yet this is clearly not the case, since all kinds of non-literary discourses (as we have seen) use figurative language. A more useful metaphor for thinking about how metaphor is used in different kinds of language is to imagine a spectrum of language types, ranging from discourses that consist mostly of literal usages and dead metaphors through to discourses that are highly conscious and highly innovative in their use of metaphor. Literature is generally at the highly conscious and highly innovative end of this spectrum, but we should be wary of thinking that only the vivid and strikingly new metaphors count in literature. Such metaphors are often important and require imaginative inferencing responses from the reader. Nonetheless, not all literary texts are necessarily trying to break new ground in their use of figurative language, or at least not all the time. Sometimes, indeed, it is the quieter, almost imperceptible metaphors – those we might easily fail to notice – that do a lot of important work in a literary text. To become good readers of literature, we need to be alert to the subtle metaphors as well as to those that shout in our face.

One of the effects of becoming alert to metaphor is that it suddenly seems as if metaphor is everywhere. However, while it is true that metaphor is everywhere, there is a danger that inexperienced readers will start seeing metaphors where there are none. To avoid this, a good rule of thumb (to use a metaphor) is to say 'if it can be read literally, then take it as literal – only read something as a metaphor if it can't be taken literally'. While this is a good general rule, however, it is not failsafe. Sometimes a text may make use of the ambiguity that can arise when something can equally be taken as literal or as metaphorical. The power of the lyrics at the end of U2's 'Bullet the Blue Sky' (*The Joshua Tree*, 1987) comes from the way they make it possible for the phrase 'the arms of America' to be both literal (weapons) and metaphorical (human, embracing arms) at the same time. Sometimes it might be possible to read something literally, but there are subtle hints elsewhere in the text that it needs to be read metaphorically. In other words, reading for metaphor sometimes has to take the whole text – or at least the immediately surrounding text – into context.

ACTIVITY 10.1

This activity will focus on Toru Dutt's 'Our Casuarina Tree' (India, 1878):

> Like a huge Python, winding round and round
> The rugged trunk, indented deep with scars
> Up to its very summit near the stars,
> A creeper climbs, in whose embraces bound
> No other tree could live. But gallantly   5
> The giant wears the scarf, and flowers are hung
> In crimson clusters all the boughs among,
> Whereon all day are gathered bird and bee;
> And oft at nights the garden overflows
> With one sweet song that seems to have no close,   10
> Sung darkling from our tree, while men repose.
>
> When first my casement is wide open thrown
> At dawn, my eyes delighted on it rest;
> Sometimes, and most in winter, – on its crest
> A gray baboon sits statue-like alone   15
> Watching the sunrise; while on lower boughs
> His puny offspring leap about and play;
> And far and near kokilas hail the day;
> And to their pastures wend our sleepy cows;
> And in the shadow, on the broad tank cast   20
> By that hoar tree, so beautiful and vast,
> The water-lilies spring, like snow enmassed.

But not because of its magnificence
Dear is the Casuarina to my soul:
Beneath it we have played; though years may roll,   25
O sweet companions, loved with love intense,
For your sakes shall the tree be ever dear!
Blent with your images, it shall arise
In memory, till the hot tears blind mine eyes!
What is that dirge-like murmur that I hear   30
Like the sea breaking on a shingle-beach?
It is the tree's lament, an eerie speech,
That haply to the unknown land may reach.

Unknown, yet well-known to the eye of faith!
Ah, I have heard that wail far, far away   35
In distant lands, by many a sheltered bay,
When slumbered in his cave the water-wraith
And the waves gently kissed the classic shore
Of France or Italy, beneath the moon
When earth lay tranced in a dreamless swoon: 40
And every time the music rose, – before
Mine inner vision rose a form sublime,
Thy form, O Tree, as in my happy prime
I saw thee, in my own loved native clime.

Therefore I fain would consecrate a lay   45
Unto thy honour, Tree, beloved of those
Who now in blessed sleep for aye repose,
Dearer than life to me, alas! were they!
Mayst thou be numbered when my days are done
With deathless trees – like those in Borrowdale,   50
Under whose awful branches lingered pale
'Fear, trembling Hope, and Death, the skeleton,
And Time the shadow' and though weak the verse
That would thy beauty fain, oh fain rehearse,
May Love defend thee from Oblivion's curse.   55

(Note: in the last stanza, Dutt alludes to and quotes from Wordsworth's poem
'Yew Trees' (1815).)

1   Highlight or underline all the uses of figurative language that you can
     find in this poem and give each usage its appropriate label (similie,
     personification, etc.).

     1.1   Choose one of the metaphors you have identified and analyse it by
            using the methods described above: (a) identify vehicle, tenor and

ground; (b) is it implicit or explicit? (c) is it concretive, animistic or humanizing? (d) is it extended – i.e. are there other vehicles or non-literal terms in the poem that come from the same semantic field?

2   Try to rewrite the first stanza in order to eliminate all similes and metaphors. What is the difference between your stanza and Dutt's?

   2.1   What kind of image of the tree do Dutt's similes and metaphors create in this stanza?

3   In the third stanza (line 23), the speaker stresses that the tree is dear to her 'not because of its magnificence'. Focus closely on the metaphors and similes of the third stanza in order to find out why the tree is dear to her. (You could also look at the first four lines of the last stanza.)

   3.1   Do the vehicles of the important similes and metaphors in the third stanza come from (a) the same semantic field, or (b) related semantic fields, or (c) different semantic fields?

   3.2   Where would you locate these important metaphors on a scale ranging from vitally new metaphors at one end and dead metaphors at the other end? What do you learn from this?

4   In what way does the use of apostrophe in stanzas three, four and five confirm or challenge your interpretation of the poem?

5   Is 'deathless' (stanza five, line 50) metaphorical or literal? How will the tree become deathless? How does the wish that the tree should become 'deathless' relate to the overall meaning of the poem?

6   In the course of answering these questions have you: (a) discovered more metaphors and similes than you did when you answered question 1? or (b) realized that some of the metaphors and similes you identified in answering question 1 are not actually metaphors or similes? What do you learn from this?

Reading

Abrams, M.H. (1993) *A Glossary of Literary Terms*, 6th edn, New York and London: Harcourt Brace Jovanovich.

Furniss, T.E. and Bath, M. (1996) *Reading Poetry*, London: Longman, Chapters 5–6.

Glucksberg, Sam (with Matthew S. McGlone) (2001) *Understanding Figurative Language: From Metaphors to Idioms*, Oxford and New York: Oxford University Press.

Kövecses, Zoltán (2002) *Metaphor: A Practical Introduction*, Oxford and New York: Oxford University Press.

Lakoff, G. and Johnson, M. (1980) *Metaphors We Live By*, Chicago, IL: University of Chicago Press, especially pp. 3–40.

Leech, G. (1969) *A Linguistic Guide to English Poetry*, London: Longman, pp. 147–65.

Lodge, D. (1977) *The Modes of Modern Writing*, London: Edward Arnold.

Richards, I.A. (1936) *Philosophy of Rhetoric*, Oxford: Oxford University Press, Chapters 5–6.

Sacks, S. (ed.) (1979) *On Metaphor*, Chicago, IL: University of Chicago Press.

Unit 11

Irony

11.1 Verbal irony

Verbal irony is a use of language where we do not literally mean what we say; instead we imply an attitude of disbelief towards the content of our utterance or writing. As an example of verbal irony, consider this first sentence of Jane Austen's novel *Pride and Prejudice*.

> It is a truth universally acknowledged, that a single man in possession of a good fortune, must be in want of a wife.

To understand how verbal irony works, we need to consider the construction of the meanings that we communicate when we speak or write. A communicated meaning can be analysed into two component parts: (1) a proposition and (2) an attitude towards that proposition. A proposition is a statement about the real world or about some fictional world. The sentences we produce typically encode propositions by containing specific words in a specific order; to be able to speak and understand sentences of a language is to be able to encode and decode a proposition into and from the sentences of that language. However, both our thoughts and hence the meanings we communicate consist of something more than just basic propositions; attached to each proposition is an attitude, usually known as a **propositional attitude**, which expresses the speaker's or writer's relation to that proposition. The most common attitude is belief, but there are other attitudes as well – differing in strength (e.g. basic belief as opposed to strong commitment) as well as in polarity (e.g. belief as opposed to disbelief). If I have an attitude of belief towards a proposition, then that proposition is true for me.

This is relevant for irony, because in irony a speaker or writer produces a proposition that is *not* true for him or her. In normal (non-ironic) communication, I communicate two things: a proposition and my attitude towards that proposition, which is that I believe the proposition to be true. In verbal irony, I communicate a proposition and a different kind of attitude: that I do not believe the proposition to be true. There is no difference in the proposition itself; the difference is in the attitude that I communicate. Verbal irony is successful when the writer or speaker provides sufficient evidence to indicate that his or her attitude is one of disbelief rather than the expected attitude of belief. In the quoted sentence from Austen, the author actually communicates two propositions, one inside the other, and makes it clear that she believes neither of them. One proposition is 'a single man in possession of a good fortune, must be in want of a wife', and this proposition is contained inside 'It is a truth universally acknowledged, that a single man in possession of a good fortune, must be in want of a wife.' The larger proposition, by asserting so strongly the truth of the contained proposition, only serves to indicate the writer's own disagreement with both of them.

For irony to function as intended, the writer or speaker must be sure that the reader or hearer will be able to recognize that an attitude of disbelief is being communicated; since this is not the normal state of affairs, there must be something odd about the text in order to give clues that the author disbelieves what he or she is saying. Here the oddness of the text is both in the exaggerated claims to certainty made for the proposition and the fact that the proposition itself is not at all clearly true; for it to be universally acknowledged, we too would have already accepted it as true but we do not.

In irony we should generally interpret the speaker/writer to be saying not only that he or she does not believe the proposition but that someone else might believe it to be true. Thus the ironist communicates both his or her own attitude (of disbelief) along with implying a different attitude (of belief) attributed to someone else – whether that someone else is identifiable or not. In the case of this proposition, we can straightforwardly assign this thought to one or more of the characters in the novel (and hence partly understand their actions through this belief). Irony often involves the implication that the speaker or writer shares with us an amused attitude towards the misguided characters who believe the proposition.

We now consider another example of verbal irony from George Eliot's novel *Middlemarch* (1871) (discussed in MacCabe (1981)):

> Some who follow the narrative of his experience may wonder at the midnight darkness of Mr Dagley; but nothing was easier in those times than for an hereditary farmer of his grade to be ignorant, in spite somehow of having a rector in the twin parish who was a gentleman to the backbone, a curate nearer at hand who preached more learnedly than the rector, a landlord who had gone into everything, especially fine art and social improvement, and all the lights of Middlemarch only three miles off.

A proposition we can derive from this sentence is 'Given the educated social environment in which he lives, it is surprising that Mr Dagley (the farmer) has remained so ignorant'. We know this to be verbal irony because we know that this proposition is both disbelieved by the writer and attributed to other (misguided, unnamed) people, towards whom the writer has an amused attitude. How do we know that this is irony: that is, that the writer does not hold an attitude of belief towards the proposition? The irony is signalled largely by the exaggerations in the passage: by emphasizing the proposition excessively, the writer warns us that she is not committed to it. There are basically two kinds of exaggeration here: first, expressions of extremity as in 'midnight darkness', 'nothing was easier', 'preached more learnedly than the rector', 'gone into everything', 'all the lights of Middlemarch'; and, second, a repetitive list, stacking up to produce a long sentence. In addition, we probably also bring our knowledge of the world, and perhaps of the novel as it has previously developed, to contradict the proposition derived.

There are different varieties of verbal irony, though all work in basically the same way, whereby an attitude of disbelief is implicitly communicated. Sarcasm is a kind of verbal irony in which, typically, an exaggerated tone of voice communicates the attitude of disbelief. Note however that, while the tone implies disbelief, this is nevertheless implicit: the speaker does not actually *say* that they do not believe what they are saying. In irony the attitude of disbelief is always implicitly communicated rather than explicitly communicated. The first sentence of *Pride and Prejudice* would not be ironic if it was written as 'Some of the characters in this book incorrectly believe that it is a truth universally acknowledged, that a single man in possession of a good fortune, must be in want of a wife.' Irony thus involves some tension between what is said and what is meant.

(A final comment: note that 'verbal' means 'using language' and does not mean the same as 'oral', which means 'using spoken language'; hence verbal irony exists in both speech and writing.)

11.2 Situational irony

Situational irony involves a conflict between what two different people (or two groups of people) know. The participant in events understands them in a way that is not correct, while the viewer or audience to the events understands them differently but correctly, such that their understanding conflicts with the participant's understanding. The viewer or audience is able to do this because they have an advantage over the participant, usually by virtue of being outside the situation of the participant. The participant is 'subject to situational irony', where 'situational irony' can be understood as a way of an audience describing events relative to a participant. An understanding of the kinds of situational irony is largely a recognition of the different ways of being 'outside the situation of the participant'. This is rather different from verbal irony, but we will see at the end of this section that there are some connections.

The participant can be a child, or some other individual who is developmentally or inherently unable to fully understand their situation, while the audience is developmentally more advanced than the participant – an older child, or an adult, for example. An example is Henry James's *What Maisie Knew* (1897). The child Maisie reports events in the adult world without fully understanding them, but we as adults can reintepret her descriptions in the light of our adult understanding of kinds of event; thus we recognize Maisie as 'subject to situational irony'. Situational irony can also separate a child character from a child reader; many children's books expect their readers to recognize that the child character is unable to understand their own situation, and that this understanding relates to their limits as children; the ten-year-old readers of Jacqueline Wilson's *The Suitcase Kid* (1992) are expected to understand more about the ten-year-old character Andrea's situation than she herself can understand; and part of this understanding is that the child reader is – like all readers – always outside the situation of the characters in the book. Thus a reader may be able to overcome the developmental limits associated with a child of their own age, by virtue of the superior position of being a reader. Even very young children's books encourage this: Beatrix Potter's illustrations to *The Tale of Peter Rabbit* (1902) encourage the child to identify to some extent with the animal characters (by putting the child looking at the picture at an eye-height just above that of the rabbits), and to see the rabbits as like the children themselves, while also enabling them to see the rabbits from the outside, permitting the assignment of situational irony. Another kind of 'limited' participant might include someone with a cognitive impairment that prevents them fully understanding their situation; this might include the autistic narrator of Mark Haddon's *The Curious Incident of the Dog in the Night-time* (2003) or the cognitively impaired narrator of book 1 of William Faulkner's *The Sound and the Fury* (1929). Finally, the participant might be non-human, and so unable to understand their situation (in comparison with us, as humans); they might be an alien, or an animal.

These ways of separating the reader from the participant are all ways of Othering the participant: that is, defining the participant not just as different but also as less than us. But these Othered participants can also encourage us to read the situational ironies in reverse, so that we identify with the character in the book as having a special kind of knowledge that we as readers lack; it is as though we temporarily depart from our own culturally contextualized selves to inhabit the fictional characters and then look back at ourselves and thereby subject ourselves to situational irony. Thus a child or animal in a book may by their difference be able to understand our adult human situation in ways that we ourselves cannot understand; now we are caught inside the situational irony and presented as such by the characters in the book. The *Harry Potter* books work in this way, encouraging the child reader to identify with the Othered 'wizards' and to look back at humans as limited and unable to understand the complexities of the world we live in. Similarly, in many novels a 'foreigner' comes to our society and, because of their impaired familiarity with it (which in some ways subjects them to situational irony), they describe our society in ways that show that we also do not fully understand our situation, thus subjecting us to situational irony; an example of this would be George Mikes's *How To Be an Alien* (1946), an Othering description of British society in the 1950s written for a British audience from the perspective of a Hungarian immigrant.

Another way of being outside the situation of a participant is to be historically later than the participant. The historical irony here arises because the participant's understanding of what events mean is contrary to a later, better and fuller understanding of them. Similarly, a participant may have convictions about how events will play out in (their) future, but from our later perspective we know that they will play out very differently.

Dramatic irony can be understood as a sub-kind of situational irony, most prototypically found in the theatre. A character on stage and involved in a dramatic action has a specific belief that the audience knows to be false. Typically, that incorrect belief will be about some crucial component of the plot, and hence the dramatic irony functions as a narrative mechanism:

Pedro: Sure I had dwelt forever on her bosom –
                But stay, he's here.
          [*Enter Belvile dressed in Antonio's clothes.*]
Florinda *(aside)*:   'Tis not Belvile; half my fears are vanished.

In this extract from Aphra Behn's play *The Rover* (1677), Florinda has a belief about an event that is incorrect; the audience, from their vantage point 'outside the situation' of the stage knows that in fact Belville has entered the stage. A writer may use the physical arrangement of the stage – with sightlines accessible to the audience but not to the characters – to distinguish the situations of the characters and the audience and hence to create dramatic irony.

All these examples of situational irony have in common that the irony is created by a difference in situation and knowledge between the participants in events on the one hand and the audience to those events (us) on the other hand. The irony is not created by a person as such, but can be attributed to the events themselves as they occur. (Of course the events themselves might have been created by a playwright or novelist, but this is ignored in thinking of these ironies as having no human 'causer'.) Instead of being attributed to a person, situational irony can be attributed to notions such as fate (in French it is called 'ironie du sort' – irony of fate), or time, or history, or life (as in 'life's little ironies'), or circumstances, or indeed anything: the first quote in the *OED* for this meaning of irony refers to 'the irony of war' (that it is better to fire an arrow at the horse than at the rider).

11.3 Mechanisms of irony

What makes verbal irony different from lying? A person who speaks or writes communicates both a proposition and his or her attitude towards that proposition. In both verbal irony and lying, the communicator has an attitude of disbelief towards the proposition. In verbal irony that attitude of disbelief is made clear (by various signals), while in lying the disbelief is concealed. For irony to be successful, the audience/readership must be able to recognize that there is a true attitude of disbelief towards a proposition expressed by the text. In principle, any kind of evidence might be used to indicate that there is a true attitude of disbelief towards the proposition; in this section we briefly consider some of the more common kinds of evidence.

One kind of evidence involves a contradiction between what the text tells us and what we already know. Unless there is good reason to abandon our previous beliefs, we will therefore adopt an attitude of disbelief towards the text. This is not enough on its own to give rise to irony, though: on its own, this might just generate a decision that the author has made a mistake. Thus we must be convinced that the author also shares the beliefs that we brought to the text. A second kind of evidence for irony comes from exaggeration and overemphasis, including hyperbole, emphatic (insincere) statements of belief, extensive use of superlatives, or exaggerations in speaking (as in typical sarcasm). Overemphasis functions to communicate the irony in the quote from Jane Austen with which we began.

Overstatement is an instance of a more general way in which a text signals the presence of irony, which is by some kind of disruption. In most texts it is possible to distinguish the normal characteristics of the text from the disruptive characteristics. In a rhyming poem, the rhymes are the default case and any failure to rhyme would be disruptive; in prose, a rhyme would be disruptive where rhyme is not expected. (The terms 'unmarked' and 'marked' are sometimes used to characterize the normal and disruptive elements of the text, respectively). Looking for disruptions in a text is always a useful way of entering into and beginning to understand the workings of a text, and the manipulation of disruptions can be a powerful communicative tool. To indicate the presence of irony, the text can be disrupted in various ways. Internal inconsistency is one kind of disruption that is fairly characteristic of irony. A common example of this second type is where the register of the text changes unexpectedly; in this case, we say that the voice of the text is inconsistent. In Henry Reed's poem 'Naming of Parts' (1946), there are at least two registers: some of the lines are spoken as if by a military instructor and some as if by a dreamy romantic. Yet there is no explicit change of speaker. In this case, the irony comes from the fact that the two registers express different attitudes that contradict one another and yet the whole poem seems to come from a single source; thus one attitude must be false.

11.4 Uncertain ironies

Irony is sometimes clear, but sometimes we feel that a writer or speaker is communicating propositions that we think they are unlikely to believe, but we do not have clear evidence either to think that they are being ironic or that they are lying. Problems in identifying or interpreting irony can arise when author and reader are separated by major differences in what they know – if, for example, they are separated by major differences in time or place or culture. Because one of the ways of marking irony is for the text to contradict what we already know, the identification of irony can depend on our (culturally dependent) knowledge. In some cases, the fact that cultural or subcultural differences can be a barrier to irony can be exploited by an author. Dick Hebdige once proposed that the new wave song 'Heart of Glass' by Blondie is capable of being read ironically (given a certain subcultural 'punk' awareness) or non-ironically (in mainstream culture), thus maximizing its audience. Perhaps the barriers to cross-cultural interpretation of irony explain the claim that is sometimes made that people in a certain foreign culture 'lack the capacity for irony', because irony is difficult to recognize across cultures given its dependence on culturally dependent knowledge. Nevertheless, given that irony is an exploitation of some very basic characteristics of human communication, irony should be possible in every language and every culture, even if outsiders have difficulty in identifying or interpreting it.

The difficulties just mentioned are the consequence – often accidental – of cultural difference. But difficulties in the identification or interpretation of irony can also be built into the workings of a text. Thus it is possible to find texts that are apparently ironic (e.g. what is said contradicts what we know), where there is a narrator, but where it is difficult to judge whether the narrator is the victim of a structural irony (i.e. a naive narrator, unaware of the ironies) or whether instead the narrator is to be understood as producing verbal irony (and hence is aware of the irony); Samuel Beckett's fiction and plays often present a problem of this kind. Similarly, texts might have overt ironies where there are two opposing voices within them, each taking different attitudes towards a proposition, but where it is difficult to decide which of the two voices is the voice of truth. These problems are characteristically found in modernist texts, where there may be many competing voices.

As an illustration of some of the more complex possibilities of irony, consider part of Shelley's poem 'Ozymandias' (1819). This is a poem that – we assume deliberately – generates a number of unresolvable interpretive problems, among which is the identification and attribution of the irony in the inscription cited in lines 10–11:

9   And on the pedestal these words appear:
10   'My name is Ozymandias, king of kings:
11   Look on my works, ye Mighty, and despair!'

The inscription is found on a pedestal, surrounded by fragments of a statue and otherwise 'nothing besides remains' in the desert where it stands. If the inscription is to be interpreted as 'Despair because even my great works will come to nothing' then it is not ironic at all; it is correctly believed by all parties concerned. If alternatively the inscription is to be interpreted as 'Despair because my works are so great' then this proposition is falsely believed by Ozymandias, and correctly disbelieved by us (because the works have now vanished over the course of time). However, even if we identify the text as ironic, there is still a problem of attribution, because it is not clear what attitude is taken by the sculptor – the person who has written these words on the statue: did the sculptor believe or disbelieve the proposition 'Despair because my works are so great'? It is not clear that these questions can be answered: whether there is an irony, and how exactly the attitudes are to be attributed. These uncertainties are characteristic of Shelley's work in general, and in particular of this poem, which is rich in uncertainties.

11.5 Why use irony?

It is possible for us to say something that we do not believe to be true, and by so doing to communicate a rich range of meanings that we *do* believe to be true. This is the basis for verbal irony as a communicative practice.

Irony might, for example, be used to express a particular world view that we can never really be certain in our knowledge and beliefs. Even the simplest and most straightforward ironies (as in the Austen text cited earlier) demonstrate the existence of incorrect certainties; and more complex ironies such as those found in Shelley's poem can create a sense of the impossibility of being certain of anything.

While irony can destabilize, it can also have stabilizing functions. Thus Austen uses irony to confirm the authority of a particular voice (the narrator's own voice) as the voice of truth. Furthermore, because irony requires the reader to bring a certain kind of **background knowledge** to the text in order to make sense of it, irony can require the reader to make certain assumptions in order to interpret the text: in order to understand Austen's first sentence we are forced to take on a set of attitudes towards women, men, marriage and society, which the novel will then manipulate.

ACTIVITY 11.1

This is the beginning of H.G. Wells's novel *The War of the Worlds* (1898) (note the date):

No one would have believed in the last years of the nineteenth century that this world was being watched keenly and closely by intelligences

greater than man's and yet as mortal as his own; that as men busied themselves about their various concerns they were scrutinised and studied,
perhaps almost as narrowly as a man with a microscope might scrutinise
the transient creatures that swarm and multiply in a drop of water. With
infinite complacency men went to and fro over this globe about their little
affairs, serene in their assurance of their empire over matter. It is possible
that the infusoria under the microscope do the same. No one gave a
thought to the older worlds of space as sources of human danger, or
thought of them only to dismiss the idea of life upon them as impossible
or improbable. It is curious to recall some of the mental habits of those
departed days. At most terrestrial men fancied there might be other men
upon Mars, perhaps inferior to themselves and ready to welcome a
missionary enterprise. Yet across the gulf of space, minds that are to our
minds as ours are to those of the beasts that perish, intellects vast and
cool and unsympathetic, regarded this earth with envious eyes, and slowly
and surely drew their plans against us. And early in the twentieth century
came the great disillusionment.

The planet Mars, I scarcely need remind the reader, revolves about the
sun at a mean distance of 140,000,000 miles, and the light and heat it
receives from the sun is barely half of that received by this world. It must
be, if the nebular hypothesis has any truth, older than our world; and
long before this earth ceased to be molten, life upon its surface must have
begun its course. The fact that it is scarcely one seventh of the volume
of the earth must have accelerated its cooling to the temperature at which
life could begin. It has air and water and all that is necessary for the
support of animated existence.

Yet so vain is man, and so blinded by his vanity, that no writer, up to
the very end of the nineteenth century, expressed any idea that intelli-
gent life might have developed there far, or indeed at all, beyond its
earthly level. Nor was it generally understood that since Mars is older
than our earth, with scarcely a quarter of the superficial area and remoter
from the sun, it necessarily follows that it is not only more distant from
time's beginning but nearer its end.

1   Explain why we might say that Wells develops 'situational irony' in this
     passage.

2   Are there examples also of verbal irony? If so, does the verbal irony
     interact with the situational irony?

3   What evidence does Wells offer the reader that the text is ironic.

4   Who is being 'Othered' in this passage.

5   What purposes might the irony serve? If you know anything about science fiction more generally, discuss some of the ways in which Wells's use of irony is here typical of the genre.

Reading

Fabb, N. (1997) *Linguistics and Literature*, Oxford: Blackwell, Chapter 10.
Furniss, T.E. and Bath, M. (1996) *Reading Poetry*, London: Longman, Chapter 8.
Leech, G. and Short, M. (1981) *Style in Fiction*, London: Longman, pp. 277–80.
MacCabe, C. (1979) *James Joyce and the Revolution of the Word*, London: Macmillan.
Muecke, D.C. (1970) *Irony and the Ironic*, London: Methuen.
Sperber, D. and Wilson, D. (1995) *Relevance: Communication and Cognition*, Oxford: Blackwell, Chapter 4.

Unit 12

Juxtaposition

12.1 Verbal (and poetic) juxtaposition

Juxtaposition may be defined simply as the placing of elements side by side. In communication the juxtaposition of meaningful elements is both a routine and essential practice in the composition of messages – literary or otherwise. Sentence construction, for instance, relies upon observing close constraints in the way words are put together and significant alterations in meaning can result from simple changes in the ordering or placement of items in a sentence.

The term juxtaposition, however, can also refer to a rhetorical technique that goes beyond the simple placement of communicative elements side by side. In this more specialized sense, juxtaposition can be defined as:

combining together two or more communicative elements in ways that emphasize the discontinuities or differences between them, thereby provoking some surprise or puzzlement at their close placement.

Some simple principles of juxtaposition can be illustrated at work in the following translations of seventeenth- and eighteenth-century Japanese **haiku**:

Haiku 1

Harvest moon:
On the bamboo mat
Pine tree shadows.

Haiku 2

Wooden gate,
Lock firmly bolted:
Winter moon.

Each poem consists of three short lines, and in both cases the sense of the poem seems to rest on three separate elements – 'moon', 'mat' and 'shadows' in one; 'gate', 'lock' and 'moon' in the other. These elements are juxtaposed in such a way that the links between them are not very obvious. Neither of the poems, for instance, consists of a fully formed sentences and so the reader is required to make an interpretive effort to fill in the gaps and spell out the connections between the main elements. This effort is accentuated by the division of each poem into two sections around a major punctuation mark – a colon. In each case there is only an implicit connection between the elements on either side of the colon. Although it is possible to see a causal relation between a harvest moon and pine tree shadows, the lack of explicit connections forces the reader to make an inferential leap. The connection between a locked wooden gate and a winter moon demands greater interpretive effort. In each poem an element from nature has been juxtaposed with an element from culture – the moon with a bamboo mat, or the moon with a bolted gate – thus creating a tension in each poem between its first and second part. Haiku poems typically revolve around a tension or puzzle produced by juxtaposing (without further explanation) a natural phenomenon with an event or object more closely related to the human world. This can be seen in two further examples:

Haiku 3

Spring rain:
Soaking on the roof
A child's rag ball.

Haiku 4

Overnight
My razor rusted –
The May rains.

Like the earlier examples, these poems require the reader to supply the unstated connection between their elements. They could be taken as implying repectively:

A child's rag ball was soaking on the roof *because of* the spring rain

Overnight my razor rusted *because of* the May rains

However, these kinds of explicit statements fail to do justice to the possibilities of the original texts. By leaving the precise relations between elements unstated, the communicative possibilities of these short poems are increased; the very disparity of the elements that have been juxtaposed generates – in the absence of explicit connections – a kind of communicative charge.

The poems are translations from Japanese texts of the seventeenth and eighteenth centuries, but similar techniques can be identified in more contemporary Western poetry. The following poem by Ezra Pound could be seen as influenced by the haiku form:

L'ART, 1910

Green arsenic smeared on an egg-white cloth,
Crushed strawberries! Come let us feast our eyes.

Here we find the startling juxtaposition of something toxic (arsenic) with something delectable (strawberries), and something green with something red. Simultaneously, things more normally defined by taste and toxicity are transformed into a publicly visual experience ('Come let us feast our eyes'). And note of course that the title makes these juxtaposed elements emblematic of a historically defined movement. At the core of the poem, however, is a pattern of juxtaposition not dissimilar to haiku. Indeed, the associations are deliberate: 'L'ART, 1910' was written when Pound was a leading figure in the 'Imagist' movement (roughly 1910–20), in which a group of writers in Britain and the United States attempted to develop a new form of poetry that was strongly influenced by haiku (especially its use of stark, unexplained juxtaposition). This new form of poetry can be seen as an early example of modernism – a period (1910–40) of experimentation in all the arts in which the juxtaposition of startlingly different elements was a characteristic technique. Much of T.S. Eliot's poetry (such as *The Waste Land*, 1922) juxtaposes a wide range of different kinds of linguistic material (quotations from Wagner's operas, biblical language, diaries, language heard in a public house, etc.). However, although juxtaposition was particularly common in the verbal and visual arts of the first half of the twentieth century, it is not confined to them; it may be found in texts (literary and non-literary) from many periods and cultures (as witness, for instance, the haiku discussed above). The technique of juxtaposition may be seen to underpin the following two examples from the contemporary Scottish poet, Alan Spence:

mouse tracks
across the frozen lard
in the frying pan

       remembering
       my father's death –
       cold november rain

          (from *Five Haiku*, 1986)

Juxtaposition is also used to startling effect in the following poem by Margaret Atwood (1971):

You fit into Me

you fit into me
like a hook into an eye

a fish hook
an open eye

12.2 Visual juxtaposition: film

The use of juxtaposition based on tension between communicative elements is not limited to verbal texts. Indeed, one early theoretician of film – the Soviet director, Sergei Eisenstein (1898–1948) – in his account of **montage** (selection, cutting, piecing together as a consecutive whole) made discontinuity between successive shots central to his account of how film should work. In contrast to the dominant strand of cinematic development associated with commercial cinema and Hollywood, in which editing aspires to continuity and smoothness of transition between shots, early Soviet cinema, particularly that of Eisenstein, attempted to produce collisions rather than continuity between successive shots in order to create quite startling juxtapositions. Eisenstein argued that, by introducing a gap or tension between successive images, it was possible to generate meaning beyond that contained within the shots themselves. For instance, in two famous images from consecutive shots in Eisenstein's film *Battleship Potemkin* (1925), the first image shows a medium close-up of a woman's face wearing pince-nez or glasses, and the second image presents the same woman, but now the eye is bleeding and the pince-nez is shattered. The overall effect is that of a shot hitting the eye, even though the latter action is not explicitly displayed. These images are part of a larger episode, commonly referred to as the 'Odessa Steps sequence', in which soldiers brutally attempt to put down a popular uprising. Images of boots marching down steps and of rifle volleys are intercut with images of a child's pram rolling unattended down the steps and a small boy being trampled underfoot. (Parts of this sequence may be viewed at http://www.carleton.edu/curricular/MEDA/classes/media110/Severson/potemkin.htm.)

As well as creating a powerful sense of movement and confusion, these stark juxtapositions force the viewer to make the connection between the soldiers' actions and the suffering of the defenceless people. In this way, montage as a collision between images can here be seen as replicating larger contradictions between contending social forces. Indeed, juxtaposition for Eisenstein was part of a self-consciously Marxist and dialectical approach to film-making, not only emphasizing discontinuity between images but (like

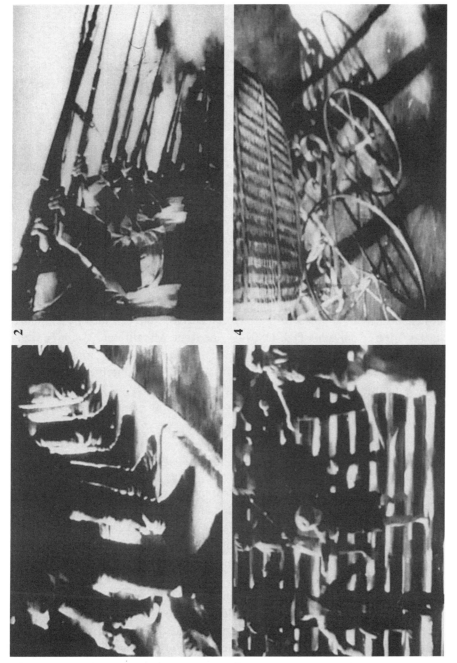

Figures 12.1–12.4 Images from the Odessa Steps sequence, *Battleship Potemkin* (Sergei Eisenstein, 1925)

Bertolt Brecht in the theatre) also demanding the active interpretive engagement of the audience.

12.3 Sequential versus simultaneous juxtaposition

Visual juxtaposition in film, video and TV mostly works by exploiting a sense of surprise or shock in the juxtaposition of successive images. Where media depend upon items occurring in series, they may be said to rely upon temporal or sequential juxtaposition. The images from Eisenstein's film are good examples of sequential juxtaposition, since their meaning depends on the very order in which the elements are presented; any change in the order either changes the meaning or results in nonsense (imagine the effect of reversing the sequence of the two images from *Battleship Potemkin*).

However, juxtaposition is also used in other kinds of media that do not unfold in sequence through time, but that are spatial (e.g. photographs, paintings, cartoons). Pictorial art is a case in point. A precise analogue to Eliot's technique of literary **bricolage** in *The Waste Land*, discussed above, may be found in pictorial art of the twentieth century. Collage, for instance, is an abstract form of art in which photographs, pieces of paper, string, etc. are placed in juxtaposition and glued to the pictorial surface. **Surrealism**, as exemplified in the work of Salvador Dali (1904–89) or René Magritte (1898–1967), often depicted quite unrelated items in the same pictorial space, creating an atmosphere of dream or fantasy. Here, for instance, is how Magritte described his famous painting, *Time Transfixed* (1938) (see Figure 12.5), in which a steam locomotive emerges from an empty fireplace on whose mantlepiece rests a clock with its hands at 12.43:

> I thought about painting a picture of a locomotive. Given that possibility, the problem was this: how to paint the picture in such a way that it evoked mystery . . . the mystery that has no meaning . . . The image of the locomotive is immediately familiar, so its mystery passes unnoticed. To bring out its mystery another immediately familiar and hence unmysterious image – that of the dining room fireplace – was combined with the image of the locomotive . . . suggesting the mystery of beings that normally strike us (by mistake, through habit) as familiar . . .

In such cases, the juxtaposed elements are simultaneously present for interpretation, we take them in at a glance and the order in which they are read seems not to affect the overall meaning. We can therefore say that such media use simultaneous juxtaposition. As with verbal composition, such techniques – though prevalent – are not restricted to the twentieth century in its modernist phase. The pictures of the Flemish painter, Hieronymous Bosch

Figure 12.5
René Magritte's *Time Transfixed* (La durée poignardée) 1938 – Oil on canvas, 147 × 98.7 cm, Art Institute, Chicago (Joseph Winterbottom collection)

(*c.*1450–1516), depicting the delights of heaven and the horrors of hell, are full of startling – sometimes grotesque and fantastic – juxtapositions.

Any visual composition, of course, is bound to include elements placed side by side. In this sense whatever occurs within the same visual frame has been 'juxtaposed', if only in rather weak terms. However, as we pointed out earlier, the notion of juxtaposition is best reserved for cases where the relation between elements goes beyond the obvious, where it defies easy explanation and where the reader or viewer is called upon to supply an inferential connection. Magazine advertising often uses juxtaposition in the sense we are using it here. The advertisement in Figure 12.6, for example, juxtaposes two basic elements within a unified two-page spread – a wrist watch and an aeroplane propeller.

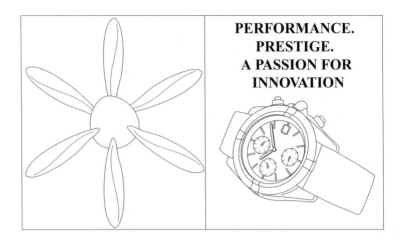

PERFORMANCE.
PRESTIGE.
A PASSION FOR
INNOVATION

Figure 12.6 Advertisement for Breitling watches

At first sight there is no obvious reason why such objects should be put together. Indeed, the very absence of an obvious connection poses a puzzle to the reader – an **enigma** that requires some interpretive effort to solve. The juxtaposition within the same visual field implies some correspondence between the objects – circular motion, perhaps, polished metal, precision engineering or, maybe, accuracy. Were it not for the segments of verbal text distributed among the visual elements, the transfer of meanings from one object to the other would be fluid and indeterminate; thus the words within the pictures serve to anchor the meanings and determine the direction of transfer. The product label and logo, both on the watch and in the bottom right-hand corner of the two-page spread, establish this as an advert – with the watch as the focused commodity for sale (rather than the propeller). The watch is presented as being in some (positive) way like the propeller, with which it shares admirable qualities. The banner legend across the top of the right-hand page fixes what these positive exemplary attributes could be: 'PERFORMANCE. PRESTIGE. A PASSION FOR INNOVATION'. The Breitling watch is presented as being like the propeller in these respects. Other parts of the text reinforce these connections: 'For over a century' (we are told) 'BREITLING has shared aviation's finest hours', with further references to the watches being 'ultra-precise' and 'ultra-reliable', and to their meeting the highest standards of 'sturdiness and functionality' – qualities somehow associated with the burnished metal propeller.

Since juxtaposition here invites the reader to compare the juxtaposed items, we can suggest that visual juxtaposition works in a similar way to metaphor (See **Unit 10**). The visual and verbal links invite us to transfer selected attributes of the juxtaposed object to the commodity being advertised (just as a metaphor demands that we transfer selected attributes from vehicle to tenor).

Sometimes these kinds of transfer can work in an ironic or semi-humorous fashion. Consider the juxtaposition in Figure 12.7. In the original a finely polished and elaborately carved string instrument – an Indian sitar – has been juxtaposed with a single bottle of beer in such a way that it dwarfs and partially conceals it – though still leaving the product label, 'Beck's', legible. How can such superficially different objects be related to each other? In terms of music, art, ornament, tradition? The caption in the original, which reads 'Unmistakable German Craftsmanship' in the top left-hand corner of the page, offers a solution. Despite the way in which the sitar with its Indian craftsmanship has been fore-grounded visually in the advert, the caption draws attention to the simple, half-concealed, bottle of beer. The values of elaborate, traditional craftsman-ship embodied in the sitar have been humorously transferred to the bottle of beer – so as to suggest that the beer has been as lovingly and individually crafted as the instrument.

In the examples of juxtaposition examined earlier, it was noticeable that juxtaposition operates by generating meanings that are somehow 'beyond' or 'between' the elements that are juxtaposed. In the haiku and imagist poems,

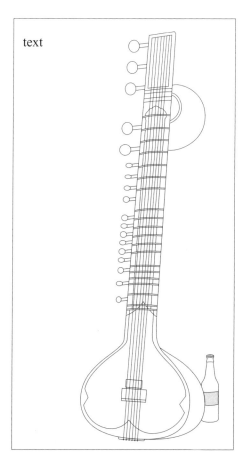

Figure 12.7
Advertisement for Beck's beer

Figure 12.8 Advertisement for Budweiser beer

the lack of a definite connection between images seems to open them up to a multiplicity of interpretations. However, when elements are juxtaposed in an advertising image, the accompanying text often plays an important role in fixing a preferred reading of the image. In the advertisements examined above, the captions are necessary to narrow down the range of communicative possibilities. This suggests that juxtaposition is both a powerful and an unpredictable device to use, since advertisers often find it necessary to control the possible interpretations it might generate. Does the advert in Figure 12.8 work, for instance, without the original caption (King of Beers) at its head?

12.4 Some effects of juxtaposition

It is not possible to predict one single effect for all cases of juxtaposition, but we can point to a range of characteristic, sometimes overlapping, effects. We have already seen that juxtaposition tends to open up a plurality of possible meaningful connections between juxtaposed elements precisely because simple and straightforward connections are omitted. Juxtaposition can also produce a characteristic sense of tension or incongruency, as in Pound's imagist poem given above: 'Green arsenic smeared on an egg-white cloth, /

Crushed strawberries!'. This incongruency typically demands of the reader some extra effort at comprehension.

Juxtaposition can therefore be thought of as a rhetorical strategy. We have already seen that in some instances juxtaposition works in a way similar to metaphor. This is supported by a humorous serial juxtaposition that is often used in films: the first image typically shows two people beginning to make love and is then cut to an image of, say, volcanoes erupting or fireworks exploding. The juxtaposition of the second image with the first asks us to imagine that there is a metaphorical relation between the couple's lovemaking and eruptions or fireworks (the second image becomes a metaphor for the first).

Some of the other effects of juxtaposition can be summarized as various kinds of irony (see **Unit 11**).

12.4.1 Tragic irony

An example of tragic irony may be found at the end of Shakespeare's *King Lear* (1606), where Edmund's dying attempt to revoke his command that Cordelia be murdered and Albany's supplication 'The gods defend her!' are immediately juxtaposed with Lear's arrival carrying Cordelia dead in his arms:

EDMUND: He hath commission from thy wife and me
                     To hang Cordelia in the prison, and
                     To lay the blame upon her own despair,
                     That she fordid herself.
ALBANY: The gods defend her! Bear him hence awhile.

Edmund is borne off
Enter Lear with Cordelia dead in his arms; Edgar, Captain and others following

LEAR: Howl, howl, howl . . . .

The juxtaposition of Cordelia's death (and Lear's reaction to it) with Albany's prayer ('The gods defend her!') reinforces the tragic effect here and ironically casts doubt on the very efficacy of prayer. Thus one of the effects of juxtaposition is to undermine or call into question one element through the immediate proximity of the other.

12.4.2 Comic irony

Sometimes the incongruity of the juxtaposition leads to a humorous effect. In radio broadcasting, mixing between alternative sources (e.g. live studio talk and pre-recorded announcements or commercials) can lead to laughably unintended juxtapositions, as in the following examples:

> 'It's time now, ladies and gentlemen, for our featured guest, the prominent lecturer and social leader, Mrs Elma Dodge ...' *(accidental cut to Superman)* ... 'who is able to leap tall buildings in a single bound.'

> 'So remember, use Pepsodent toothpaste, and brush your teeth ...' *(Cut in to cleansing product commercial)* ... 'right down the drain!'

In these examples it is important that the cut-in text provides a grammatically well-formed completion of a sentence begun in the initial text, even though its topic in each case is discordantly at odds with that already established by the initial text. Humourous juxtaposition is often deliberately employed as a textual strategy in comic texts (as in the mixing of different registers: see **Unit 7**).

12.4.3 Destabilizing irony

When elements from recognizably different texts are deliberately rather than fortuitously mixed in with each other, a sense of irony can be created that goes beyond calling one element into question by its juxtaposition with another. In the following example from *Ulysses* (1922), James Joyce intersperses the description of a place with fragments of a formulaic prayer:

> Stale smoky air hung in the study with the smell of drab abraded leather of its chairs. As on the first day he bargained with me here. As it was in the beginning, is now. On the sideboard the tray of Stuart coins, base treasure of a bog: and ever shall be. And snug in their spooncase of purple plush, faded, the twelve apostles having preached to all the gentiles: world without end.

'Drab abraded leather', 'base treasure of a bog' and 'snug in their spooncase of purple plush' are phrases unlikely to occur outside the context of literary descriptions. On the other hand, the fragments 'As it was in the beginning, is now', 'and ever shall be' and 'world without end' clearly belong to a prayer. These two types of text (or the two registers they use) normally operate in very different contexts – the sacred and the secular – but here they are starkly juxtaposed. It would simplify matters if we could claim that this juxtaposition merely calls the prayer into question by inserting it into a secular context; but counterpointed, as they are in this passage, the sacred and the secular simultaneously call each other into question. One way of understanding the presence and relevance of the prayer fragments in the passage is to suppose that they comprise thoughts in the consciousness of the first person narrator (see **Unit 21, Narrative point of view**), but there is no explicit signal that this is the case, or no reporting clause such as 'The unchanging nature of the room recalled to mind the oft-repeated formula like some ironic echo: "As it was in the beginning, is now …".' In addition, the weaving together of these different strands of text blurs the boundaries between description of external objects and events and internal states of consciousness. It also – and perhaps more interestingly – destabilizes the text, so that we are no longer certain where different parts of it are coming from. There is no longer a single, authoritative, narrative voice making clear to us where one element or fragment stands in relation to another.

Although simple juxtaposition is a general feature of communication, its special use as a rhetorical device to startle the viewer or reader seems particularly noticeable in twentieth-century art forms, including both pictorial fine art and poetry. It also finds its way into film and advertising images as a pervasive technique for intriguing, mystifying and holding the viewer. It is a specialized invitation to read into the message meanings that are only there by implication because of the lack of an explicit connection between the elements that are juxtaposed. Its effects are multiple; but a sense of irony, humour, surprise or enigma is often produced in our reading of it. Like other literary and artistic techniques, juxtaposition can be used (in the words of Magritte) to evoke 'the mystery of beings that normally strike us only as familiar'.

ACTIVITY 12.1

1   Cut-up poems are made by juxtaposing elements drawn from two or more pre-existing texts in order to create effects of tension or incongruity. Below are two extracts from the beginning and end of Adrian Henri's 'On the Late Late Massachers Stillbirths and Deformed Children a Smoother Lovelier Skin Job', which is presented as a 'Cut-up of John Milton Sonnet XVIII On the late Massacher in Piedmont/TV Times/CND leaflet' ('CND' stands for 'Campaign for Nuclear Disarmament').

The seven-day beauty plan:
Avenge O Lord thy slaughter'd saints, whose bones
Will cause up to 1 million deaths from leukaemia
Forget not, in thy book record their groans
Now for the vitally important step. Cream your face and
        neck a second time
No American president world-famous for beauty creams
responsible for the freedom and safety of so many young offenders
TODAY'S MEN OF ACTION
The Triple Tyrant Macmillan Kennedy Watkinson
The West governments are satisfied as to the moral necessity
        to resume Racing from Newmarket
    …

This baby's eyes and nose had merged into
one misshapen feature in the middle of its
forehead, lost 6″ from Hips
sufferers can now wear fashion stockings
Early may fly the Babylonian woe
followed by
TOMORROW'S WEATHER
The Epilogue
close down.

1.1 Relying on features of language and style, try to identify the source of each phrase or line (i.e. whether it is from Milton's sonnet, the *TV Times* or the CND leaflet).

1.2 Pick out three examples of juxtaposition and try to describe the effect of each one.

1.3 What is the overall effect of the use of juxtaposition in this poem?

2 Construct a cut-up poem of your own by (a) selecting two short texts (one of which should be a poem), (b) cutting them up into fragments, and (c) weaving them together in order to achieve irony, humour, surprise, enigma or effects that are similar to Henri's poem.

For the best results do not use two texts of the same type (two poems, or two adverts, etc.). The reason for choosing a poem as one of your source texts is to help establish a semblance of poetic form in your cut-up poem, but the other text needs to be significantly different in order to create effects of tension and incongruency. Use the same wording as the original texts but you need not use the whole of each text nor follow the original order.

When you have finished your cut-up poem, try to answer the following questions:

2.1 What guided your choice of texts?

2.2 How did you decide where to divide them up into into fragments?

2.3 What principles guided your attempt to reconstitute them as a cut-up poem (e.g. Why did you use the material you included? Why did you not use other material? Why did you juxtapose the material in the way you did?).

2.4 What kind of overall effect do you think you've achieved?

Reading

Burgin, V. (1976) 'Art, Common Sense and Photography', in S. Hall and J. Evans (eds) (1999) *Visual Culture: The Reader*, London: Sage/Open University, pp. 41–50.

Eisenstein, S. (1979a) 'The Cinematographic Principle and the Ideogram', in G. Mast and M. Cohen (eds) *Film Theory and Criticism*, Oxford: Oxford University Press, pp. 85–100.

Eisenstein, S. (1979b) 'A Dialectic Approach to Film Form', in G. Mast and M. Cohen (eds) *Film Theory and Criticism*, Oxford: Oxford University Press, pp. 101–22.

Eliot, T.S. (1922) *The Waste Land*, in T.S. Eliot (2005) *Complete Poems and Plays*, London: Faber & Faber.

Shklovsky, V. (1917) 'Art as Technique', in D. Lodge (ed.) (1988) *Modern Criticism and Theory: A Reader*, London: Longman, pp. 16–30.

Unit 13

Intertextuality and allusion

13.1 Allusion

An 'allusion' occurs when one text makes an implicit or explicit reference to another text. In an explicit verbal allusion an actual quotation is made and signalled with quotation marks. In an implicit verbal allusion, no signal is given and the original wording is sometimes changed to suit the new context. Thus the opening of Wordsworth's *The Prelude* (1805) alludes to the end of Milton's *Paradise Lost* (1667) without actually quoting from it:

> The earth is all before me: with a heart
> Joyous, nor scared at its own liberty,
> I look about, and should the guide I choose
> Be nothing better than a wandering cloud,
> I cannot miss my way.
> *(The Prelude*, I, 15–19)

> The World was all before them, where to choose
> Their place of rest, and Providence their guide:
> They hand in hand with wand'ring steps and slow,
> Through Eden took their solitary way.
> *(Paradise Lost*, XII, 646–9)

13.1.1 Allusion as a means of establishing a relation to a cultural or literary tradition

Allusion serves to place a text within the textual network that makes up a cultural tradition. Because of this, allusion can be used simply as a way of adding cultural value to a text. This is a common device in advertisements. For example, in the *Observer* magazine of 8 May 1988, there are four advertisements that use allusions in their captions, including: a Renault car advertised with the caption 'A room of my own', and Cadbury's Bournville chocolate advertised with the caption 'If Chocolate be the food of Gods, Heaven must be in Birmingham'. One of the reasons for making such allusions is that they are thought to invoke some of the cultural connotations of the source text and, by a process of transference, bestow them on the product being promoted. Thus, in the first example (which has a picture of a woman in a Renault car), women are being encouraged to buy a Renault car by suggesting that it will grant them some of the independence that Virginia Woolf was seeking for women in *A Room of One's Own* (1929). Such allusions can also serve to flatter readers – giving those who recognize the allusion the illusion of being superior to those who don't even realize that an allusion is being made. The Cadbury's advertisement therefore implies that it is only 'highly cultured' people – those with the 'good taste' to recognize an allusion to Shakespeare (the first line of *Twelfth Night*) – who will fully appreciate Bournville chocolate. Curiously, the advertisements in the *Observer* magazine of 20 February 2005 are contrastingly light on allusions, except for 'South American *Odyssey*' (advertising a holiday in South America) – and, even in this example, it is perhaps not necessary for readers to realize that this is a reference to one of Homer's epics, since the word 'odyssey' has come to mean any long, eventful journey (sixteen nights, in this case!).

Allusions are also used in the titles of newspaper and magazine articles. The *New Scientist* magazine of 20 March 1999 includes the following titles: 'Forever Young' (article about the youthfulness of *New Scientist* readers); 'The Long Goodbye' (article about the extinction of the North Atlantic right whale); 'Something Rotten ...' (article about bluebottles); 'For Your Ears Only' (article about radio); 'Trouble in Paradise' (article about ecological loss in Caribbean islands); and 'Where No Chip Has Gone Before' (article about Motorola). Here the allusions are primarily to pop songs, films and television, reaching back to the 1970s or before, and to well-known literary texts. We might understand the consistency in the range of these allusions as a product of authorship, arising from the identity of the magazine's editor (perhaps one person with a particular kind of cultural knowledge writes the titles). At the same time, this consistency also positions the reader by telling the reader who recognizes the allusions that this magazine is for him or her – that is, for a person of a certain age and with a certain range of cultural knowledge.

13.1.2 Varieties of allusion

Texts may allude to other texts in a variety of ways, of which these are the most common:

1   Through a verbal reference to another text (as in the way *The Prelude* refers to *Paradise Lost* through a similarity of phrasing).

2   Through **epigraphs** (an inscription at the beginning of the text). T.S Eliot's poem 'The Hollow Men' (1925) has an epigraph taken from Joseph Conrad's *Heart of Darkness* (1899/1902): 'Mistah Kurtz – he dead'. This invites the reader to look for a significant relationship between the poem and the novel – which is perhaps that both texts suggest there is hollowness at the heart of European 'man' in the early twentieth century.

3   Through names of characters. Thus the name Stephen Dedalus, the central character in James Joyce's *A Portrait of the Artist as a Young Man* (1914), refers to Daedalus, a character in Greek mythology who 'made wings, by which he flew from Crete across the archipelago . . . his name is perpetuated in our daedal, skillful, fertile of invention' (*Brewer's Dictionary of Phrase and Fable*).

4   Through choice of titles. Thus the title of William Faulkner's novel *The Sound and the Fury* (1929) is an explicit allusion to Macbeth's despairing claim that life is nothing but 'a tale / Told by an idiot, full of sound and fury, / Signifying nothing' (Shakespeare, *Macbeth* (1606), V, v, 26–8).

13.1.3 Allusion in film, TV and music

The process of allusion is not confined to literature and advertisements, but may be found in most cultural and artistic forms. Music may allude to earlier music (e.g. Stravinsky's allusions to Bach, or the Beatles' allusions to the French national anthem and 'Greensleeves' in 'All You Need is Love'). A complex example is presented by the band Big Daddy, who released a record called *Sgt. Peppers* (1992) – a reworking of the Beatles' *Sgt. Pepper's Lonely Hearts Club Band* (1967) performed entirely using instruments and musical styles of the 1950s. The Beatles' original record itself alludes to, and reworks, 1950s' music (among other kinds of music), but when Big Daddy re-performed it as a 1950s' record, styles merely alluded to in the original became the songs' dominant style. Woody Allen's films frequently make allusions to literature and to other films: *Play It Again Sam* (1972) is a striking example that makes a series of allusions to *Casablanca* (1942). Francis Ford Coppola's *Apocalypse Now* (1979) exists within a complex network of allusions to Conrad and Eliot: it is in essence a rewriting of *Heart of Darkness*, but towards the end the Kurtz character (played by Marlon Brando) reads Eliot's poem 'The Hollow Men' – which reverses the relationship between *Heart of Darkness* and 'The Hollow Men' noted earlier. A combination of musical and narrative allusion indicates that the television series *Star Trek Voyager* (1995) is a version of *The Wizard of Oz* (1939): the TV theme tune begins with a five-note motif that, stripped of its initial note, is the beginning of the film's most famous song 'Somewhere Over the Rainbow', while the film's basic story is reproduced in the television series – which is about a spaceship that is captained by a woman and crewed by individuals who represent accentuated traits but lack certain qualities; the ship and crew are swept into another part of the galaxy, where they kill the 'wicked witch' who brings them there and then try to get home. Even characters' clothing in the TV series can be part of the set of allusions to the film: the alien creature 'Neelix' is dressed and whiskered like a munchkin in the film.

13.1.4 Allusion signals a relationship between texts

An adequate reading of a literary or other cultural text will need to recognize the significance of the ways it interacts with earlier texts. This involves trying to work out the similarities and differences between the two texts that are momentarily brought together by an allusion. By choosing the title *The Sound and the Fury*, Faulkner is presumably inviting us to compare the events and themes of his novel with Macbeth's nihilistic despair. In *A Portrait of the Artist*, the name Stephen Dedalus invites the reader to look out for parallels between the novel and the story of Daedalus. Is there some connection with the notion of flight? Or is the emphasis on Stephen's aspirations to be an artist (skilful, fertile of invention), or on failure (since Icarus, his son, dies), or on the father–son relation (death of the son because the father's ingenuity fails)? A reading that approached the novel with this range of questions in mind would probably find that each of them is relevant in some way.

13.1.5 A way of reading allusions

Thomas Hardy's novels can often seem overloaded with allusions, but some of them are charged with a significance that an adequate reading cannot afford to pass by. In *Tess of the D'Urbervilles* (1891), for example, Alec d'Urberville, Tess's eventual seducer, makes an allusion that, if she had spotted it, might have allowed Tess to avoid her tragedy. Early on in the novel, Tess's impoverished parents send her to work for a rich family to whom they mistakenly think they are related in some way. Tess's new employer, Mrs d'Urberville, who knows nothing of the supposed kinship, sets her to work looking after her poultry and bullfinches. One of the responsibilities involved in looking after the bullfinches is to whistle to them in order to 'teach 'em airs'. Alec, Tess's so-called cousin, spies her vainly attempting to practise whistling and takes this as an opportunity to flirt with her:

> 'Ah! I understand why you are trying – those bullies! My mother wants you to carry on their musical education. How selfish of her! As if attending to these curst cocks and hens were not enough work for any girl. I would flatly refuse if I were you.'
> 'But she wants me particularly to do it, and to be ready by tomorrow morning.'
> 'Does she? Well then – I'll give you a lesson or two.'
> 'Oh no, you won't!' said Tess, withdrawing towards the door.

> 'Nonsense; I don't want to touch you. See – I'll stand on this side of the wire-netting, and you can keep on the other; so you may feel quite safe. Now, look here; you screw up your lips too harshly. There 'tis – so.'
>
> He suited the action to the word, and whistled a line of 'Take, O take those lips away'. But the allusion was lost upon Tess.

The editor of the Macmillan edition of Hardy's novel provides an endnote that tells us that Alec is alluding to the first line of the Page's song in Shakespeare's *Measure for Measure* (1604), Act IV, scene 1. But this information, in itself, is not enough to allow us to understand the full import of the allusion. Without an understanding of the significance of the song in the context of *Measure for Measure*, the allusion remains lost upon us as well as upon Tess. It is only when we compare the situation in the novel with the situation in the text being alluded to that the significance of the allusion becomes apparent. Peter Hutchinson (1983) makes a succinct analysis:

> The narrator may be suggesting that Tess is simply ignorant of the source . . . If we too are ignorant of this, we may assume that the reference is merely a means of contrasting Alec's worldliness with Tess's simplicity and uncultured existence. This is certainly part of its function, but the fact that the narrator terms the whistling an 'allusion' may suggest that the original context of the song has some bearing on the present situation. In retrospect [when Tess has been seduced by Alec and abandoned by Angel Clare] we can see that it clearly does: the Boy sings these lines to Mariana when she has become a seduced and abandoned victim.

Thus the fact that the allusion is lost upon Tess proves fatal for her; a full understanding of the allusion thus adds to our sense of the text's tragic irony (once we know how the novel ends).

It is possible to identify at least three separate stages in this analysis of the allusion in *Tess of the D'Urbervilles*:

1   The first step is to recognize that an allusion has been made in the first place. In Hardy's novel, this is made easy because we are told that 'the allusion was lost upon Tess', but not all allusions are so explicit. To a certain extent the ability to spot an implicit allusion is largely dependent on the reader having read the text being alluded to (thus the reader will have the feeling of having read something vaguely similar and will proceed from there). However, spotting an allusion is not so wholly dependent on chance as this suggests; it is often possible to detect the presence of an allusion because it will usually stand out in some way from the text that surrounds it – perhaps through differences of style or register (see **Unit 7**). For example, Ernest Hemingway quotes the seventeenth-century poet John Donne in the title of his novel *For Whom the Bell Tolls*

(1940), but we do not need to know this fact in order to recognize that the title uses a more archaic and 'literary' phrasing than Hemingway usually employs.

2   The second task is to trace the allusion. In the example from *Tess of the D'Urbervilles* the editor does this job for us, and in some instances we will be familiar enough with the allusion to go straight to the original text; but in most cases we will have to do some detective work. The most obvious way to trace the allusion is to use the Internet. For example, a Google search on the words 'Take, O take those lips away' takes us almost instantly to many websites that quote the whole lyric and give the information we need. In the past, the process of hunting an allusion was much more laborious and usually involved a trip to the reference section of the library to consult concordances or dictionaries of quotations. If this failed, it was often a matter of educated guesswork.

3   The third step involves a close reading of the section of the source text in which the word or phrase originally appears, together with some investigation of its significance in the text as a whole. At this stage you should try to work out the similarities and differences between the source text and the text being read. This should help you to establish why the allusion is being made and whether there is an ironic or parallel relation between the texts. Only by such a careful consideration of the source text (as the example from *Tess of the D'Urbervilles* demonstrates) can we be aware of the full implications of an allusion.

13.2 Intertextuality

Intertextuality is used in literary criticism to describe the variety of ways that texts interact with other texts; in particular, the notion of intertextuality stresses the idea that texts are not unique, isolated objects but are actually made out of numerous other texts, both known and unknown. Allusion is a form of intertextuality that works largely through verbal echoes between texts; however, texts may also interact with one another through formal and thematic echoes and through recycling the voices and registers of other literary texts and the general culture that they exist within (see **Unit 7, Language and context: register**).

13.2.1 Intertextuality through genre

The very idea of genre – that texts can be divided into different groups according to certain shared characteristics – necessarily involves a degree of interconnection between texts (see **Unit 4, Recognizing genre**). No text is an island. Any poem, for example, will draw on certain poetic conventions that will distinguish it from prose (even if only to undercut or resist those conventions).

The idea that texts belong to intertextual 'families' is even truer of the various sub-genres, such as the sonnet. The sonnet was developed in Italy and was introduced into English poetry in the sixteenth century. Its first practitioners in English generally followed the formal and thematic conventions established by Italian poets such as Petrarch: thus most sonnets have fourteen lines of **iambic pentameter** (close to Petrarch's *endecasillabo* metre) arranged into an elaborate rhyme scheme and – at least in the Renaissance – tend to have a male speaker who addresses his words to an unavailable woman to whom he professes eternal love. Following the example of Petrarch, English Renaissance poets – such as Spenser, Sidney and Shakespeare – tended to arrange their love sonnets into sonnet sequences that chart the changing fortunes and feelings of the male sonneteer in his quest for his beloved. Although the thematic range of the sonnet has been greatly extended since then, the form continues to be associated with the unrequited passion of a male speaker for an unavailable woman. Thus Edna St Vincent Millay's sonnet, 'I, Being Born a Woman and Distressed' (1923), is intertextually related to the sonnets of the past not only because it conforms to the formal requirements of the sonnet, but because it reverses and flouts these thematic conventions:

> I, being born a woman and distressed
> By all the needs and notions of my kind,
> Am urged by your propinquity to find
> Your person fair, and feel a certain zest
> To bear your body's weight upon my breast:
> So subtly is the fume of life designed,
> To clarify the pulse and cloud the mind,
> And leave me once again undone, possessed.
> Think not for this, however, the poor treason
> Of my stout blood against my staggering brain,
> I shall remember you with love, or season
> My scorn with pity, – let me make it plain:
> I find this frenzy insufficient reason
> For conversation when we meet again.

Millay's speaker is clearly a woman who informs a man she has had sex with that she is so far from feeling eternal love for him that she feels no urge even to make conversation with him when they meet again. Part of the impact of the poem arises from the fact that the woman rejects the role conventionally ascribed to women in such situations. But the poem's full impact can only be registered by a reader who realizes that it uses the sonnet form in order to transgress those thematic conventions we have come to expect in sonnets. Thus part of the meaning of the poem derives from the intertextual relationship it sets up between itself and the sonnet tradition.

13.2.2 Intertextuality through parody

A second way in which intertextuality occurs specifically through genre is in parody, satire and mock forms. These sub-genres rely upon intertextual relations with other genres for their effect. For example, Alexander Pope's *The Rape of the Lock* (1712/14) depends upon the reader's familiarity with the conventions of the epic genre that it mocks. Thus the poem opens:

> What dire offense from amorous causes springs,
> What mighty contests rise from trivial things,
> I sing – This verse to Caryll, Muse! is due.

These lines echo the ritualistic opening gesture of the epic mode – an example of which can be seen in the opening lines of *Paradise Lost*:

> Of man's first disobedience, and the fruit
> Of that forbidden tree, whose mortal taste
> Brought death into the world, and all our woe,
> With loss of Eden, till one greater man
> Restore us, and regain the blissful seat,
> Sing heavenly Muse . . .

As its opening indicates, *The Rape of the Lock* uses these epic conventions in order to treat a 'trivial' event in high society (a man snips a lock of hair from a woman's head) as if it were an epic matter.

From these examples, we can see that part of the significance of a literary text exists not within itself but in the relationships it sets up with other texts. These examples also show that the intertextual dimensions of cultural texts can only have effects and meaning through the active knowledge that a reader brings to them. Thus Pope's poem has a much-reduced impact on readers unfamiliar with the tradition it parodies.

13.2.3 The changing role of intertextuality

Between the Middle Ages and the end of the eighteenth century education in Britain was limited to a privileged minority and was based on the study of the literature of ancient Greece and Rome (the 'classics'). Authors assumed that their readers would recognize allusions to the 'authorities' (the classics, Aristotle, the Bible), and tradition was valued at least as much as innovation. For example, in the 'neoclassical' period (roughly 1660–1785), authors demonstrated their respect for classical writers by writing thematic and formal imitations of them. Examples include Andrew Marvell's 'An Horatian Ode' (1681) and Alexander Pope's 'Imitations of Horace' (1733–9).

In the Romantic period (roughly 1790–1830), however, with its emphasis on 'originality' in a period in which literacy and education in the vernacular (i.e. English rather than the classical languages) began to increase rapidly, the importance of the 'classics' as authorities began to dwindle. The relation of authors to past texts became less that of reverential imitation and more an attempt to break with the past. Wordsworth's allusions to *Paradise Lost*, for example, both acknowledge Milton's importance and register Wordsworth's rebellion against him (Wordsworth begins where Milton ends).

13.2.4 Intertextuality and originality

The fact of intertextuality and allusion thus raises questions about originality: how far do literary texts originate in an author's mind and how far are they composed out of other literature? In modernist literature (roughly 1910–40), allusion becomes a constitutive principle of composition. If T.S. Eliot's *The Waste Land* (1922) is read alongside the notes Eliot printed with it, we get a sense of the poem as a collage of quotations from and allusions to other texts. In the postmodernist period (roughly 1960 to the present), writers such as Angela Carter (e.g. *The Magic Toy Shop* (1967)) and Umberto Eco (e.g. *The Name of the Rose* (1980)) seem to have set aside attempts to be original in the narrow sense in order to participate in an intertextual free-for-all in which the possibility that all writing is allusive and/or intertextual is celebrated for its own sake.

13.2.5 Post-structuralist accounts of intertextuality

Traditional literary criticism is often concerned with the texts that influenced a particular writer: influence is most usually established through tracing allusions. If an editor spots an allusion, he or she will typically say something like 'Keats is thinking of Shakespeare's *Venus and Adonis* here'. But this assumption begs a number of questions: how do we know that? What if the allusion were unconscious? Or accidental? Or created by the editor's own associations? What if texts inevitably interact and reading is necessarily an intertextual process? For post-structuralist theorists such as Julia Kristeva and Roland Barthes, all language usage is inevitably intertextual in several senses: first, because individuals do not originate or invent language – we are always born into a language or languages that precede us; and, second, because without pre-existing forms, themes, conventions and codes there could be no such thing as literature at all. For Barthes (1971), 'a text is . . . a multi-dimensional space in which a variety of writings, none of them original, blend and clash. The text is a tissue of quotations drawn from the innumerable centers of culture.' In claiming this, Barthes transforms the idea of literary or cultural tradition from being a selected body of earlier work available as a stable resource behind the text into a potentially infinite network of links and echoes between texts of all kinds. Such a theory of intertextuality is radically different from traditional understandings of the functions and significance of allusion.

13.2.6 Intertextuality in children's literature

Our initiation into intertextuality begins with the very beginning of our encounter with stories as children. The formulaic opening 'Once upon a time' signals to the young reader or listener that this is the beginning of a story because he or she has encountered that formula before. It signifies because it is intertextual. Many children's books are intertextual in that they draw on and revise the kinds of plots, characters and settings that children become familiar with through listening to and reading other texts. This is the case with some of the most successful and innovative of children's books. The *Harry Potter* series (1997–), for example, mixes the genre conventions of two long-standing children's genres – fantasy (with wizards and witches, and so on) and the boarding school story (which goes back to *Tom Brown's Schooldays* (1857) and includes classic series such as Enid Blyton's *Malory Towers* (1946–51)). Children do not have to be conscious of these intertextual relations in order to understand and enjoy the *Harry Potter* series, though subliminal recognition of them may contribute to the pleasure. A more complex example is Philip Pullman's *His Dark Materials* series (1995–2000), which draws on Blake in order to reread and critique the Book of Genesis, Milton's *Paradise Lost*, C.S. Lewis's *The Chronicles of Narnia* (1950–6) and institutionalized Christianity in general. While many of Pullman's young readers may have read *The Chronicles of Narnia*, not many will have read Genesis, Milton or Blake or be wholly aware of the theological issues that *His Dark Materials* engages with. Nonetheless, *His Dark Materials* has been hugely successful with young readers and can be understood and enjoyed at the level of character and plot alone. In this case, the allusions and intertextual context seem to produce two levels of reading, with adult or more widely read readers being able to understand Pullman's trilogy in a different way to those who don't realize the texts' intertextual significance.

ACTIVITY 13.1

This activity looks at another sonnet by Edna St Vincent Millay:

> We talk of taxes, and I call you friend;
> Well, such you are, – but well enough we know
> How thick about us root, how rankly grow
> Those subtle weeds no man has need to tend,

> That flourish through neglect, and soon must send
> Perfume too sweet upon us and overthrow
> Our steady senses; how such matters go
> We are aware, and how such matters end.
> Yet shall be told no meagre passion here;
> With lovers such as we forevermore
> Isolde drinks the draught, and Guinevere
> Receives the Table's ruin through her door,
> Francesca, with the loud surf at her ear,
> Lets fall the colored book upon the floor.

As with many sonnets, this sonnet is divided into an octave (first eight lines) and a sestet (last six lines); this division or *volta* (turn) is marked by the rhyme scheme and by the word 'Yet' at the beginning of the ninth line.

1   Read the first eight lines carefully and try to identify: (a) the speech situation (who is speaking to whom); (b) what the speaker is saying to the person spoken to (the addressee); and (c) how the use of metaphor indicates a particular attitude towards, or representation of, what the speaker is talking about.

2   Read the last six lines carefully and underline or highlight all potential allusions.

   2.1   Using the Internet and/or appropriate reference books, do a search on the key words of each potential allusion in order to confirm whether or not it is an allusion.

   2.2   For each allusion that you discover: (a) take notes about what the Internet source or reference book says about the source of the allusion; (b) where possible, try to read the original text or texts that Millay's poem is alluding to; and (c) work out the relevant similarities between the source text and Millay's poem.

   2.3   What is the overall function or effect of the allusions in the sestet of Millay's sonnet?

3   What is the relationship between the sestet and the octave in Millay's sonnet?

4   How does Millay's sonnet relate to the general conventions of the sonnet genre?

5   How does Millay's sonnet relate to the general conventions of love poetry?

Reading

Barthes, R. (1968) 'The Death of the Author' and (1971) 'From Work to Text', in Vincent B. Leitch (ed.) (2001) *The Norton Anthology of Theory and Criticism*, New York and London: Norton.

Bate, J. (1970) *The Burden of the Past and the English Poet*, London: Chatto & Windus.

Bloom, H. (1973) *The Anxiety of Influence*, Oxford: Oxford University Press.

Eliot, T.S. (1919) 'Tradition and the Individual Talent', in Vincent B. Leitch (ed.) (2001) *The Norton Anthology of Theory and Criticism*, New York and London: Norton.

Gilbert, S. and Gubar, S. (1979) *The Madwoman in the Attic*, New Haven, CT: Yale University Press.

Hutchinson, P. (1983) *Games Authors Play*, London: Methuen.

Renza, L.A. (1990) 'Influence', in F. Lentricchia and T. McLaughlin (eds) *Critical Terms for Literary Study*, Chicago, IL: Chicago University Press, pp. 186–202.

Unit 14

Authorship and intention

It seems obvious to assume that a text is created by an author (or by a group of authors). It also seems obvious to assume that an author (or group of authors) has a particular intention about how that text should act on a reader and how it should be interpreted. The concepts of author and intention appear to be central, even indispensable, notions that offer a necessary point of origin and guide to meaning for any given text. Indeed, it is our sense that a text (or art object) was designed by human agency that encourages us to believe that it will be worthwhile spending time interpreting it. And the goal of our interpretive efforts, we assume, is to discover the author's intention. Despite these common-sense assumptions, however, the concepts of author and intention are less straightforward than they seem.

14.1 The author

14.1.1 A brief history of the author

Our assumptions about authorship and intention are related to assumptions about what an author does in creating a text. One historically influential view is that the author is a sort of skilful craft worker, who draws on and reworks the conventions of the cultural tradition but always remains less important than that tradition. This view is associated with literary practices and criticism in Europe broadly from the Middle Ages up to the eighteenth century. The neo-classicism of the eighteenth century, for example, placed emphasis not so much on an author's originality as upon the way a text conforms to the conventions of classical literature (the literature of classical Greece and Rome) and to established ideas. This outlook is summarized in Alexander Pope's definition of good poetry (true wit) in 1711: 'True wit is Nature to advantage dress'd; / What oft was thought, but ne'er so well expressed' (*An Essay on Criticism*, II, 297–8).

Toward the end of the eighteenth century, however, the intellectual and artistic movement known as Romanticism developed a significantly different view of the author and of creativity, with particular emphasis on the individual imagination and on inner feelings. The Romantics held that an author discovers original material for creative work somewhere inside himself or herself rather than in the tradition. In 1800, William Wordsworth defined poetry as 'the spontaneous overflow of powerful feelings' ('Preface to *Lyrical Ballads*'). Thus the author becomes the guarantor of what might be called the text's authenticity (original, sincere, natural). The Romantic view of the author became very influential throughout nineteenth-century Europe and beyond. It survives today as a popular 'common-sense' assumption about artistic creativity.

Criticism of the Romantic view of authorship and creativity characterized the modernist aesthetic theory of early twentieth-century Europe and the United States. In his influential essay 'Tradition and the Individual Talent' (1919), the poet and critic T.S. Eliot effectively resurrected and modified pre-Romantic views of the author in order to attack the Romantic focus on individual creativity. Eliot argues that the individual poet's mind is and should be subservient to the literary tradition, which he defines as the 'existing monuments' of the whole literature of Europe from Homer to the present. For Eliot, the popular interest in a poet's individuality and personal emotions is misguided, and he proposes instead that we should focus on what he calls 'significant emotion, emotion that has its life in the poem and not in the history of the poet'. In effect, Eliot is calling for a shift in attention from poets to poetry, and suggesting that a poem's originality is derived not from the inner life of the poet but from the way it both fits into and modifies the literary tradition. Eliot's thinking significantly influenced a whole generation of writers and scholars, especially the New Critics who taught in British and American universities from the 1940s onwards.

In the 1970s, a number of critical groups in Europe and the United States began to examine what we might call the politics of authorship. This involved investigating the way marginalized groups, such as female, black, working-class or gay writers, have had to struggle in order to represent particular, marginalized social experiences. One area in which such work has been particularly influential is feminist literary history, which has drawn our attention to many women writers from the past who had been lost to modern readers. One of the reasons for the disappearance of these authors is that, in certain historical periods and places, it was considered improper for women to be published authors. As a consequence, some eighteenth-century and nineteenth-century women novelists were published anonymously or under a male pen name (e.g. Charlotte Brontë as Currer Bell).

From the late 1960s onwards, post-structuralist theory – especially in the writings of Michel Foucault, Jacques Derrida and Roland Barthes – attempted to do away entirely with the notion of the author and authorial intention. In an essay provocatively called 'The Death of the Author' (1968), Barthes makes the following key suggestions:

1   The author is, by definition, absent from writing (in contrast with speech, which generally implies the presence of the speaker).
2   A text is not a unique artefact, emerging through a kind of immaculate conception from a writer's brain. Rather, the conventions and language that make up the text (any text) are available to the writer precisely because they have been used before (see **Unit 13, Intertextuality and allusion**). A text is 'a tissue of quotations', 'a multi-dimensional space in which a variety of writings, none of them original, blend and clash'.
3   Barthes claims that 'Classic criticism has never paid any attention to the reader; for it, the writer is the only person in literature.' This focus on the writer is an exercise of institutional control: 'to give a text an Author . . . is to impose a limit on that text'.
4   Barthes therefore seeks to transform reading into a productive practice in which the reader is liberated from the process of discovering, or pretending to discover, what the author intended. For Barthes, a text's meaning is generated in the creative, playful processes of reading, not of writing.
5   Encapsulating these arguments, Barthes concludes that 'the birth of the reader must be at the cost of the death of the Author'.

The notion of the author's 'death' is not, of course, to be taken literally. By announcing the **death of the author** Barthes was attempting to kill off the tendency in literary criticism and educational institutions to use the notion of the author, and his or her supposed intentions, to limit the interpretive possibilities of reading. The continuing influence of Barthes's essay points to the fundamental nature of the questions he poses: questions about the symbolic role played by the author and by authorial intention in imposing a kind of law on what might otherwise be a free play of interpretation.

Barthes' announcement of the birth of the reader was taken up in other theoretical developments, particularly the Reader–Response criticism that began to emerge in the late 1960s and 1970s in the work of Wolfgang Iser and Stanley Fish. As Fish developed his theory he assigned a smaller and smaller role to both the author and the text itself, even suggesting at one stage that the reader is the 'author' of the text that he or she reads – a banishment of the role of the author that is even more radical than Barthes's. Yet the report of the death of the author seems to have been an exaggeration. Many literary theorists, critics, students and general readers seem unable or unwilling to accept that reading can proceed without consideration for authorial intention. In recent years, there have been at least two book-length announcements of the 'return' or 'resurrection' of the author (see Burke, 1998 [1992] and Irwin, 2002). The critical debate about authorship and its impact on theories and practices of reading looks set to continue as long as the category of 'the author' remains viable.

14.1.2 Modern media and the future of authorship

An emphatic illustration of the complexity of authorship is offered by texts typically created by a team or group of people, such as films, television programmes, theatrical performances or music CDs. Contributions to a film text may be made by many people, including actors, camera operators, lighting and set designers, script writers and editors, make-up artists, directors, producers and even test audiences in some cases. Nonetheless, we tend to assume that a film's 'author' is its director, who is supposed to have final artistic control. This view played a central part in the *politique des auteurs* developed by the French *Cahiers du cinéma* in the 1950s, and in the related *auteur* theory of Andrew Sarris in the United States (see Caughie, 1981). In this view, an 'auteur' (an especially valued director such as Alfred Hitchcock) is considered to be the person who expresses his or her personal vision coherently across the corpus of films that he or she makes. In other words, it seems as if we want to hold on to the notion of the author even in creative processes that involve teamwork.

The case of film mentioned here relates largely to studio forms of production in which high production costs mean that there are limited opportunities for individuals to play the central part of 'author'. The same is true in other instances of corporate production of contemporary media (consider, for example, the credit list on any commercial multimedia CD-ROM). But the recent development of digital technologies of media production means that an increasing amount of cultural texts of various kinds can now be produced on personal computers and in home studios. The implications of these developments for our notions of authorship are as yet unpredictable. One view is that the new media technologies allow anyone and everyone to become an author (anyone can have a home page, post material on the Internet and become a 'blogger'). A second view suggests that the new interactive media technologies will eventually remove the need for a clear-cut concept of authorship altogether.

14.2 Intention

The concept of the author is closely bound up with the notion of intention. Critical appeals to the notion of authorial intention are often made in order to authenticate the critic's particular interpretation. But such appeals also indicate the anxiety that, if there was no way of accessing authorial intention as a guarantor of textual meaning, there would be no limit to the kinds of meanings that might be found, no way of judging whether we are misreading or over-interpreting, and no clear reason ever to stop reading the same text in endlessly different ways. But is this anxiety well founded? And if not, what factors other than authorial intention might serve to guide or limit interpretation? The history of literary criticism has typically approached the problem of textual meaning by focusing on three different aspects of the reading situation: the notion of authorial intention; the conventional forms or codes of the text itself; and the attribution or ascription of meaning by readers (or viewers). Different theories of interpretation typically differ in the respective degrees of priority they accord to one or more of these three elements. A consideration of these three aspects of reading can open up usefully different perspectives on the role of intention in shaping the meanings of a text.

14.2.1 Authorial intention

In the eighteenth century in particular, literary works were considered to be products of conscious intention. This assumption led to a particular way of reading, as encapsulated in another of Pope's couplets in his *Essay on Criticism*: 'In every work regard the writer's end / Since none can compass more than they intend' (II, 255–6). At the close of the eighteenth century, however, Romantic writers began to claim that authors are not always fully conscious of the meaning or implications of their own literary works because they were produced in moments of 'inspiration'. The Romantic poet William Blake, for example, claims that, although John Milton tells us that he set out in *Paradise Lost* to 'justify the ways of God to men', the poem itself reveals that Milton was actually 'of the Devil's party without knowing it'. Yet the Romantics' rejection of conscious intention still allows for interpretation to be anchored in authorial intention – as long as authorial intention is taken to include unconscious elements, such as the mysterious workings of the poetic imagination, that are not always readily available for conscious reflection, even by the author him- or herself.

In the early twentieth century, the view that creation emerges out of unconscious meanings or impulses not always available to conscious attention was given fresh impetus by psychoanalysis. Sigmund Freud, C.G. Jung and others suggested that we are never fully conscious of our intentions because the unconscious mind can have an effect on what we say – and on what we don't say – without our being aware of it. For Freud and Jung – though in different ways – the unconscious mind plays a major part in artistic creativity. Yet no agreed answer exists to the question of how far these claims undermine appeals to authorial intention. In some traditions of criticism and theories of interpretation (e.g. in **hermeneutics**), intention has continued to play an important part in claiming validity or legitimacy for textual interpretations. What seems certain, however, is that, in the light of psychoanalysis and other intellectual developments sceptical of authorial intention, straightforward confidence in the role played by intention in fixing meaning (for instance, the kind of confidence implicit in Pope's couplet) can no longer be justified.

14.2.2 Intention versus the conventional forms or codes of the text itself

One common argument against the notion that the author's intention is the ultimate arbiter of a text's interpretation comes from the fact that meaningful forms are shared, social property. The words of a language, for example, exist and have conventional meanings before any particular speaker or writer uses them.

One development of this insight in literary criticism is the claim that the meanings of texts should be discoverable within texts themselves rather than by searching beyond them for an author's intention. A particularly influential formulation of this view is the New Critical argument in W.K. Wimsatt and M.C. Beardsley's essay 'The Intentional Fallacy' (1946). Concentrating on poetry (though similar arguments might be made about novels, films or other text types), Wimsatt and Beardsley set out the following reasons for not going outside the text in the search for authorial intention:

1   In most cases it is not possible to find out what the poet intended.
2   We are primarily interested in how a poem works, not what was intended.
3   A poem is a public rather than a private thing because it exists in language – which is by definition social rather than personal. The author does not own the text once it has been made public, and therefore does not have eternal authority over its meaning.
4   A poem's meaning can only be discovered through its actual language, 'through our habitual knowledge of the language, through grammars, dictionaries, and all the literature which is the source of dictionaries, in general, through all that makes a language and culture' (Wimsatt and Beardsley, 1946).
5   'If the poet succeeded in doing [what he intended], then the poem itself shows what he was trying to do' (Wimsatt and Beardsley, 1946).

The last of these points indicates, however, that Wimsatt and Beardsley were not rejecting the notion of authorial intention per se. They were, instead, trying to reject the practice of trying to look for intention outside the text itself – in diaries, anecdotes, biographies and so on. For Wimsatt and Beardsley, a successful poem embodies what its author intended. If we need to look outside the text to discover the author's intention, then the poem has failed to embody its author's intention and is therefore not worth bothering with.

A more radical development of the notion that meaning does not originate in the intentions of individual minds but in the shared conventions of language can be found in the structuralist literary theory that emerged in France in the 1960s. Developing Ferdinand de Saussure's claim in the early twentieth century that individual speech acts are made possible by a pre-existing language system that is shared by all users of the language, structuralism argued that individual literary texts are made possible and meaningful by a pre-existing literary system made up of conventional techniques and devices, such as the conventions of genre and the general symbolic codes of the culture. Structuralist literary theory minimized the role of the author and authorial intention in order to focus on the way individual literary texts relate to and help us understand the pre-existing literary system.

14.2.3 Inferencing: the attribution of meaning (and authorial intention) by readers

At the outset of this unit we said that it is our sense that a text (or art object) was designed by human agency that encourages us to believe that it will be worthwhile spending time interpreting it. This remains the case, even if we take into account the various critiques of authorship and intention that we have examined. Even if the unconscious mind does have an impact on literary creativity (and on everyday language usage), the conscious mind also plays a crucial role. Even if the author's conscious mind is reduced to juggling the promptings of the unconscious mind on the one hand and mixing and reworking available codes and conventions on the other, it remains the case that successful authors do this with great skill and with conscious intentions about the effects and meanings of the resulting text.

Reading a text generally begins, then, by assuming that an author (or a group of authors) has designed that text in order to communicate meanings and effects that a reader will find it rewarding to discover or respond to. (If we were presented with a literary text written entirely by a computer, would we read it in the same way that we do texts written by human beings?) Assuming that the effort will be worth it, an interpreter searches for a text's relevant implications by focusing on aspects of the text itself and of the immediate context (what kind of text is this? in what form does it appear? where is it from? who is its author? and so on). In addition, the interpreter may need to draw on more specific cultural knowledge that the text is also drawing on. Such interpretive activities allow the interpreter to select – often quickly and without conscious effort – the meaning that the speaker is likely to have foreseen in formulating the utterance or text in that way rather than any other.

The process of inferencing that we are describing here can be illustrated by a fictional example. Imagine the following dating ad in a magazine: 'Captain Kirk seeks Lieutenant Uhura to boldly go on voyages of discovery. Report to the command deck. Box 162.' The immediate context is the magazine's 'soul mate' column: the column is recognizably one of a type in which men and women seek to establish long-term romantic relationships, and the reader assumes that this text is one of that type. To understand this particular advert, however, the reader has to access another kind of specific, culturally formed background knowledge – in this case the second or third *Star Trek* TV series (or one of the films). Thus the reader draws on general cultural assumptions plus more specific intertextual references that trigger what might be called 'subcultural' assumptions. If a reader is able to interpret this ad in this way it reveals that both the reader and the author are co-members of a restricted subculture. In other words, reader and author have something in common, and this might indicate that they may be compatible romantic partners.

Such an account of interpretation therefore combines aspects of 'coded' meaning with a further level of inference. Decoded meanings are used as input into an inferential process of filling out and constructing a relevant meaning in the particular context inferred for the text by the interpreter. To the extent that the text-producer and interpreter share assumptions that can be activated in interpretation, the interpreter's computation of meaning is likely to resemble the author's intention. Where assumptions mobilized differ significantly, however, the interpretation produced is likely to diverge from authorial intention. In the case of some texts or utterances (especially poetry, religious or mythical discourse, or other kinds of figurative or evocative language), the search for relevant meanings may produce a wide range of weakly implied meanings that border on meanings not intended by the author at all. In addition, in constructing a reading of a text or utterance, of any sort, the interpreter can always make inferences that will not have been in any way intended (or even foreseen) by the author. Such inferences may produce 'symptomatic' interpretations that generate meanings for the text that are highly relevant to the reader – and possibly of great interest in the reader's context – regardless of what the author may or may not have been trying to say. As a consequence, it would seem that, while the process of inferencing offers a good account of what readers actually do when trying to work out an author's intention, it is not a fail-safe process and does not provide us with a clear-cut way of deciding between authorial intention and the reader's own projections onto a text.

14.3 Ways of reading authorship

We have seen that the notion of authorship is problematic, and that appeals to or attempts to discover authorial intention are equally problematic. Although our interest in authors and authorial intentions seems to persist in spite of these problems, we therefore need to be hesitant, when interpreting any text, in claiming that we have uncovered what the author meant or intended. One way of avoiding some of the more obvious pitfalls is to distinguish carefully between authors, on the one hand, and narrators and characters, on the other. The contemporary novelist Margaret Elphinstone, who is a colleague of three of the writers of this textbook, sometimes receives letters from enthusiastic readers who confuse the characters and narrators of her books with the author herself. The following ways of reading will help readers to avoid making such mistakes.

14.3.1 Narrator, implied author and poetic speaker

The author of a literary text needs to be distinguished from the imaginary person who is supposed to 'speak' it. In novels, we differentiate between the author and the first person or third person narrator (the fictional person who narrates it). This distinction is clear enough in the case of the main narrator of Gloria Naylor's *Bailey's Café* (1992):

> I can't say I've had much education. Book education. Even though high school back in the twenties was really school; not what these youngsters are getting away with now . . . I went to kindergarten on the muddy streets in Brooklyn; finished up grade school when I married Nadine; took my first diploma from the Pacific; and this café, well now, this café is earning me a PhD. You might say I'm majoring in Life.

The narrator here differs from the author in several ways: the narrator is male (Naylor is female); the narrator went to school in the 1920s (Naylor was born in 1950); the narrator has not had much book education (by the time *Bailey's Café* was published Naylor had a BA in English from Brooklyn College, an MA in Afro-American Studies from Yale, had taught in various universities, and had published four highly regarded novels).

In poems, too, we often need to distinguish between the poem's author and its **poetic speaker**, narrator or persona. For one thing, while the poet may be regarded as the creator of the poem, the speaker is clearly one of its devices or techniques – a formal choice made by the poet. This distinction is often important even in first person Romantic poems, despite the emphasis in Romanticism on individual authorial expression. In the first stanza of Wordsworth's 'Lucy Gray' (1800), for example, which recounts the story of a young girl who drowned in a canal in a snowstorm, it might seem natural to assume that the speaker is Wordsworth himself:

> Oft had I heard of Lucy Gray:
> And, when I crossed the wild,
> I chanced to see at break of day
> The solitary child.

Yet scholars have revealed that this poem is not based on Wordsworth's own experience but on Wordsworth's sister Dorothy's recollections of a real incident that occurred during a period of her childhood when she was separated from her brother and living in a different part of England. In other words, Wordsworth could never have seen Lucy Gray in real life. Although the poem implies that the speaker encounters Lucy's ghost, who continues to haunt the moors where she died, it seems clear that this is a fictional encounter. This is not to say that the poem is based on a lie, but to say that the poem recounts an imaginary incident and that we therefore need to see the 'I' of the poem not as Wordsworth himself, but as a kind of imaginary Wordsworth – a persona.

14.3.2 Authorial irony and the implied author

One reason for distinguishing between author and narrator is that some narrative texts may present us with a narrator who is subject to authorial irony or **structural irony** (see **Unit 11**) by being shown to be unreliable at some level – perhaps in terms of his or her ability to understand events or in terms of his or her moral position. For example Huck, the narrator of Mark Twain's novel *Huckleberry Finn* (1884), is presented from the beginning as being unable fully to understand his own situation, including the fact that he himself is a fictional character:

> You don't know about me, without you have read a book by the name of *The Adventures of Tom Sawyer*, but that ain't no matter. That book was made by Mr Mark Twain, and he told the truth, mainly. There was things which he stretched, but mainly he told the truth.

The novel was published in 1884, but it is set 'forty to fifty years previously' – that is, before the American Civil War led to the emancipation of American slaves. Huck is presented as sharing a conventional view that slavery is natural, even though this conflicts with his personal friendship for an escaped slave called Jim. As the narrator of the novel, Huck explicitly expresses the moral confusion that results – worrying, for example, about Jim's plan to emancipate his children from slavery. Ironically, Huck is shocked by hearing Jim

> coming right out flat-footed and saying he would steal his children – children that belonged to a man I didn't even know; a man that hadn't ever done me no harm.

Huck subsequently recognizes that he would feel just as bad if he betrayed Jim to the authorities, and so abandons his attempt to resolve what for him is a moral dilemma. To suggest, however, that Huck's predicament is a moral dilemma for the novel itself, or for its real author, would be a serious misreading. Huck's interior monologue is both comic and tragic in its limited viewpoint and in its aping of the flawed logic and morality that helped sustain slavery. Since Huck cannot see the irony that his own reasoning reveals, there seems to be a higher-level viewpoint in the novel that is not available to Huck himself. We might describe this viewpoint as a post-Civil War perspective that exposes the ironic contradictions and limitations of a pre-Civil War narrator whose love for an individual slave does not allow him to see the problem with slavery in general.

In order to capture the sense that there is another point of view hidden behind or above Huck's, which allows us to glimpse a 'true' moral position that differs from Huck's ironized version, we need to employ a concept such as the **implied author**. The implied author needs to be distinguished from the real author because the implied author is not the original producer of the text but rather an *effect* of the text – an impression that it produces. The implied author, then, can only ever be a critical fiction – a rationalization of the impression we have in reading a novel (or perhaps in viewing a film) that we are being confided in by some specific human consciousness. Thus the idea of the implied author already presumes an understanding of novels as a kind of intimate speech. It might be, therefore, that the implied author is more the product of a particular way of reading than a way of reading in its own right. Furthermore, the distinction between implied author and real author is sometimes difficult to sustain in practice. It seems almost inevitable to say that the post-Civil War consciousness that is exposing the ironic dilemmas of the narrating character in *Huckleberry Finn* is none other than Mark Twain himself. Nonetheless, it also needs to be stressed that this is not a claim about authorial intention: a close reading of the text reveals that the text itself is working to ironize Huck's dilemma, even though there are no voices in the text from which that irony appears to originate. Thus it is possible to say that the text ironizes its own narrator, but problematic to claim that this was Twain's intention.

14.3.3 Ways of reading authorial games

Literary texts can be seen as elaborate games that authors and readers play together. Authors are continually reviving old games and making up new ones, and readers need to learn to identify these games and learn how to play them. In the Gothic novels that flourished in the second half of eighteenth-century Britain, for example, authors would often pretend that the novels they had written were actually ancient manuscripts that they had found and had edited for the general public to read. Most readers quickly learned that this game, presented in prefaces supposedly written by an 'editor', was part of the fiction and one of the conventions of the Gothic novel. Twenty-first century novelists also play versions of this game, especially in historical fiction. In *Voyageurs: A Novel* (2003), for example, Margaret Elphinstone begins her novel about a Quaker's voyage to North America in the eighteenth century with an 'Editor's Preface' in which the 'editor', who is mischievously identified as 'MNE', supposedly discovers a manuscript, written by the central character, which becomes the basis of the book. Yet, despite the fact that *Voyageurs* is subtitled '*A Novel*', many readers have assumed that Elphinstone really did find such a manuscript. In other words, it is important not to confuse such fictional 'editors' with real authors. Again, such an 'editor' is part of the text, part of the fiction, not the text's creator.

14.3.4 Does the identity of the author matter?

Knowing information about an author can often hinder rather than aid inter-pretation. Once readers discover that the Romantic poet Samuel Taylor Coleridge was addicted to opium they tend to see nothing else in his poems except the effects of that addiction. In other instances, making discoveries about an author's identity may have positive effects. For example, the realization that the nineteenth-century realist novelist George Eliot was actually a woman – Mary Ann Evans (1819–80) – may enhance or subtly change our response to her novels' moral analysis of nineteenth-century England. On the other hand, a great deal of ink has been wasted over the question of whether Shakespeare really wrote the plays and poetry that have been attributed to him or whether 'Shakespeare' was a pseudonym for another, more educated or higher-class person from the period. In this case, it does not seem to matter that we know little about Shakespeare the man: the texts themselves do the talking.

Having said this, it is inescapably the case that the name of the author is an important factor in the experience of reading. Knowing that we are reading a text by 'Shakespeare' has an impact – whether positive or negative – on our responses to that text. This is likely to be the case with all the 'great' or canon-ical writers we encounter. In a sense, the name of the author on the cover of a book is part of that book and shapes the way we read it. Different names will have different effects according to whether the author is famous or rela-tively unknown, whether or not we have read other books by the same author, or whether the author is male or female, from the past or the present, and so on. The name of the author – together with information on the cover – might signal his or her geographical or ethnic origins. Also, given the fact that the name of the author may carry such a range of influential connotations, we need to consider the contrary experience of reading anonymous texts, or texts that have been worked on by more than one author. And there are some cases where knowing the actual identity of an author concealed behind a nom-de-plume might have a significant impact on our response to a text. A stark example of this arises with the erotic classic *Story of O* (Paris, 1954), by 'Pauline Réage'. Given that the novel follows the experiences of a woman who subjects herself entirely to the whims of her 'master', it would seem important to know whether the text was written by a man or a woman – whether, that is, the name 'Pauline Réage' was a pseudonym for a male writer. In fact, as www.storyofo. co.uk reveals, this question has appeared urgent for many readers:

> The *Story of O* has surrounded itself with secrecy, mystery, and conjec-ture for fifty years. When it was published in Paris in 1954 it provoked all sorts of scandals and for forty years the true identity of its author 'Pauline Reage' (actually Dominique Aury) was kept secret by a handful of friends close to the writer. Speculation concerning the author's iden-tity produced many candidates, among them André Malraux, Henry de

Montherlant, Andre Pieyre de Mandiargues, Raymond Queneau, and Jean Paulhan for whom, it turns out, the book was actually written. The fact that it was written by a woman gives the novel, it has been said, a special 'diabolical' aura.

It is revealing that readers assumed that the real author of the novel must have been a man and that the revelation that it was actually a woman made the story seem all the more 'diabolical'. Yet the fact that it was written by a woman could be said to make it less 'diabolical' in that this knowledge allows us to see the book as a woman's bold exploration of aspects of female sexuality rather than as a man's fantasy about the exploitation of women.

ACTIVITY 14.1

The following text was written, anonymously, in France during the thirteenth century. In form, it is a motet (a musical composition for two, three or four voices, with each voice singing different words). The text – whose author remains unknown – was translated from Old French by Carol Cosman.

> I am a young girl
> graceful and gay,
> not yet fifteen when
> my sweet breasts may
> begin to swell;
>
> Love should be my contemplation,
> I should learn its indication,
>
> But I am put in prison.
> God's curse be on my jailor!
>
> Evil, villainy and sin
> did he
> to give up a girl like me
> to a nunnery;
>
> A wicked deed, by my faith,
> the convent life will be my death
>   My God! for I am far too young.
>
> Beneath my sash I feel the sweet pain.
> God's curse on him who made me a nun.

This activity concentrates on questions about who the author of the text might be (allowing for an informal use of the word 'author' to describe production of a text in the circumstances that are likely to have existed). You may find evidence as to the writer's identity in features of the text, in the description given at the beginning of the activity, or in what you know or can guess about historical circumstances of thirteenth-century France and about people of the time and the sorts of opportunities open to them.

1   Give any evidence that you can find (or can construct for yourself) for thinking that the speaker of the text is also the author.

2   Give any evidence that you can find (or construct for yourself) for thinking that the speaker of the text is *not* the author.

3   Are there aspects of your response to the poem that you believe are affected by the fact that it is (a) anonymous, (b) written for more than one voice, (c) written in the thirteenth century, and (d) a translation by a specific, named translator?

4   Now temporarily assume that the author is not, in any direct way, the speaker. Present any evidence that you can find (or construct) in support of the idea that the author was (a) a woman, or (b) a man.

5   Below are simple descriptions of two hypothetical authors. For each, describe how believing that this was the identity of the author would change how you read the poem (and the effects the poem has on you):

(a)   imagined author X = a 25-year-old male
(b)   imagined author Y = a 15-year-old female

Pay particular attention to sorts of effect you think may have been intended or anticipated by the author of the text, and sorts of response you are making to the text that could not have been anticipated by the text's author.

Reading

Burke, S. (ed.) (1995) *Authorship: From Plato to the Postmodern: A Reader*, Edinburgh: Edinburgh University Press.

Burke, S. (1998 [1992]) *The Death and Return of the Author: Criticism and Subjectivity in Barthes, Foucault and Derrida*, 2nd edn, Edinburgh: Edinburgh University Press.

Caughie, J. (ed.) (1981) *Theories of Authorship: A Reader*, London: Routledge & Kegan Paul and the British Film Institute.

Irwin, William (ed.) (2002) *The Death and Resurrection of the Author?*, Westwood, CT and London: Greenwood Press.

Leitch, Vincent B. (ed.) (2001) *The Norton Anthology of Theory and Criticism*, New York and London: Norton. See all the essays on authorship, including the essays by Barthes, Eliot, Foucault, and Wimsatt and Beardsley mentioned in this unit.

Newton-de Molina, D. (ed.) (1976) *On Literary Intention*, Edinburgh: Edinburgh University Press.

Unit 15

Positioning the reader or spectator

The meaning of a text is produced in a complex negotiation between the reader and the text. It cannot be said that one contributes more than the other, and much recent theorizing suggests a finely balanced negotiation between the two in terms of who or what determines the interpretation or meaning that the reader arrives at. Nevertheless, although it is clear that readers bring a great deal of background information with them, which they use in order to construct a 'reading' of a text, the focus of this unit is on the way that texts address or position their readers. Texts address readers in a variety of ways, either by directly addressing them, or by indirectly encouraging them to agree with certain statements.

15.1 The implied reader

It is important to distinguish between the actual reader of any text and its **implied reader**. The actual reader is any person who reads the text, but the implied reader is an ideal or optimum figure that the text anticipates or constructs. In this sense, the implied reader is rather like a role that the real reader is encouraged to adopt, providing a 'position' from which the real reader can interpret the text. For example, in the following extract from Joseph Conrad's *Heart of Darkness* (1902), the main narrator (Marlow) makes the following statement:

> It is queer how out of touch with truth women are. They live in a world of their own, and there has never been anything like it, and never can be. It is too beautiful altogether, and if they were to set it up it would go to pieces before the first sunset. Some confounded fact we men have been living contentedly with ever since the day of creation would start up and knock the whole thing over.

Marlow is the main protagonist and narrator of this novel, and in general his views are not overly challenged by other views. It seems as if he as narrator and character is given a position from which the 'truth' of the situation is given (Rimmon-Kenan, 1983; Toolan, 2001). The role that the reader is called upon to adopt here – that of the implied reader – is in fact a masculine role: this is cued for the reader by the use of 'we men', a reference that includes Marlow and a group of men that comprises his audience on board a boat, together with the novel's male readers. It is also cued by the reference to 'women' as 'they', which signals to the reader that the narrator is referring to a group to which 'we' do not belong. The reader here may also be drawn into agreeing with what is said about women, since the statements are not modified in any way by qualifying phrases such as 'I think' or 'Maybe', or by counter-statements from Marlow's listeners. The narrator's views about women come from a position in which it is 'common sense', a 'matter of fact', that 'women . . . are out of touch with truth', that 'they live in a world of their own' and so on. In this way, there-fore, we can say that the (actual) reader of *Heart of Darkness* is drawn into a position (that of the implied reader) where the obviousness of these stereotypes about women may be taken for granted.[1] However, that is not to say that we as readers have to agree with these views and we may well distance ourselves as real readers while recognizing the position of the implied reader.

15.2 Direct address

Most texts present themselves as ignoring the presence of a reader. Yet some texts do address the reader in a direct manner, for example, by calling him or her 'dear reader' or 'you'. Advertisements in particular often address the reader in a very direct manner, as the following caption in *New!* magazine demonstrates:

> Copy these A-listers and get your hair to shine by nourishing it both inside and out.
>
> (*New!*, April 2005)

This calls upon the reader directly by first ordering her to 'copy' celebrities, addressing her as 'you' and by referring to 'your hair'. It makes assumptions about the reader that she can be included in a group of people who are concerned about their hair shining and it also assumes that she would like to emulate famous celebrities who have shining hair. Some texts also address only a small proportion of their potential audience, as in the following advert for the Chocolate Tasting Club:

> ATTENTION ALL CHOCOLATE ENTHUSIASTS! WHY DO WE LOVE IT SO MUCH? YOUR CHOCOLATE BLISS POINT EXPLAINED. THE MOST DELICIOUS DRINKING CHOCOLATE YOU WILL EVER TASTE.

Since this advert was distributed fairly widely, it might be assumed that it is addressing all people who like chocolate; however, nearly all of the images within the advertisement are of women eating chocolate. Furthermore, this notion that the advert is primarily addressed to women is affirmed since the language used is that of sexual seduction ('good chocolate seduces . . . flooding our senses with a deep pleasure'; 'voluptuous . . . lusciously wicked') and there is a history of adverts that equate chocolate with sexual stimulation for women Thus, while the direct address is to 'we' and 'you', the implied reader is in fact restricted to women who like chocolate. Thus, the real reader and the implied reader may not always match up. However, as will be argued in the next section, although the reader is relegated to the position of an 'overhearer', this still may have an effect on him or her, by encouraging them to agree with particular statements or ideas.

Direct address can also be found in novels. Mark Twain's *The Adventures of Huckleberry Finn* (1884), for example, begins with Huck as narrator introducing himself to the reader: 'You don't know about me, without you have read a book by the name of *The Adventures of Tom Sawyer*, but that ain't no matter.' The narrator of Herman Melville's *Moby Dick* (1851) begins by inviting the reader to 'Call me Ishmael' and then takes the reader on an imaginary journey, asking the reader to look and to respond to rhetorical questions. Sometimes, novels address the reader as 'reader' – the most famous example is perhaps the first sentence in the last chapter of Charlotte Brontë's *Jane Eyre* (1847): 'Reader, I married him.' Such strategies of direct address work to position the reader in relation to the text and to the narrator, although the precise implications of this need to be worked out in each case.

Even plays, which generally present the action and dialogue as if there were no audience or reader, may sometimes include a character who directly addresses the reader/audience. Such a character, sometimes operating as the **chorus**, is often detached from the play's action and acts as a type of narrator. The chorus in Shakespeare's *Henry V* asks the members of the audience to use their imagination to help the players present large-scale historical actions on the stage:

> . . . let us, ciphers to the great account,
> On your imaginary forces work.
> Suppose within the girdle of these walls
> Are now confined two mighty monarchies.

Yet, we need to be wary of assuming that all instances in which a text addresses someone in the second person (you) are directly addressing the reader. In poetry, for example, instances of direct address are more likely to refer to what is called the 'addressee' than to the reader. In other words, many poems are addressed to someone other than the reader.

15.3 Indirect address

While some texts address their readers directly by the use of 'you', others engage the reader in more subtle ways by the use of **indirect address**. An important aspect of the use of indirect address is the invocation of background knowledge and assumptions. All texts, even the most simple and explicit, assume some degree of shared knowledge between the reader and the producer of the text. Sometimes, these knowledges or ideas are presented as if the reader is bound to agree with them, or are based upon implicit assumptions that prove difficult to object to.

For example, in an advertisement for Lil-lets tampons, which is headlined 'Lil-lets: the art of the self-protection' and which shows in the background two women engaged in martial arts, it is assumed that the reader will bring to bear quite particular background assumptions about menstruation. The advertisement shows a ball and chain in the foreground, representing the women as being imprisoned by periods, together with the statement 'the small key to freedom'. It is assumed that the reader will agree with the implicit assertion that periods are imprisoning, that menstruation is something that women want to be 'discreet' about, and that Lil-lets are a way out of this imprisonment (represented by Lil-lets as a key to the clasp on the chain). Even those women who do not in fact see their periods in such a negative way will, in order to make sense of the text, be led to draw on this shared knowledge about menstruation. (See Laws, 1990, for further discussion.)

15.4 Dominant readings

Recent theorizing of interpreting texts, particularly in cultural/media studies, has drawn on Stuart Hall's work on encoding and decoding (Hall, 1973; Van Zoonan, 1994). This assumes that the message that is encoded in the text by the author is not the same as the message that is decoded by the reader. However, it is possible to argue that there are clues to what might constitute a **dominant reading**, that is, the reading that seems to be self-evident; it is the one that is ratified by common sense or by other ideologies that are available within the society of the time. Thus, rather than simply assuming that the reader will have certain knowledges to make sense of the text, the dominant reading makes sense only through drawing on larger 'stories' circulating through society. For example, many texts have a dominant reading that accords with conventional notions of femininity.

In an advertisement for Lancôme eye make-up, the dominant reading is that women who want to look like the person depicted should use Lancôme eye make-up. On the right of the advertisement there is a representation of a beautiful woman and to the left are the words 'L'origine. Pebble grey, moss green, cedar wood, senna brown. These are the subtle harmonies of original colour, colours drawn from Nature herself.' Below this there is a representation of the eye make-up and this is linked to the depiction of the woman by Lancome's trademark rose motif.

In order to make sense of this advertisement, we have to decode a range of elements: first, that the natural is good. This is signalled by the inclusion of reference to colours that are 'drawn from Nature herself' and named after natural substances (pebble grey, cedar wood). It is also signalled by the inclusion of the Lancôme trademark, which is a white stylized rose running horizontally across the image, linking the woman and the make-up. The juxta-position (see **Unit 12**) of the woman, natural elements, the supposedly 'natural' make-up and the fact that Nature is referred to as 'her' produces a dominant reading of this text, which offers itself for interpretation in ways that suggest the following kinds of connections between elements:

- the make-up is coloured in the same way as nature;
- natural ingredients are good;
- feminine women have a special relationship with nature;
- women who would like to be thought to be feminine will buy the make-up.

These are not statements that the text makes explicitly, but in order to make coherent sense of this very fragmented text the reader has to draw on these larger discourses about femininity and its relation to the natural. In this way, therefore, ideological assumptions that circulate and constitute systems of shared knowledge allow the preferred sense of a particular text to seem self-evident.[2]

While a text will normally proffer one particular preferred or dominant reading, there is always the potential for other, contrary readings of the same text, as will be explored later. However, in order to make sense of the text as a coherent whole, the dominant reading is the one that readers can generally recognize easily and that they may therefore choose, unless they have political or personal reasons for challenging this reading.

15.5 Gender and positioning

The space or position that a text offers to a reader from which it makes most sense may be of various kinds, but one kind of position that has received particular attention of a critical and searching kind relates to the gender of the reader.

15.5.1 Positioning of the reader as male

Feminists such as Judith Fetterley (1981) and Elaine Showalter (1977) argue that, when women read literature, they often read as men, precisely because literature often constructs the implied reader as male. Thus, women readers often assent to background assumptions that are actually the shared assumptions of males, masquerading as a kind of general knowledge that 'we all know' to be true. So, for example, when women readers read the passage from Conrad cited on page 183, they may read it without questioning the sexism contained in the text since it accords with stereotypical background assumptions.

In the text below – an advertising flyer for Trippet's Nail and Tan – there are a number of assumptions about girls that the reader has to agree with in order to make sense of the text:

> Lost for an idea for a children's party ? Look no further. Trippet's nail and tan are now available for children's beauty parties. £12 per head (includes goody bag). Treatments available – mini manicure and polish, nail art, mini facial, make-up samplings, temporary body tattoos. Full makeover for party girl.

First, the reader has to assume that children's parties could include such things as body tattooing and that girls should be trained in this way to see that they need to have beauty treatments. It assumes that, in much the same way as boys are given parties that involve swimming or ten pin bowling, girls' sense of enjoyment should come from concentrating on their appearance. This background knowledge is not made explicit, but the reader is forced to construct it and the reader may feel some sense of disjuncture between their own sense of what is appropriate for children and the seemingly 'common-sense' assumptions about girls that are articulated here.

Similarly, in film theory it has been argued (see Mulvey, 1981) that women characters in many Hollywood films are posed as objects 'to-be-looked-at'.[3] The camera focuses on women characters from the perspective of male characters, and it is often a very sexualized vision of the women that is produced. This means that women spectators watching these films have to watch them as if they were male voyeurs. This may be a pleasurable experience for women spectators, but it may also make the woman spectator complicit with assumptions about women that she may not ordinarily share (see Stacey, 1994).

15.6 The resisting reader

At the same time, no account of the positioning of the reader would be complete without some attention to the way readers may also generate alternative readings. One influential approach to alternative readings is that developed by

Judith Fetterley (1981) around the term the **resisting reader**, that is, a reader who does not accept the assumptions and knowledges that the text presents in the dominant reading, but resists them to construct an oppositional reading. Both male and female readers can read critically or oppositionally, as Jonathan Culler (1983) has shown, but it is often more in a woman's interest to read in this way. Thus with the Conrad text discussed earlier (pp. 183–4), a resisting reader will focus on the assumptions that seem to make the text intelligible (for example, by focusing on the use and effects of 'they' and 'we').

In the following extract from a song by Neil Hannon of The Divine Comedy (1997) it is possible to trace two distinct readings, a dominant reading and a resisting reading:

If . . .

If you were the road I'd go all the way
If you were the night I'd sleep in the day
If you were the day I'd cry in the night
'Cause you are the way the truth and the light
If you were a tree I could put my arms around you
And you could not complain
If you were a tree I could carve my name into your side
And you would not cry, 'cause trees don't cry

If you were a man I'd still love you
If you were a drink I'd drink my fill of you
If you were attacked I would kill for you
If your name was Jack I'd change mine to Jill for you
If you were a horse I'd clean the crap out of your stable
And never once complain
If you were a horse I could ride you through the fields at dawn
Through the day until the day was gone
I could sing about you in my songs
As we rode away into the setting sun

If you were my little girl I would find it hard to let you go
If you were my sister I would find it doubly so
If you were a dog I'd feed you scraps from off the table
Though my wife complains
If you were my dog I am sure you'd like it better
Then you'd be my loyal four-legged friend
You'd never have to think again
And we could be together 'til the end.

The dominant reading of this song is shaped by a series of conditional propositions that involve the reader and the narrator in a series of statements that map out a position whereby the singer and the audience are assumed to share certain attitudes towards romance. The reader is directly addressed here, so that he or she has to decide as to whether he or she takes up the position of the 'I' or the 'you', the addresser or the addressee. However, the content of the song is not simple: at one and the same time, the singer articulates an excessively romantic form of love, while ironizing the grounds on which those romantic utterances are made. In some ways, the singer, in true postmodernist fashion, can be seen to be pushing the expression of romantic feeling beyond the realms of current discursive norms in that, instead of comparing the person he loves to flowers and birds, he compares her to horses and dogs. In this lies the humour of the song since the singer uses the sort of language that is generally not permissible within romantic songs (for example, 'crap') and also makes statements such as 'If you were a man I'd still love you'. In this reading of the song, the singer is making excessive, humorous statements that the reader is expected to find ironizing and funny.

The resisting reading of this song would take issue with this position of postmodernist ironizing, since its playful instability seems to offer no basis from which to criticize the song. However, in this seemingly playful song, the woman is objectified just as in more openly sexist songs – she is represented as a loyal dog who is given scraps, a passive horse who is ridden, a tree on whom the singer carves his name, or a drink that is consumed by the singer (albeit in this slightly distanced, conditional form). Perhaps the oddest line in the song is in the final stanza: 'If you were a dog I'd feed you scraps from off the table / Though my wife complains'. If the loved one were a dog she would be loyal and would 'never have to think again'. Female agency is deleted in this song, even though on the surface it seems to be gesturing towards a more playful and anti-sexist interpretation.[4]

Resisting readings may be produced for most texts, and may focus on the representation of a range of issues, such as race, class and sexual preference. For example, Cora Kaplan has questioned the way that white women have assumed that Alice Walker's *The Color Purple* refers to women in general rather than Black women in particular, and she challenges the universalizing discussions there have been of the book, which erase the discussion of race issues that the text raises (Kaplan, 1986). Lesbian readers might argue for a foregrounding of the elements in the text that focus on the female characters' love for one another (Hobby and White, 1991). In a similar way, some post-colonial theorists have begun to reread canonical literary texts in order to focus on elements such as slavery and complicity in colonialism, which earlier readers of the texts in the past have overlooked or tried to ignore (Said, 1993). Other post-colonial critics have analysed the way that Eurocentrism pervades much of the representational practices within Western culture (Shohat and Stam, 1994).[5] Adopting such an approach, the reader can first trace and describe the dominant reading of the text and then refuse this particular position in order to focus on other elements of the text. In this way, the reader is positively enabled and encouraged to assume power and responsibility in relation to the text and to the determination of its meaning. Instead of the traditional view of the reader as a passive recipient of information, the reader is enabled to construct meaning for him- or herself.

ACTIVITY 15.1

The following is a horoscope from the *Observer* Magazine (2005) for Libra and Aquarius:

Libra: There's quite a change unfolding now, what with the professional pressure back on and some patient, tender handling of your personal life being called for. Take care with your words; this week they can carry extra clout and can hurt. The Libran Moon on Friday/Saturday brings emotional issues to a combustible climax; you might as well go for broke, in every respect except financially.

Aquarius: Work: even if you are not in education, a teaching role plays in your favour. You'll have to bi-locate like a Gemini in order to field imminent information overload. Good time to sign contracts, do deals. Home: about to become one heck of a sight busier. Romance, not tonight Josephine – but you can raise quite a rumpus come Friday and Saturday. Yes, you wild thing. Enjoy.

1 Construct a number of different readers' lives for whom these predictions could be made to fit (i.e. someone thinking of leaving a relationship; someone thinking of changing jobs; for example, consider the range of interpretations for, in the Aquarius section, 'a teaching role plays in your favour' and, in the Libra section, 'you might as well go for broke').

2 Find evidence for things the readers of this horoscope share (for example, income, class, age, relationship).

Notes

1 It might be asserted that on the whole Marlow as a narrator is less than reliable, and therefore these statements cannot be taken at face value; however, his assertions about women do not seem to be subject to the same questioning as other statements that he makes in the novel.

2 There are further assumptions that are perhaps even more deeply embedded in the message of the text to do with race, and these are really at a higher discourse

level of interpretation. The fact that Black models are rarely used in advertisements for beauty products entails that femininity, or at least the seemingly universal femininity that is referred to in this advertisement, is constructed as white femininity.

3   The model in the Lancôme advertisement we discussed previously has adopted the position of a woman who is to-be-looked at, in that she is not engaging in eye contact with the implied reader, but is presenting herself as an aesthetic object.

4   I would like to thank Keith Green and Jill LeBihan for bringing this example to my notice.

5   Eurocentrism is the form of thinking that makes an implicit assumption that other countries are lacking in relation to a Western norm. This involves viewing other countries not in their own terms, but weighed against Western criteria, such as industrial development and scientific achievement, which in other environments are not appropriate. Thus, small-scale self-sufficient communities in Latin America are judged to be lacking because they have not developed a certain type of technology appropriate to the Western world.

Reading

Fetterley, J. (1981) *The Resisting Reader: A Feminist Approach to American Fiction*, Bloomington, IN: Indiana University Press.

Mills, S. (ed.) (1994) *Gendering the Reader*, Hemel Hempstead: Harvester Wheatsheaf.

Mills, S. (1996) *Feminist Stylistics*, London: Routledge.

Toolan, M. (2001) *Narrative: A Critical Linguistic Introduction*, 2nd edn, London: Routledge.

Van Zoonan, L. (1994) *Feminist Media Studies*, London: Sage.

Poetic form

Unit 16

Rhyme and sound patterning

In the process of reading words on a page, we translate visual marks (letters) into mental representations of sounds (phones, or phonemes). English uses a 'phonetic-alphabetic script' in which letters stand for sounds, or serve to represent particular patterns of sound. For example, the letter 'p' in 'pin' stands for a single sound (which we write phonetically as [p]); the two letters 'th' in 'thin' stand for a single sound (which we write phonetically as [θ]); the letter 'i' in 'time' stands for a combination of sounds called a diphthong (which we write phonetically as [a ɪ]). We can represent the way a word is made up of sounds using a phonetic script, and so can compare the letter-spelling of a word with the phonetic structure of the word:

letter-spelling:	thing	queen	come
phonetic structure:	θ ɪ ŋ	k w i n	k ʌ m

In this unit we are interested in the phonetic structure of words rather than their spelling. Because of the relatively small number of distinct sounds used in a language, the sounds of a text inevitably occur and recur as we read. and make up a kaleidoscope of repetitions and permutations. In casual conversation and most kinds of written texts, this repetition of sounds occurs for the most part apparently randomly, ordered only by the historical accidents governing which sounds make up which words. However, it is also possible for speakers and writers to organize the sounds of utterances in more systematic ways – ranging from motivated but irregular instances through to fully predictable patterns – in order to achieve certain effects. Many different types of discourse employ such sound patterning: poetry, jokes, slogans, proverbs, advertising copy, sound-bites in political speeches and interviews, pop lyrics, rapping, etc.

16.1 The structure of the syllable

In **Unit 17** we will see that the metrical form of a poem involves control over the syllables of the line, and syllables are also relevant for the organization of sound patterning. Rhyme and alliteration, the two basic kinds of sound patterning, involve different parts of the syllable. A syllable is divided into three parts (of which only the nucleus is essential): the onset, the nucleus and the coda. Table 16.1 illustrates this division of the syllable into three parts, using monosyllabic words.

Table 16.1

Onset	Nucleus	Coda	
b	a ɪ	t	bite
f	a ɪ	t	fight
pl	a ɪ	t	plight
spl	æ	t	splat
p	e ɪ	st	paste
p	e ɪ		pay
	æ	t	at
	a ɪ		I

This table shows us several things about syllables and sounds.

1   An onset can have anything from zero to three consonants, while a coda usually has between zero and two consonants. But there is always a nucleus.

2   The number of written letters before or after the nucleus is irrelevant; syllable structure is a matter of sound and not spelling and so both 'bite' and 'fight' have a one-consonant coda.

3   While the nucleus of a syllable is almost always a vowel, there are some written vowels that are not syllable nuclei because they are not pronounced as vowels: thus 'paste' is a monosyllalic word based on the nucleus vowel [a], and the final written 'e' is irrelevant to the syllable structure.

The nucleus of the syllable is usually a vowel. Sometimes the nucleus of the syllable is a diphthong, which is two vowels pronounced together as in 'wheel', which is a single-syllable word with a two-vowel diphthong as its nucleus (in phonetic representation it is [i ə]). The nucleus can also be a highly 'sonorant' consonant; sonorance is a vocal quality of vowels, but some consonants such as [r] and [l] and the nasal consonants [m] and [n] also have sonorance and so they can be syllable nuclei. For example, the word 'bottle' has two syllables, the second of which has [l] as its nucleus.

16.2 Types of sound pattern: types of rhyme and types of alliteration

We can group the various kinds of sound patterning into larger groups, which we can call types of rhyme and types of alliteration. Types of rhyme involve the end of the syllable, while types of alliteration involve the beginning of the syllable.

Strict rhyme involves the [nucleus+coda]. Thus 'bite', 'plight' and 'fight' (from Table 16.1) could all rhyme, because they have the same nucleus and coda. Where just the [nucleus] is repeated, and the coda varies, this is 'assonance'. While 'I' does not rhyme with 'bite' because the coda is different, the identity of nucleus makes this an example of assonance. Where just the [coda] is repeated, and the nucleus varies, this is 'consonance'. Though 'at' does not rhyme with 'bite' because the nucleus is different, the similarity of coda makes this an example of 'consonance'. Various issues relating to rhyme can be examined by using the following stanzas.

> Hail to thee, blithe spirit!
> Bird thou never wert,
> That from heaven, or near it,
> Pourest thy full heart
> In profuse strains of unpremeditated art.
>
> Higher still and higher,
> From the earth thou springest
> Like a cloud of fire;
> the blue deep thou wingest,
> And singing still dost soar, and soaring ever singest.
>   (Percy Bysshe Shelley, 'To a Skylark', 1820)

In the first stanza there is an exact repetition in 'heart' and 'art', which is a rhyme (because nucleus+coda are the same in both words). Is 'wert' part of the same rhyme? One question we might ask is whether Shelley *pronounced* this word as he pronounced 'heart': vowels have changed in the course of the history of English, and a pair of words might once have rhymed even if they do not rhyme now. (However, a check of a contemporary edition of Walker's Pronouncing Dictionary shows that 'wert' and 'heart' are listed at that time as having different pronunciations, at least in one standard accent of English.) If he did not pronounce these words alike, then we could describe this as an example of consonance with 'heart': consonance is the repetition of just [coda], here the final consonant [t] (or [rt] if the r is pronounced as it is in some accents). It is often the case that a consonance is 'upgraded' to count as a rhyme, if there is supportive evidence. If we look at the rest of the poem – including the second stanza quoted here – we find that the second, fourth and fifth lines characteristically rhyme with each other, and this gives us some reason to think of the 'wert'/'heart' match as a slightly defective rhyme rather than as a true consonance. In this way we see that – just as in metre – the abstract description of the form as 'rhyme' conceals some variation in actual pronunciation. We might similarly allow 'spirit' and 'near it' to count as rhyme; here we have a shared sequence of nucleus-onset-nucleus-coda, thus involving two syllables. This kind of rhyme, where two syllables are involved and where the first syllable is stressed and the second is unstressed is called a **feminine rhyme**. Rhymes involving just a final stressed syllable are called masculine rhymes. Rhyme is often used systematically in English verse, and we say that a poem can have a 'rhyme scheme', which for this poem would be written down as ABABB for each stanza, showing which lines rhyme in each five-line stanza. Some types of rhyme scheme have their own names: AABBCC, etc. patterns are called 'couplets' and AAABBB, etc., 'triplets'. Combinations of specific metres with specific rhymes also have specific names: the combination of iambic pentameter with (rhyme) couplets is called 'heroic verse', while the use of iambic pentameter *without* rhyme is called 'blank verse'. Special types of stanza also have specific rhyme schemes, and poetic genres such as the sonnet have specific rhyme schemes. Finally, remember that sounds (not spellings) produce rhyme, so 'cough' rhymes with 'off', not with 'plough'. Words like 'cough' and 'plough', whose spelling suggests they ought to rhyme, are called 'eye-rhymes'.

The second major class of sound patterning is **alliteration**, which in its prototypical form involves repetition of the onset, as in 'paste' and 'pay', or 'plaster' and 'plight'. For the most part in English, we can say that there is alliteration if just the first consonant in the onset is repeated. This is the kind of alliteration we see in Shelley's poem: 'pourest' and 'profuse' and 'blithe' and 'bird'. In a stricter variant the whole onset must be repeated, so that 'blithe' and 'bird' would not alliterate with each other, but 'blithe' and 'blood' or 'bide' and 'bird' would alliterate. In a third variant, the onset must be in the first stressed syllable of the word, which can be seen in the notion of the 'three Rs': 'reading, writing and arithmetic'. Here the 'r' in each word is the complete onset of the first stressed syllable in the word (in 'arithmetic' this syllable is the second actual syllable in the word). A fourth variant of alliteration involves not only the onset but also the nucleus, as in 'cash' and 'carry'. Leech (1969) calls this 'reverse rhyme'; it is the standard type of alliteration (or reverse rhyme) in, for example, Finnish and Mongolian poetry (but is not common in English poetry). If we look at the alliteration in Shelley's poem we see that, although it is quite widespread, it is not systematic: we could not talk about an 'alliteration scheme' to parallel the rhyme scheme in the poem. In fact, English poetry has not had systematic alliteration since the medieval period (it is the rule in Old English poetry, was revived in the Middle Ages, and is occasionally imitated in later poetry). In analysing alliteration it is particularly important to remember that you are analysing sounds and not letters: 'seek' and 'shape' do not alliterate with each other because they begin with different sounds (even though their spelling makes them look similar). There is, however, a tradition of using line-initial (or stanza-initial) letters as an organizatory device; while this is not a kind of alliteration, because it uses letters and not sounds, it is worth noting. The Latin poem *Altus Prosatur* (written in Iona in the sixth century) has each stanza beginning with a different letter of the alphabet, and is called an 'abecedarian' poem.

Thus we can broadly distinguish between rhyme as the repetition of the end of the syllable (and usually the end of the word) as opposed to alliteration as the repetition of the beginning of the syllable (and usually the beginning of the word). It is technically possible to have both the beginning and the end of the syllable repeated; this is called 'pararhyme' (and sometimes also called 'consonance') and is seen in 'send' and 'sound', or 'beat' and 'bite'.

16.3 The significance of sound patterns

So far, we have simply identified possible patterns and presented ways of describing them. In order to investigate how such patterns work as a stylistic resource, we need now to consider what kind of significance or function they might have. Five alternative possibilities are presented below. Each possibility should be considered for each case of sound patterning identified in a text:

(1)   Patterning may serve no particular function, and be simply the accidental result of a random distribution of the small number of distinct sounds that make up the language. This is especially likely in spontaneous conversation. It is also likely where there is some closeness in the text between instances of the sound taken to create the effect: functional sound patterning depends on proximity between the words involved, since readers (or listeners) are unlikely to recognize sounds repeated far apart. Moving to a more formal type of description (see Fabb, 1997), we can express this another way by saying that a closeness constraint seems to operate on some or all kinds of sound patterning, and that this closeness constraint seems required in order to ensure that such patterning is noticeable or perceptually 'salient'.

(2)   Patterning may serve a 'cohesive' function, bonding words together as formulaic, fixed phrases or units. This extra bonding at the level of sound can enhance the memorability of an utterance, as in riddles, catch phrases and proverbs ('action-packed'; 'a stitch in time saves nine'; 'be Indian, buy Indian', etc.).

(3)   Patterning may have the effect of emphasizing or 'foregrounding' some aspect of the text. Sometimes patterning that involves repetition serves to make a passage seem as though it expresses great feeling, as is often the case in political rhetoric. Sometimes the physical existence of the utterance as a linguistic

construct is emphasized, as in the case of tongue twisters such as the alliterative 'Peter Piper picked a peck of pickled peppercorns'. Notice incidentally that the alliteration here is set against a kind of counter-alliteration (the [p] sound and the [k] sound are made at opposite ends of the mouth), which is what creates the tongue twister.

(4) Patterning may have the effect of creating or reinforcing a parallelism. In this case, words that are linked together on the basis of shared sounds will also be linked in terms of their meanings (they typically have similar or opposite meanings). This technique is common in jokes, advertising and some types of poetry (e.g. Augustan verse). Consider, from this point of view, such phrases as 'chalk and cheese' and 'cash and carry'; or recall Blake's 'marks of weakness, marks of woe', for an example of this effect in Romantic poetry (see **Unit 3, Analysing units of structure**).

(5) Patterning may contribute **sound symbolism**. Such effects are based on a belief that the sounds that make up words are not arbitrarily related to their meaning, as most linguists think, but are motivated in some way by being loaded with resonance or connotational value.

A number of points are worth noting about the notion of sound symbolism:

(a) The linguistic view that the sounds of language are arbitrary is supported by evidence such as the fact that the same meaning is expressed in different languages by words with very different sounds ('tree', 'arbre', 'Baum', etc.), and that the sounds of words change over time. Such evidence suggests that sounds are merely conventional aspects of the formal system of a language.

(b) The view that sounds in language may have symbolic meanings or expressive effects, on the other hand, is based on a musical belief that sound itself carries meaning, as well as on the idea that individual sounds are felt differently because the way we make them with the voice differs for each sound. Consider three types of much-discussed evidence for this:

(i) Here are three imaginary but possible 'words': 'la', 'li' and 'lor'. If you had three tables of different sizes to label with these words, which would you call which? Research has shown that most people – across a wide range of different cultures – label the small table 'li', the middle-sized one 'la' and the largest 'lor'. This tendency probably reflects the fact that sounds are made differently in the mouth: 'lor' is a 'big' sound (mouth open, tongue back, large mouth cavity); 'li', by contrast, is a 'small' sound (mouth relatively closed, tongue up and forward, etc.).

(ii)   Some groups of words have both their sound and their general area of meaning in common (this effect is traditionally called 'onomatopoeia'): 'clatter', 'clang' and 'clash' all suggest one thing striking against another; 'sneeze', 'snore', 'snooze' and 'sniffle' are all to do with breathing through the nose and might be considered to sound like the actions they refer to (though consider 'snow' and 'snap' as counter-examples).

(iii)   Consider the hypothesis of a gradience of linguistic sounds, from 'hard' through to 'soft'. The so-called hardest sounds include [p], [b], [t], [d], [k] and [g] (these are technically called stops or plosives and all involve completely stopping breath coming out of the mouth, then releasing it suddenly). The so-called softest sounds are the vowels (which do not impede the air-flow out of the mouth at all, but simply reshape it), plus sounds like those commonly produced from the letters 'w' and 'l'. The idea that words contain hard and soft sounds is sometimes then used as the basis for making an equation between sound and meaning.

(c)   Sound symbolism involves attributing conventional meanings or resonances to sound patterns. In Keats's famous line in 'To Autumn' (1820), 'Thou watchest the last oozings hours by hours', the repeated 's' and 'z' sounds are often taken to represent the oozing of cider in the press. In an equally well-known line from Tennyson, 'The murmuring of innumerable bees' ('The Princess' [1853]), the repeated 'm' sounds are taken to represent the sound of bees. These associations of sound and meaning are not fixed, however: the sounds 's' and 'z' could equally be taken to stand for the buzzing of bees if they were in a poem about bees. Meaning thus contributes significantly to the apparent effect of sound symbolism in a poem.

16.4 Making interpretations on the basis of sound patterns

Having looked at how sound patterns may function, we need to consider how the identification of sound patterning can be used in ways of reading, and to assess some of the possibilities and problems involved in doing this.

Understanding the conventions of many idioms or genres requires that we recognize aspects of their use of sound patterning. Contemporary rapping involves rhyming as one of its main organizational principles; and headlines and advertising slogans have characteristic ways of using sound patterns. Many texts written within established literary traditions draw on conventions of sound patterning (and sometimes sound symbolism) as a conventional compositional resource. Traditions of interpretation of these texts also draw on the same network of conventions.

The conventional register of poetic language has itself fluctuated through-out its history in terms of its use of sound patterning. Some periods and poets have preferred highly complex effects, such as Gerard Manley Hopkins, whose sound patterning is evident in the opening lines of 'The Windhover' (1877; published 1918):

I caught this morning morning's minion, king
Dom of daylight's dauphin, dapple-dawn-drawn Falcon, in his riding
Of the rolling level underneath him steady air, and striding
High there, how he rung upon the rein of a wimpling wing
In his ecstasy!

Such complexity of sound patterning contrasts strongly with, for instance, Wordsworth's aspiration for poetic language (or 'diction') to approximate to the ordinary language of speech, famously presented in the 'Preface to *Lyrical Ballads*' (1802) roughly half a century earlier. We should nevertheless be careful about generalizations about the contribution made by sound patterning to poetic styles. This is partly because sound patterning intersects in complex ways with rhythm and other aspects of register; it is also partly because writers are not always consistent in their practice.

Wordsworth's co-authorship of the *Lyrical Ballads* with Samuel Taylor Coleridge, for instance, did not stop Coleridge less than two decades later producing one of the most celebrated instances of intricate sound patterning in English verse – the first lines of 'Kubla Khan' (1816):

In Xanadu did Kubla Khan
    A stately pleasure-dome decree:
Where Alph, the sacred river, ran
Through caverns measureless to man
    Down to a sunless sea.

Earlier in this unit, we named various types of sound pattern that can emerge in a text. These labels are useful if they help us to describe sound patterning; but in the actual analysis of texts it often seems that there are no clear-cut boundaries between sound effects. Rhyme, assonance and consonance are mixed together not as a repertoire of separate devices but in a texture of complex and interconnected patterning. Consider the lines from 'Kubla Khan' above in this respect. If you try simply to list instances of sound patterning, you quickly run into difficulties (including difficulties that are the result of language variation as well as language change). Does the vowel in 'Khan' in the first line, for instance, assonate with 'Kubla' (and possibly with 'Xanadu')? Or does it rhyme with the first vowel in 'Xanadu'?

In attempting to interpret sound patterns, it is useful to distinguish between fairly systematic and predictable patterns that serve to define a form (such as rhyme schemes and local kinds of ornamentation), and patterns that have locally marked effects and seem to have expressive or symbolic functions (such as extra memorability or special suggestiveness). One problem with trying to interpret this second kind of pattern is that the expressive or symbolic significance of sound effects cannot simply be read off from a text in a series of mechanical equations between sound and sense (see the examples from Keats and Tennyson on p. 201). A sequence of words beginning with the same sound may suggest one thing in one context and quite a different thing in another. The context and meanings of words that appear to create local, expressive effects should therefore take priority. Only after considering these is it safe to suggest ways in which the sound might support (or perhaps undercut) the sense.

More generally, it is rarely, if ever, possible to prove an effect of sound patterning or sound symbolism. Caution is therefore needed in putting forward interpretive arguments based on the connotations or symbolic qualities of sounds. Arguments regarding the expressive or symbolic qualities of sound in a text are persuasive only when they are based on some mutual reinforcement that can be shown between properties of the text at different levels (between its sounds, grammatical structures, vocabulary, etc.), rather than when appeals are made either directly to fixed symbolic values for sounds, or to a reader's personal sense of a sound's resonance.

Finally, when writing about a text, there is little point in simply listing aspects of its sound patterning (e.g. its rhyme scheme, or the fact that two words alliterate). Comments along these lines only become interesting when linked to one of two kinds of argument: either as a contribution to the identification of a genre or form, where for some reason this is in question or worth establishing; or else to support a case for some local interpretation, where the evocative effect of the sound connects with other indicators of what is meant.

ACTIVITY 16.1

These are the final two stanzas of Edmund Spenser's *The Faerie Queene* (1609):

> When I bethinke me on that speech whyleare,
> Of *Mutability*, and well it way:
> Me seemes, that though she all unworthy were
> Of the Heav'ns Rule; yet very sooth to say,
> In all things else she beares the greatest sway.
> Which makes me loath this state of life so tickle,
> And loue of things so vaine to cast away;
> Whose flowring pride, so fading and so fickle,
> Short *Time* shall soon cut down with his consuming sickle.

> Then gin I thinke on that which Nature sayd,
> Of that same time when no more *Change* shall be,
> But stedfast rest of all things firmely stayd
> Upon the pillours of Eternity,
> That is contrayr to *Mutabilitie*:
> For, all that moueth, doth in *Change* delight:
> But thence-forth all shall rest eternally
> With Him that is the God of Sabbaoth hight:
> O thou great Sabbaoth God, graunt me that Sabaoths sight.

1 Identify the rhyme scheme of the stanzas. Identify masculine versus feminine rhymes, and say whether you think there is any significance or pattern to the choice of one or the other.

2 Identify the examples of alliteration in the text. Is a specific type of alliteration used here, or a mixture?

3 Which key words in the stanzas participate in alliteration (or rhyme), and which key words do not? Can this be explained?

4 Discuss the ways in which the author uses sound patterning (rhyme and alliteration) to indicate that the last few lines of the poem are indeed the final lines of the poem.

Reading

Fabb, N. (1997) *Linguistics and Literature*, Oxford: Blackwell.

Furniss, T.E. and Bath, M. (1996) *Reading Poetry: An Introduction*, London: Longman, Chapter 4.

Leech, G. (1969) *A Linguistic Guide to English Poetry*, London: Longman, Chapter 6.

Verse, metre and rhythm

The rain is raining all around	iambic tetrameter
It falls on field and tree,	iambic trimeter
It rains on the umbrellas here,	iambic tetrameter
And on the ships at sea.	iambic trimeter

(Robert Louis Stevenson,
'Rain', 1885)

This is an example of metrical verse. It is verse because it is divided into lines. It is specifically *metrical* verse because each line belongs to a 'metre' (here iambic tetrameter, or iambic trimeter), which partially controls how many syllables there are in the line and what the rhythm of the line is. In order to understand English metre, it is first necessary to understand the two aspects of English words that are controlled by metres: syllables, and relative stress on syllables.

17.1 Syllables and stress

Syllables can be thought of as 'beats' in speech, such that, for example, a word of three syllables such as 'umbrellas' consists of three beats and you can represent it by tapping three times with your fingers (try tapping 'umbrellas' on the table). In English, a syllable is usually based around a vowel or diphthong (two vowels spoken together) or triphthong (three together), which is called the 'nucleus' of the syllable: see **Unit 16, Rhyme and sound patterning** where we look at sounds in more detail. However, a syllable can also be based on vowel-like consonants such as 'l' or 'n' or 'r', so that a two-syllable word like 'bottle' actually has its second syllable based on 'l'.

Monosyllables

1 syllable: in, up, man, heart, score, feet, words, smelt, death, wheat, hope

Polysyllables

2 syllables: ready, pieces, upset, apple, without, ending, fearsome, Scotland

3 syllables: readiness, undertake, manicure, randomness, gentlemen

4 syllables: monstrosity, repulsiveness, menagerie, telescopic, dissertation

5 syllables: unreality, fortification, structuralism, nationality, philosophical

6 syllables: encyclopaedia, psychotherapeutic

7 syllables: environmentalism, autobiographical

Some words have alternative numbers of syllables (e.g. 'literature' usually has 3 but can be pronounced with 4; 'Wednesday' can be pronounced with 2 or 3), and dialects can differ in this way. (To test your understanding of syllable counting, describe each line in the poem above in terms of how many syllables there are in each word; for example the first line has 1-1-1-2-1-2. Then count up the syllables in each line. You should find that there are 8+6+8+6.) One characteristic of being metrical is that the number of syllables in each line is controlled (with some permitted variation); thus an iambic tetrameter line normatively has 8 syllables, and an iambic trimeter line normatively has 6 syllables, as here. This places a constraint on composition; in this metre the 1-syllable word 'field' could not be replaced by the 2-syllable word 'garden' without the line becoming here unmetrical. As a way of visually representing the organization of the line into syllables, we suggest writing an asterisk (or x) under each syllable in the line:

```
The rain is raining all around
 *   *   *   *   *    *   * *

It falls on field and tree,
*    *    *   *     *     *

It rains on the umbrellas here,
*    *    *   *   * *   *   *    *

And on the ships at sea.
 *   *   *   *    *   *
```

(Tip: if you are writing a representation like this using a computer, choose a monospaced font such as *Courier*, where each letter has the same width; this will make it much easier to match the asterisk with the nucleus of the syllable in the line above. Do not use the tabs key.)

The second aspect of metricality involves the placement of stress. In any sequence of syllables, some syllables carry greater 'stress' than others: the syllable with greater stress is experienced as more prominent (e.g. louder). This is true of all the polysyllables in the list above, where, for example, it is possible always to designate one syllable as systematically the most strongly stressed, and in any given accent of English this syllable will always carry the strongest stress within its word, irrespective of the words around it. In dictionaries of English the syllable with greatest stress relative to other syllables has an inverted comma put before it in its representation of pronunciation, and we can do this for the words in the above list: r'eady, r'eadiness, monstr'osity, unre'ality, encyclop'aedia, environm'entalism. (Try doing this for all the words in the list, and check in a dictionary if you are unsure.) When words are put together, the relative strength of syllables can also vary between words; thus in a sequence of monosyllables you will find that some monosyllables (e.g. the nouns) have more stress than others (e.g. the article 'the' or the preposition 'of' tend not to be stressed relative to surrounding words). When you tap out a word, you should find that you can tap loudest on the syllable with greatest stress. Stress is also manifested as higher pitch and greater length, and these may also be audible on the stressed syllables in addition to greater loudness. Furthermore, syllables with very weak or no stress are often reduced in 'vowel quality' such that they are no longer clearly distinguishable from other vowels and may also be shortened. (The extent to which this happens depends on dialect: some kinds of Welsh and Scottish English for example have less reduction of unstressed vowels than some kinds of English English.) In the poem below, we have indicated with an inverted comma where the stressed syllables in polysyllables are: these syllables are also underlined, and they must have stress. And we have underlined monosyllables that are likely to have stress in a performance of the line (but some variation is permitted here):

```
The rain is r'aining all ar'ound
 *   *    *   *     *   *   *  *

It falls on field and tree,
*    *    *   *     *    *

It rains on the umbr'ellas here,
*    *    *   *   * *     *   *   *

And on the ships at sea.
*   *   *   *     *   *
```

17.2 Iambic feet

The striking thing about the stresses in this poem is that they tend to be two syllables apart; only the third line fails to show this pattern (and even here we could choose to stress 'the' and so make the rhythm fully regular). This suggests that, as far as the organization of stress is concerned, the syllables are grouped into pairs. Furthermore, it is clearly the final (rightmost, second) syllable in each pair that tends to have stress. A group of syllables like this is called a **foot**, and because the ones in this poem are pairs and the final syllable in the pair is stressed they are called 'iambic feet'. Feet are divided off in the diagram below by putting brackets after every second asterisk, so that the asterisks – representing syllables – are grouped into pairs. This is a 'scansion' of the line – a representation of its metrical structure:

```
The rain is raining all around
 *  *)  *   *)  *   *)  *  *)        four iambic feet

It falls on field and tree,
 *   *)   *   *)   *      *)          three iambic feet

It rains on the umbrellas here,
 *   *)   *    *)*  *)  *   *)    four iambic feet

And on the ships at sea.
 *   *)   *   *)   *    *)          three iambic feet
```

The right bracket separates off two asterisks as a pair, but it is actually 'bracketing' the rightmost asterisk in each pair. We use this to indicate that this asterisk, and the syllable it represents, is the 'head' of the foot – the syllable that is more likely to carry stress than the other syllable in the foot. It can be seen that the heads – the 'bracketed' syllables in the above scansion of the line – tend to be stressed syllables, the ones that are underlined.

Now we come to the difference between the rhythm of the line and its metre. The first and third lines are in the same metre – they are both 'iambic tetrameter' (the name for a line with four iambic feet). However, they have slightly different rhythms, as can be seen by looking at the pattern of stressed and unstressed syllables. The rhythm of the line is indicated by underlinings in the line itself, while the metre of the line is indicated under the line by the asterisks and brackets that indicate foot structure. The rhythm is what the line sounds like; the metre is the abstract organization to which the rhythm approximates. The metre of each line in this poem is given a name, such as 'iambic tetrameter', which indicates (1) the type of foot in the line, here iambic, and (2) how many feet there are in the line. Tetrameter means that there are four feet, while trimeter means that there are three.

Now consider the relation between the rhythm and the metre. First, note that, while stressed syllables tend to be heads of feet (and vice versa), there are some heads that are not stressed. In particular, the word 'the' in the third line is unlikely to be stressed in performance, though there is nothing actually stopping a performer from stressing it. Furthermore, the final line could have at least two other fairly natural sounding stress patterns in performance, either stressing 'and' instead of 'on', or stressing neither 'and' nor 'on':

```
And on the ships at sea.
*   *)  *   *)  *   *)

And on the ships at sea.
*   *)  *   *)  *   *)
```

These variations tell us, first, that there is no requirement that a stressed mono-syllable should be a head of a foot, and, second, that a head of a foot need not be a stressed syllable. Thus there is potential variation between the rigid (unpronounced) pattern of the metre and the pronounced pattern of the rhythm; it is possible that we match the abstract pattern (the metre) in our head against the actual pattern (the rhythm) that we hear, giving various kinds of complex mismatch, which are sometimes called 'metrical tension'.

A metre is named after the type of foot and the number of feet in the line. These are the names for numbers of feet. So far we have seen iambic trimeter and iambic tetrameter.

dimeter	two feet
trimeter	three feet
tetrameter	four feet
pentameter	five feet
hexameter	six feet
heptameter	seven feet

17.3 Other kinds of foot

There are four kinds of foot in English: two binary feet and two ternary feet:

iambic foot (iamb)	two syllables, final is head
trochaic foot (trochee)	two syllables, initial is head
anapaestic foot (anapaest)	three syllables, final is head
dactylic foot (dactyl)	three syllables, initial is head

For example, here are some lines organized in trochaic feet (but with varying numbers of feet in each line):

In the bleak mid-winter
Frosty wind made moan,
Earth stood hard as iron,
Water like a stone;
Snow had fallen, snow on snow,
Snow on snow,
In the bleak mid-winter
Long ago.

(Christina Rossetti, 'In the bleak mid-winter', 1872)

Here, scanned, are three lines from the poem (note that the third of these lines permits various other possible rhythms, some closer to the metre and some further from the metre). The bracketed asterisk is now the initial asterisk in each foot: this is the head, the syllable most likely to be stressed:

```
Snow had fallen, snow on snow,      = trochaic tetrameter (4 feet)
 (*   *  (* *      (* *    (*

Snow on snow,                        = trochaic dimeter (2 feet)
 (*  *   (*

In the bleak mid-winter              = trochaic trimeter (3 feet)
 (*  *   (*   *   (*  *
```

In these lines we see something new: a foot at one end of the line contains one syllable when it might be expected to contain two. This is called 'catalexis'; it is one of the permitted variations in English, where a foot can be 'short' at one end of the line. In trochaic metres the short foot comes at the end of the line (in iambic metres it comes at the beginning).

Now we look at some lines in a metre where the syllables are grouped into triplets for rhythmic purposes:

```
Mummies and skeletons, out of your stones;
 *) *    *      *)* *    *)  *    *    *)

Every age, every fashion, and figure of Death:
 *   * *)   *   *  *) *    *    *)*   *   *)

The death of the giant with petrified bones:
  *  *)   *    *  *)*   *    *) * *    *)

The death of the infant who never drew breath.
  *  *)   *    * *) *    *   *)*    *    *)
```

(Thomas Lovell Beddoes, 'Song by the Deaths', 1829)

The stressed syllables tend to be three syllables apart. Furthermore these are three-syllable feet in which the final syllable tends to be stressed (and so is the head). Three-syllable feet (triplets) with a final head are anapaests, so this is in an anapaestic metre (actually anapaestic tetrameter because there are four anapaestic feet in each line). Note that the initial foot in the line is sometimes one syllable, sometimes two and sometimes three, thus showing different possibilities for catalexis, which thus permits variation between lines. Metres are rigid systems that nevertheless open up various 'loopholes' for variation (in length or rhythm) in this way. Another kind of variation can be seen in the fact that, while there is a general tendency for the head of the foot to be stressed, other syllables can sometimes be stressed as well, as 'every' in the second line shows. Finally, if we look at the first line we can see that the likely stressing of 'out' is to some extent a performance decision that is forced on us by the metre.

Finally we consider the fourth kind of foot, dactyls, which are initial-headed triplets. These are quite rare in English:

```
Look at her garments
(*   *   *  (*   *

Clinging like cerements;
 (*   *     *    (* * *

Whilst the wave constantly
 (*       *   *  (*   *    *

Drips from her clothing;
 (*      *   *   (*   *
```

(Thomas Hood, 'The Bridge of Sighs', 1844)

In these lines, which are in dactylic dimeter (two dactylic feet in each line), the final foot in the line sometimes falls short. We can tell that these are dactyls, first because the stressed syllables tend to fall three syllables apart, and second because the stressed syllable comes first. Note again various possibilities for rhythmic variation: we might want to stress 'wave' in performance even though it is not the head of a foot. Lines that are in the same metre can thus vary in length and in rhythm.

17.4 Rhythm, metre and 'foot substitution'

Much literary criticism that refers to the metrical form of a poem uses a notion of 'foot substitution'. We will explain shortly why we do not endorse this practice, but first we explain it.

```
Eye Nature's walks, shoot folly as it flies,
 *    *)*      *)      *   *) * *) *   *)
```

This line is in iambic pentameter because it has five iambic feet (binary feet with the rightmost syllable the head). In explaining what a head of a metrical foot was, we earlier said that it 'tended' to be a stressed syllable, but that it need not be. Our assumption was that a line is all in one kind of foot, and does not vary foot type within the line, and that any mismatches between the rhythm of the line and the metre of the line should be recognized as variations – as a gap opening up between the rigid metre and the more flexible rhythm. In this particular line, there are mismatches involving the first and fifth syllables (both of which carry stress but are not heads) and the eighth syllable (which does not carry stress but is a head).

The notion of 'foot substitution' changes the metrical form to match the rhythm, by replacing feet with other types of foot:

```
Eye Nature's walks, shoot   folly as     it flies,
 *    *)*      *)      *    *) * *)    *    *)
iamb      iamb        iamb    iamb     iamb     'template'
spondee   iamb              spondee pyrrhic iamb   'substitutes'
```

The substitutions here include a spondee (a foot with two heads) and a pyrrhic (a foot with no heads) – two types of 'mutant' foot that are found in English verse only as substitutions. This approach to feet implies that feet are a component of the *rhythm* of the line. We suggest that this is not the case: feet are a component of the metre of the line, but the rhythm – the actual performance of the line – is not composed from specific types of foot; instead the rhythm of the line can be thought of as approximating to the metre of the line. We think foot substitution is not a good idea, partly because it confuses rhythm and metre, and partly because it is terminologically over-complex (it requires more than the four basic feet) and describes details that do not clearly have any significance: what do we know when we know that the line begins with a 'spondee'? The only occasions when the notion of 'foot substitution' is potentially useful are when it is used to describe very common rhythmic variations, of which the most common is for an iambic line to begin with a 'stressed–unstressed' sequence:

> I cannot rest from travel: I will drink
> Life to the lees: at times I have enjoy'd
> Greatly, have suffer'd greatly, both with those
>
> (Alfred Tennyson, 'Ulysses', 1842)

All the feet in every line are iambic, but *rhythmically* the second and third of these lines begin with a stressed–unstressed sequence that is 'in counterpoint' to the right-headed iambic foot. If this sequence was systematic across the line the line would be trochaic; as it is only in the first foot this is sometimes called 'trochaic substitution' or 'trochaic inversion'. There is no actual substitution, but the term is a useful reminder of a common pattern.

17.5 Extra (and missing) syllables in the line

We have seen that, at one end of the line, there can be one or two missing syllables, a phenomenon called 'catalexis' (where a metrical foot falls short). We now look at three ways in which lines of exactly the same metre can vary by having additional syllables in the line. The first of these is the opposite of catalexis; while the line can have one or two syllables fewer at one end, at the other end it can have one or two syllables extra, *which do not count for metrical purposes*. Because they do not count they are called 'extrametrical' and are not included in feet. In iambic verse, where extrametricality is fairly common, one extra syllable can optionally appear at the end of the line:

> With fingers light the lingering breezes quiver
> Over the glowing of the still, deep river,
> Whose water sings among the reeds, and smiles
> 'Mid glittering forests and luxuriant isles.
>
> (John Ruskin, untitled, 1836)

The first line would be grouped into five pairs (iambic feet) and a final unfooted or 'extrametrical' syllable. The extrametricality of the final syllable is cued by the fact that it is in a 'feminine rhyme' (where the last stressed syllable in the line is not the last syllable in the line):

```
With fingers light the lingering breezes quiver
 *    *) *    *)     * *)   *    *) *    *)*
```

This line also illustrates a second way in which a syllable can be 'extra'. The word 'lingering' has three syllables but here it counts as two; this means that one syllable is ignored when grouping them into metrical feet. It is possible to mark out these 'ignored' syllables (while remembering that they do not affect the actual foot size) by writing a different kind of symbol beneath them (we use a delta, a little triangle, to mark uncounted syllables):

```
With fingers light the lingering breezes quiver
 *    *) *    *)     * *) Δ *    *) *    *)*
```

The seventeenth-century poet John Donne made very extensive use of the principle of not counting some syllables (particularly vowels before vowels), to the extent that some readers found it very difficult to work out the relation between the performed rhythm of the poem and the actual metre:

> Since she whom I loved hath paid her last debt
> To nature, and to hers and my good is dead,
> And her soul early into heaven ravished,
> Wholly in heavenly things my mind is set.
> Here the admiring her my mind did whet
> To seek thee God; so streams do show the head;
> But though I have found thee, and thou my thirst has fed,
> A holy thirsty dropsy melts me yet.
> But why should I beg more love, when as thou
> Dost woo my soul for hers, offering all thine:
> And dost not only fear lest I allow
> My love to saints and angels, things divine,
> But in my tender jealousy, dost doubt
> Lest the world, flesh, yea devil put thee out.
>
> (John Donne, 'Sonnet 17', c.1607)

Consider, for example, the second line, which should be scanned like this:

```
To nature, and to hers and my good is dead,
 *  *)*    *)   Δ *   *)  *  *)  *   *)
```

One syllable is not counted ('to' before 'hers') and Donne compounds the difficulty by having a rhythm that is some way from the periodic pattern of the iambic pentameter metre of the line, such that syllables that would not be thought of as carrying stress such as 'and' are in head positions. (Try scanning the rest of the poem – you will find that it is entirely in iambic pentameter.) Both of these ways of having 'extra' syllables are fairly common in ordinary English verse, particularly iambic verse.

However, there is another way of having 'extra' syllables that constitutes an entirely new metre – one we have not seen before. This metre has been given many names: 'ballad metre', 'Christabel metre', 'dol'nik' or 'iambic-anapaestic metre'. We call it 'loose iambic' metre because we think the feet are actually iambs, with one extra syllable permitted between a pair of iambs. It is found in much folk poetry (particularly ballads and nursery rhymes), in art poetry that imitates folk poetry, such as William Blake's *Songs of Innocence and Experience* (1794), and in much twentieth-century metrical verse. Here is a nursery rhyme that illustrates the metre:

A frog he would a-wooing go,	loose iambic tetrameter
Heigh ho! says Rowley,	loose iambic trimeter

> Whether his mother would let him or no.   loose iambic tetrameter
> With a rowley, powley, gammon and spinach,   loose iambic tetrameter
> Heigh ho! says Anthony Rowley.   loose iambic trimeter (?)

('The love-sick frog, 1809)

If we look at the line 'With a rowley, powley, gammon and spinach' we can see why the metre is sometimes called 'iambic-anapaestic'. What seems to happen in this metre is that we get a mixture of iambic and anapaestic feet. This is not just a matter of monosyllables permitting variation: the polysyllables also participate in this, and their stressed syllables can be one or two syllables apart in the same line:

```
With a r'owley, p'owley, g'ammon and sp'inach,
 *     *   *) *      *) *      *) *  *       *)*
```

In the loose iambic metre, the rhythm and the metre are much more closely related than in the metres we have seen before; 'counterpointing' of a varying rhythm against a strict metre does not happen here. Instead, the rhythm largely determines where the heads of feet fall: as a general principle, wherever there is a strongly stressed syllable in the line, this is treated as the head of a foot (and hence has a right bracket put after it). The strongly stressed syllables can be at most three syllables apart; they can also be two syllables apart, and often there is a combination of the two as in the line quoted above. But it is also possible for two strongly stressed syllables to be next to each other, in which case they build shorter-than-usual feet, here feet containing just one syllable:

```
Heigh ho! says R'owley,
 *)    *)  *     *) *
```

Notice that there is also an extrametrical syllable at the end of the line. Because rhythm determines metre to some extent here, different performances can give the line different metrical forms; here are two alternatives for the last line (we prefer the first, but acknowledge the possibility of the other one):

```
Heigh ho! says 'Anthony R'owley.
 *    *) *   *) * *   *) *   loose iambic trimeter

Heigh ho! says 'Anthony R'owley.
 *)   *) *   *) * *   *) *   loose iambic tetrameter
```

The poet Gerard Manley Hopkins developed a version of this metre that permits even longer stretches between heads (of three or more syllables), and called it 'sprung rhythm'.

17.6 Free verse

Metrical verse is verse in which the line's length is measured by counting sylla-bles in pairs or triplets. Verse whose lines are not measured in this way is non-metrical verse, and in English most non-metrical verse is more specifically **free verse**. In free verse, there is not any special principle to determine how the text is divided into lines. Consider for example these lines from William Blake's 'Vala, or the Four Zoas':

> They sing unceasing to the notes of my immortal hand.
> The solemn, silent moon
> Reverberates the living harmony upon my limbs,
> The birds & beasts rejoice & play,
> And every one seeks for his mate to prove his inmost joy.

Why is this text divided into lines as it is? There is no common structural prin-ciple based on the linguistic form of the poem (some lines are sentences but others are not, some end on pauses while others do not, etc.), and there is no rhyme or sound patterning or parallelism that consistently organizes the lines in the way that a metre consistently organizes lines. This lack of any consistent reason to divide the text into lines means that it is 'free verse'; the King James Bible is a good source of verse of this kind, and is a likely influence on Blake. In the twentieth century, free verse has become a very common type of verse.

17.7 What to look for in verse

Verse is interesting for a number of reasons. Metrical verse is characterized by a degree of formal complexity perhaps greater than that found in any other aspect of literature; for this reason, some researchers have suggested that the possibility of composing metrical verse reflects deep aspects of how we process language. This is much debated, and there is still no general agreement on how best to understand how metres work.

In the reading of specific verse texts, one of the questions often worth asking is whether the different kinds of constituent structure match or mis-match. In verse, the major constituent is the line. The language of the text is also divided into major constituents – sentence, subordinate clauses and phrases – and it is worth asking whether in a particular text line endings are matched with major linguistic constituent endings. Matches or mismatches might give rise to aesthetic effects of **coherence** or complexity, and their use might reflect the aesthetic attitudes of the time. An example of mismatch, where the line ending interrupts a syntactic constituent (a phenomenon called 'enjambment') can be found in William Wordsworth's *The Prelude* (1805):

> And there, with fingers interwoven, both hands
> Press'd closely, palm to palm, and to his mouth
> Uplifted, . . .

In both first and second lines a noun phrase is interrupted, with the noun coming at the end of the line and a modifying phrase (contained in the same phrase as the noun) coming at the beginning of the next line. Mismatches between syntactic and line structure are common in this text, but much less common in poetry of the preceding century, with its different aesthetic aims. Compare the following lines from a poem by John Brown published in 1776:

> ... Now every eye,
> Oppressed with toil, was drowned in deep repose;

Here, too, we have a noun separated from its modifier by a line break. Though superficially similar, the major difference is that the modifying phrase is separated from the noun by a comma, and in fact constitutes additional information about an already established phrase 'every eye'. Thus it is not as coherently bound to the preceding noun as the modifiers in the Wordsworth text, where the modifiers crucially express what the body parts are doing and hence are very tightly bound to the noun in the preceding line. Thus there is no reason to describe the Brown text as involving enjambment.

ACTIVITY 17.1

For each text below, name the metre (type of foot, and number of feet in line). For each text, every line of the text is in the same metre; you are likely to find the metres increasingly difficult to analyse as you work through this exercise.

As a very rough reminder, these are the characteristic rhythms corresponding to each type of metre:

one-TWO-one-TWO-one-TWO, etc. = iambic

ONE-two-ONE-two-ONE-two, etc. = trochaic

one-two-THREE-one-two-THREE-one-two-THREE, etc. = anapaestic

ONE-two-three-ONE-two-three-ONE-two-three, etc. ('waltz time') = dactylic

varying between one-two and one-two-three = loose iambic

Text A

Airly Beacon, Airly Beacon;
Oh the weary haunt for me,
All alone on Airley Beacon,
with his baby on my knee!

(Charles Kingsley, 'Airly Beacon', 1847)

Text B

The choking Frog sobbed and was gone
The Waggoner strode whistling on,
Unconscious of the carnage done,
Whistling that waggoner strode on –

Whistling (it may have happened so)
'A froggy would a-wooing go.'
A hypothetic frog trolled he,
Obtuse to a reality.

(Christina Rossetti, from 'A Frog's Fate', 1885)

Text C

'I wish I had feathers, a fine sweeping gown,
And a delicate face, and could strut about Town!'
'My dear – a raw country girl, such as you be,
Isn't equal to that. You ain't ruined,' said she.

(Thomas Hardy, from 'The Ruined Maid', 1866)

Text D

In Siberia's wastes
The ice-wind's breath
Woundeth like the toothèd steel;
Lost Siberia doth reveal
Only blight and death.

(James Clarence Mangan, from 'Siberia', 1845)

Text E

Ay, because the sea's the street there; and 't is arched by . . .
    what you call
. . . Shylock's bridge with houses on it, where they kept the carnival:
I was never out of England – it's as if I saw it all.

(Robert Browning, from 'A toccata of Galuppi's', 1855)

6   Somehow a tyrannous sense of a superincumbent oppression
    Still, wherever I go, accompanies ever, and makes me
    Feel like a tree (shall I say?) buried under a ruin of brickwork.

(Arthur Hugh Clough, from *Amours de Voyage*, 1858)

Reading

Attridge, D. (1995) *Poetic Rhythm: An Introduction*, Cambridge: Cambridge University Press.

Fabb, N. (2002) *Language and Literary Structure*, Cambridge: Cambridge University Press, Chapters 1, 2 and 4.

Fabb, N. and Halle, M. (2007) *The Meter of a Poem*, Cambridge: Cambridge University Press.

Furniss, T.E. and Bath, M. (1996) *Reading Poetry: An Introduction*, London: Longman, Chapter 2.

Fussell, P. (1979) *Poetic Meter and Poetic Form*, New York: McGraw-Hill.

Unit 18

Parallelism

18.1 Kinds of parallelism

Parallelism exists where two close or adjacent sections of the text are similar. The similarity usually involves one or both of structural similarity, where the sentence structures are similar, and lexical similarity, where the words are similar (or opposite) in meaning. The limit case of similarity is exact repetition, but in most cases of parallelism there is partial exact repetition and partial difference:

> so in the agonies of Death, in the anguish of that dissolution, in the sorrows of that valediction, in the irreversableness of that transmigration, I shall have a joy which shall no more evaporate than my soul shall evaporate, a joy that shall pass up and put on a more glorious garment above, and be joy superinvested in glory.
>
> (John Donne, 'Sermon at St Paul's', 1625)

Here, for example, there is a parallelism between 'in the anguish of that dissolution' and 'in the sorrows of that valediction'. These two sections of text are structurally similar (as can be seen by the identitical parts: 'in the ... of that ...') and, where they differ, the words are similar in meaning: 'anguish' and 'sorrows' on the one hand, and 'dissolution' and 'valediction' (saying goodbye) on the other.

Parallelisms can be distinguished by which level of textual material they involve. At the level of narrative structure, we can talk about the parallelism between plots, or a parallelism between characters. The component parts of a narrative include distinct sub-plots, episodes, characters and objects, and all of these types of component can be involved in parallelism. Thus, for example, it is not uncommon for a sub-plot to parallel a main plot (as for example in Shakespeare's *A Midsummer Night's Dream* (1596)). A narrative might be

219

in groups of parallel episodes, possibly organized according to some numerical principle such as 'in pairs' or 'in triplets' (e.g. three incidents of one kind, followed by three incidents of another). And it is common to have characters in a narrative who are similar at some level of abstract description but who are opposites on the surface; there may be a parallelism between the hero and the villain.

At the level of linguistic structure we can also distinguish kinds of parallelism: 'lexical parallelism' is a parallelism in meaning, involving words (hence 'lexical'); 'syntactic parallelism' (parallelism in sentence structure) is a parallelism in form, and is a parallelism between two sections of text that have the same syntactic components; and 'phonological parallelism' is parallelism involving sounds. There are basically two kinds of phonological parallelism. The most common type of phonological parallelism in English literature involves coherent 'clumps' of sound such as the end or beginning of a syllable, and is exemplified by rhyme and alliteration (see **Unit 16: Rhyme and sound patterning**). There is another type of phonological parallelism, which is developed systematically in some literary traditions; this is a parallelism between two longer and disconnected sequences of sounds and could be called sound-pattern parallelism. Examples of this are found in the technique of *cynghanedd* ('harmony') in Welsh poetry, where a sequence of consonants in the first half of the line is repeated in the second half of the line; the Welsh-born poet Gerard Manley Hopkins adapted this technique in some of his English-language poems.

Most parallelisms have two members (called 'binary parallelisms'), while some have three parts ('ternary parallelisms') or more. The extract from *Hiawatha* below is characteristic of the text as a whole in having an extended (here four-part) parallelism. Lines 2 and 3 are two members of a two-part (binary) parallelism; and line 4 contains within it a binary parallelism. Lines 4–8 are members of a four-part parallelism:

Should you ask where Nawadaha
Found these songs so wild and wayward,
Found these legends and traditions,
I should answer, I should tell you,
'In the bird's-nests of the forest,
In the lodges of the beaver,
In the hoofprint of the bison,
In the eyry of the eagle!'
        (Henry Wadsworth Longfellow,
          Song of Hiawatha, 1855)

The words that constitute the members of a parallelism are often different but are usually related in meaning in some way. A pair or larger set of words that belong to the same 'area' of meaning are said to belong to the same 'semantic field'. A semantic field is a set of words with various kinds of relation to one another, including similarity of meaning (synonymy), part-to-whole relations (a hyponym is a part relative to a whole) and opposition of meaning (antonymy). Where the two meanings are interpreted as in opposition, then we have 'polar parallelism' (because the words are at opposite poles as far as meaning is concerned). Anther kind of parallelism is non-polar parallelism:

> Five years have past; five summers, with the length
> Of five long winters!
> (William Wordsworth, 'Tintern Abbey', 1798)

```
    Five        years                       have past;
    five        summers,  with the length /
Of  five  long  winters!
```

In this example, we have a triple parallelism, where the first two members are in a whole-to-part relation (a year contains a summer), and the next two members are in polar opposition (summer is opposite from winter). Polar parallelisms often draw on pre-existing stereotyped oppositions in the culture, such as the culture versus nature opposition, or man versus woman.

In parallelism, members need not be structured identically. One member of the parallelism can have a 'gap' called an 'ellipsis', where the missing word or words can be filled in from context. Thus consider this proverb:

> Excellent speech becometh not a fool;
> Much less do lying lips a prince.
> (Proverbs, 17, 7)

This can be laid out as follows, to bring out the parallelism:

```
              Excellent speech becometh not  a fool; /
    Much less do lying lips                  a prince.
```

The second member of the parallelism is missing its verb, but it is easy to complete it as 'become' (here meaning 'suit' or 'fit'), so that the second member can be read as 'much less do lying lips *become* a prince'. Ellipsis can involve the second member of a parallelism, but it can also involve the first member.

A **chiasmus** (or chiasm) is a syntactic parallelism where the order of parallel elements is reversed. ('Chiasmus' comes from the Greek 'chi', which is the name for the Greek letter χ, thus symbolizing the crossing over of the parts.)

> Oft did the harvest to their sickle yield,
> Their furrow oft the stubborn glebe has broke;
> (Thomas Gray, 'Elegy Written in a
> Country Churchyard', 1751)

```
Oft   did    the harvest  to  their sickle  yield,
A            B                C             D

Their furrow  oft    the stubborn glebe  has broke;
C             A      B                   D
```

Here, 'the harvest' and 'the stubborn glebe' (mass of earth) are lexically parallel because they both relate to the earth, and 'their sickle' and 'their furrow' are lexically parallel because they both relate to the human modification of the earth, but the two parallel pairs are changed in order from line to line, and hence are an example of chiasmus. Note that another 'crossing' (though not a strict chiasmus) involves 'did ... yield', which is parallel to 'has broke', where the former member is split in the line.

18.2 Analysing parallelism

As a sustained example of parallelism, consider the beginning of *An Essay on Man* (1733) by Alexander Pope:

> Awake, my St. John! leave all meaner things
> To low ambition, and the pride of kings.
> Let us (since life can little more supply
> Than just to look about us and to die)
> Expatiate free o'er all this scene of man;
> A mighty maze! but not without a plan;
> A wild, where weeds and flow'rs promiscuous shoot;
> Or garden, tempting with forbidden fruit.
> Together let us beat this ample field,
> Try what the open, what the covert yield;
> The latent tracts, the giddy heights explore
> Of all who blindly creep, or sightless soar;
> Eye Nature's walks, shoot folly as it flies,
> And catch the manners living as they rise;
> Laugh where we must, be candid where we can;
> But vindicate the ways of God to man.

We work out the parallelisms by laying it out again, this time with parallel sections put one above the other where possible. Where there are parallelisms between more distant parts of text, this is also partially reflected in layout but more difficult to see (e.g. between 'leave all meaner things' and 'expatiate free o'er all this scene of man'). The slashes indicate line boundaries. The text has been divided into four sections, which are internally consistent as regards meaning (see **Unit 3, Analysing units of structure**). You should be able to analyse any parallelistic text in this way yourself – you do not need any special knowledge (e.g. of grammar), but can do it on the basis of looking at meanings alone. (Tip: if you are doing this yourself on a computer, use a monospaced font such as *Courier* to control vertical alignments, and avoid using the tabs key.)

```
A
          Awake, my St. John!
          leave                 all meaner things /

To    low          ambition,
and   the pride    of kings. /


B
Let us
(since life can little more supply / Than just to look about us
                                      and to die) /
          Expatiate free o'er    all this scene of man; /

   A mighty maze!    but not without a plan; /
   A          wild,    where weeds
                         and flow'rs promiscuous shoot; /
Or          garden, tempting with forbidden fruit. /


C
Together
let us    beat                     this ample field, /

Try what the open,
   what the covert yield; /

   The    latent   tracts,
   the   giddy    heights   explore /
Of all who blindly    creep,  or
          sightless   soar; /

   Eye    Nature's walks,
   shoot  folly                   as   it    flies, /
And catch  the manners    living  as   they   rise; /


D
   Laugh                     where we must,
   be candid                 where we can; /
But vindicate the ways of God
                 to man. /
```

(Note: 'expatiate' means both to wander freely and to write about at length; 'wild' here is used as a noun; section C describes a hunting practice, beating the field to drive game into view.)

By laying out the poem in this way, we can see clearly some of the ways in which parallelism works:

1   Note the placement of line endings; we often find that a member ends at the end of a line; we also find that two members often share the same line. Thus parallelism varies in how it operates relative to line boundaries, but generally respects or is aware of line boundaries.
2   The parallelisms are generally binary (two members), but ternary parallelisms (three members) have a tendency to come at the ends of the sections we identified (sections B, C and D). These sections were distinguished on the basis of each having a unified meaning, but we can see that there is also a formal cue to the end of the section, using a ternary rather than binary parallelism.
3   There are some chiasms (though not many), most prominently 'low ambition' and 'the pride of kings', where we have an AB:BA pattern, if we interpret 'low' to be opposite to 'kings'.
4   Parallelism is sometimes very obvious and sometimes less so; we might suggest that the whole text has a parallelism involving members that are exhortations or commands: 'leave all meaner things' finds a parallel in section B, '(let us) expatiate free o'er all this scene of man', in section C, 'let us beat this ample field', and in section D, 'laugh ... be candid ... vindicate the ways of God to man'.
5   Parallelism does not necessarily respect syntactic (grammatical) structure. Thus the adjective 'low' functions as the opposite of the noun 'kings', and hence different word classes are involved. Also, members are not coherent syntactic units, as in 'Try {what the open:: what the covert} yield' – these would only be coherent syntactically if they were structured as 'Try {what the open yields :: what the covert yields}'. Parallelism thus largely respects syntactic structure but sometimes violates it.
6   The text is threaded with a semantic field of 'looking', which involves 'look about us', 'blindly', 'sightless' and 'eye', and this semantic field crosscuts the parallelisms as a kind of extended parallelism of its own.
7   There are some stereotyped parallelisms, here most clearly the parallelism between the words 'God' and 'man', which is very common in English poetry. Implicitly there is also a culture–nature parallelism (also very common elsewhere) in, for example, the {wild :: garden} opposition.

We can sum up the formal operations of parallelism in this text by saying that parallelism is an organizatory principle, which correlates to some extent with other organizatory principles in the text such as lineation and syntactic structure, but which also is in 'counterpoint' to these. (This was a notion we introduced also in talking about the relation between rhythm and metre in poetry, where there is often a correlation but also the possibility of counterpoint; see **Unit 17**.) In itself, this formal complexity is part of the goal of the poem, as in much poetry: the display of compositional skill. But the poem also has a meaning; it is an 'essay on man', and hence the oppositions between man and animals, culture and nature, and God and man, which are generated through the parallelisms, are formal ways in which this essay is composed.

18.3 The functions of parallelism and the variety of texts in which it is found

Parallelism is a 'formal practice'. When we say this, we mean that parallelism is a way of organizing the material from which a text is made – both the forms of the language (the words and sentence structures) and the meanings of the text. As a formal practice it is widespread. It is found in many English texts, and indeed in texts in all languages. For some languages, it appears to play an organizatory role in verse equivalent to (and usually instead of) metrical form. Thus Mongolian verse, ancient Semitic verse (e.g. Hebrew, Egyptian, Akkadian), South African verse traditions (e.g. Xhosa, Tswana), Indonesian verse traditions, Central and South American Indian verse traditions and so on all have parallelism as a fundamental structural principle, where it is expected that components of the verse will systematically and thoroughly engage as members of parallelisms (Jakobson calls this systematic parallelism 'canonic parallelism'). It is also found in different genres of text: in English we find it not only in poetry such as Pope's, which is designed for pleasure, but also in religious texts (such as the Bible), in advertising, in political speeches and so on. Here is a text from a political speech, laid out to show the parallelisms:

```
I have a dream
    that one day on the red hills of Georgia,
        the sons of former slaves
      and the sons of former slave owners
    will be able to sit down together at the table of brotherhood.


I have a dream
    that one day even the state of Mississippi,
                    a state
            sweltering with the heat of injustice,
            sweltering with the heat of oppression,
        will be transformed into an oasis of freedom
                            and justice.
```

```
I have a dream
     that my four little children
     will one day live in a nation where they will not be judged
          by the color of their skin
     but by the content of their character.


I have a dream
          today!
```

(Martin Luther King, speech at the Lincoln Memorial,
Washington DC, 28 August 1963)

Aspects of parallelism particularly worth noting in this text include the high amount of repetition, and the fact that the four-unit section is ended with a unit that, unlike the others, does not have internal parallelism: 'I have a dream today!'. Here we see a similar use of formal difference to mark the end of a section (in the Pope poem, the formal difference involved not less parallelism but more parallelism).

Why is parallelism so common in texts (cross-linguistically), and why is it used in specific texts or groups of texts? It is very difficult to find an answer to this question. Literary studies is, however, a discipline that encourages speculation, and 'trying out' possible answers. Hence we can speculate on the functions of parallelism; that is, we can provide a *functional* explanation of a *formal* practice. We need always to remember that functional explanations of formal practices can seem very convincing on the basis of almost no evidence; they appeal to common-sense views, and thus should be treated with caution.

The influential linguist and literary theorist Roman Jakobson suggested that parallelism functions to draw attention to form. He suggested that this worked by choosing as members two items that normally would be *alternatives* and putting them one after another. Thus 'blindly creep' and 'sightless soar' (from Pope's poem) are alternative ways of describing a living thing's movement, and, instead of stating one or the other, Pope states both in sequence. Jakobson claims that this draws attention to the formal characteristics of 'blindly creep' and 'sightless soar': that we notice the words themselves, and are aware of the possibilities of what can be said – of the system of language itself. Jakobson says that, when our attention is drawn in this way to language itself (thus taking some portion of attention away from what is being communicated *by* the language), the forms of the text are performing a specific function, which he called the 'poetic function'. The poetic function is dominant in poetry, though it is also a function that can be found performed in non-literary texts as well.

Parallelisms in a text can correspond to stereotyped parallelisms – and particularly polar parallelisms (oppositions) – in a culture, and by so doing they can both reinforce and indeed construct such cultural parallelisms. Pope's poem draws on the stereotyped oppositions between human and animal, culture and nature, and human and God; whether or not he reinforces these oppositions or undermines or renegotiates them is a matter that a reading of the whole poem might seek to establish. Claude Lévi-Strauss is a structural anthropologist who has argued that certain structures of parallelism (and specifically opposition) might be fundamental to the way that cultures think. This suggests that parallelistic texts that draw on and transform stereotyped parallelisms might function as more general ways of thinking about the world; not just about the overt topics (such as culture and nature) that they seem to be fixed on.

Parallelism between the text and something outside the text can also be seen in texts like the following, which would be said by a parent to a small child, the parent tapping the child's face while saying the text.

What is said	What gestures are carried out
`Here sits the Lord Mayor,`	Touch forehead
`Here sit his men,`	Touch eyes
`Here sits the cockadoodle,`	Touch right cheek
`Here sits the hen,`	Touch left cheek
`Here sit the little chickens,`	Touch tip of nose
`Here they run in,`	Touch mouth
`Chin chopper,`	Chuck under chin
`chin chopper,`	Chuck under chin
`chin chopper,`	Chuck under chin
`chin`	Chuck under chin

(Nursery rhyme, 1846; cited in Opie, 1951)

Though this is a simple text, it has an interesting complexity, which relates to 'here they run in'; should this be paired with 'here sit the little chickens' (given the paired gestures otherwise found), or is it indeed part of a four-part set with the previous three lines, parallel to the three+one chucking in the final part? In fact, the parallelism structure is formally somewhat unstable at this point, just before the gestures shift from touching to more aggressive or ticklish chucking – a kind of textual anxiety or excitement on the edge of the exciting final gestures.

For most texts we feel that the text must hold together as a whole: it must be 'coherent'. Coherence is partly a matter of interpretation: the reader or listener can impose coherence on a text that in itself might seem not to be coherent. But coherence can also be fostered by text-internal devices that are called 'cohesive devices'. (Halliday and Hasan (1976) is a sustained examination of some of the words and phrases that foster cohesion in this way.) Parallelism might function as a cohesive device – a way of making the text seem coherent. As an example of this, consider the use of parallel plots (e.g. main and sub-plot) in a narrative – a type of narrative parallelism where one story is parallel to the other. In many episodic television programmes, the hour-long, self-contained episode may run several parallel plots; often the coherence of the episode will be bolstered by implicit similarities between the themes raised by each plot.

Parallelism, along with other formal practices (such as metre), might be a way of making a text easier to remember. This might be one reason why laws can be formulated in parallel structures, why political and persuasive texts have parallel structures, and why religious texts have parallel structures. Perhaps this is one of the reasons that proverbs (such as that quoted on p. 221) and other kinds of 'wisdom literature', cross-linguistically, often have parallelistic structures: these are short texts that are memorized, and the parallelism may help memorization.

Finally, parallelism might be explained in terms of intertextuality or allusion (see **Unit 13**). It is always possible that there is no inherent relation between a formal practice and the function it performs: it may be that a formal practice is just used because someone else used it before. Here, it is worth considering the influence of the Bible, for example in the English 'Authorized version' translation. In the eighteenth century, the first theorist of parallelism, Robert Lowth, described how the original Hebrew texts (those that were translated into English as the 'Old Testament') were governed by parallelism. (This is a characteristic of many other texts of the ancient Near East, including Egyptian texts.) The translation into English preserves the principle of parallelism, such that it is possible to open the English Old Testament at any page and find examples of parallelism. Here is an example:

```
      Every     valley                   shall be exalted,
  and every     mountain
                and hill                  shall be made low:

  and           the crooked              shall be made straight,
  and           the rough places                     plain:

  And           the glory of the Lord shall be revealed
  and           all flesh                shall see it together:
  for           the mouth of the Lord hath spoken it.
```
(Isaiah 40, 4–5 (AV))

Because the Bible has parallelism, parallelism carries a certain cultural value with the consequence that a text can acquire cultural value by using parallelism. Perhaps this is another reason for the widespread use of parallelism in political (and advertising) discourse: the speaker is claiming the kind of authority associated with the Bible by borrowing its formal practices. The extract from King's speech (p. 225) is soon followed by his quoting this passage from the Bible, thus connecting his speech both formally and in content (and morally and religiously) with the Bible.

This activity uses a poem by Emily Dickinson, written about 1863:

> Because I could not stop for Death –
> He kindly stopped for me –
> The Carriage held but just Ourselves –
> And Immortality.
>
> We slowly drove – He knew no haste
> And I had put away
> My labor and my leisure too,
> For His Civility –
>
> We passed the School, where Children strove
> At Recess – in the Ring –
> We passed the Fields of Gazing Grain –
> We passed the Setting Sun –
>
> Or rather – He passed Us –
> The Dews drew quivering and chill –
> For only Gossamer, my Gown –
> My Tippet – only Tulle –
>
> We paused before a House that seemed
> A Swelling of the Ground –
> The Roof was scarcely visible –
> The Cornice – in the Ground –
>
> Since then – 'tis Centuries – and yet
> Feels shorter than the Day
> I first surmised the Horses' Heads
> Were toward Eternity –

(Note: a 'tippet' is a garment (for the shoulders), and 'tulle'and 'gossamer' are materials. A 'cornice' is a decorative structure below the ceiling of a room.)

1 Write this poem out to show the parallelisms (using the method shown for *An Essay on Man* (p. 223) in this unit). How does the structure of the parallelisms relate to the other structural aspects of the text: the division into stanzas, and the division into lines?

2 For the lexical parallelisms, distinguish polar parallelisms (opposites) from non-polar parallelisms. How do the lexical parallelisms, both polar and non-polar, help develop and clarify the meaning of the poem as we read it from first to last stanza?

3   Identify any chiasms. How do chiasms help structure the poem, and develop its meaning?

4   Is sound systematically or significantly organized in this poem (e.g. rhyme, alliteration or other forms of sound patterning, including sound pattern parallelism)?

Reading

Fabb, N. (1997) *Linguistics and Literature*, Oxford: Blackwell, Chapter 6.
Fox, J.J. (ed.) (1988) *To Speak in Pairs: Essays on the Ritual Languages of Eastern Indonesia*, Cambridge: Cambridge University Press.
Halliday, M.A.K. and Hasan, R. (1976) *Cohesion in English*, London: Longman.
Jakobson, R. (1988) 'Linguistics and Poetics', in D. Lodge (ed.) *Modern Criticism and Theory: A Reader*, London: Longman, pp. 32–57.
Leech, G. (1969) *A Linguistic Guide to English Poetry*, London: Longman, Chapter 5.

Unit 19

Deviation

In this unit we explore a common feature of the language of literature – its tendency to deviate from everyday norms of communication. Literary language, especially poetry, differs from everyday language in its deliberate manipulation and exploitation of linguistic norms or rules. We consider briefly the types of linguistic rule that underpin ordinary communication and then explore ways in which these are manipulated in literary communication. The unit concludes with a consideration of what purpose is served in literary communication by breaking linguistic norms or rules.

19.1 Convention and deviation in everyday language

Everyday verbal communication depends upon following the underlying rules (or grammar) of the language. (**See Unit 3, Analysing units of structure**.) When linguists study a language, their aim is to describe these rules or norms and thereby account for our capacity to achieve mutual intelligibility when we are using the same language with each other. Linguists emphasize that the rules they describe are constitutive of language use and need to be distinguished from prescriptions such as 'don't split your infinitives', 'don't drop your aitches' or 'say "it is I" rather than "it is me"', which are merely a kind of linguistic etiquette and bear little relation to the underlying grammar that makes communication possible.

19.1.1 Components of grammar and types of linguistic rule

Linguists commonly distinguish between three levels at which a language is organized – the levels of substance, form and meaning. Substance refers to the physical medium in which expression takes place – articulated sounds in speech or marks on paper in writing. Form refers to how these sounds become organized into words, and words into sentences. Meaning refers to the propositions that become encoded in form and substance. Each level has a different subsection of the grammar associated with it, each subsection being constituted by different kinds of rules. The level of substance (sounds or letters) is analysed in terms of phonological or graphological rules (pronunciation and spelling). Form – the patterning of words into sentences – is analysed in terms of syntactic rules. And meaning is studied through semantics. The overall picture may be summed up in the following diagram:

G	Substance	Articulated sounds	Phonology
R		Marks on paper	Graphology
A	Form	Words	Vocabulary
M		Words combined	Syntax
M		into sentences	
A	Meaning	Propositions	Semantics
R			

For the linguist, formulating the grammar for a language consists of stating what rules govern its operation at each of the three main levels. Thus, there are phonological or graphological rules that state permissible patterns at the level of substance: in English, for instance, we do not find the sound /n/ followed immediately by /g/ at the beginning of a word. There are rules of syntax that govern how words combine into sentences: in English, for instance, definite articles ('the') come before the noun, not after ('the car', not 'car the'). And there are semantic rules governing the properties of propositions (such as, one cannot properly promise or predict things that have already happened).

In practice, of course, the grammar, or rule system, is not always rigidly observed. In rapid speech, for instance, we constantly make mistakes – slips of the tongue, false starts, unfinished sentences, and other kinds of production error. But our background awareness of the rule system helps us decipher or edit out these mistakes so that in practice we are hardly aware of them. Children learning their first language also – unsurprisingly – make mistakes. They build up the adult grammar or rule system by degrees, using interesting approximations to it on the way. These mistakes (e.g. 'me go home') are much more than random errors. Children make similar kinds of approximation, in the same developmental order, as they build up the adult rule system. Finally, in addition to performance errors and developmental errors, other kinds of mistake may be traced to particular kinds of impairment (such as aphasia or dyslexia) with particular disruptions to the rule system. In all these cases, however, the linguistic errors or deviations that result are unintended; and speakers attempt to avoid them.

There is, however, a further class of deviation, of a qualitatively different kind, comprising playful departures from the rule system. An everyday example of manipulating an aspect of the rule system – in this case that of spelling – may be found in 'text-messaging', or SMS, where 'be' becomes 'B', 'you' becomes 'U', 'great' becomes 'GR8', and 'BCNU' means 'be seeing you'. At one level these departures from normal spelling may be seen simply as speed and economy measures; but there is undoubtedly a considerable measure of inventiveness, innovation and play involved, as in F2F ('face to face') or H2CUS ('hope to see you soon'). Although this kind of deliberate, rule-breaking playfulness undoubtedly occurs in everyday contexts of communication, it is particularly common in literature. Indeed, the language of literature can be seen as dominated by two overarching principles: rule-breaking on the one hand and rule-making on the other. In **Units 16–18 (Rhyme and sound patterning**, **Verse, metre and rhythm**, and **Parallelism**), we have looked in detail at rule-making or the superimposition of extra patterning in the language of literature. In the remainder of the present unit we focus on its antithesis – rule-breaking, or deviation.

19.2 Convention and deviation in literature

As we have just suggested, literature – to a greater or lesser extent – separates itself from other uses of language by deliberately bending the rules of everyday communication. Indeed, the literary institution could be seen as operating within a spectrum constituted by degrees of linguistic deviation, so that some authors, periods and genres are more deviant than others. The literature of the first half of the twentieth century, for instance, probably involved more conscious linguistic experimentation, and hence deviation, in literature than, say, that of the first half of the eighteenth century.

The pleasure we experience from linguistic deviation in everyday language depends upon our knowledge of the norms or conventions of ordinary usage: deviation only becomes pleasurable and interesting when we know what it deviates from. The same is true of deviation in literature. In this case, however, there is a complicating factor. In literature, deviation may operate against the background of two sets of norms:

1   the conventions or norms of ordinary usage;
2   the conventions or norms of the literary system itself.

Indeed, what is at first deviant and 'original' in literature can quickly become conventional – which is why writers continually invent new kinds of deviations in the attempt, as Ezra Pound put it, to 'make it new'.

We will now examine some common types of linguistic deviation in literature, considering examples of deviation in substance, form and meaning.

19.2.1 Deviation in substance

In modern as opposed to traditional, pre-literate societies, literature exists primarily as a body of printed works rather than as a set of oral performances. Since the principal mode of literary expression in English is now written rather than spoken, it follows that, where we get deviation at the level of substance, this is primarily a matter of typography, layout, punctuation and spelling. Poetry routinely adopts modes of layout that are peculiar to itself – relatively short lines indented on the page, and so on; but this has itself become a poetic convention against which even more extreme deviations can be measured. The following poem by Edwin Morgan, for example, takes liberties with many aspects of substance simultaneously – principally features of typography, layout and punctuation (1967):

Message clear

```
    am                 i
                                  if
i am                       he
     he r         o
     h      ur    t
     the re              and
     he       re     and
     he re
 a                     n   d
      th   e   r               e
i am       r                   ife
                  i n
          s       ion and
 i                        d    i e
   am    e res    ect
   am    e res    ection
                      o         f
      the                       life
                      o         f
    m   e                 n
          su re
      the                 d    i e
```

```
i        s
         s    e  t    and
i am the    sur          d
   a   t   res     t
                      o           life
i am  he r                          e
i a                ct
i           r   u       n
i  m   e  e        t
i                  t              i e
i           s      t    and
i am th                 o      th
i am     r                a
i am the   su          n
i am the   s         on
i am the  e   rect on        e if
i am      re           n    t
i am        s          a        fe
i am       s    e    n      t
i     he  e                d
i    t e   s      t
i          re           a  d
   a    th  re           a  d
   a         s     t on            e
   a   t   re            a  d
   a    th  r        on            e
i          resurrect
                        a       life
i am                 i  n       life
i am      resurrection
i am the resurrection and
i am
i am the resurrection and the life
```

Perhaps the most deviant feature of this text is the way in which the conventional method of using spaces to indicate the boundaries between words in the written medium has been violated by using them within words as well as between them. Moreover, not only do the spaces seem to be randomly distributed with no respect for word-boundaries, they also vary in length. This deviation may seem trivial in itself, but it makes the text initially difficult to read and understand because the conventional signals about how letters combine together to make up words have been abandoned. It is only as we approach the final line – perhaps on a second or third reading – that we recognize that all the previous lines are variations on the last line in that they delete some of its letters, leaving blank spaces instead. The letters that remain in each line are thus placed in exactly the same position as they appear in the last line. Yet, if the resulting irregular spacings are carefully negotiated, these apparently random letters can be read as words and phrases. By doing this, we discover that every line anticipates the last line not only by selecting letters from it, but also by making a series of statements ('i act', 'i am the sun', etc.). These statements, it turns out, can be interpreted as partial but congruent versions of the message of the final line – 'I am the resurrection and the life'. The title, 'Message Clear', initially might seem to be an ironic comment on the struggling reader, but by adopting a different way of reading the deviations begin to make sense so that the 'message' finally begins to become 'clear'.

Deviation of substance is not restricted to poetry but may also be found in novels such as Laurence Sterne's *Tristram Shandy* (1759–67), James Joyce's *Finnegans Wake* (1939) or Alasdair Gray's *Lanark* (1981).

19.2.2 Deviation in vocabulary

Deviation in vocabulary occurs in literature when new words are deliberately created for particular effect. This may be done in various ways, but the most straightforward strategy is simply the pasting of words or elements of words together into new combinations. Many words in English have been formed in this way:

fortunate	=	fortune+ate
unfortunate	=	un+fortune+ate
unfortunately	=	un+fortune+ate+ly
unusually	=	un+usual+ly
uncool	=	un+cool
breakfast	=	break+fast
laptop	=	lap+top

We can see from these examples that even the small elements or affixes – such as un-, -ate and -ly – can have a fairly predictable meaning in the structure of a word: the affix un- usually means 'not'; -ate usually suggests 'quality'; and -ly usually suggests 'manner'. These basic patterns of meaning and word construction allow us to make sense of words that we have never encountered before, but they also give poets manifold opportunities for innovation. When the Victorian religious poet and Jesuit priest, Gerard Manley Hopkins, refers in *The Wreck of the Deutschland* (1875) to the sea as 'widow-making, unchilding, unfathering deeps', he is using the ordinary possibilities of affixation and compounding to form 'one-off' neologisms or new words, providing him with a resource for conveying in a particularly compressed fashion the way in which the sea can take husbands from their wives, children from their parents and fathers from their children. Similarly, when T.S. Eliot in *The Waste Land* (1922) puts a neologism into the mouth of the blind seer Tiresias, so that he says 'And I Tiresias have foresuffered all', our knowledge of the conventional function of 'fore-' means that we are able to derive a meaning for 'foresuffer'. (Tiresias is presumably claiming that his prophetic powers mean that he not only 'foresees' events but also suffers or endures them before they occur.) Thus, we make sense of neologisms in the same way that we make sense of other kinds of deviation – through using our implicit knowledge of the underlying conventions of the language. These principles enable the production and understanding of puns in everyday life, and they help us to at least attempt to interpret the radical deviations in word formation found in *Finnegans Wake*:

> I have just (let us suppraise) been reading in a suppressed book – it is notwithstempting by measures long and limited – the latterpress is eminently legligible and the paper, so he eagerly seized upon, has scarsely been buttered in works of previous publicity wholebeit in keener notcase would I turf aside for pastureuration.

In this comparatively mild example of the novel's lexical deviations, Joyce employs what Lewis Carroll called 'portmanteau' words (because they pack several meanings into one word): 'notwithstempting', for example, can be read as containing both 'notwithstanding' and 'not tempting'.

Lexical deviation of a less exalted kind may also be found in comedy, such as Ronnie Barker's television sketches that featured Dr Small Pith, 'president of the loyal society for the relief of the sufferers of pismonunciation'. Here is the beginning of one of his appeals:

> *Ronnie Barker*: Good evening. I am the president for the loyal society for the relief of sufferers from pismonunciation; for the people who cannot say their worms correctly. Or who use the wrong worms entirely, so that other people cannot underhand a bird they are spraying. It's just that you open your mouse, and the worms come turbling out in wuk a say that you dick knock what you're thugging a bing, and it's very distressing.

Here, although we find the occasional neologism (turbling, thugging), much of the comic effect derives from substituting one word for another on the basis of similarities in pronunciation (worms for words, mouse for mouth, underhand for understand, spraying for saying, etc.) to incongruous effect. This is lexical deviation on a large scale, though dependent on establishing a clear frame within which both the item (e.g. words) and its substitute (e.g. worms) can be simultaneously evoked.

19.2.3 Deviation in syntax

Conveying one's meaning depends not only on one's choice of word as opposed to another but on how these are arranged in sentences. Indeed, if words are to make sense there are strong constraints on the ways in which they can be combined into sentences. (See **Unit 3, Analysing units of structure**.) These constraints are called the syntax of the language and all language users are subject to them. The importance of syntactic conventions in English can be demonstrated by how relatively small shifts in word order and combination can significantly alter the meaning of sentences. In the following example the change from a statement to a question is brought about by a simple change in the order of the initial two items, the Subject and Verb:

This is the ten o'clock news.

Is this the ten o'clock news?

Poets, no less than other language users, have to subscribe to syntactic constraints if they are to be understood; even when they deviate from them, they depend upon our tacit knowledge of the conventions that are broken in order to achieve their effects. In poetry, inversions of normal word order are quite common, may be motivated by considerations of rhyme and rhythm, and are tolerated if not too blatantly intrusive. Consider the following:

Silent is the house: all are laid asleep:
One alone looks out o'er the snow-wreaths deep ...
(Emily Brontë, 'The Visionary', 1846)

A more conventional order would be:

The house is silent: all are laid asleep:
One alone looks out over the deep snow-wreaths ...

This more conventional order, however, misses those opportunities for patterning in rhyme and metre that were taken by the poet. In effect, the poet's extra patterning in phonology has gone hand in hand with deviation in normal word order. An extended example of deviant word order may by found in the following poem by E.J. Scovell (1907–99):

The Paschal Moon

At four this April morning the Easter moon –
Some days to full, awkwardly made, yet of brazen
Beauty and power, near the north-west horizon
Among our death-white street lamps going down –

I wondered to see it from a lower storey
Netted in airy twigs; and thought, a fire
A mile off, or what or who? But going higher
I freed it (to my eyes) into its full glory,
Dominant, untouched by roofs, from this height seen
Unmeshed from budding trees; not silver-white
But brazed or golden. Our fluorescent light,
That can change to snow a moment of the young green
In the maple tree, showed ashen, null and dead
Beside such strength, such presence as it had.

Formally, this poem conforms to most of the conventions of the sonnet genre. There are fourteen lines; and, despite some half rhymes (moon/down; dead/had) (see **Unit 16, Rhyme and sound patterning**), the rhyme scheme is that of an English sonnet, with three quatrains (abba, cddc, effe) and a concluding couplet. Indeed, in meeting the requirements of the sonnet form, this poem deviates markedly from the normal word order of English. When making statements, for instance, the English clause or sentence tends to follow a pattern of Subject followed by Verb followed by Object (as, for instance, in 'Ellen Macarthur [S] broke [V] the record [O]'). (It is for this reason that English is sometimes described as an SVO language.) The opening of the poem, however, deviates from this usual syntactic pattern. If we try and turn it into something closer to everyday English it might read like this:

> I wondered to see the Easter moon at four this April morning from a lower storey, netted in airy twigs, going down among our death-white street lamps near the north-west horizon, awkwardly made, yet of brazen beauty and power, some days to full.

This version of the content of the poem restores the more normal order of core constituents of an English clause or sentence: the Subject comes first (in this case 'I'), followed by the Verb (or Verb Phrase) ('wondered to see') and then the Object ('the Easter moon'). These elements are followed here by syntactically optional elements relating to time, place and circumstance of the action ('at four this April morning from a lower storey . . .', etc.). In the poem, however, the conventional order of the main elements is reversed, giving first the syntactically non-essential elements, relating to circumstances, and delaying specification of the Object. We do not encounter the Subject and the main Verb of the first sentence until line 5. Only then does the structure and sense of the poem's first sentence fall into place and become evident to the reader.

This kind syntactic 'suspensefulness' is unusual in everyday speech and, although it does occur in writing, is more typical of poetry, especially where the poet – as here – is working against, or within the self-imposed limits of, a tight poetic form. In short, the unusual or deviant syntax may be explained as the result of the pressures exerted by the constraints of the sonnet form on the syntactic shaping of the sentence.

The diction of the poem is also curious. There are turns of phrase that would be surprising in everyday prose. Again we can compare the opening of the poem with a second attempt at an everyday, prose rendering of its content:

> I was surprised to see at four o'clock in the morning – around Easter time – the moon silhouetting the outline of a tree, descending among white street lamps near the north-west horizon. It was not yet a full moon, was awkwardly made, and was of brazen beauty and power.

Some of the phrasing of this everyday prose version and the poem itself may be compared in the opposing columns below:

'I wondered to see'	'I was surprised to see';
'netted in airy twigs'	'silhouetting the outline of a tree'
'some days to full'	'not yet a full moon'

In every case the phrasing of the poem seems deviant by comparison with the more usual linguistic choices that we could make. For instance words that combine more usually with *wondered* are as follows:

wondered + if
wondered + what
wondered + why

On an intuitive basis, bearing in mind our everyday immersion in ordinary usage, the combination *wondered + to* (as in the poem) seems unusual. We can test this empirically by checking the frequency of occurrence of this combination in a large corpus of English text such as the Collins Online Birmingham University Corpus of English (COBUILD). This corpus, which may be searched online for the likely occurrence of phrases, is composed of fifty-six million words of contemporary spoken and written text – including books, newspapers, magazines and transcribed speech from everyday conversation and radio. (For further details see www.collins.co.uk/Corpus/CorpusSearch.aspx.) In this corpus *surprised to see* (as in our prose version) occurs more than a hundred times; but *wondered to see* (as in the poem) occurs not at all. Although *wondered + to* does occur, it does so only in combinations such as *I wondered to what extent* or *I wondered to what degree*.

Similarly, 'netted in airy twigs' is a highly distinctive word combination in the poem. By searching again the COBUILD corpus of everyday English usage we find that 'netted' occurs most usually either in angling contexts or in relation to money, prizes and other financial gains, as in:

netted the carp
netted five bream
netted this eleven pounder

having netted £66 million from the re-release
Black netted £73 million profit by selling shares

By contrast, 'netted in' is extremely rare. Here is one example from the corpus:

The foal lay bloody and inert in the muck, half *netted in* the amniotic
sack, its visible eye open and opaque.

Significantly, the use here verges on the metaphorical – like the example in the
poem.

Two further examples in Scovell's poem are the title, 'Paschal Moon', and
the reference to the moon's 'brazen beauty and power'. 'Paschal' is a word that
pertains to the Jewish festival of Passover and the related Christian festival of
Easter. It typically combines in religious contexts with words such as 'joy',
'mystery' and 'optimism', but not with 'moon'. 'Moon' typically combines with
words such as 'full', 'half' and 'blue'. The phrase, 'Paschal Moon', combining
the notion of lunar cycle with that of Judaeo-Christian religious festival is most
likely unique to this particular poem. It certainly does not occur in the fifty-
six million words of text that make up the COBUILD corpus.

Similarly, 'brazen beauty' is a distinctive phrase tending to be out of step
with everyday usage. In the COBUILD corpus we find typical phrases such as:

brazen cheek
brazen deception
brazen boasting
brazen denial
brazen crooks
brazen con-man

Thus, a common association of 'brazen' is with negative activities – e.g. deception, boasting, crookery. In the poem, however, we find precisely the opposite
kind of association in its unusual combination with 'beauty'. Indeed, a
COBUILD search reveals that the combination 'brazen beauty', while undoubtedly a possible combination in grammatical terms, occurs only once within the
corpus. ('A stunning brunette, whose *brazen beauty* makes Raquel with her
blonde curls, baby blue eyes and little-girl voice look rather ridiculous in
comparison.')

Generally, therefore, we see the poet avoiding common usage and opting
for combinations that are rare, distinctive and unusual. Indeed, the combination, 'the brazen beauty and power' of the moon, provides one route to a

paradox at the heart of the poem. The paschal moon is depicted as dominant, a thing of beauty and power and of glory and strength – most unlike the ashen, fluorescent street lamp. When, however, we look at the actions associated with her, she is invariably on the receiving end of them: she is 'awkwardly made', 'netted in airy twigs', 'freed' and 'seen unmeshed'. The nearest thing to a positive action attributed to the moon occurs in the last few words of the poem: 'such presence as it had'. So we have a tension between the moon contemplated, experienced and acted upon by others while simultaneously being a thing of power and beauty. Indeed, its power emerges from within this contradiction as integral to its very being rather than a quality discernible in its actions or behaviour. This complex meaning is nowhere simply asserted by the poem but is the cumulative outcome of sets of unusual linguistic choices and patterns that deviate from the patterning of everyday speech and writing. Indeed, if the poem consisted simply of unusual word choices, we as readers might easily just give up on it, finding its linguistic peculiarities rebarbative. If, however, its unusual choices can be seen to cohere within an overarching interpretation, the extra efforts demanded of readers may come to seem worth-while – a sign, then, of the work's literary value.

19.2.4 Deviation in semantics

All the cases of literary deviation that we have considered so far have conse-quences for meaning and interpretation: breaking the rules of punctuation, for instance, affects the way we read and make sense of a text. However, it is also possible to find cases of direct manipulation of conventional meanings in them-selves. Joseph Heller's novel, *Catch 22* (1961), is particularly rich in this kind of deviation. Set during the Second World War, it gets its title from the famous paradox (Catch 22) that is used by the authorities in the novel to keep American fliers flying an ever-increasing number of bombing missions. Although fliers can appeal to be grounded on grounds of insanity,

> [t]here was only one catch and that was Catch 22, which specified that a concern for one's own safety in the face of dangers that were real and immediate was the process of a rational mind. Orr was crazy and could be grounded. All he had to do was ask; and as soon as he did, he would no longer be crazy and would have to fly more missions. Orr would be crazy to fly more missions and sane if he didn't, but if he was sane he would have to fly them. If he flew them he was crazy and didn't have to; but if he didn't want to he was sane and had to.

Conventionally, the expressions 'sane' and 'crazy' are opposite in meaning. Part of the fascination (and the humour) of *Catch 22* is the way in which it constructs conditions under which such opposites can both be true at the same time. Love and hate are conventionally opposite, yet the novel tells us that

'Dunbar loved shooting skeet because he hated every minute of it and the time passed so slowly.' Many examples of semantic deviation in the novel are structured like jokes in two parts:

> Doc Daneeka was Yossarian's friend
> and would do just about nothing in his power to help him.

This profusion of semantic anomalies in the opening chapters of *Catch 22* helps to create the impression of a world in which war has undermined the rational basis of social and moral action.

Another, more fundamental, way in which literature produces and exploits semantic deviation in meaning is through its use of figurative language, since figures of speech can be thought of as deviations from literal meaning (see **Unit 10, Metaphor** and **Unit 11, Irony**). Figures of speech play a large part in other kinds of discourse, but there they tend to become conventional and we lose our sense of their 'deviance'. In literature, on the other hand, figurative language tends to be freshly minted and calls attention to the way it deviates from literal usage or conventional figures.

19.2.5 Literature as deviant discourse

Perhaps the most fundamental kind of deviation that characterizes literature stems not so much from its manipulation of linguistic rules, but from peculiarities in the way it relates to the world at large. These peculiarities include:

1   the way that literary texts construct imagined worlds;
2   the way that literary texts construct imagined speakers;
3   the way that literary texts address imagined addressees.

Most kinds of discourse – news, problem-pages, research reports, gossip or even advertising – operate under certain conditions of truth; we expect their assertions to be true, or at least to amount to a reasonable claim. Literature, on the other hand, is full of things that look like assertions about the world but that actually contradict our everyday sense of what the world is like. Literary discourse, then, is deviant in the sense that it is non-referential and, even when it claims to refer to things in the world, we are not expected to take those claims seriously. Take, for instance, the opening sentence of George Orwell's novel, *Nineteen Eighty-Four* (1949):

> It was a bright cold day in April and the clocks were striking thirteen.

To a British readership, the notion of there being a bright cold day in April may be completely unremarkable, but the fact that the same sentence tells us that 'the clocks were striking thirteen' serves to place the events of the novel outside that readership's everyday world (since clocks in public places in Britain don't habitually strike thirteen). Furthermore, although for many years the title of the book (written 1948, published 1949) looked forward to a date in the future, the past **tense** of the first sentence refers backwards as if to events that have already happened. Yet most readers would not interpret the first sentence as the beginning of a factual record of events that had really happened but would realize that Orwell's point was that such events could conceivably come to pass.

However, it is not just the way that literature refers to non-existent entities that marks its peculiarity as a discourse. The narrators of novels and the speakers of poems are as fictional as the events that are presented. When Julian Barnes uses a woodworm to retell the Biblical story of Noah's Ark from an unusual angle in *A History of the World in 10½ Chapters* (1989), he follows a long tradition of using non-human narrators in literary narratives. The speaker of Sylvia Plath's poem 'Elm' (1962) is a tree.

In the case of poetry in particular, literature's whole mode of address turns out to be deviant since it typically addresses someone (or something) other than the reader. During the Romantic period, for instance, there are poems that directly address a rose, a skylark and even a piece of pottery (a Grecian urn):

> O Rose, thou art sick
>
> > (Blake, 'The sick rose', 1794)

> Hail to thee blithe spirit!
>
> > (Shelley, 'Ode to a skylark', 1820)

> Thou still unravished bride of quietness
> > (Keats, 'Ode on a Grecian urn', 1820)

Addressing entities that are incapable of talking back may have become a fairly unremarkable literary convention (known as 'apostrophe'), but it is worth noting how deviant this is by comparison with everyday conditions of discourse. We might swear at the cat when it gets under our feet, but we don't write an elaborate note to it – not, at least, unless we're writing poetry.

19.3 Effects and implications of literary deviation: defamiliarization

We have seen that literature is a discourse that reworks the conventions and codes of the language and is potentially deviant in a range of different dimensions. This does not mean, however, that literature has nothing to say about the ordinary world we live in. On the contrary, its use of deviation allows us to see that world from unfamiliar and revealing angles (Russian Formalist critics called this effect defamiliarization). The philosopher Ludwig Wittgenstein (1889–1951) wrote that 'the limits of my language mean the limits of my world' (*Tractatus Logico-Philosophicus*, 1922). In everyday communication we are usually content to leave intact the limits of our language and therefore of our world. Literature, by contrast, extends the boundaries of our taken-for-granted world and allows us to think and feel it afresh by systematically deviating from conventional linguistic practices and habitual modes of expression. Literature may be seen as a domain of linguistic experiment in how to say new things by bending the rules of the system. By subverting the commonsense bonds between utterances and their situations of use it allows us to explore new kinds of identity, forms of relationship and ways of seeing the world.

ACTIVITY 19.1

Here are two quite separate poems by the American poet, Emily Dickinson (1830–86). The first is about a storm, the second concerns death. They deviate from everyday English in various respects.

Text A

The Clouds their Backs together laid
The North begun to push
The Forests galloped till they fell
The Lightning played like mice

The Thunder crumbled like a stuff
How good to be in Tombs
Where Nature's Temper cannot reach
Nor missile ever comes

Text B

I heard a Fly buzz – when I died –
The Stillness in the Room
Was like the Stillness in the Air –
Between the Heaves of Storm –

The Eyes around – had wrung them dry –
And Breaths were gathering firm
For that last Onset – when the King
Be witnessed – in the Room –

I willed my Keepsakes – Signed away
What portion of me be

Assignable – and then it was
There interposed a Fly –

With Blue – uncertain stumbling Buzz –
Between the light – and me –
And then the Windows failed – and then
I could not see to see –

1   Underline some instances of deviation in punctuation in both poems. In
     what respects are they deviant and what effect or effects can you attribute
     to the deviations?

2   Identify one instance of unusual word order in the first poem. Can you
     suggest what motivates the deviation and what might be gained by the
     unusual word order?

3   The following are representative kinds of word combination, extracted
     from the COBUILD corpus, involving the phrase 'to push':

you don't even need a free hand to **push** the button to open the door

Any attempt to **push** the boat upwind at more than 18 knots resulted

have surrendered after a drive by the army to **push** them out of the eastern part of the country.

She lay in bed, swallowing, trying to **push** back the acid bile that rose in her throat.

From this position, try to **push** your hands further away from you and hold the

Pressure is put on the upper arm to **push** it to the floor whilst the opposite hip is

and holding it while you attempt to **push** it into further extension.

good crack in his left eye before he managed to **push** her away from him.

that some boundaries exist. We continue to **push** boundaries in any new relationship throughout

coming in with lots of money and trying to **push** people around.

He's extraordinary – he learned how to **push** a can of pineapple chunks through someone's

right at the end of the session to **push** Coulthard's team mate Damon Hill into third

longer effective and couldn't bring myself to **push** the line. This commitment to a product line is

and the spell was broken. They all began to **push** their chairs back and reach for plates

(COBUILD Corpus Concordance Sampler,
www.collins.co.uk/Corpus/CorpusSearch.aspx)

3.1 What is distinctive about the way the phrase 'to push' is used in the
     second line of the first poem above?

3.2 What is unusual about the phrase 'the forests galloped'?

3.3 Identify some unusual combinations from the second poem and
     comment upon their effects.

4   In what crucial way is the second poem deviant as discourse? What advan-
     tage does the poet gain from this deviation?

Reading

Erlich, V. (1969) *Russian Formalism: History – Doctrine*, The Hague: Mouton.

Garvin, P. (ed. and trans.) (1964) *A Prague School Reader in Aesthetics, Literary Structure and Style*, Washington, DC: Georgetown University Press.

Leech, G. (1969) *A Linguistic Guide to English Poetry*, London: Longman, Chapters 2 and 3.

Lemon, L.T. and Reis, M.J. (eds) (1965) *Russian Formalist Criticism: Four Essays*, Lincoln, NE: University of Nebraska Press, especially the Chapter by Shklovsky (1921) 'Sterne's *Tristram Shandy*: Stylistic Commentary', pp. 25–57.

Widdowson, H. (1975) *Stylistics and the Teaching of Literature*, London: Longman.

Widdowson, H. (1992) *Practical Stylistics: An Approach to Poetry*, Oxford: Oxford University Press.

Narrative

Unit 20

Narrative

In this unit we examine narrative. Narratives are stories involving a sequence of related events. There are various kinds of relationship between events in a narrative. The most obvious kind is where one event causes another. Such causal connections link one event with another and function partly to give unity to the narrative, and partly to enable the narrative to draw moral conclusions about the consequences of actions.

In the simplest narrative texts, there is a single series of events with causal connections between them. More complex narrative texts might be compounded from simple narratives, with two or more simultaneous narratives (perhaps as plot and sub-plot), or with narratives in sequence that are only loosely connected, perhaps through sharing the same basic character (this is the structure of **picaresque** narratives).

20.1 Narrative form and narrative content

Much thinking about narrative distinguishes between two dimensions or layers of interest, which we will call 'narrative form' and 'narrative content'. The content of a narrative is a collection of represented events, along with the participants in those events, and the circumstances of those events. The form of a narrative is the way in which those events are represented through a particular narrative medium (usually spoken or written language, and/or images). Many components of a narrative show a tension between content and form, as we shall see in this unit.

The distinction between content and form is realized in different ways for different aspects of narrative. If we consider narrative events, we can distinguish between the content order of events and the form order of events. The 'content order' is the chronological order of events (events in the sequence in which they supposedly 'really' occurred). The 'form order' is the order in which the narrative presents these events to us. In the simplest narratives, the presentational or form order is the same as chronological or content order: thus form order = content order. In fact, if there is nothing to tell us otherwise, we just assume that the orders are the same and hence that, if we are told first one thing and then another, the first thing we heard about happened first and the second thing happened second. Thus, if a narrative simply states:

> The queen died. The king died.

we typically assume that the queen died before the king and that probably the latter's death was a result of the former. However, it is also possible for narratives to present events out of chronological sequence. For instance:

> The king died. Only a month earlier the queen had died in child birth.

The presentation of events (the order in which they are narrated) does not match their chronological occurrence. There is thus a mismatch between form order and content order, with content being reordered. Complex narratives, such as we find in film or the novel, often tend to manipulate the presentation of events. Detective fiction, for instance, may begin with the crime and spend the rest of the narrative uncovering the chain of events behind it. Flashbacks in film also manipulate form order and content order. Thus, for example, the film *Sunset Boulevard* (1950) begins with a body floating in a pool; the next images we see represent events that occurred earlier than the first image of the body in the pool.

There are various terms used to describe the distinction between form order and content order in a narrative; one terminological distinction is between 'story' (= the content order of events, the order in which they supposedly happened) and 'discourse' (= the form order of events, the order in which they are presented to us in the narrative as it is told.)

A mismatch between content order and form order is an example of an 'aesthetic strategy', a strategy that might typically be used in creating an aesthetic object such as a novel, film, oral narrative, etc. It is never possible to pin down a single function for an aesthetic strategy; instead, it might perform any one of a number of functions. The strategy of mismatching content order and form order might be used to create enigmas (we are told the consequences before we are told how they were achieved), to create suspense (the order of events is interrupted by a flashback), to help organize our understanding of the content (crucial background history is delayed until we need to be told it) and so on. The Russian Formalists, a group of theorists working in the early twentieth century, focused their energies on an attempt to establish what makes a text 'literary'; one basic idea was that a text is literary to the extent that our attention is drawn to its aesthetic strategies. One very noticeable aesthetic strategy is a mismatch between form order (which they termed *sjuzhet*

– something like 'story' above) and content order (which they called *fabula,* something like 'discourse' above); hence such a mismatch helps define a text as literary.

A mismatch between form and content can have consequences for narrative pace. Minor events in the narrative can be dwelt on at length and major events treated briefly or compressed. Spelling out minor events in detail can give the effect of slowing down – retarding – the narrative. Conversely, condensed treatment of a crucial event seems to speed the narrative up.

Orwell's account of an execution in Burma ('A Hanging', 1931) deals with events that last only about half an hour. The prisoner is picked up at eight and is pronounced dead by eight minutes past eight. Orwell's account, however, dwells in detail on small events that retard the progress to the execution: a dog runs out to interrupt the procession; the prisoner steps aside to avoid a puddle; his final prayer seems to last for ever.

Here is how Orwell dwells on one of these moments that retard the narrative:

> And once, in spite of the men who gripped him by each shoulder, he stepped slightly aside to avoid a puddle on the path.
>
> It is curious, but till that moment I had never realized what it means to destroy a healthy, conscious man. When I saw the prisoner step aside to avoid the puddle, I saw the mystery, the unspeakable wrongness, of cutting a life short when it is in full tide. This man was not dying, he was alive just as we were alive. All the organs of his body were working – bowels digesting food, skin renewing itself, nails growing, tissues forming – all toiling away in solemn foolery. His nails would still be growing when he stood on the drop, when he was falling through the air with a tenth of a second to live. His eyes saw the yellow gravel and the grey walls, and his brain still remembered, foresaw, reasoned – reasoned even about puddles. He and we were a party of men walking together, seeing, hearing, feeling, understanding the same world; and in two minutes, with a sudden snap, one of us would be gone – one mind less, one world less.

But when the end finally comes, it comes swiftly:

> Suddenly the superintendent made up his mind. Throwing up his head he made a swift motion with his stick. 'Chalo!' he shouted almost fiercely.
>
> There was a clanking noise, and then dead silence. The prisoner had vanished, and the rope was twisting on itself.

So, just as dwelling on some events can slow the narrative down, compressing major events can give the impression of acceleration. We get the effect of the narrative decelerating when things are described very slowly (an effect also seen in slow motion sections of films); and narratives can also accelerate or jump when two events separated in the narrative content by major gaps in time are placed next to each other. A strategy of this kind is used by Woolf in *To the Lighthouse* (1927). Various functions are possible for this aesthetic strategy, which again exploits the difference between narrative form and narrative content.

'Narrative coherence' amounts to our recognition that we are being told one unified story – which means that we understand why we are told every event, we understand how events fit together, and, if there are any sub-stories inside the main story, these sub-stories make sense in terms of the overall story, perhaps as commenting on it (e.g. sub-plots in a Shakespeare play or a story one character tells another). An interesting test for coherence in a narrative is to try formulating the narrative as a whole as a single sentence, or even as a single word; this exercise can bring out quite abstract kinds of coherence (the title might carry out this function). Even the author of the narrative may not always find this easy to do. F. Scott Fitzgerald went through a series of titles for his most famous novel, including *Among the Ash-Heaps and Millionaires*, *Trimalchio in West Egg*, *Trimalchio* and *The Golden-Hatted Gatsby*, before finally settling for *The Great Gatsby* (1925). In retrospect, his final choice seems to capture the core meaning of the novel in ways eluded by the earlier attempts. One of the distinctions between form and content in a narrative is that form is inherently more coherent than content. If we take narrative content to be analogous to the way reality is, then we acknowledge its complexity, density and multiplicity; reality is a mess rather than a single coherent thing, and narrative content takes on this implied messiness. In contrast, the organization of narrative content by selection and ordering, which is part of the construction of narrative form, is the creation of order, a fitting together, a making sense, and in general a creation of coherence. Narratives tend to move from a lack to a resolution, a particular kind of beginning to a particular kind of end, but these are formal characteristics that give the narrative its coherence; the implied reality represented by the narrative (the narrative content) lacks any coherent movement from a particular kind of beginning to a particular kind of end – this is imposed upon it by the process of narration.

Finally, another possible kind of mismatch between narrative form and narrative content comes when we consider 'narrative point of view' (see **Unit 21**). Events in narrative content just occur; they do not occur from a particular point of view. However, in a particular narrative, the selection of events and the way in which they are described will interact with the choice of a **focalizer** from whose perspective the events are described. In Henry James's classic ghost story, *The Turn of the Screw* (1898), crucial events are presented to us from the perspective of the governess. From her perspective the children in her charge are in danger of demonic possession from ghostly apparitions; but readers may wonder if the apparitions are merely figments of the governess's neurotic imagination. It is difficult to decide what actually happens in the narrative because of the overriding position given to the governess's point of view. In *The Turn of the Screw* the point of view is that of a character who is supposedly involved in the events (and hence has a particular angle on them). In other cases the narrator stands outside the events of the story.

The use of a narrator is thus an aesthetic strategy, which, like all such strategies, can be used in various ways and for various purposes. Point of view might be switched in the course of the narrative (a technique systematically used by the author Philip K. Dick, or in the film *Rashomon* (1951) for example); the consequence might be, again, that we become uncertain about the narrative content because it alters depending on point of view. Also, because narrators are fictional constructions, it is possible to invent narrators who are fantastic in various ways; so an animal may be a narrator, or a dead person (the body in the pool in *Sunset Boulevard* is also its narrator).

In this section we have seen that differences between narrative form and narrative content can be exploited in aesthetic strategies. In some cases, the narrative form is rigidly constrained but variation is possible in narrative content as in flashbacks, while in other cases it is the content that is constrained and the form that is unconstrained as in narrative pace acceleration and deceleration. In other cases, the narrative content simply lacks a characteristic that can be found in narrative form, such as narrative coherence and narrative point of view. In the next section we look at how events themselves, and the participants in those events, also show a tension between narrative form and narrative content.

20.2 The typicality of characters and events

The raw material of narrative consists of events with their accompanying actors and circumstances. These, we have suggested, comprise the basic content of a narrative, which becomes shaped into form by ordering and reordering their sequence and by the choice of point of view. However, one of the characteristics of narratives is that the events themselves are often stereotyped, with the genre of the narrative to some extent requiring certain kinds of typical event – a marriage, a murder, a chase, a disguise uncovered, a false accusation, etc. The very typicality of events moves them from the level of narrative content to the level of narrative form – they are among the components from which a narrative form is built. Hence, there is a conflict for events between the tendency towards typicality (a formal characteristic) and the demands for the individuality, uniqueness and realism that are associated with narrative content. A marriage in a narrative is (supposedly) a specific marriage, which really happens in all its complex and individual details in the fictional world; but, at the same time, it is a typical event with all its individuality stripped off – a building block of the narrative, perhaps as one of the components that helps end the narrative. Typical events in a narrative are called **motifs**. Folklorists catalogue motifs in folktales (naming and numbering them, tracing their occurrence across storytelling history).

Just as events in a narrative are both individuated and typical, so also characters in a narrative are both individual and typical. On the one hand, characters are representative of supposedly real people in the fictional world represented by the narrative. On the other hand, characters can also be seen as parts of the mechanism that drives the narrative from beginning to end; in this sense they can be labelled depending on their function in the narrative (this is the characters as elements of narrative form). This approach is particularly associated with Vladimir Propp, who suggested that typical characters in Russian fairy tales perform typical functions. Propp identifies a character function on the basis of the character's involvement in specific types of event; for example, for Propp, the 'hero' is the character function of the character who, in the fairy tales under discussion:

- is forbidden to do something;
- is sent off to resolve a lack;
- acquires a magical object;
- fights the villain;
- is marked (e.g. injured, or given something like a ring);
- is pursued;
- arrives somewhere unrecognized;
- is married and ascends the throne.

Propp lists seven character-functions, not all of which are clearly useful in all narratives. However, one in particular, 'the donor', does appear to be found in many kinds of narrative. One specific character is often particularly important in enabling a narrative to move from lack to fulfilment. Donor (= giver) is the name given to this character, and typically the donor(-function) will give the hero(-function) some object that enables the hero to conclude the narrative by restoring the lack. In Propp's fairy tales the gift is often magical (a cloak of invisibility, or a special weapon), but if we move beyond fairy tales to more realistic narratives we still find that there may be something magical about the gift (e.g. it may function unexpectedly, like a Bible carried in a shirt pocket that deflects a bullet). A typical type of donor is an old person who gives the hero(-function) something in exchange for a favour. Sometimes the gift is simply information (as when the dying character in a thriller gasps out crucial information with his or her last breath).

When we seek Propp's character functions in more realistic texts, we may need to adapt them in this manner, interpreting the name of the character function rather abstractly. Thus 'the princess' is just the character who is sought for by the hero, possibly because that character has been snatched by a villain. This means that the princess might for example be a kidnapped young boy; if the only family member otherwise involved is the boy's mother then she might be classified as 'the father of the princess'. This is the power of Propp's approach: it enables us to understand the characters functionally in terms of their role in the narrative rather than just realistically in terms of their identity.

Narratives permeate culture as a way of making sense, packaging experience in particular ways for particular groups and audiences. Thus, as part of the self-representations and imaginings of a culture, an individual can be classified on the basis of some characteristic – race, ethnic group, gender, age, sexuality, size, skin colour, etc. It is interesting to look at the relationship between a particular classificatory characteristic of a character and the function played by that character in the narrative. For example, in many contemporary American films an African-American character has the function of donor. The donor typically has a minimal presence in the narrative (usually appearing briefly) but has a crucial role in enabling it to develop and come to a conclusion. In any particular film, we could interpret the use of an African-American donor as making a historical claim: that African-Americans function as donor for the development of the 'narrative' of the US economy. Or we could interpret it in terms of a contradictory position taken by the film with regard to racism, since it enables racial discrimination at the level of employment (the actor gets a small part) while carrying a positive message at the level of meaning (without this African-American character the narrative could not be resolved).

20.3 The narrative arc: from lack to resolution

Narratives are typically about change. We can think of a change like this:

situation A   changes to   situation B

The changes are often brought about by human actions, and the notion that actions are causes that have effects is an important part of many narratives. Often in a narrative the changes that take place – particularly the important ones – can be understood in terms of situation A being a lack or disruption, which is restored or resolved by situation B. So we can think of many narratives as having arcs like this:

situation A   changes to   situation B

lack   leads to   restoration

The lack may occur when a family member leaves home; this lack may be restored when a family is reunited at the end (it need not be exactly the same people; the crucial point is that a lacking family is replaced by a restored family). Or the lack may be the theft of an object, which is hunted and finally recovered. The lack may be a personal lack; the hero or heroine may begin in ignorance and end in wisdom, or begin in isolation and end in community. There are many other variations on the pattern of lack and restoration, and the movement from one to the other is often the driving force of a narrative.

One very important aspect related to the unity and coherence of a narrative is its achievement of 'closure'. Closure is the 'tying up' of the narrative, whereby loose ends are dealt with, problems solved and questions answered. The restoration of a lack is a form of closure. Few narratives are completely without closure (if they are, we think of them as experimental or avant-garde), though, because most narratives involve plenty of lacks and plenty of restorations, there is typically some lack of closure – a few issues (though not usually central ones) may not be resolved. Sometimes the narrative ends with closure but at the very end of the text a new lack may open up again; the text in its conclusion opens up a new narrative (perhaps leading to a new text – a sequel – that will bring closure to the lack that begins the new narrative). The existence or non-existence of closure often reveals a moral or ideological position. For example, if a narrative can be closed by the major male and female characters getting married, the narrative potentially carries a message about the virtues of marriage. Along similar lines, we could look at what constitutes or causes a 'lack' or a disruption in the terms of a particular narrative: if the absence of the father at the beginning of a film constitutes its initial lack, then the narrative can be read to mean that nuclear families should stay together.

We can exemplify some of these points by looking at some aspects of the narrative of N. Scott Momaday's novel *House Made of Dawn* (1966), about a young American Indian man after the Second World War and his relationship with his culture; as in many narratives, the novel is concerned with an interior change in the hero from lack to fulfilment (in this case the change is emphasized by the fact that the narrative is constructed to parallel an all-night healing ceremony). The novel is divided up into a one-page prologue and four numbered sections. The prologue is echoed in the last page of the novel in that both parts describe a runner (the hero); they are somewhat distinct from the development of events in the narrative, and we could call one the 'orientation' and the other the 'coda' (see next section). After the orientation, the narrative begins with the return home of the hero from the war; we can interpret this as an inversion of the common opening in which the hero leaves home. Normally leaving home is seen as disruptive, but in this novel the hero is unable to fit into the home that he returns to, and so his *return* is the creation of a lack or a disruption. At the end of the novel, the hero walks out of the village, so providing a mirror-image of the beginning. However, he is now integrated into the culture. In the prologue (the orientation) he runs alone; at the end he runs with others. These lacks and closures are to do with movement between the village and the surrounding landscape (a culture–nature opposition: see **Unit 18, Parallelism)**; the closure of the novel involves the unifying of the two, a unity expressed in the title *House Made of Dawn*.

20.4 How narratives begin and end

We have looked at ways in which narrative form is a management of the narra-tive content it represents. We now consider some of the ways in which the narrative form is a response to the context of narration, and in particular how narratives are started and finished. We can call the movement from lack to resolution the 'narrative proper'. The text of the narrative may begin before the lack is revealed, and may end some time after the lack is resolved. This extra material functions to lead into and out of the narrative proper. The hearer or reader must enter into a narrative, and must then exit from the narrative at the end, and there are characteristic strategies for achieving this entry and exit; we first consider some 'entry strategies' and then some 'exit strategies'.

Entry strategies include the title of the narrative and material quoted from elsewhere (an epigraph); these may function to set the leading idea of the narrative – the single notion that gives the narrative coherence. There may occasionally be an initial 'abstract', which is a summary of what is to come. Very often, the text begins by setting the scene; this is called the 'orientation' of the narrative, and may include a representation of the place where the narra-tive is to take place and perhaps some initial details about the characters. Orientations can be stereotyped; fairy tales may begin with a stereotyped orien-tation 'Once upon a time there was . . .', and many films begin with the camera travelling over a city towards a particular locality.

Exit strategies are ways of ending the text once the lack has been resolved. This material is generally called the 'coda'; it can contain elements that mirror the 'abstract' (e.g. a final summary) or the 'orientation' (by describ-ing some kind of departure from the scene). It can also be stereotyped, as in the fairy-tale coda 'And they all lived happily ever after . . .'. Codas sometimes fill a historical gap between an explicitly historical narrative content and now, the time of narrating and reading/hearing; thus a film might end by telling us what happened to various characters between the end of the narrative proper and now.

━━━ ACTIVITY 20.1

1   Choose a nineteenth-century novel. You will need to read* the novel for this exercise.

* This activity can be understood in part as asking you to read different parts of a novel in different ways – a useful skill. Approaches to reading sometimes distinguish (1) close reading: reading every word carefully; (2) skimming: reading quickly through a whole text in order to get a sense of the whole, skipping chunks that you judge to be less crucial to your needs; or (3) scanning: reading quickly while looking for particular things in the text. This exercise asks you to read closely the beginning and the end of the novel, while requiring you to skim the rest (so that you have a sense of the overall structure of the rest of the novel, while paying relatively little attention to detail).

2   Why does the novel have this particular title? In answering this, consider (a) whether the title is an aid in the interpretation of the novel, (b) whether it creates initial expectations that are important for the reading of the novel, and (c) whether it has this title for marketing reasons.

3   Outline the structure of the beginning of the novel, distinguishing the following components (if they exist), or any other components you think are relevant: title, prologue or abstract (introducing a text in an author's voice, perhaps summarizing some of what is to come); epigraph (= a quotation); orientation, beginning of the narrative proper, etc.

    3.1   Comment on any continuities or blurred boundaries between these components.

    3.2   If any of these components are absent, and you think there is some interest in their absence, comment on it.

    (You will need to make your own decision about how far into the novel the 'beginning' extends.)

4   Does the ending of the novel relate in any ways to the beginning of the novel? Describe all the links you can find (e.g. you might expect a restoration at the end of lacks that were indicated at the beginning, and you might also find certain kinds of 'return' to the situation described at the beginning).

Reading

Briggs, K. (1970) *A Dictionary of British Folk Tales in the English Language*, London: Routledge & Kegan Paul.

Fabb, N. (1997) *Linguistics and Literature*, Oxford: Blackwell, Chapters 7–8.

Finnegan, R. (1992) *Oral Traditions and the Verbal Arts: A Guide to Research Practices*, London: Routledge.

Murray, J.H. (1997) *Hamlet on the Holodeck: The Future of Narrative in Cyberspace*, Cambridge, MA: MIT Press.

Onega Jaén, S. and Garcia Landa, J.A. (eds) (1996) *Narratology: An Introduction*, London: Longman.

Propp, Vladimir (1968) *Morphology of the Folktale*, Austin, TX: University of Texas Press.

Toolan, M. (2001) *Narrative: A Critical Linguistic Introduction*, 2nd edn, London: Routledge.

Unit 21

Narrative point of view

21.1 'Story' and 'narration'

In most theories of narrative two main dimensions or levels are identified. The first consists of the basic events or actions, in the chronological order in which they are supposed to have happened, together with the circumstances in which the actions are performed. This level is sometimes referred to as the 'story'. The second level includes the techniques and devices used for telling the story to the reader. This latter level is sometimes referred to as 'discourse' (see **Unit 20, Narrative**) but also as 'narration'. In effect, these two levels may be seen as corresponding to the distinction between the tale itself and the manner in which it is told – a distinction that is based upon our intuitive recognition that the same tale can be told in different ways.

21.2 Point of view and narration

The term 'point of view' in the discussion of prose fiction has been used in a variety of ways (see Fowler, 1986; Simpson, 1993, 2004). It can be used literally to refer to visual perspective – the spatial position and angle of vision from which a scene is presented. It can also be used, metaphorically, to designate the ideological framework and presuppositions of a text (e.g. 'the point of view of the emergent bourgeoisie', or 'a male perspective'). Finally, it can be used as a term for describing and analysing distinctions between types of narration – the different types of relation of the teller to the tale in any narrative. It is this relationship – between point of view and narration – that will be examined in this unit.

The simplest distinction that we can make in discussing point of view is between two types of narration – a first person 'I-narration' and a third person

261

'they-narration'. Thus, if we take a narrative event such as 'the end of a relationship', the same event could be narrated in at least two ways:

> She texted him that it was all over (third person).

Or:

> I texted him that it was all over (first person).

The terminology, first person versus third person, is based upon the grammatical distinction between three persons. In describing the grammar of the personal pronoun system in English (I, you, he, she it, we, you, they), items that refer to, or include, the speaker (I, we) are termed 'first person'. Items that refer to the addressee (you) are termed 'second person'. Items that refer to anyone or anything other than the speaker and the addressee are termed 'third person'.

Given the options in the pronoun system, we might wonder if second person narration ever occurs. In fact, although it is extremely rare, some examples do exist – the best known being perhaps Italo Calvino's *If on a Winter's Night a Traveller* (1981). The reason why second person narration is so rare relates to the ease with which both first person and third person reference can be restricted to figures in a narrative and the converse difficulty in making the second person refer only to a figure in the tale: the second person always somehow points to, or constructs for itself, an addressee. Thus:

> You texted him that it was all over,

sounds like a question to a co-conversationalist rather than a description of a narrative event. Accordingly, we will deal only with features of first versus third person narration.

21.2.1 First person narration

First person narration may be found in a wide range of novels otherwise different in style and period. Novels such as Daniel Defoe's *Robinson Crusoe* (1719), James Hogg's *The Private Memoirs and Confessions of a Justified Sinner* (1824), Charlotte Brontë's *Jane Eyre* (1847), Mark Twain's *Huckleberry Finn* (1884), Philip Roth's *Portnoy's Complaint* (1967) and Alice Walker's *The Color Purple* (1983) are all told in the first person. Indeed, in the case of Robinson Crusoe, the very chapter headings emphasize the use of the first person: 'I Go to Sea', 'I Am Very Ill and Frighted', 'I Sow My Grain', 'I Am Very Seldom Idle'. In this example, and in most of those listed above, the I-narrator is also the central protagonist of the tale, so that the person central to the action of the story is also telling it.

For example, the 'Private Memoirs and Confessions of a Sinner' (which is the central narrative of *The Private Memoirs and Confessions of a Justified Sinner*, framed before and after by 'The Editor's Narrative', also narrated in the first person) begins as follows:

> My life has been a life of trouble and turmoil; of change and vicissitude; of anger and exultation; of sorrow and of vengeance. My sorrows have all been for a slighted gospel, and my vengeance has been wreaked on its adversaries. Therefore in the might of heaven I will sit down and write . . . I was born an outcast in the world, in which I was destined to act so conspicuous a part.

It concludes with the impending death of the sinner and a series of farewells:

> Farewell, world, with all thy miseries; for comforts and joys hast thou none! Farewell, woman, whom I have despised and shunned; and man, whom I have hated; whom, nevertheless, I desire to leave in charity! And thou, sun, bright emblem of a brighter effulgence, I bid farewell to thee also! I do not now take my last look of thee, for to thy glorious orb shall a poor suicide's last earthly look be raised. But, ah! Who is yon that I see approaching furiously – his stern face blackened with horrid despair! My hour is at hand. – Almighty God, what is this that I am about to do! The hour of repentance is past, and now my fate is inevitable – *Amen, for ever!* I will now seal up my little book, and conceal it; and cursed be he who trieth to alter or amend!

Thus, in the 'Private Memoirs and Confessions of a Sinner' the sinner's life is coterminous with the narrative, which is told by him in the first person as the very figure who acts 'so conspicuous a part' in the tale.

First person narration, however, can be used in a quite different way where the story is told not by the central protagonist but by a subsidiary character. Indeed, the 'Private Memoirs and Confessions of a Sinner' is framed – as we have said – by just such a first person narration, purportedly that of the editor and discoverer of the 'confessions' narrative that the sinner had completed just before his death.

F. Scott Fitzgerald's *The Great Gatsby* (1922) is a well-known case of the tale being told through the first person narration of a subsidiary character. Although Nick, the narrator, tells the story in the first person, he remains on the margins of the main events, which involve the central figure – Jay Gatsby himself – whose story is thus told from some degree of narrative distance. Here, for instance, is Nick describing Gatsby and Daisy, whose reunion he has helped – almost unwittingly – to make possible:

> As I went over to say goodbye I saw that the expression of bewilderment had come back into Gatsby's face, as though a faint doubt had occurred

to him as to the quality of his present happiness. Almost five years! There must have been moments even that afternoon when Daisy tumbled short of his dreams – not through her own fault, but because of the colossal vitality of his illusion. It had gone beyond her, beyond everything. He had thrown himself into it with a creative passion, adding to it all the time, decking it out with every bright feather that drifted his way. No amount of fire or freshness can challenge what a man can store up in his ghostly heart.

As I watched him he adjusted himself a little, visibly. His hand took hold of hers, and as she said something low in his ear he turned toward her with a rush of emotion. I think that voice held him most, with its fluctuating feverish warmth, because it couldn't be overdreamed – that voice was a deathless song.

They had forgotten me, but Daisy glanced up and held out her hand; Gatsby didn't know me at all. I looked once more at them and they looked back at me, remotely, possessed by intense life. Then I went out of the room and down the marble steps into the rain, leaving them there together.

Nick's narration does contain some confident, almost poetic, assertions – usually about life: for instance, 'No amount of fire or freshness can challenge what a man can store up in his ghostly heart'; or 'that voice was a deathless song'. However, it is also full of circumspect observation ('I saw that . . .', 'As I watched him . . .', 'I looked once more at them . . .'), where the truth of the events that are described is not certain: 'I saw that the expression of bewilderment had come back into Gatsby's face, *as though a faint doubt* had occurred to him'; or 'There *must have been* moments'; or 'and as *she said something low* in his ear he turned toward her with a rush of emotion'; or '*I think* that voice held him most'. Indeed, the two deaths that separately constitute the spring of the tragedy and its **dénouement** each happen, so to speak, 'off camera' since Nick is present at neither event.

First person narration, therefore, usually has in-built restrictions, especially when told from the viewpoint of a minor character, though even a central character will be ignorant about some of the things happening around him or her. Whatever its restrictions, however, it projects the reader clearly inside the consciousness of someone in the story giving us the events from a defined observer's position.

21.2.2 Third person narration

Third person narration, by contrast, can be used in such a way that we are not particularly aware of the role of the narrator, who remains outside the action of the tale. In such writing the narration seems to operate as a simple window on the events of the story; and, because the role of the narrator is carefully effaced, this mode of narration acquires a reputation for impersonal, but all-seeing, objectivity. The opening of William Goldings's *Lord of the Flies* (1954) is of this type, in the way it introduces an unnamed boy, who is presented from the outside:

> The boy with fair hair lowered himself down the last few feet of rock and began to pick his way towards the lagoon. Though he had taken off his school sweater and trailed it now from one hand, his grey shirt stuck to him and his hair was plastered to his forehead.

As third rather than first person narration this presents quite different opportunities for readers to align themselves with the story. 'The boy with fair hair' is clearly presented to us at this moment as if observed from without. Indeed, it would be hard to re-cast any of this into first person from the boy's perspective: for instance 'my hair was plastered to my forehead' sounds odd precisely because the boy would simultaneously have to be the subjective agent of the narration and object of its scrutiny. He'd have to be looking at himself.

The opening passage of the novel continues (still in the third person) as follows:

> All round him the long scar smashed into the jungle was a bath of heat. He was clambering heavily among the creepers and broken trunks when a bird, a vision of red and yellow, flashed upwards with a witch-like cry; and this cry was echoed by another.

Although the narration remains in the third person, the sensations described shift to being – in part at least – those of the boy. It could be the boy who feels the long scar in the jungle as a bath of heat and who sees the red and yellow of the bird and who hears its 'witch-like cry'. Indeed, these sentences do not sound as odd as the earlier part of the passage if transformed into the boy's first person narration: for instance, 'All round me the long scar smashed into the jungle was a bath of heat' reads quite appropriately.

In this respect, third person narration is potentially more flexible and enjoys a technical advantage over first person narration. First person narrators have to provide a warrant for knowing the details that they narrate. However, if the narrator is not defined and named, operating instead anonymously in the third person, the narrative does not have to provide a warrant for presenting everything and anything that is going on in the story, whether it is inside the mind of a character or not.

Moreover, it is important to recognize that there are contrasting possibilities within third person narration, which we may sum up in terms of the following oppositions:

INTERNAL versus EXTERNAL

RESTRICTED KNOWLEDGE versus UNRESTRICTED KNOWLEDGE

Internal/External: The example of third person narration given above from *Lord of the Flies* begins by observing characters and events from outside (externally). But third person narration may also provide access to the (internal) consciousness of characters by telling us how they think and feel. Much of D.H. Lawrence's *Lady Chatterley's Lover* (1928), for instance, despite its title, adopts Connie Chatterley's perspective rather than that of her lover, Mellors. The following passage (despite its third person narration) is – with its emphasis on Connie's feelings – fairly representative of the novel as a whole:

> Now she came every day to the hens, they were the only things in the world that warmed her heart. Clifford's protestations made her go cold from head to foot. Mrs Bolton's voice made her go cold, and the sound of the business men who came. An occasional letter from Michaelis affected her with the same sense of chill. She felt she would surely die if it lasted much longer.
>
> Yet it was spring, and the bluebells were coming in the wood, and the leaf-buds on the hazels were opening like the spatter of green rain. How terrible it was that it should be spring, and everything cold-hearted, cold-hearted. Only the hens, fluffed so wonderfully on the eggs, were warm with their hot, brooding female bodies! Connie felt herself living on the brink of fainting all the time.

Although this passage, like the rest of the novel, is consistently in the third person, it is nonetheless devoted primarily to the inner sensations of the person it describes. Indeed, rhetorically it is structured around a simple, basic opposition in Connie's sensations between warmth and cold (equivalent to life and death). Significantly, it is difficult to read the penultimate sentence as the narrator's comment. It makes most sense as a piece of free indirect thought (see **Unit 22, Speech and narration**) belonging in part at least to Connie herself. Third person narration, therefore, has the option of being internal or external, sometimes switching within the same text.

Restricted/Unrestricted: A second distinction may be made in third person narration between narration with no restrictions on the knowable (so-called 'omniscient narration'), and narration with restrictions on the knowable. Indeed, in third person narration we tend to assume that narration is omniscient unless there are indications to the contrary, usually in the foregrounding of a character who – though given to us in the third person – offers a position from which events can be known. Consider the following passage from Henry James's short novel *Daisy Miller* (1879), in which the heroine is observed for

us (by a subsidiary character – a young man named Winterbourne who is sympa-
thetically attracted to Daisy) in conversation with an Italian companion ('her
cavalier', or gallant), named Giovanelli:

> Winterbourne stood there: he had turned his eyes towards Daisy and her
> cavalier. They evidently saw no-one; they were too deeply occupied with
> each other. When they reached the low garden-wall they stood a moment
> looking off at the great flat-topped pine-clusters of the Villa Borghese;
> then Giovanelli seated himself familiarly upon the broad ledge of the
> wall. The western sun in the opposite sky sent out a brilliant shaft through
> a couple of cloud bars; whereupon Daisy's companion took her parasol
> out of her hands and opened it. She came a little nearer and he held the
> parasol over her; then, still holding it, he let it rest upon her shoulder, so
> that both their heads were hidden from Winterbourne. This young man
> lingered a moment, then he began to walk. But he walked – not towards
> the couple with the parasol; towards the residence of his aunt, Mrs
> Costello.

In places this passage could be read as simple, omniscient, unrestricted third
person. For instance, the following fragment, taken in isolation, seems to be
from no one individual's perspective:

> The western sun in the opposite sky sent out a brilliant shaft through a
> couple of cloud bars; whereupon Daisy's companion took her parasol out
> of her hands and opened it. She came a little nearer and he held the
> parasol over her.

However, placed in a larger context this event is clearly framed from
Winterbourne's perspective: 'he had *turned his eyes towards* Daisy and her cavalier. They *evidently* saw no-one.' And, later, with the opening of the parasol:
'their heads were hidden from Winterbourne'. Restricting at crucial moments
our observation of a central action to what a subsidiary character can see is
an important structural device in the novel (as so often in James). Like
Winterbourne, we are left at this moment in the narrative in a state of uncertainty concerning the exact nature of Daisy's relationship (sexual or merely
flirtatious?) with her cavalier (courtly gentleman or lover?).

    Other indications of limited knowledge include phrases of doubt, such as
'it seemed/appeared/looked as if'. The following paragraph, for example, from
a story by Nadine Gordimer, uses several signals of doubt (such as 'no doubt',
'somehow' and the question form: 'Hadn't he written a book about the Bay
of Pigs?'):

> The voice of the telephone, this time, was American – soft, cautious – no
> doubt the man thought the line was tapped. Robert Greenman Ceretti,

from Washington; while they were talking, she remembered that this was the political columnist who had somehow been connected with the Kennedy administration. Hadn't he written a book about the Bay of Pigs? Anyway, she had certainly seen him quoted.

It is no accident, of course, that this kind of narrowing down of a potentially omniscient narration should come in a narration that aligns itself strongly with the consciousness of one character, even while remaining third person. It is important to recognize, therefore, that third person narration need not always embody objectivity. It can quite easily work from subjective, internal and restricted positions.

21.3 Focalization

We can see, therefore, that the distinction between first person and third person narration is not sufficient in itself to account for different types of point of view. An additional complication arises from the fact that most prose fiction is not stable or homogeneous in the point of view that it adopts, so that it can be quite misleading to describe a story as 'told externally in the third person' (which would imply that this was a consistent point of view throughout). Even Ernest Hemingway, who might be thought an exemplar of the external third person viewpoint, does in practice use a variety of modes of narration, often within the same text, which allow for subjective and internal points of view. Because of this instability in point of view, some accounts of narrative (e.g. Bal, 1985; Rimmon-Kenan, 1983; and Simpson, 1993) have refined the account of point of view by developing the notion of 'focalization'. Focalization refers to the way in which a text represents the relationship between who 'experiences' and what is experienced. The one who experiences is termed the 'focalizer', and who or what the focalizer experiences is then called the 'focalized'. Focalization falls into two main types: external focalization, where an anonymous, unidentified voice situated outside the text functions as focalizer; and character focalization, where phenomena are presented as experienced by a character within the story.

It is possible then to map shifts and tendencies in focalization within any one text by using the following simple notation:

F'r	=	Focalizer
E	=	External
C	=	Character
1	=	First person
3	=	Third person
F'd	=	Focalized phenomenon

Thus:

External focalizer	=	EF'r
Character focalizer (first person)	=	CF'r1
Character focalizer (third person)	=	CF'r3
Focalized phenomenon	=	F'd

Take the following idealized examples of differing focalization from three hypothetical narrations:

(1) Despite closing the windows, I could hear noises from the beach all that sleepless night.

(2) Even with the windows closed, she could not shut out the noises from the beach.

(3) Even with the windows closed, the noises from the beach were audible all night.

In each example, 'noises from the beach' are the focalized phenomenon, hence [F'd]. In (1) 'I' is the focalizer, hence [CF'r1]. In (2) 'she' is the focalizer, hence [CF'r3]. In (3) no-one is identified as the focalizer and the noise is reported by an unidentified narrator from a position potentially outside the constructed world of the fiction, hence [EF'r]. Thus, the focalization structure of the three examples may be rendered in notational terms as follows:

(1) CF'r1('I')   → F'd ('noises from the beach')

(2) CF'r3('she') → F'd ('the noises from the beach')

(3) EF'r   → F'd ('the noises from the beach')

These examples, as if from separate narrations, have been constructed to display differences of focalization. In practice, focalization within a narrative text tends to shift from sentence to sentence and sometimes can alter even within the same sentence. In the later history of the novel it is hardly ever stable and consistent throughout a text. The advantage of the notation lies in the way it can be applied to display these focalization shifts in terms of who is experiencing what and how from sentence to sentence.

Crucial evidence for deciding who is focalizing is the presence or absence of verbs of experiencing such as 'look', 'see', 'touch', 'smell', etc. Consider the following example from Rosamund Lehmann's *The Weather in the Streets* (1936) (the sentences have been numbered):

(1) She [Olivia] ran down to the next floor, telephoned for a taxi, then opened the door of Etty's bedroom, adjoining the sitting room. (2) Silence

and obscurity greeted her; and a smell compounded of powder, scent, toilet creams and chocolate truffles.

In the first sentence Olivia and her actions are focalized from without by an unidentified focalizer. In the second sentence, however, the smell and the silence are impressions that belong to Olivia rather than to the external focalizer of the first sentence. The focalization shifts therefore from external focalization (EF'r) to character focalization (CF'r). This can be summed up as follows:

Sentence 1: EF'r (unspecified) → F'd (Olivia)

Sentence 2: CF'r3 (Olivia/She) → F'd (silence, smell, etc.)

Similar shifts can be detected in the following passage from the same book:

(3) Between stages of dressing and washing she [Olivia] packed a hasty suitcase. (4) Pack the red dress, wear the dark brown tweed, Kate's cast off, well-cut, with my nice jumper, lime green, becoming, pack the other old brown jumper – That's about all.

Again, the extract begins as externally focalized, but in the second sentence there is a switch to Olivia's 'inner speech' or thoughts, as she does her packing (presented in 'free indirect style': see **Unit 22, Speech and narration**). Moving into the character's consciousness in this way entails a change of focalization from external focalization to character focalization. Here again, we can summarize:

Sentence 3: EF'r (unspecified) → F'd (Olivia packing)

Sentence 4: CF'r1 (Olivia/my) → F'd (Olivia packing)

On this occasion, the notation helps to highlight, not just a shift in focalization, but the way in which Olivia in this passage comes to be the focalizer of her own actions. For a moment she is the object of her own subjective consciousness in a way that is both intimate and distanced. In ways such as these, the concept of focalization can become an important supplement to notions of point of view because it prompts close attention to the shifts, developments and balances within point of view within a particular text. *The Weather in the Streets,* for instance, moves between external focalization and character focalization that is centred primarily on Olivia, who figures sometimes as third person, sometimes as first person. These subtle variations help construct her as at once somehow both subject and object of the narrative.

Focalization can in this way be studied in terms of how it is realized from one sentence to another in a text. It may be observed at the level of the form of the text. But focalization at a deeper level is more than this. Patterns of focalization are at once the expression and construction of types of both consciousness and self-consciousness. In that respect, *The Weather in the Streets* is very much a novel of the first half of the twentieth century. It is quite distinct, for instance, from *Robinson Crusoe*, even though Crusoe also figures as both subject and object of his own narrative. The relentless 'I' of Crusoe's narrative seems to present the human subject as individual, stable, unified and separate. The shifting patterns of focalization in *The Weather in the Streets* on the other hand seem to present an idea of subjectivity as split and dispersed at the very moment that it becomes possible to grasp it in a self-conscious way.

ACTIVITY 21.1

The following text is the complete version of a story by Ernest Hemingway. It is narrated in the third person and involves two main protagonists, a man and a woman.

A Very Short Story

One hot evening in Padua they carried him up on to the roof and he could look out over the top of the town. There were chimney swifts in the sky. After a while it got dark and the searchlights came out. The others went down and took the bottles with them. He and Luz could hear them below on the balcony. Luz sat on the bed. She was cool and   5
fresh in the hot night.

Luz stayed on night duty for three months. They were glad to let her. When they operated on him she prepared him for the operating table; and they had a joke about friend or enema. He went under the anaesthetic holding tight on to himself so he would not blab about   10
anything during the silly, talky time. After he got on crutches he used to take the temperatures so Luz would not have to get up from the bed. There were only a few patients, and they all knew about it. They all liked Luz. As he walked back along the halls he thought of Luz in his bed.   15

Before he went back to the front they went into the Duomo and prayed. It was dim and quiet, and there were other people praying. They wanted to get married, but there was not enough time for the banns, and neither of them had birth certificates. They felt as though they were married, but they wanted everyone to know about it, and   20
to make it so they could not lose it.

Luz wrote him many letters that he never got until after the armistice. Fifteen came in a bunch to the front and he sorted them by the

dates and read them all straight through. They were all about the
hospital, and how much she loved him and how it was impossible   25
to get along without him and how terrible it was missing him at
night.

  After the armistice they agreed he should go home to get a job so
they might be married. Luz would not come home until he had a good
job and could come to New York to meet her. It was understood he   30
would not drink, and he did not want to see his friend or anyone in
the States. Only to get a job and be married. On the train from Padua
to Milan they quarrelled about her not being willing to come home
at once. When they had to say good-bye, in the station at Milan, they
kissed good-bye, but were not finished with the quarrel. He felt   35
sick about saying good-bye like that.

  He went to America on a boat from Genoa. Luz went back to Pordenone
to open a hospital. It was lonely and rainy there, and there was
a battalion of arditi quartered in the town. Living in the muddy, rainy
town in the winter, the major of the battalion made love to Luz, and   40
she had never known Italians before, and finally wrote to the States
that theirs had been only a boy and girl affair. She was sorry, and she
knew he would probably not be able to understand, but might some
day forgive her, and be grateful to her, and she expected, absolutely
unexpectedly, to be married in the spring. She loved him as always,   45
but she realized now it was only a boy and girl love. She hoped he
would have a great career, and believed in him absolutely. She knew
it was for the best.

  The major did not marry her in the spring, or any other time. Luz
never got an answer to the letter to Chicago about it. A short time   50
after he contracted gonorrhea from a sales girl in a Loop department
store while riding in a taxicab through Lincoln Park.

1   Read through the story and then try altering the mode of narration by
    transposing the text into first person narration from the woman's point
    of view. (Thus, 'Luz sat on the bed' becomes transposed to 'I sat on the
    bed.)

2   Write down any peculiar or incongruous sentences that result from this
    transposition and try and detail the grounds on which they are peculiar.

3   Now transpose the text into first person narration from the man's point
    of view. (Thus, 'they carried him up on to the roof' becomes transposed
    to 'they carried me up on to the roof'.)

4   Note again any peculiarities or incongruities that result.

5   Which transposition of point of view has worked best and why? What
     does it suggest about the original, third person mode of narration? Did
     it involve an implicit bias; and, if so, in favour of whom? What other
     textual mechanisms might support this bias?

Reading

Bal, Mieke (1985) *Narratology: Introduction to the Theory of Narrative*, Toronto:
    Toronto University Press.
Branigan, E. (1984) *Point of View in the Cinema*, New York: Mouton.
* Fowler, R. (1986) *Linguistic Criticism*, Oxford: Oxford University Press, Chapter 9,
    pp. 127–46.
Furniss, T.E. and Bath, M. (1996) *Reading Poetry: An Introduction*, London: Longman,
    Chapter 7.
* Rimmon-Kenan, S. (1983) *Narrative Fiction: Contemporary Poetics*, London: Methuen,
    Chapter 6, pp. 71–85.
Scholes, R. (1982) *Semiotics and Interpretation*, New Haven, CT: Yale University Press.
Simpson, P. (1993) *Language, Ideology and Point of View*, London: Routledge.
Uspensky, B. (1973) *A Poetics of Composition*, Berkeley, CA: University of California
    Press.

Speech and narration

Characters and events are the building blocks of narratives, as we saw in **Unit 20**. In narratives (as in life) characters leave home, fall in love, wake and sleep, live and die. However, characters also speak: they argue, seduce, cajole, flatter and entertain each other; and storytelling – whether in the novel or in the everyday anecdote – reflects this: it relies on the expressive and dramatic potential of speech and quotation. The spoken narrative has specialized strategies for capturing the speech of characters. The storyteller, for instance, can mimic tones of voice and pitch to convey emotion and even to distinguish between one speaker and another. Here, for instance, is a fragment of anecdote told by a young casualty doctor:

> They come bustin' through the door – blood is everywhere
> on the walls
> on the floor
> everywhere
> [raised pitch]
> It's okay Billy it's okay we're gonna make it
> [normal voice]
> What's the hell wrong with you?
> We look at him. He's covered with blood y'know?
> All they had to do was take a wash cloth at home and go like this
> [pause for wiping action]
> and there'd be no blood . . .

The teller of the tale switches between narration of action and the speech of protagonists. Indeed, in spoken narratives pivotal moments in the action are often marked by this kind of embedding of enacted dialogue. The successful performance of the tale requires the performance of the voices of those who inhabit it in order to best bring it alive for the audience.

In written narrative, speech is no less important than in oral narrative; but writers have needed to evolve specialized techniques to tackle the management and embedding of characters' voices and speech within the narrative as a whole.

22.1 Speech and writing

Writers must find ways of replacing the expressive possibilities of voice with techniques for quotation, for the presentation of speech and for the identification and individuation of speakers – techniques of the kind that developed slowly in the history of the novel. They are, it must be stressed, highly conventionalized: writers of narratives rarely attempt to render in detail actual, 'real-time', conversational speech, or **dialogue**. For one thing, conversation is full of false starts, repetitions, pauses, unfinished sentences and self-correction, so real-time speech can look messy on the page. Here, for instance, is someone in ordinary conversation talking about arrangements for making telephone calls from a payphone:

> well you see (.) I'm sure it would have
> I'm sure it would have been possible
> if they had known anyone who was a post office engineer
> to install (.) a um er (.) rig
> so that the the (.)
> where you can actually dial from the from the from that phone (.)
> er and if you (.) but that could be you know locked away
> and the er something like that (.)
> so that you could actually dial from that one
> by-pass the coin mechanism

A written version of this snatch of conversation – smoothing out the apparent disfluencies – might look like this:

> I am sure it would have been possible, if they had known anyone who was a post office engineer, to install the type of pay-phone where you can, if you wish, use a key to by-pass the coin mechanism and still dial out.

This generally is what writers of narrative do: in the first place they tend to conventionalize the raw immediacy of speech – even where, as we saw in **Unit 6, Language and place**, and **Unit 9, Language and society**, a writer accentuates the difference between narrative voice and character voice by attributing vernacular forms to characters and reserving standard dialect for narration.

22.2 Types of speech presentation in prose fiction

In addition writers have evolved various ways of presenting the speech of characters, which vary from giving as much autonomy to words of a character as possible (rendering them, as it were, directly) to filtering a character's speech through the report of the narrator – or another character – thus rendering them indirectly.

22.2.1 Free direct speech

In free direct speech there is hardly any ostensible intrusion or filtering by the narrator. We know, however, that we have switched from the words of the narrator to the words of a character through various clues such as indentation on the page and the use of quotation marks, but there is little description of whose words they are or how they are spoken. They are allowed to speak for themselves. Here is an extract of free direct speech from Doris Lessing's *The Golden Notebook* (1962). Note the absence of any reporting clauses such as 'he said', 'she replied':

> They talked about his work. He specialised in leucotomies:
> 'Boy, I've cut literally hundreds of brains in half!'
> 'It doesn't bother you, what you're doing?'
> 'Why should it?'
> 'But you know when you've finished that operation, it's final, the people are never the same again?'
> 'But that's the idea, most of them don't want to be the same again.'

22.2.2 Direct speech

Direct speech is enclosed within quotation marks, like many examples of free direct speech, but it is introduced by, or presented in the context of, a reporting clause (such as *she said/declared/commanded/asserted*, etc.):

> She said: 'Well there's nothing I can say to that, is there?'
> He leaned forward and said: 'I'm going to give you another chance, Anna'.
>
> (Doris Lessing, *The Golden Notebook*, 1962)

This strategy makes a clear distinction between the words of the narrator ('He leaned forward and said') and the words of a character ('I'm going to give you another chance, Anna.'); and it opens up possibilities for comment or evaluation (implicitly or explicitly) by the narrator on the character. Thus, in the exchange above, the details of manner supplied by the narrator – as well as the words themselves – suggest a vaguely intimidating move in the dialogue. We have the words of the characters; but we also have – through the words of the reporting clause – the narrator's perspective.

22.2.3 Indirect speech

Indirect speech shifts the perspective yet further from the speaker to the narrator. It differs from direct speech in various ways:

1   quotation marks are dropped;
2   some kind of subordinating **conjunction** such as *that* may be used;
3   there is a switch from first and second person pronouns (for example *I* or *you*) to third person (*she, he, they*);
4   there is a shift in the tense of the verb 'backwards' in time (e.g. from *is* to *was*);
5   temporal expressions shift backwards in time (e.g. *now* becomes *then*);
6   **demonstratives** shift from close to distant ones (e.g. *here* becomes *there*).

Following these guidelines, the piece of dialogue in direct speech from *The Golden Notebook*, given above, can be transformed into indirect speech simply as follows:

> She said that there was nothing she could say to that. He leaned forward and said that he was going to give her another chance.

Notice that the narrative voice is now more dominant than before with a consequent attenuation of the immediacy of the original dialogue. In the following passage from George Mackay Brown's novel *Beside the Ocean of Time* (1994) the author alternates between direct and indirect speech:

> It was to an island satiated with festival that the three mysterious strangers came. In those days, the country people went out of their way to be pleasant and welcoming to visitors, but those men, from first setting foot on Norday, didn't seem to care what the islanders thought of them. They climbed through fences and trespassed on the Glebe and the Bu. Simon Taing of the Bu came out and remarked that the gentlemen were in his barleyfield. They looked at the farmer coldly, and made some measurements and set up a tripod, right there in the middle of the barley, and looked in all directions through some kind of an instrument, and one of them spoke some numbers, and another made notes in a large notebook. Lucky, the Bu collie, didn't like the look of them, it seemed, for he went circling behind the man with the theodolite and suddenly made a grab at the man's trouser-leg. 'Keep that brute under control,' the man taking notes said ... Simon Taing called in the dog, and said that Lucky had never been known to seize anyone before – all the same, it was his land

they were trespassing on, his barley, the winter bread of the people, and
he would be glad to know what they were there for, anyway . . . The three
men paid no attention to the farmer.

The utterance of the man taking notes, 'Keep that brute under control', carries
more force than the utterances of the farmer, Simon Taing, which on each
occasion here are presented in indirect speech.

22.2.4 Free indirect speech

This is a mixed form, consisting partly of direct speech and partly of indirect
speech, where – because of the suppression of some of the distinguishing signals
– it is difficult to separate the voice of the narrator from the voice of the character. In the following short extract from Chapter 16 of Dickens's novel,
Dombey and Son (1846–8), we find 'backshifting' of tense ('the motion of the
boat . . . *was* lulling him to rest'), as well as some pronoun shift ('me' becomes
'him'); these characteristic features of indirect speech emphasize the presence
of a narrator who filters the speech of characters. At the same time some
sections sound close to the direct speech of the character (e.g. 'how bright the
flowers growing on them, how tall the rushes!'):

> Presently he told her the motion of the boat upon the stream was lulling
> him to rest. How green the banks were now, how bright the flowers
>   growing
> on them, and how tall the rushes! Now the boat was out at sea but
>   gliding
> smoothly on. And now there was a shore before him. Who stood on the
>   bank!

It is a fairly simple matter, involving few changes, to switch the free
indirect speech of this passage into direct speech, thereby moving it closer to
the perspective of the character:

> Presently he told her: 'The motion of the boat upon the stream is lulling
> me to rest. How green the banks are now, how bright the flowers
>   growing
> on them, and how tall the rushes! Now the boat is out at sea but gliding
> smoothly on. And now there is a shore before me. Who stands on the
>   bank!'

Free indirect speech is thus an ambiguous mode in that it blurs the distinction
between a character's speech and the narrative voice; this ambiguity has made
it attractive to novelists from Jane Austen onwards. Some writers – such as
Joyce in *Dubliners* (1914), or Austen in *Emma* (1816) – are especially known
as exponents of free indirect speech. As a technical device it offers writers a

way of presenting words that seem to come from inside and outside a character simultaneously. Such words can be given the emotional weight of the character's perspective, while at the same time preserving a degree of narrative distance or ironic detachment from the character.

22.2.5 Speech and thought

Many of the distinctions discussed above apply also to the representation of characters' thoughts in narrative, so much so that in many respects thought may be considered as a kind of 'inner speech'. Thus the different modes of presenting both speech and thought can be represented in a table that shows the different degrees to which a character's speech or thought can be filtered through the narrator:

FREE DIRECT SPEECH/ THOUGHT	UNFILTERED BY NARRATOR ('Come here tomorrow')
DIRECT SPEECH/ THOUGHT	SOME FILTERING (She said to him 'Come here tomorrow.')
FREE INDIRECT SPEECH/ THOUGHT	MORE FILTERING (She said to him to come tomorrow)
INDIRECT SPEECH/ THOUGHT	MOST FILTERING (She said that he was to come there the next day)

Because of the connection between modes of presentation and relative closeness to or distance from the viewpoint of the character or of the narrator, modes of presenting speech in prose fiction are more than merely technical accomplishments that allow for variety in the handling of characters' voices. Each possibility has a different effect, and seems to carry a different value ranging from allowing the character to speak as if in his or her 'own words' to filtering them through the perspective of the narrator. If, for instance, free indirect speech lends itself to the creation of ironic distance between the words of the character and those of the narrator, free indirect thought on the other hand can create a sense of empathy with the character. These different kinds of interplay between the voice of the narrator and the speech of a character make the issue of speech presentation important not just for its own sake but also for the way in which it connects with other topics such as 'point of view' in fiction (see **Unit 21**).

22.2.6 Genre and the presentation of speech

Subtle differences in the presentation of speech can also serve as indicators of different 'genres' of prose fiction (see **Unit 4**). Consider, for example, the following reporting clauses that frame direct speech (they are all drawn from within a few pages of each other in a single novel; the speech itself has been omitted):

'. . .,' she replied sharply
'. . .,' she stuttered
'. . .,' she wailed gaspingly
'. . .,' he murmured huskily
'. . .,' she asked as calmly as she could
'. . .,' he said with chilly emphasis
'. . .,' he countered silkily

Readers familiar with the genre will no doubt instantly recognize these as coming from popular romance (they are quoted from Susan Napier's *The Counterfeit Secretary: A Vivid Story of Passionate Attraction,* published by Mills and Boon (1986)). The way in which the manner of the speech has been foregrounded in the reported clauses through adverbial phrases such as 'gaspingly', 'huskily', 'with chilly emphasis' and so on, is genre-specific to such popular romance. This can be seen by comparing these reporting clauses with the way speech is presented in the following short scene from Nancy Mitford's 'literary' novel *The Pursuit of Love* (1945):

'*Allô – allô.*'
'Hullo.'
'Were you asleep?'
'Yes, of course. What's the time?'
'About two. Shall I come round to see you?'
'Do you mean now?'
'Yes.'
'I must say it would be very nice, But the only thing is, what would the night porter think?'
'*Ma chère*, how English you are. *Eh bien, je vais vous le dire – il ne se fera aucune illusion.*'
'No, I suppose not.'
'But I don't imagine he's under any illusion as it is. After all, I come here for you three times every day – you've seen nobody else, and French people are quite quick at noticing these things, you know.'
'Yes – I see –'
'*Alors, c'est entendu – à tout à l'heure*'.

Both *The Counterfeit Secretary* and *The Pursuit of Love* are concerned with romantic relationships, and dialogue in both works as an important vehicle for registering fluctuations in degrees of emotional attachment. This makes the differences in the ways dialogue is handled all the more striking. *The Counterfeit Secretary* uses some free direct speech; but a great deal of the dialogue is direct speech, where information about the manner of the speaker is foregrounded in explicit narrative comment. *The Pursuit of Love* makes much more use of free direct speech, in which the words of characters have to achieve their own significance without being mediated by a direct comment from the narrator. Comparison between the two techniques suggests that, for popular romance, the shifting grounds of emotional attachment may be carried in the manner of the speech as much as by the speech itself. For readers of *The Pursuit of Love*, on the other hand, the ebb and flow of emotional confrontation is to be deciphered in the nuances of the very wording of the dialogue itself. Such differences function as formal markers of generic distinctness; they may also signal differences in attitudes towards language and meaning in the 'implied readerships' of the two works (See **Unit 15, Positioning the reader or spectator**). The implied readership of *The Pursuit of Love* is, for instance, more class-based than that of *The Counterfeit Secretary*. The extract from the former presupposes not only some knowledge of the French language (very much a minority skill in Britain in 1945, restricted mostly to the middle and upper classes) but also – for its humour to be intelligible – some acquaintance with the distance between French and English sexual mores of the time. Free direct speech, furthermore, may be seen as making greater demands of the reader, since the significance of the dialogue has to be extracted from the wording of the speech itself without interpretive signposts regarding tone and manner being supplied by the narrator. Thus, the differences in the narrative presentation of speech in prose fiction may correlate with broader distinctions between popular and minority genres.

In this unit we have explored how writing and speech – because of the very different circumstances in which they are produced – constitute very different modes of communication. We then considered how particular conventions have arisen in written storytelling, or prose narration, for the rendering of speech. Different techniques for presenting speech (as well as thought, as a kind of 'inner speech') were examined; and some suggestions were made as to the different effects associated with the different techniques. Finally, it was proposed that there may also be generic differences associated with the adoption of one mode of speech presentation rather than another.

ACTIVITY 22.1

Since 'thought' may be considered as a kind of 'inner speech', the presentation of thought – for the purposes of this activity – is treated as similar to the presentation of speech. Direct speech, for example, is similar in its presentation to direct thought – except that the kind of reporting verb will be different:

> *Direct speech*:
> She said, 'Well there's nothing I can say to that, is there?'

Direct thought:
She thought, 'Well there's nothing I can say to that, is there?'

In the following extract from Doris Lessing's *The Golden Notebook* (1962), two characters – Tommy and Anna – are having a confrontation. Tommy is the adult child of Anna's close friend; he is challenging Anna about her writing – specifically about her way of organizing her work in four notebooks.

'Don't put me off, Anna. Are you afraid of being chaotic?'
Anna felt her stomach contract in a sort of fear, and said, after a pause: 'I suppose I must be.'
'Then it's dishonest. After all, you take your stand on something, don't you? Yes you do – you despise people like my father, who limit themselves. But you limit yourself too. For the same reason. You're afraid. You're being irresponsible.' He made this final judgement, the pouting, deliberate mouth smiling with satisfaction. Anna realised that this was what he had come to say. This was the point they had been working towards all evening. And he was going on, but in a flash of knowledge she said: 'I often leave my door open – have you been in here to read these notebooks?'
'Yes, I have. I was here yesterday, but I saw you coming up the street so I went out before you could see me. Well I've decided that you're dishonest, Anna. You are a happy person but . . .'
'I, happy?' said Anna, derisive.

1   Identify the type of speech presentation in the following segments:

(a)   Anna . . . said, after a pause: 'I suppose I must be.'

(b)   in a flash of knowledge she said: 'I often leave my door open – have you been in here to read these notebooks?'

Try to rewrite each segment as indirect speech. Make a note of the changes that were necessary in order to do so. Compare the original with your rewritten version: are there any differences between them in terms of meaning or effect? If so, make a note of what the differences are.

2   Identify the way of presenting speech used in the following segment:

'Yes, I have. I was here yesterday, but I saw you coming up the street so I went out before you could see me. Well I've decided that you're dishonest, Anna. You are a happy person but. . .'

Try to rewrite the segment as free indirect speech. Make a note of the changes you needed to make in order to do this. Compare the original with your rewritten version: do they differ in meaning or effect? If so, how?

3   Identify the way of presenting inner-speech/thought used in the following segment:

> Anna realised that this was what he had come to say. This was the point they had been working towards all evening. And he was going on, . . .

Is there any ambiguity about how much of this extract is the character's thought, and how much is the narrator's report of, or comment upon, the events? If so, where does the ambiguity begin? How might you resolve this ambiguity? Try to rewrite the passage as direct thought ('inner-speech'). Compare the original with your rewritten version: do they differ in effect? If so, how?

4   Substitute your rewritten segments into the original, and read the whole (rewritten) passage through again. Does it work as well as the original? If not, why not? If you can offer an answer to this question, you have gone a long way towards understanding why the writer may have made those particular technical choices in the first place.

Reading

Leech, G. and Short, M. (1981) *Style in Fiction*, London: Longman, pp. 318–51.

Ong, W.J. (2002) *Orality and Literacy: The Technologizing of the Word*, London: Routledge.

Toolan, M. (2001) *Narrative: A Critical Linguistic Introduction*, 2nd edn, London: Routledge, pp. 90–145.

Narrative realism

'Realism' as a critical term is sometimes taken to signify a relationship between a text and reality that is felt to be immediate and direct. Examples of realism are typically chosen from genres such as 'the nineteenth-century novel', 'the Hollywood film' and 'popular fiction'. An alternative way of thinking about realism has developed within more recent critical theory, however, and that is to see it as marked out by the adoption of specific devices or formal techniques for producing a sense of the 'real'. Realism is thus a style that need not be considered to have any necessary reference to an external reality. It is possible, therefore, to make a distinction between *realistic*, commonly used to mean something like ' close to how I see reality' or 'life-like', and *realist*, in the more technical sense of conforming to conventions for passing something off as real, so that even future-fantasy or science fiction could be seeing as drawing on conventions of realism stylistically or formally. Realistic is an evaluation of a piece of prose whereas realist is an assessment of the formal elements of a prose narrative.

23.1 The traditional view of realism

Realism is both the name of a literary movement involving primarily novels, which flourished between about 1830 and 1890 and included, for instance, George Eliot as one of the major British exponents, and a particular 'genre' (see **Unit 4**) of writing in which certain formal features of realist texts are displayed. This was the view held by realist writers and many critics until recently. Within the traditional critical view it is possible to see realism in two ways: either as a direct imitation of the facts of reality, or as a special recon-struction of the facts of reality, which Eric Auerbach (1953) calls **mimesis**. In the first of these views of realism it is seen as a style of writing that acts as a simple window onto the world, mirroring events, almost as if the writing is a direct transcription of events in the real world. In mimesis, while the reader recognizes the vision of reality that is represented in the narrative, since it includes elements from external reality with which he or she is familiar, it is a more generalized or universalized version of reality than that which the reader habitually experiences, and it is this that is thought to be of most value. Mimesis does not simply describe 'a' reality, but teachers readers about 'reality' in general.

In **Unit 4, Recognizing genre**, we looked at the possibility of listing characteristics of particular genres. In the traditional view, the characteristics of realism revolve particularly around its subject matter and its message or moral intentions. The subject matter of realist novels is generally concerned with what is considered in the West to be 'ordinary life' – centring on the home, on work and on human relationships. Most of the events described are not about heroic deeds but are, rather, the seemingly ordinary events within the lives of ordinary people, their emotions, their relationships, etc. One of realism's aims is to present ordinary people as complex and multifaceted. Although realist texts are about individual characters and their lives, their message – often developed in terms of a secular, socially based morality – is supposed be true for all readers.[1]

23.1.1 Language, reality and representation

In such an approach to realism, there is not generally much attention to the language of the text; in fact it is often seen to be **non-self-reflexive language**, that is, it does not draw attention to itself as language. Rather, the language is treated merely as a transparent medium for the transmission of the message, as if it were capable of simply reflecting reality. However, it is clear that the relation between texts, particularly literary texts, and reality is far more complex than simply reflection or idealization. As Leech and Short state: 'The myth of absolute realism arises from a mistaken attempt to compare two incomparable things: language and extralinguistic realities' (1981, p. 152). Realist texts are, after all, only verbal constructs, and yet it is this essentially textual nature that is often ignored in traditional critical discussions of realism. It is for this reason that some critics have turned to analysing not the relation between words and the material world outside the text but the relations between words within the text.

23.1.2 How traditional realism shapes ways of reading

The traditional view, by which realist texts are assumed to describe the reality of a period or a place, is common in the criticism and teaching of texts, and is often tied into stereotypical views of the place of particular people in reality. Realism is firmly linked to stereotypical notions of authenticity, whereby certain experiences or individuals are deemed to be more 'real', or closer to 'life' than others. The so-called 'gritty' realism of a novel about working-class life in the inner city, for example, is often considered to be more authentic than a close examination of refined middle-class behaviour in north London. Many texts are assumed to be realist for these stereotypical reasons. For example, novels written by women are often interpreted, when they are included on university courses, as though they were autobiographical (drawing upon the stereotypical notion that women are restricted to the private sphere and to descriptions of the personal, intimate intricacies of relationships); novels by working-class writers are read as documentary accounts (according to a stereotype in which working-class people see everyday reality as it really is but are unable to transcend the particularity of that view); or novels by Black writers are read as documenting personal struggles against oppression, rather than being concerned with larger, more universal issues that concern both white and Black people.

23.2 The structuralist view

Structuralist critics such as Roland Barthes (1986) and David Lodge (1977) have helped to shift attention from the relationship between the text and reality to the textual qualities of realism, and have shown that the notion of literary convention is very important in the construction of realist novels. In this view, whether or not a text is realist (that is, has the formal characteristics of realism) is not related to whether it is realistic (that is, whether it seems to the reader to approximate to some notion of reality), but to whether it uses conventional techniques to produce a **reality effect**.[2]

23.2.1 Conventions

Literary texts are generally constructed according to a system of textual conventions or rules; our notion of which genre a text belongs to is largely founded on the recognition of the particular set of conventions that the text is drawing on (see **Unit 4, Recognizing genre**). When a writer decides to produce a realist narrative, there is already a set of conventions in place governing the choices to be made. For example, he or she will be constrained by a number of conventions that govern the production of such a narrative: (1) events in the text are arranged in a roughly chronological order; (2) there are complex, 'rounded' developed characters who develop throughout the narrative; (3) there is generally a narrator who will constitute a consistent position within the text; (4) there will be an ending that will draw the various strands and sub-plots in the narrative together; and (5) events will be included on the basis of clear relevance to plot development. Point (3) is particularly important, as we shall see. The presence of a reliable or omniscient narrator creates a hierarchy of discourse that seems to guarantee that at least one view of the events in the novel offers us a view of the 'truth' or the 'real'. Although these conventions of realism can be experimented with and altered, as they invariably are in novels, they nevertheless exist as the basis for the construction of realist texts.

23.2.2 Characteristics of realism

David Lodge (1977) suggests that realist texts achieve their effect not so much because they are like reality as such, but because they resemble in their conventions texts that we classify as non-fictional. He takes two separate descriptions of capital punishment, one by George Orwell entitled 'A Hanging' and one that appeared in *The Guardian* newspaper. Lodge analyses the similarities between the realist fiction and the non-fictional report: (1) in neither case are features of language foregrounded so that they become the focus of attention; (2) the narrator does not draw attention to his or her role in interpreting events – the events, rather, seem to speak themselves or to present themselves to the reader without mediation; and (3) there is an emphasis on detailed description of the context of the event (the exact time, place and setting) and of the preparation for the execution. It is almost impossible, Lodge argues, to distinguish one text from the other purely on the basis of strategies that they adopt to depict the event. From this he concludes that realist texts draw on the same conventions used to construct non-fictional texts in order to convince the reader that they are describing reality. This strategy accrues some authority to realist texts. Lodge thereby suggests a working definition of realism in literature as: 'the representation of experience in a manner which approximates closely to descriptions of similar experience in non-literary texts of the same culture' (1977, p. 25).

In a similar way, as discussed in **Unit 22, Speech and narration**, it is clear that dialogue is represented in literature, particularly in realist narrative, according to a set of conventions, rather than with reference to the way that people speak in real life. Many elements of actual speech are omitted when speech is represented in prose narrative (for example, hesitation, interruption, repetition), while other elements are included to signal to the reader that they are reading 'real speech' (for example, inverted commas, the use of colloquialism).

Other conventions that govern the production of realist narrative concern the inclusion of descriptive passages. Roland Barthes has noted that in most classic realist texts there is a proliferation of descriptive detail. Although narratives in general tend to include a descriptive section that sets the scene in which the actions take place, Barthes points to the presence in realist narratives of details that seem to be included for the sole purpose of signalling to the reader that it is 'the real' that is being described. For example, in the following extract from *The Well of Loneliness* by Radclyffe Hall (1928), some of the description serves the purpose of setting the principal character within a certain social class (the estate is 'well-timbered, well-cottaged'; there are two large lakes in the grounds; the house has 'dignity and pride'; and so on), but other elements seem to be included in the text simply because of the conventions of realist texts:

> Not very far from Upton-on-Severn – between it, in fact, and the Malvern Hills – stands the country seat of the Gordons of Bramley; well-timbered, well-cottaged, well-fenced, and well-watered, having in this latter respect, a stream that forks in exactly the right position to feed two large lakes in the grounds. The house itself is of Georgian red brick, with charming circular windows near the roof. It has dignity and pride without ostentation, self-assurance without arrogance, repose without inertia; and a gentle aloofness that, to those who know its spirit, but adds to its value as a home.

The aside in the first sentence – 'between it, in fact, and the Malvern Hills' – serves no discernible informational purpose as such, and functions simply to give a sense of the real. Similarly, the description of the house as being built of Georgian red brick and as having circular windows seems excessive. These elements of the passage may thus be seen to function as what Barthes terms 'realist operators', producing a 'reality effect' (that is, they signal to the reader that this is a realist text), and helping to reinforce for the reader a sense that the text is well anchored to some recognizable reality.

Barthes also suggests that many realist texts implicitly draw upon a **cultural code**, which is a set of statements that must be decoded by the reader according to a set of conventions that the reader already knows, and shares with the writer. These are statements that appeal to background knowledge, stereotypes and so-called common-sense knowledge, and that either appear self-evident or, it is assumed, the reader will recognize and assent to them. For example, *The Well of Loneliness* continues:

> To Morton Hall came the Lady Anna Gordon as a bride of just over twenty. She was lovely as only an Irish woman can be, having that in her bearing that betokened quiet pride, having that in her eyes that betokened great longing, having that in her body that betokened happy promise – the archetype of the very perfect woman, whom creating God has found good.

This description of Anna is presented as if the reader will instantly recognize that it fits the stereotype of the perfect woman. The reader is supposed to draw upon background assumptions about the loveliness of Irish women, and to recognize the elements about Anna's eyes and body that the text presents as self-evidently constituting perfection in women (that is, having quiet pride, embodying happy promise and so on). It is presented as information that 'we all know'. In this way, in drawing on this kind of background knowledge we are, Barthes would claim, drawing upon the cultural code, using the term to indicate an organized repository of common-sense knowledge and stereotypes. It is through the cultural code that realist texts confirm certain conventional views of reality (which may have only slight correspondence with the way things actually are); in this way, realist texts are creating rather than reflecting realities, and one way of reading realist texts is to see them as shaping (rather than reflecting) our views of the real. Not only this, but they tend to reaffirm the status quo and the self-evident quality of stereotypical knowledge.

A further convention in realist texts is that they have narrative 'closure' – that is, at the end of the narrative the problems that the text presents are resolved. In nineteenth-century realist novels plots are frequently resolved by death or marriage, and coincidence is a strong motivating factor in the way that most, if not all, of the loose ends of the plot are finally knitted together, so that the reader is left with no unresolved questions about the characters. In twentieth- and twenty-first-century realist texts, the resolutions tend to be less complete and closure is one of the conventions that writers may feel that they can experiment with or reject altogether. Writers no longer feel it necessary to employ coincidence to such an extent to bring their narratives to a close. However, for many readers, narrative closure is pleasurable, and they may feel unsatisfied or cheated if a text leaves them with too many unresolved plot elements. (See **Unit 20, Narrative**.)

23.3 Marxism and realism

Marxist criticism attaches great importance to questions of realism, and the progressive or reactionary nature of realism has been much debated in Marxist circles. (This issue has also been debated within feminist circles. See, for example, Coward (1986) for an overview.) For some critics, such as Georg Lukács (1962), realist novels can present to readers a vision of a greater harmony in the face of capitalist fragmentation; in this way, these novels can spur people to action, since they point out the problems within the present system, exposing the tensions between the individual and society in such a way as to foreground points of prevailing ideological contradiction. Lukács, indeed, championed the cause of realism against the rival claims of modernism, rejecting the latter on the grounds of its subjective, fragmentary and disconnected modes of representation, which he felt amounted to a retreat from society into pathological individualism. Bertolt Brecht, however, saw realist novels as a form of anaesthesia (Brecht, 1977). Readers become hypnotized by realist narrative and become uncritical of the values within the text and within the wider social system. As an alternative, he proposed a new form of art that would deny the reader the comforts of realist narrative and encourage him or her to act on the contradictions in capitalism. Lukács is thus closer to the traditional view, and Brecht closer to the structuralist view of realism.

23.4 Non-realist texts

Many contemporary literary texts play with the conventions of realism, either to challenge traditional notions of realism (for example, surreal, science fiction or fantasy texts) or to challenge notions of what reality is (for example, representing the perspective of narrators or characters with different or altered states of consciousness). Many of these **non-realist texts** force the reader to question both their sense of what counts as realism in a text and what is real. For example in Mark Haddon's *The Curious Incident of the Dog in the Night-Time* (2003), the central character and narrator is not the conventional middle-class educated narrator of classic realist fiction. Take for example, this extract:

> Then the police arrived. I like the police. They have uniforms and numbers and you know what they are meant to be doing. There was a policewoman and a policeman. The policewoman had a little hole in her tights on her left ankle and a red scratch in the middle of the hole. The policeman had a big orange leaf stuck to the bottom of his shoe which was poking out from one side. The policewoman put her arms round Mrs Shears and led her back towards the house. I lifted my head off the grass. The policeman squatted down beside me and said 'Would you like to tell me what's going on here, young man?' I sat up and said 'The dog is dead.' 'I'd got that far,' he said. I said 'I think someone killed the dog.' 'How old are you?' he asked. I replied, 'I am 15 years and 3 months and 2 days.' 'And what precisely were you doing in the garden?' he asked. 'I was holding the dog,' I replied. 'And why were you holding the dog?' he asked. This was a difficult question. It was something I wanted to do. I like dogs. It made me sad to see that the dog was dead. I like policemen too, and I wanted to answer the question properly, but the policeman did not give me enough time to work out the correct answer.

This extract is not a conventionally realist text, although it shares certain of the features of realism. There is a certain amount of descriptive information given about the characters, and yet this information seems not to be the type of relevant character-revealing information that we find in realist texts. Instead, the reader is presented with information about the police officers that appears random: that the policewoman has a hole in her tights and that there is a scratch on her leg; that the policeman has a leaf stuck to his shoe. This type of information seems to conform to Barthes' reality effect in that it is excessive, non-necessary information, but here its relevance to the plot or character development is in question. In a similar way, we are not informed that the character/narrator is lying on the ground but rather we are forced to work this out when he says 'I lifted my head off the grass'. We expect realist narrators to spell out what is happening clearly to the reader. The fact that the protagonist gives the police officers either too much information (about his age) or too little (about his reasons for being in the garden) leads the reader to surmise that this is not the trustworthy narrator of **classic realism**. We are forced to assume that this narrator's perspective is just one of many different views of the events and thus the hierarchy of discourses of class realism is reversed: instead of the narrator presenting us with the 'truth' of the events, here, his perspective needs to be set alongside the perspective of the police officers. Thus, contemporary texts may be non-realist in the sense that they play with the conventions of classic realism or they may be attempting to represent different 'realities', calling for different forms of representation.

ACTIVITY 23.1

The aim of this activity is to analyse two pieces of visual narrative and to identify the markers of realism and non-realism.

1   Choose two pieces of narrative, one that you would identify as an example of realism and the other an example of non-realism. Your two pieces should be from the same medium (from a novel, a short story, television, film, video, comic strip, photo-reportage, etc.). You will need to look closely and repeatedly at the texts, so if you choose a moving image you will probably need to have it on videotape.

2   Here is a reminder of some features that have been claimed to be characteristic of various different sorts of realist texts (for more detail see the unit):

- the subject matter is generally drawn from 'everyday', 'ordinary' life;
- the characters are ordinary people presented as complex individuals who are shown to be capable of change and development;
- there is a moral position from which the events are viewed;
- there is a consistent point of view from which the events are evaluated (there may be more than one but they are consistent);
- the narrator presents a non-contradictory reality;
- the narrator does not draw attention to him- or herself;
- the language used in the narrative does not draw attention to itself;
- events are arranged in roughly chronological order (there may be flashbacks, but the sequence of events is clear);
- the narrative reaches a clear resolution;
- there is detailed description of material objects (clothes, faces, furniture, etc.);
- there are realist operators (the inclusion of arbitrary details);

- • the narrative includes an appeal to the cultural code (views that we are all supposed to share).

3 Examine the 'realist' text, and check which of these characteristics are present. Add any other general characteristics of realism that occur to you as you examine the text.

4 Now examine the 'non-realist' text and check which of these characteristics are absent. Cross off the list any characteristics that this examination suggests might be characteristic of all texts (not just realist ones).

5 For the two texts you have chosen, what are the reasons you might suggest for each text drawing on or rejecting the conventions of realism?

Notes

1 It should be noted that 'ordinary' here can often turn out to refer to middle-class characters, since most novels revolve around bourgeois characters. Although there is a tradition of working-class writing where the central characters are members of the working classes, generally even now it is the middle class who are mostly represented as the 'ordinary' and therefore universal individual.
2 These problems with the nature of 'reality' largely stem from theoretical work that questions the sense of a pre-existent reality to which all individuals have the same access and apprehension. Theorists who have questioned this notion of a pre-given, agreed-upon reality that pre-dates our own individual experiencing and apprehension of it are Berger and Luckman (1966) and Michel Foucault, most notably in *The Archaeology of Knowledge* (1989) and *The Order of Things* (1970).

Reading

Barthes, R. (1986) *The Rustle of Language*, Oxford: Blackwell, pp. 141–8.
Leech, G. and Short, M. (1981) *Style in Fiction*, London: Longman, pp. 150–70.
Lodge, D. (1977) *The Modes of Modern Writing*, London: Arnold, Chapter 3, 'Realism'.
Mills, S. and Pearce, L. (1996) *Feminist Readings/Feminists Reading*, 2nd edn, Hemel Hempstead: Harvester, especially chapter on 'Authentic Realism'.
Toolan, M. (2001) *Narrative: A Critical Linguistic Introduction*, 2nd edn, London: Routledge.

Section 6

Media: from text to performance

Unit 24

Film and prose fiction

Narratives take many shapes. Both opera and soap opera depend upon narrative, as do theatre, ballet, news and documentary. At the beginning of the twenty-first century, however, there are two particularly dominant forms of fictional narrative: the visual narrative forms of cinema (and television); and the prose forms of the novel (and short story). Not infrequently, the same stories circulate between the different media, so reinforcing the distinction developed in previous units between *story* (narrative content) and *discourse* (narrative form). One of the underlying justifications for making this distinction is the observation that the same story may be told in different forms and in different media – in a novel, for instance, or as film. In this unit we explore this distinction further, by looking at some of the similarities and differences between narration in film and in prose fiction.

The early development of film as a medium is marked by the effort to capture movement photographically – as the name 'movie' of course implies. Eadweard Muybridge (1830–1904), for instance, is credited with 'The Horse in Motion', which dates from the 1870s. And many early attempts at cinematography were devoted to capturing the movements of animals or humans with an emphasis on documentary record. It is some time before film as a medium for fiction or for narrative begins to be established with *The Burglar in the Roof* (1896) and *The Life of an American Fireman* (1903). One of the curiosities of cinema's early history is the way in which, from this point onwards, film quickly became devoted primarily not just to narrative, but to fictional narrative – rather than, say, simply to song, spectacle or documentary record; so that, by the 1920s, 'movies' or 'films' showing in 'picture palaces', 'film theatres' or 'cinemas' had became established as a rival to the novel, short story or drama as a major source of narrative fiction.

Since that time, novels – and prose fiction more generally – have remained a constant source of inspiration to film-makers. Almost from inception film has drawn freely on available narratives that already existed in prose form: films such as *Gone with the Wind* (Victor Fleming, 1939), *The Maltese Falcon* (John Huston, 1941), *Moby Dick* (John Huston, 1956), *Trainspotting* (Danny Boyle, 1996), *Eyes Wide Shut* (Stanley Kubrick, 1999) and *Bridget Jones' Diary* (Sharon Maguire, 2001) were all adapted from novels. Since the first Academy Awards, more than three-quarters of the awards for best film went to films based on novels. Some novelists have proved particularly popular. There were, for instance, nearly sixty filmic adaptations of work by Dickens between the years of 1898 and 1915 alone (on average more than three a year), including eight versions of *Oliver Twist*. It has even been argued (see Wagner, 1975; and Spiegel, 1976) that certain film techniques (close focus, the flashback) were themselves anticipated in the writing of novelists such as Dickens, Conrad and James and contributed in formal terms to cinema's rapid development as a narrative medium. Yet, despite this history of interconnection, techniques of film narration and prose narration are in many ways quite different from each other; and these differences can be identified at various levels, from differences at the level of the institutions of literature and cinema to differences at the more formal level of the contrasting media themselves.

24.1 Institutional differences: literature versus cinema

Fictional narrative in prose and film has become institutionalized in quite different ways. Studio-based commercial film-making for general release is a highly capitalized institution; the cost of making a commercial film for film (and DVD, TV, etc.) can run to millions of dollars, using equipment that is costly and capital intensive. Cinema is also a highly specialized industry, requiring a large number of skilled workers (camera operators, script-writers, editors, sound and lighting technicians, etc.); so the production process can only be understood as a highly collective one involving a large range of people in different capacities. An analogous perspective applies to the process of consumption. Although videoCD and videocassette sales and rental for home viewing have complicated the picture, a major source of income for film studios remains 'box-office' receipts from public viewing in cinemas. Publicity and distribution networks provide for the screening of films in public auditoria, where they are viewed by an audience that has assembled expressly for the purpose at advertised times.

By comparison, the novel, as an institution of cultural production, is not nearly so capital intensive or industrialized. Publishing houses may be large-scale commercial enterprises, but they often depend upon more than fiction for their commercial viability. Nor is the production process so heavily centralized, as is the case with the film industry: printing, for example, is routinely subcontracted. In addition, the production of the text of a novel is much more individualistic than the production of a film. Novels are 'authored' (see **Unit**

14, Authorship and intention) and, as such, they derive mostly from a single person. Responsibility for the words on the page is always assumed to lie with the individual author. (There is nothing in the novel corresponding to the credit sequence in a film.) Authors are also much cheaper as a production entity than a film crew: millions of dollars do not have to be raised in advance in order to begin production of a novel. Significantly, consumption of the prose text mirrors its conditions of production. Again it is highly individualistic, performed independently by discrete readers operating as autonomous entities.

24.2 Differences in media: film versus prose

The commercial film has evolved as a self-contained event, for public screening, lasting about two hours, with a strong emphasis on it being widely intelligible at a single viewing. Originally, as a visual text it was based upon the continuous projection of light through moving frames onto a screen, thereby providing a high-definition image later to be accompanied by high-quality sound. As a result, it evolved as something to be viewed in semi-darkness, with direct appeal to the senses of hearing and vision; but also, typically, for public screenings projection is continuous and without interruption for the course of the film. As a public event there is therefore no possibility, under normal cinematic conditions, for control by the viewer. Spectators in the cinema are in no position to vary or control the rate of viewing. Neither interruption nor review is permitted. The spectator is caught up by the event in a continuous process. Two key points emerge from this. First, the spectator's condition – viewing images in darkness – is similar to that of someone dreaming; this favours a high degree of projection of the self into the film, or identification with particular aspects of it. Second, as a self-contained but continuously projected event, film in mainstream cinema has evolved under a regime that values easy intelligibility.

With the growing potential for digitally recording, editing and re-mastering film, a range of different distribution platforms, outside cinema, have become available. Accordingly, fiction films are no longer restricted to screenings in public auditoria but are widely available through broadcast television, online on the Internet, and on DVD. No doubt the proliferation of formats through which film is available will have long-term consequences for its formal techniques. For the moment, however, these seem to remain strongly rooted in the traditional techniques of (Hollywood) commercial cinema and in habits of collective consumption.

The novel, by contrast, presents its stories in the medium of prose writing. This favours an individual mode of consumption. Reading a prose novel is usually a solitary act, which apparently allows greater degrees of discretion and control to the individual reader. Variable levels of attention are possible, as are differing rates of reading. It is possible to skip and to review. Readers, unlike cinema-goers, can set their own pace and choose to reread at their own

convenience; and, while this approach is increasingly available for film spectatorship in DVD formats, it has not yet begun generally to affect the film form.

24.3 Formal differences: verbal sign versus visual image

The most important contrast between film and prose, however, rests on the
distinctive features of the two media and upon the different kinds of signification involved in them. Prose as a medium depends upon linguistic signs where
the relationship between the material of the sign (sounds or letters) and that
which is designated by them is quite arbitrary. The significatory medium – the
letters on the page in the case of prose – has no necessary, obvious or natural
relationship with the entities signified by it. There is no particular reason why
the letters P-I-G should be inevitably associated with the concept of a four-
legged creature that grunts and lives in a sty. The association depends simply
upon convention – upon a tacit agreement between users of the sign; and
decoding prose depends upon consciously learnt methods of interpretation.
(See **Unit 9, Language and society**, for further discussion of the arbitrary nature
of the linguistic sign.)

In film, by contrast, the signifying material (visual patterns shaped in variations of colour and of light and dark) has a much closer relationship to that
which is signified. The film (or video) image resembles in visual terms the reality
that it signifies or depicts, and so its relationship to reality seems more obvious,
direct and easily intelligible. As a medium of representation, film is composed
from **iconic** images – unlike prose, which is made up of linguistic signs.

24.4 Narration

This basic distinction between words and images is an important point of difference between the two media. Indeed, the differences between film and prose
fiction can seem to reduce to a long-established distinction in the study of narrative between 'showing' (mimesis), on the one hand, and 'telling' (diegesis) on
the other. It has even been suggested that narrative film can be thought of as
'story' without the level of narration – a tale without a teller. In what follows,
however, it is suggested that film can be thought of as a narrative medium –
even though the medium through which narration is accomplished is quite
different from that of prose.

Despite the differences between them, some important points of resemblance between film and prose fiction remain. These resemblances are best
revealed in terms of narration. In the first place, the claim that film is a non-
narrated medium is one that is difficult to sustain. For one thing it is not uncommon for the soundtrack of a film to include elements of voice-over narration
(as, for instance, in Steven Spielberg's *The Color Purple* (1985), Francis Ford

Coppola's *Apocalypse Now* (1979) or *Trainspotting* (1995)). More significantly and more persuasively, however, the way in which film is shot and edited together to construct a coherent and intelligible story follows certain basic conventions, amounting to codes of narration, or routine ways of telling, even when a personalized narrator is not evident. Film is not a completely transparent 'window' on the world of the tale: the film image should not be confused with reality. Despite their iconicity, film images are still 'signs', in that they recall or resemble a segment of reality elsewhere, without being that reality itself. Moreover, the significance of a film image always exceeds what it literally depicts or denotes. This broader significance has many aspects, and is conferred on the image in the following ways:

1   An image supplied by a shot derives significance from its place in series of shots. This is the classical principle of 'montage' (see **Unit 12, Juxtaposition**) in which the sequential juxtaposition of one shot with another produces significance that goes beyond what can be traced to the individual shots themeselves.

2   In mainstream cinema, the image is constantly supplemented by sound. Contemporary cinema typically uses immensely complex, multilayered soundtracks, which interweave several different types of sound, including music (e.g. 'motifs'), ambient or diegetic sound (e.g. traffic, rattling teacups), and voice/speech (both as character dialogue and voice-over narration).

The organization and sequencing of shots – especially in commercial cinema – are themselves subject to powerful conventions. In the presentation of dialogue in the fictional film it is rare for characters to address the camera; rather, they are filmed in various degrees of profile addressing each other. This is such a binding convention that 'the look to camera' might almost be described in film terms as 'the forbidden look'. When it does occur, it typically breaks the illusion of **naturalism**. It is more common in art cinema (in films by Jean-Luc Godard and Ingmar Bergman, for example, or Sally Potter's film *Yes* (2003)) than in mainstream cinema, though it may be found occasionally in popular television drama series (e.g. Glenn Gordon Caron's *Moonlighting*, 1985–9, Channel 4's *Sex and the City*, 1999, or BBC 2's *Rab C. Nesbitt*, 1992–9).

The practice of filming dialogue in profile is part of a larger set of conventions built up around an important organizing principle: the line of action. In its simplest form, for a scene involving two protagonists, this principle is based on an imaginary line drawn between the two characters. In mainstream cinema it is a basic convention to restrict consecutive shots in the same scene to only one side of this imaginary line. In theory, it might seem possible to set up shots from anywhere within a 360-degree circle around the space in which the filmed action occurs. In practice, however, shots are restricted to half this domain, in conformity with what then becomes known as 'the 180-degree rule'.

In shooting a scene involving dialogue, film-makers have available to them a standard repertoire of possible shots. The most common among these are mid-shots, medium close-ups and close-ups. At or near the beginning of a scene will occur a mid-shot, in which both characters figure, in order to establish the line of action (sometimes called a two-shot or an establishing shot.) As the dialogue proceeds, there will usually be a progressive focusing in on the individual protagonists, so that each is shown individually in close-up. At or near the end of a scene, a two-shot or mid-shot is often used as part of the process of bringing the scene to a close. Within the scene, then, the handling of close-ups is prepared for by the initial establishing shot, which gives the line of action. Subsequent chaining together of the close-ups develops in a form of visual counterpoint: a shot of one speaker is typically replaced by a shot of the other in a technique commonly known as 'field/reverse-field' or 'shot/counter-shot'. In the clearest cases, the speaker is observed from a position nearby, to one side or behind the listener; the position is then reversed when the speaking roles switch, the camera remaining all the time on one side of the line of action. The repertoire and combination of shots amount to a set of conventions for making the events of the narrative intelligible. As a set of conventions they are comparable in some ways to showing and in some ways to telling. In the case of filmed dialogue, for example, they are analogous to (but clearly not the same as) the reporting clauses and other methods for the presentation of speech in fictional prose narratives. The sequence of stills in Figures 24.1–3, from David Lean's film of *A Passage to India* (1978), helps to show these conventions at work.

These basic conventions are, of course, honoured as much in the breach as in the observance. They have evolved as routines that provide flexible formats for making what is seen on screen coherent and intelligible; but they are not adhered to in a rigid fashion. The shot/counter-shot does not always follow the speaker. Sometimes it includes the reactions of the listener, hence the term 'reaction shots'. Generally, however, these routines provide background norms of presentation that help guide the spectator through the time and space of the narrative on the basis of tacit knowledge of the conventions.

The notion that conventions help to supply or guarantee intelligibility is crucial here. Conventions cue us to expect certain kinds of relationship between shots so that, for instance, if in one shot we, the viewers, see a character gazing out of frame, we then interpret the next shot (whenever possible) as depicting what that character could see from the position he or she occupies. Such apparently simple mechanisms for chaining shots together help to situate us as viewers in the temporal and spatial world of the fiction, and to draw us through the narrative. In this way the 'eye' of the camera, as reflected in the angle of shots and the way in which these shots are edited into sequence, is anthropomorphized, or made to seem human. As spectators, we see from positions that could be (and sometimes even are) those of protagonists in the fiction themselves.

Figure 24.1
A Passage to India:
two-shot

Figure 24.2
A Passage to India:
field

Figure 24.3
A Passage to India:
reverse-field

It has been argued, in fact, that the position constructed for the film spectator (and the pleasures associated with being a spectator) resemble those of a voyeur – a claim that has been particularly discussed within feminist film theory, but that has also been made the subject of conscious attention by filmmakers themselves in films such as Michael Powell's *Peeping Tom* (1959) and Alfred Hitchcock's *Rear Window* (1954). One significant aspect of the notion of the voyeuristic spectator is that the camera does not just show the action of the story, like some simple recording device. It shows events in a way that is so constructed, and edited according to specifiable conventions, that it amounts – if not exactly to a narrator – then to some anthropomorphically defined, implied spectator. Indeed, for a feminist film theorist such as Laura Mulvey (1975/1989), the eye of the camera is not merely anthropomorphic, but more specifically masculine, inasmuch as it routinely constructs women within cinema as objects of male desire (see **Unit 15, Positioning the reader or spectator**).

24.5 Differences between film and prose fiction

The novel, because it operates exclusively through the medium of the verbal sign, is sometimes considered richer in its texture than film. Its relationship to reality can seem more oblique, since the world that unfolds in the novel is not given directly but is developed by the narrator and recreated in an active and controlled process of reading that allows for reflection, comparison and the gradual construction of a coherent whole. Patterns of reference and cross-reference may be built up over several hundred pages; and the whole novel may take several hours to read (perhaps ten hours for an average length novel).

Film, by contrast, can seem more immediate, but perhaps at the same time, less dense. In the case of a film adaptation of a novel, the ten hours of reading are condensed into two hours' viewing; and this viewing is required to be intelligible at a single screening. This might suggest that film is somehow a less complex, less demanding medium than the prose novel. It is, however, worth remembering that film is a multilayered medium, working with a potent combination of two modalities of expression: image and sound. The image has powerful possibilities for condensing significance: descriptive detail, character and action can be displayed simultaneously within the single shot, through codes of lighting, colour and composition, whereas prose is constrained by a sequential, piece by piece, mode of presentation. The significatory possibilities of the image are further enhanced, of course, by the various kinds of sound that constitute the soundtrack. Because of their different conditions of presentation and consumption, then, films may condense narrative material; but this does not inevitably entail simplification or mere reduction.

In conclusion, therefore, it is important to note that stories have a constructed nature, in whichever medium they are rendered. We have seen that film, no less than prose, depends on the operation of conventions – for example, rules that guide the selection of shots and their combination. Such conventions range from those governing the depiction of dialogue to those governing the depiction of a chase or the intrusion into a scene of a sinister onlooker. These filmic conventions are just as crucial for narration in film as are those that govern the representation of thought or speech (see **Unit 22, Speech and narration**) or the handling of 'point of view' in prose fiction (see **Unit 21**). Prose is governed by conventions that are linguistic in character. What is less obvious – but no less true – is that film-makers also operate according to a kind of language: the language of film.

ACTIVITY 24.1

Irvine Welsh's novel, *Trainspotting* (1993), was filmed by Danny Boyle in 1995 from a screenplay by John Hodge. In the following activity you are invited to prepare a shooting script from a passage of the novel and to compare it with a section of Hodge's screenplay.

In the extract of the novel given below the main character Renton and his friend Murphy ('Spud') are interviewed for jobs. Neither of them is serious about looking for work, but in order to maintain their claim to social security benefit ('job seeker's allowance') each of them must appear to go through the motions of job-seeking. They prepare in advance to steer a fine line between success and failure in the interview.

1 Create a shooting-script using the extract from the novel below: select and adapt material to form the dialogue for the film; and include further information about how the scenes should be shot.

2 Compare your shooting-script with the dialogue from the corresponding section of Hodge's screenplay reprinted after the extract from the novel.

3   What are the main differences between your shooting-script and Hodge's screenplay? Do they involve different interpretations and realizations of the novel? If so, in what way?

4   What are the differences between yours and Hodge's screenplays and the extract from Welsh's novel? What specific aspects from the novel cannot directly be transposed into a film version? What adjustments have been made and why? (Read the passage from the novel carefully and think back to what you have learnt about narrative prose fiction in the previous units.) What are the respective advantages and disadvantages of the two media?

Extract from Irvine Welsh's novel *Trainspotting*

2 – Process: Mr Renton (1.00 p.m.)
The trainee manager whae welcomed us wis a mucho spotty punter in a sharp suit, wi dandruff oan the shoodirs like piles ay fuckin cocaine. Ah felt like takin a rolled up fiver tae the cunt's tin flute. His biscuit-ersed face and his plukes completely ruin the image the smarmy wee shite's tryin tae achieve. Even in ma worse junk periods ah've nivir had a complexion like that, the poor wee bastard. This cunt is obviously along for the ride. The main man is the fat, stroppy-lookin gadge in the middle; tae his right thirs a coldly smiling dyke in a woman's business suit wi a thick foundation mask, who looks catalogue hideous.

This is a heavy-duty line-up for a fuckin porter's joab.

The opening gambit wis predictable. The fat cunt gies us a warm look and says: – I see from your application form that you attended George Heriots.

– Right . . . ah, those halcyon school days. It seems like a long time ago now.

Ah might huv lied on the appo, but ah huvnae at the interview. Ah did once attend George Heriots: whin ah wis an apprentice joiner at Gillsland's we did some contract work there.

– Old Fotheringham still doing his rounds?

Fuck. Select from one of two possibilities; one: he is, two: he's retired. Naw. Too risky. Keep it nebulous.

– God, you're taking me back now . . . ah laugh. The fat gadge seems tae be happy wi that. It's worrying. Ah feel that the interview is over, and that these cunts are actually going tae offer us the joab. The subsequent questions are all pleasantly asked and unchallenging. Ma hypothesis is fucked. They'd rather gie a merchant school boy with severe brain damage a job in nuclear engineering than gie a schemie wi a Ph.D. a post as a cleaner in an abattoir. Ah've goat tae dae something here. This is terrifying. Fatso sees us as a George Heriots old boy fallen on hard times, and he wants tae help us oot. A gross miscalculation Renton, you radge.

Thank fuck for spotted dick. A fair assumption tae make, considering every other part of him seems tae be covered in zits. He gets tae nervously ask a question: – Ehm . . . ehm . . . Mr Renton . . . ehm . . . can you, ehm, explain . . . eh, your employment gaps, ehm . . .

Can you explain the gaps between your words, you doss wee cunt.

– Yes. I've had a long-standing problem with heroin addiction. I've been trying to combat this, but it has curtailed my employment activities. I feel it's important to be honest and mention this to you, as a potential future employer.

A stunning *coup de maître*. They shift nervously in their seats.

– Well, eh, thank you for being so frank with us Mr Renton . . . eh, we do have some other people to see . . . so thanks again, and we'll be in touch.

Magic. The gross git pulls down a wall of coldness and distance between us. They cannae say ah didnae try. . .

3 – Process: Mr Murphy (2.30 p.m.)

This speed is el magnifico, likesay. Ah feel sortay dynamic, ken, likesay, ah'm really lookin forward tae this interview. Rents sais: Sell yirsell Spud, n tell the truth. Let's go for it cats, let's get it on . . .

– I see from your application form that you attended George Heriots. The old Heriots FPs seem to be rather thick on the ground this afternoon.

Yeah, fat-cat.

– Actually man, ah've goat tae come clean here. Ah went tae Augie's, St. Augustine's likesay, then Craigy, eh Craigroyston, ken. Ah jist pit doon Heriots because ah thoat it wid likes, help us git the joab. Too much discrimination in this town, man, ken, likesay? As soon as suit n tie dudes see Heriots or Daniel Stewarts or Edinburgh Academy, they kinday get the hots, ken. Ah mean, would you have said, likesay, ah see you attended Craigroyston?

– Well, I was just making conversation, as I did happen to attend Heriots. The idea was to make you feel at ease. But I can certainly put your mind at rest with regards to discrimination. That's all covered in our new equal opportunities statement.

– It's cool man. Ah'm relaxed. It's jist that ah really want this job, likesay. Couldnae sleep last night though. Worried ah'd sortay blow it likesay, ken. It's jist when cats see 'Craigroyston' oan the form, they likesay think, well everybody thit went tae Craigie's a waster right? But eh, ye ken Scott Nisbet, the fitba player likesay? He's in the Huns . . . eh Rangers first team, haudin his ain against aw they expensive international signins ay Souness's, ken? That cat wis the year below us at Craigie, man.

– Well, I can assure you Mr Murphy, we're far more interested in the qualifications you gained rather than the school you, or any other candidate, went to. It says here that you got five O Grades . . .

– Whoah. Likesay, gaunnae huv tae stoap ye thair, catboy. The O Grades wis bullshit, ken? Thought ah'd use that tae git ma fit in the door. Showin initiative, likesay. Ken? Ah really want this job, man.

– Look Mr Murphy, you were referred to us by the Department of Employment's Jobcentre. There's no need for you to lie to get your foot in the door, as you put it.

– Hey ... whatever you say man. You're the man, the governor, the dude in the chair, so tae speak, likesay.

– Yes, well, we're not making much progress here. Why don't you just tell us why you want this job so desperately that you're prepared to lie.

– Ah need the hireys man.

– Pardon? The what?

– The poppy, likesay, eh ... the bread, the dosh n that. Ken?

– I see. But what specifically attracts you to the leisure industry?

– Well, everybody likes tae huv a good time, a bit a enjiymint, ken? That's leisure tae me man, likesay. Ah like tae see punters enjoy them-selves, ken?

– Right. Thank you, the doll wi the makeup mask sais. Ah could sortay like, love that babe ... – What would you see as being your main strengths? she asks us.

– Er ... sense ay humour, likesay. Ye need that man, goatay huv it, jist goatay huv it, ken? Ah'll huv tae stoap sayin 'ken' sae much. These dudes might think ah'm a sortay pleb.

– What about weaknesses? the squeaky-voiced kitten in the suit asks. This is one spotted catboy; Rents wisnae jokin aboot the plukes. We have a real leopard cub here.

– Ah suppose man, ah'm too much ay a perfectionist, ken? It's likesay, if things go a bit dodgy, ah jist cannae be bothered, y'know? Ah git good vibes aboot this interview the day though man, ken?

– Thank you very much Mr Murphy. We'll let you know.

– Naw man, the pleasure wis mine. Best interview ah've been at, ken? Ah bounds across n shakes each cat by the paw.

4 – Review

Spud met Renton back in the pub.

– How did it go Spud?

– Good catboy, good. Possibly too good, likesay. Ah think the dudes might be gaun tae offer us the job. Bad vibes. One thing though, man, ye wir right aboot this speed. Ah never seem tae like, sell masel properly in interviews. Cool times compadre, cool times.

– Let's huv a drink tae celebrate yir success. Fancy another dab at that speed?

– Wouldnae say naw man, would not say no, likes.

Extract from Hodge's screenplay for the film *Trainspotting*

INT. CAFÉ. DAY

Two milkshakes clink together.

Renton and Spud and seated at a booth, dressed in their own fashion for job interviews.

RENTON
Good luck, Spud.
SPUD
Cheers.
RENTON
Now remember –
SPUD
Yeah.
RENTON
If they think you're not trying, you're in trouble. First hint of that, they'll be on to the DSS, 'This cunt's no trying' and your Giro is fucking finished, right?
SPUD
Right.
RENTON
But try too hard –
SPUD
And you might get the fucking job.
RENTON
Exactly.
SPUD
Nightmare.
RENTON
It's a tightrope, Spud, a fucking tightrope.
SPUD
My problem is that I tend to clam up. I go dumb and I can't answer any questions at all. Nerves on the big occasion, like a footballer.
RENTON
Try this.

Renton unfolds silver foil to reveal some amphetamine. Spud dips in a finger and takes a dab. He nods in appreciation as he tastes it. Renton leaves the packet in Spud's hand.

SPUD
A little dab of speed is just the ticket.

————

INT. INTERVIEW OFFICE. DAY

A Woman and Two Men (1 and 2) are interviewing Renton. His job application form is on the desk in front of them.

MAN 1
Well, Mr. Renton, I see that you attended the Royal Edinburgh College.
RENTON
Indeed, yes, those halcyon days.
MAN 1
One of Edinburgh's finest schools.
RENTON
Oh, yes, indeed. I look back on my time there with great fondness and affection. The debating society, the first eleven, the soft knock of willow on leather –
MAN 1
I'm an old boy myself, you know?
RENTON
Oh, really?
MAN 1
Do you recall the school motto?
RENTON
Of course, the motto, the motto –
MAN 1
Strive, hope, believe and conquer.
RENTON
Exactly. Those very words have been my guiding light in what is, after all, a dark and often hostile world.

Renton looks pious under scrutiny.

MAN 2
Mr. Renton –
RENTON
Yes.
MAN 2
You seem eminently suited to this post but I wonder if you could explain the gaps in your employment record?
RENTON
Yes, I can. The truth – well, the truth is that I've had a long-standing problem with heroin addiction. I've been known to sniff it, smoke it, swallow it, stick it up my arse and inject it into my veins. I've been trying to combat this addiction, but unless you count social security scams and shoplifting, I haven't had a regular job in years. I feel it's important to mention this.

There is silence.

A paper clip crashes to the floor.

————

INT. OFFICE. DAY

The same office. The same team are interviewing Spud.

SPUD

No, actually I went to Craignewton but I was worried that you wouldn't have heard of it so I put the Royal Edinburgh College instead, because they're both schools, right, and we're all in this together, and I wanted to put across the general idea rather than the details, yeah? People get all hung up on details, but what's the point? Like which school? Does it matter? Why? When? Where? Or how many O grades did I get? Could be six, could be one, but that's not important. What's important is that I am, right? That I am.

MAN 1

Mr. Murphy, do you mean that you lied on your application?

SPUD

Only to get my foot in the door. Showing initiative, right?

MAN 1

You were referred here by the Department of Employment. There's no need for you to get your 'foot in the door', as you put it.

SPUD

Hey. Right. No problem. Whatever you say, man. You're the man, the governor, the dude in the chair, like. I'm merely here. But obviously I am. Here, that is. I hope I'm not talking too much. I don't usually. I think it's all important though, isn't it?

MAN 2

Mr. Murphy, what attracts you to the leisure industry?

SPUD

In a word, pleasure. My pleasure in other people's leisure.

————

WOMAN

What do you see as your main strengths?

SPUD

I love people. All people. Even people that no one else loves, I think they're OK, you know. Like Beggars.

WOMAN

Homeless people?

SPUD

No, not homeless people. Beggars, Francis Begbie – one of my mates. I wouldn't say my best mate, I mean, sometimes the boy goes over the score, like one time when we – me and him – were having a laugh and all of a sudden he's fucking gubbed me in the face, right –

————

WOMAN

Mr. Murphy, {leaving your friend aside,} do you see yourself as having any weaknesses?

SPUD

No. Well, yes. I have to admit it: I'm a perfectionist. For me, it's the best or nothing at all. If things go badly, I can't be bothered, but I have a good feeling about this interview. Seems to me like it's gone pretty well. We've touched on a lot of subjects, a lot of things to think about, for all of us.

MAN 1

Thank you, Mr. Murphy. We'll let you know.

SPUD

The pleasure was mine. Best interview I've ever been to. Thanks.

Spud crosses the room to shake everyone by the hand and kiss them.

RENTON (v.o)

Spud had done well. I was proud of him. He fucked up good and proper.

————

INT. PUB 1. DAY

Renton and Spud meet up after the interviews.

SPUD

A little too well, if anything, a little too well, that's my only fear, compadre.

RENTON

Another dab?

SPUD

Would not say no, would not say no.

————

INT. OFFICE. DAY

The Woman and Two Men sit in silence.

————

Reading

Bordwell, D. (1985) *Narration in the Fiction Film*, London: Methuen.

Chatman, S.B. (1978) *Story and Discourse: Narrative Structure in Film and Prose Fiction*, Ithaca, NY and London: Cornell University Press.

Giddings, R., Selby, K. and Wensley, C. (1990) *Screening the Novel: The Theory and Practice of Literary Dramatization*, London: Macmillan.

Harrison, S. (2005) *Adaptations: From Short Story to Big Screen: 35 Great Stories That Have Inspired Great Films*, New York: Random House/Three Rivers Press.

McFarlane, B. (1996) *Novel to Film*, Oxford: Oxford University Press.

Rifkin, B. (1994) *Semiotics of Narration in Film and Prose Fiction*, New York: Peter Lang.

Spiegel, A. (1976) *Fiction and the Camera Eye: Visual Consciousness in Film and the Modern Novel*, Charlottesville, VA: University Press of Virginia.

The following Internet sites provide useful support to the study of film adaptation:

film.guardian.co.uk/adaptation/
web.cocc.edu/humanities/hir/film/filmadaptation.htm
www.nv.cc.va.us/home/bpool/dogwood/general.html
www.screenonline.org.uk/film/id/526560/

Ways of reading drama

25.1 The page and the stage

There are two basic ways of reading plays, based on two different conceptions of what a play is: a play may be conceived of as a dramatic performance or as a dramatic text (a piece of dramatic literature published in a book). For most actors, directors, theatre-goers, theatre critics, teachers and students of theatre studies, along with many teachers in university departments of literature, a play is something that takes place on a stage rather than on a page. Teachers of drama tend to see the printed text of a play as merely a preliminary script or set of guidelines that contributes just one element to the total living performance of the play on stage. Teachers of literature in universities similarly assume that their students need at least to try to imagine how a dramatic text's meanings and effects might be realized on stage. (See **Unit 26, Literature in performance**.)

From this point of view, reading the text of a play is quite different from reading a novel or a poem. In their student textbook *Studying Plays* (1998), for example, Mick Wallis and Simon Shepherd start out by saying:

> For many of us the business of reading a play is rather unsatisfactory because we continually have the sense that what we are looking at is only words on a page and that those words have yet to come alive in the mouths of real human beings standing on a stage. It is much more pleasant and satisfying to read a good novel, because the novel is designed to be words on a page. Open a novel and you've got everything you need in front of you; open a playtext and you have to start imagining the things that aren't there – how it might look and sound, how an audience might react.
>
> (1998, p. 1)

The notion that we need to analyse the play on the stage rather than on the page is quite compatible with some of the ways of reading developed in the present book, where we have extended the notion of reading to include not only the reading of written texts, but also the analysis of speech, songs, advertisements, films and TV, and so on. This extended notion of reading makes it perfectly possible to talk about 'reading' the products of the performative arts, such as stand-up comedy, dance or dramatic performance. Yet there are problems with the basic assumption that dramatic texts are incomplete objects that can only be made complete by being turned into theatrical texts on the stage. In this unit, we want to concentrate on exploring ways of reading dramatic texts as fully readable texts in their own right. In other words, we want to demonstrate that dramatic texts, for the most part, are as readable as novels or poems. Most of the time, we will suggest, reading dramatic texts involves employing and adapting the general reading skills and strategies developed in the present book.

25.2 Reading dramatic texts

Reading dramatic texts in their own right involves attending only to those aspects of theatrical performance that are written into the dramatic text itself. In other words, unless they are actually specified in the dramatic text, things like costume, lighting, gestures and so on are theatrical elements added to the dramatic text for the purposes of dramatic performance and are not part of the dramatic text at all. In taking this position, we are in fact echoing one of the earliest and most influential discussions of drama in the history of criticism – that of Aristotle in his *On the Art of Poetry* (fourth century BCE). Aristotle identifies six constituents in the tragic drama of classical Greece: plot, character, diction, thought, spectacle and song. However, after discussing the first four constituents, he more or less dismisses the last two as more to do with theatrical production than with drama per se:

> Of the remaining elements, the music is the most important of the plea-surable additions to the play. Spectacle, or stage-effect, is an attraction, of course, but it has the least to do with the playwright's craft or with the art of poetry. For the power of tragedy is independent both of perform-ance and of actors, and besides, the production of spectacular effects is more the province of the property-man than of the playwright.
>
> (1965, p. 41)

In accord with this, we are suggesting in this unit that the power of dramatic texts is independent both of performance and of actors and that most of the theatrical devices and techniques that are employed in a production of a play are 'pleasurable additions' rather than intrinsic elements of the play itself.

In order to support our claims, we will begin by looking at a passage from Shakespeare's *Othello* (*c*.1602), which Wallis and Shepherd analyse in their attempt to demonstrate that it is essential to think of dramatic texts as scripts for theatrical performance. *Othello* is set in Venice and Cyprus and focuses on the tragic downfall of Othello, a Moor (a Muslim from North Africa) who has entered military service as a general with the Duke of Venice. For reasons that never become entirely clear, Iago – Othello's 'Ancient' (his ensign or standard bearer) – hates Othello and tries to destroy him. Iago convinces Othello that he is a trustworthy ally and then induces him to believe that his wife Desdemona has been unfaithful. When Othello is finally brought to believe that Desdemona has betrayed him by having an affair with Cassio (his honourable lieutenant), he accuses Desdemona of being a whore and then leaves the stage. Desdemona – who the reader/audience knows is innocent – is bewildered and thrown into despair by Othello's behaviour. At this point, Iago and his wife Emilia (who is Desdemona's faithful maid) enter the stage. The audience/reader knows that Iago is a villain and has duped Othello, but, while his wife is beginning to suspect him, Desdemona still thinks of Iago as Othello's loyal servant. Desdemona therefore turns to Iago for help:

> O God, Iago,
> What shall I do to win my lord again?
> Good friend, go to him, for, by this light of heaven,
> I know not how I lost him. Here I kneel:
> If e'er my will did trespass 'gainst his love,
> Either in discourse of thought or actual deed,
> . . .
> Comfort forswear me! Unkindness may do much,
> And his unkindness may defeat my life
> But never taint my love.
>
> (*Othello*, IV, ii, 150–63)

Wallis and Shepherd point out that 'Here I kneel' is an implicit stage direction – in other words, it serves to guide the actor playing the part (Wallis and Shepherd, 1998, p. 10). Indeed, Wallis and Shepherd are correct in saying that, although Shakespeare's plays include a minimum of explicit stage directions, they do tend to embed implicit stage directions in the characters' speeches. At the same time, however, 'Here I kneel' works for the reader as well as for the actor because it allows the reader to imagine Desdemona's posture and its implications in context. In other words, the sentence works on the page as well as on the stage. The same may be said for the main points that Wallis and Shepherd make about the passage:

> if we ... note that [Desdemona] is kneeling, we start to see that
> Shakespeare is here constructing a formal picture, an emblem, rather like

that in a stained-glass window ... But the total stage picture is of Iago manipulating Desdemona into her posture of defeat, and revelling in it. Surrounding the emblem of innocence is the emblem of villainy and deception. This double emblem is part of the way in which this scene produces meaning for an audience. Here, then, is clear evidence of the importance of remembering always that the dramatic text is a script for activity on a stage.

(1998, p. 4)

This impressive piece of analysis offers good insight into how Shakespeare's play is working in this scene. However, while Wallis and Shepherd claim that the passage, and their analysis, is evidence of the need to regard the written text as a prescription for dramatic staging, it is equally possible to say the opposite. In the first place, their analysis is based entirely on the written text itself, rather than on a performance, and is convincing because the reader can see the evidence for it in the written text alone (and does not need to see or even imagine a performance). The scene, then, produces these meanings for a reader as well as for a potential audience. Such a reader can imagine how the scene might look and work on a stage, but the point is that *he or she does not have to do so*. A reader can just as well imagine that the scene takes place in Cyprus. In other words, the process of reading and interpreting this passage need not be essentially different from reading an equivalent passage in a novel.

25.2.1 Dramatic or situational irony

Surprisingly, Wallis and Shepherd neglect to discuss what might be thought of as a specifically dramatic technique or effect in this passage from *Othello* – that is, 'dramatic irony' (see **Unit 11**). Dramatic irony has been defined as:

> a plot device according to which (a) the spectators know more than the protagonist; (b) the character reacts in a way contrary to that which is appropriate or wise; (c) characters or situations are compared or contrasted for ironic effects, such as parody; or (d) there is a marked contrast between what the character understands about his acts and what the play demonstrates about them ... Tragedy is [especially] rich in all forms of dramatic [irony]. The necessity for a sudden reversal or catastrophe in the fortunes of the hero means that the fourth form of [irony] (form d) is almost inevitable.
>
> (Preminger and Brogan, 1993, p. 635)

Dramatic irony, then, is produced when an audience knows something important that one or more of the characters in a play do not know. If the character did have this knowledge, it would change his or her behaviour and/or attitude towards other characters. In a comedy, this can produce humour at the expense of the uninformed characters. In a tragedy (like *Othello*) it usually leads to a tragic dénouement (the character or characters only find out what they need to know when it is too late). In *Othello*, dramatic irony is produced because the virtuous characters (Othello and Desdemona) are fooled by Iago into believing that he is also virtuous and doing his best to help them, when the audience knows the opposite to be the case. In the scene we are examining, the audience knows that Iago is the cause of Desdemona's suffering and therefore sees or experiences dramatic irony when she kneels before him and supplicates him to help her.

Dramatic irony would seem to be an inherently theatrical effect in that it is produced by the difference between what the characters on stage know of their situation and what the audience knows. Yet it is perfectly possible for a reader to experience a similar ironic effect. An attentive reader of the passage (provided that he or she has read the rest of the play up to this point) will recognize or experience the same sense of tragic irony that an audience will. This is because written texts (novels, dramatic texts and so on) employ techniques of 'situational irony' (see **Unit 11**) whose conditions are virtually the same as dramatic irony. Indeed, M.H. Abrams defines dramatic irony as an effect produced by narrative as well as drama and as available to readers as well as spectators (1993, p. 99). Thus the 'double emblem' that Wallis and Shepherd refer to may be seen by an audience or imagined by a reader. In the first case it will produce dramatic irony; in the second case it will produce situational irony. In other words, there is no need for the reader to remember 'that the dramatic text is a script for activity on the stage'. While a dramatic text can be read in that way, it can equally be read on its own terms – with apparently no loss of meaning or effect.

25.3 The formal analysis of drama

Instead of saying that the distinctive feature of dramatic texts is that they are designed for, or only achieve their full realization in, theatrical performance, it is more useful to define dramatic texts in purely *formal* terms in ways that bring out their differences from narrative prose fiction and most kinds of poetry. Basically, following Aristotle (1965, p. 34), the three main genres of literature can be distinguished from one another by the different ways in which they present themselves as speech or present the speech of the characters they construct. The distinctive formal feature of lyric poetry is that it presents itself as the unmediated speech of a first person speaker. The distinctive formal feature of narrative prose fiction is that it typically presents itself as the speech of a number of different characters mediated to us through a narrator. Drama differs from lyric poetry and narrative fiction in that it typically presents itself to us as the direct speech or dialogue of a number of different characters without a mediating narrator. Thus the scene from *Othello* examined above continues with Iago responding to Desdemona's supplication as follows:

> IAGO   I pray you, be content, 'tis but his humour;
>   The business of the state does him offence
>   And he does chide with you.
> DESDEMONA If 'twere no other –
> IAGO   'Tis but so, I warrant.
>
>   (*Othello*, IV, ii, 167–70)

In this exchange, there is no narrator to mediate the characters' speech or to guide the reader: there are no reporting clauses ('she said, anxiously') or descriptions of the characters and their behaviour ('she knelt with her head in her hands'). Thus reading dramatic texts can be more demanding than reading narrative prose fiction since the reader is required to picture what is happening or to gauge the characters' emotions or motives by picking up on the clues embedded in the characters' speech (as in 'Here I kneel'). But it is usually perfectly possible for a reader to do this without needing to see or imagine the scene acted out on a stage.

25.4 Narrative in dramatic texts

The suggestion that drama can be characterized as dialogue unmediated by narration is a useful one, but it does need to be qualified. In fact, dramatic texts make use of a variety of narrative devices or strategies that perform a number of functions: guiding actors, directors or set designers; guiding an audience; or guiding readers.

25.4.1 Implicit and explicit stage directions

As we have seen, characters' speeches can contain implicit stage directions ('Here I kneel') that do two things at once: they guide actors, and they guide readers by performing a narrative function. Explicit stage directions can also be read both as guidelines for stage performance and as functioning like a narrative voice. In the scene from *Othello* that we are examining, the text continues as follows:

> IAGO   'Tis but so, I warrant.
>   [*Trumpets.*]
> Hark how these instruments summon to supper.
>
>   (*Othello*, IV, ii, 170–1)

In a novel, this passage might have been written as follows:

> 'Tis but so, I warrant,' Iago replied. As he was speaking they heard the sound of trumpets calling them to supper.

In the naturalist and realist drama of nineteenth-century Europe (involving largely middle-class audiences watching the critical breakdown of middle-class life as if through a transparent 'fourth wall' of a living room), stage directions became more extensive and began to resemble the narrative voice of the realist novels of the period. One of the reasons for this was that such plays were beginning to be published before they were performed and so began to be written as self-sufficient texts independent of dramatic performance. Henrik Ibsen's *A Doll's House* (1879), for example, begins with two paragraphs of stage directions. The first paragraph describes in detail a middle-class, late nineteenth-century drawing room in which all the on-stage action will take place; the second paragraph describes Nora Helmer arriving back from a Christmas shopping trip. Such extensive and detailed stage directions offer directors, set designers and actors explicit instructions about staging the play. But they also read not so much as a description of a theatrical set but of an actual drawing room with real people in it. For example, the first two sentences of the second paragraph are as follows (in an English translation first published in 1961):

> The front door-bell rings in the hall; a moment later, there is the sound of the front door being opened. NORA comes into the room, happily humming to herself. She is dressed in her outdoor things, and is carrying lots of parcels which she then puts down on the table, right.

This passage is mostly indistinguishable from the kind of narrative **exposition** that features in the nineteenth-century realist novel, except that: (1) it is in present rather than past tense; (2) the narrative voice seems confined to the room; and (3) the table is said to be 'right' – that is, stage right.

25.4.2 Narrative exposition in dialogue

Another way in which dramatic texts can include narrative elements is to have the characters themselves present the reader/audience with narrative exposition in dialogue with other characters. Thus, when Iago says to Desdemona 'Hark how these instruments summon to supper', he says it as much for the reader/audience as for Desdemona (who presumably knows what the trumpets signify). More crucial passages of narrative exposition often occur in characters' speeches at the beginning of plays in order to help the reader/audience understand what is going on – as in Iago's speech in the opening scene of *Othello*:

RODRIGO	Thou told'st me
	Thou didst hold [Othello] in thy hate.
IAGO	Despise me
	If I do not. Three great ones of the city,
	In personal suit to make me his lieutenant,

> Off-capped to him, and by the faith of man
> I know my price, I am worth no worse a place.
> But he, as loving his own pride and purposes,
> Evades them, with a bombast circumstance
> Horribly stuffed with epithets of war,
> And in conclusion
> Nonsuits my mediators. For, 'Certes,' says he,
> 'I have already chose my officer.'
> And what was he?
> Forsooth, a great arithmetician,
> One Michael Cassio, a Florentine
>
> (*Othello*, I, i, 5–19)

Iago's speech fills in part of the story of what has occurred before the opening scene: Iago had attempted – through the intercession of friends in high places – to get a position as Othello's lieutenant, but Othello rejected him because he had already chosen Cassio for this position. In telling this to Rodrigo, Iago is also telling it to the audience or to the reader – and providing one motive for his hatred of Othello.

25.4.3 The chorus as narrator

Another way that narration may be presented in drama is through the use of a 'chorus'. In the tragic drama of classical Greece, the chorus consisted of twelve to fifteen men who sang odes as part of the dramatic performance. The chorus would also deliver speeches – spoken either as a group or by the leader – that constituted a kind of commentary on the action. Since the classical period, the chorus has largely disappeared from drama, though it has occasionally been used in original and effective ways. Shakespeare uses a chorus (consisting of a single person) in *King Henry V* (*c*.1599) to deliver a **prologue** at the beginning of each act and an **epilogue** at the end of the final act. Shakespeare's chorus directly addresses the audience, carrying out a number of functions and producing a variety of effects. He encourages the members of the audience to accept that the necessarily limited action that takes place on the stage represents the large-scale events of war between England and France involving ships, armies, horses, battles and so on: 'Think, when we talk of horses, that you see them / Printing their proud hoofs i'th' receiving earth' (*Henry V*, prologue to Act I, 26–7). In doing this, the chorus serves to highlight that this is a play, not real life: 'Admit me Chorus to this history / Who prologue-like your humble patience pray, / Gently to hear, kindly to judge our play' (*Henry V*, prologue to Act I, 33–5). Shakespeare's chorus also works as a narrative voice for the audience/reader, as in the prologue to Act 2 in which he describes England preparing for war:

Now all the youth of England are on fire,
And silken dalliance in the wardrobe lies.
Now thrive the armourers, and honour's thought
Reigns solely in the breast of every man.
                    (*Henry V*, Prologue to Act II)

The chorus device has occasionally been used in plays since Shakespeare, including Milton's *Samson Agonistes* (1671) and T.S. Eliot's *Murder in the Cathedral* (1935). Indeed, it underwent something of a revival in the twentieth century precisely because of the way it foregrounds theatricality and hence breaks with the naturalistic illusion of late nineteenth-century drama. In *The Threepenny Opera* (1928), for example, Bertolt Brecht employs a chorus-type 'Narrator' who introduces each act and delivers a prologue to the whole play that includes the well-known song 'Mack the Knife'. Brecht used choruses – along with a range of other theatrical devices – to produce an **alienation effect** in the audience. Brecht's plays tend to disrupt the audience's tendency to become uncritically absorbed in the theatrical spectacle because he felt that this was akin to the way the people of Europe were being mesmerized by fascism and/or capitalism in the period, both of which used a kind of mass theatre to manipulate the masses (today, TV advertising is simply the most explicit version of this process).

The fact that a chorus serves to foreground the theatrical process and produce an alienation effect, preventing the audience from consuming the represented events as if they were real, would appear to make it an inherently theatrical device whose effects need to be experienced in live theatre. Yet we have seen that the chorus is also a kind of narrator for someone reading the play as a dramatic text; and, for a reader used to the playful foregrounding of the narrative situation in postmodernist novels, even the anti-realist, alienating commentary of a chorus like La Corbie in Liz Lochhead's *Mary Queen of Scots Got Her Head Chopped Off* (1989) does not make the dramatic text unreadable.

25.5 The representation of thoughts or inner speech in drama

One of the characteristic strategies of novels is to give us access to the thoughts or inner speech of characters (in ways explained in **Units 22** and **23**). Drama does this through the use of a device called **soliloquy**. A soliloquy is 'A speech delivered by a character alone onstage, speaking to himself or herself, or to the audience' (Worthen, 2000, p. 1488). As such, it is clearly a theatrical device rather than a representation of human behaviour (although some people do talk to themselves when alone). The importance of the device is that it appears to give us access to what the character is really thinking and so allows us to compare this with what the character says to other characters. (We tend to think that a character reveals the truth in a soliloquy because he or she is not at that moment attempting to deceive another character – though a soliloquizing character might attempt to deceive the audience or be self-deceived.) The soliloquy thus presents the reader/audience with knowledge that is not available to other characters and may hence play a role in the generation of dramatic or situational irony. At the end of Act One of *Othello*, for example, Iago delivers the following soliloquy:

> I hate the Moor
> And it is thought abroad that 'twixt my sheets
> He's done my office. I know not if't be true,
> But I for mere suspicion in that kind
> Will do as if for surety. He holds me well,
> The better shall my purpose work on him.
> Cassio's a proper man: let me see now,
> To get his place, and to plume up my will
> In double knavery. How? How? let's see:
> After some time to abuse Othello's ear
> That he is too familiar with his wife.
> He hath a person and a smooth dispose
> To be suspected, framed to make women false.
> The Moor is of a free and open nature
> That thinks men honest that but seem to be so,
> And will as tenderly be led by th' nose
> As asses are.
> I have't, it is engendered! Hell and night
> Must bring this monstrous birth to the world's light.
> (*Othello*, I, iii, 385–402)

In this soliloquy Iago offers the reader/audience another reason for his hating Othello: the rumour that Othello has had sex with his wife. To get revenge, he will make Othello believe that Cassio has had sex with Desdemona, which will serve both to destroy Othello's happiness and bring down Cassio. By allowing the reader/audience to know more about what Iago is doing than the other characters do, this soliloquy enables the generation of tragic irony.

However, although the soliloquy is an important dramatic device that can have resonant theatrical effects on stage, it is also akin to the representation of thought in novels and, as such, would appear to be as perfectly readable to a reader of the dramatic text as it is to the audience of the theatrical text.

25.6 Dramatic devices that are written into the dramatic text but only work on the stage

We have been suggesting throughout this unit that most of the devices, tech-niques and conventions that are thought to characterize the dramatic perform-ance of plays are also discernible to readers of dramatic texts. Such readers inevitably draw on their experience of seeing live theatre (or drama on TV or in films), but they also employ and modify the ways of reading that are used in reading novels and poems. However, having argued this, we also need to recognize that there are dramatic techniques and devices that are written into dramatic texts but that can only be fully effective in dramatic performance. Like some of the other devices we have looked at, these devices tend to shatter the illusion that a play is a slice of real life by foregrounding the techniques of theatrical performance itself. As such, they are predominantly used in anti-realist drama – especially in the plays of the last fifty years or so that critique the naturalism/realism both of late nineteenth-century drama and of contem-porary popular drama (as seen in mainstream films and TV soaps). The differ-ence between these devices and the ones we have already looked at is that, while they are discernible to the reader (they are written into the dramatic text) they can only work for an audience seeing a stage performance.

25.6.1 Breaking the identity between actor and character

In naturalist or realist drama, the tendency is to disguise the difference between character and actor in order to make the overall play more 'realistic'. The casting process therefore involves choosing actors who appear appropriate for the part in terms of sex, age, racial identity and so on, and the acting process involves the actor trying to identify with the character (a process formalized in the techniques of 'method acting' developed by Konstantin Stanislavsky at the turn of the twentieth century and enshrined in Hollywood cinema). Yet such assumptions have not always held in the history of the theatre. From ancient Greece up to the Renaissance, for example, there were no female actors and female roles had to be played by male actors (female actors did not appear on the English stage until after the restoration of the monarchy in 1660). Such **cross-dressing** was not written into the dramatic texts produced in these periods but was a social and theatrical convention. As such, it would not have appeared odd to audiences, who in any case were not necessarily looking for a 'realistic' one-to-one relationship between actors and characters. Similarly, in staging *Othello* it is unlikely that Shakespeare's company would have felt the need to get a Moorish actor to play Othello. (Until quite recently, it was commonplace for white actors to play Othello with blacked faces.) It has become the norm today, without violating the texts, for female actors to play Shakespeare's female characters and for black actors to play Othello. However, in the 'post-modernist' drama of the last fifty years or so there has been a tendency to include devices and techniques in dramatic texts that serve to expose and accentuate discrepancies between actors and characters.

25.6.2 Role doubling

One technique that serves to break the identification between actor and character (and between audience and character) is that of **role doubling**, or the 'practice of using one actor to play more than one part' (Worthen, 2000, p. 1487). Prior to nineteenth-century naturalism it was probably quite common for an actor to play two or more parts for reasons of economy. In productions of the decidedly non-realist *Peter Pan* (first performed in 1904), it became customary for the same actor to play Mr Darling and Captain Hook – a practice that underlines the oedipal elements in the play. Yet these examples of role doubling were production decisions and were not written into scripts. In Brecht's *The Good Person of Setzuan* (1943), by contrast, the text specifies that the same actor should play both the prostitute Shen Teh and her male 'cousin', Shui Ta (a character she has herself invented, out of self defence, to be her alter ego). In this instance, role doubling is not simply a fashionable device used to spice up a production, but is written into the dramatic text itself and clearly relates to the play's investigation of gender stereotypes, capitalism and the theatre itself.

Role doubling is now a fairly common technique in contemporary non-realist drama, but it is most interesting when it is being used to dramatize the critical issues that the play is dealing with. An intriguing example can be found in Athol Fugard's *Valley Song* (1996; published 1998), set in a small village in South Africa shortly after the end of apartheid. There are three characters in this play: a white South African man simply called 'The Author'; a coloured farmer in his seventies called Abraam Jonkers (also known as Buks); and Buks's seventeen-year old granddaughter Veronika. However, only two actors are required because the dramatic text specifies that 'The role of the Author and Buks must be played by the same actor' – a use of role doubling that has many resonances both within the play and in the post-apartheid world that the play addresses. 'The Author' buys a derelict house that includes a farm with a piece of land, the cultivation of which has sustained Buks's family over several generations. 'The Author' and Buks are thus potentially in conflict with one another, and yet the fact that they are played by the same actor suggests both that there is some significant kinship between them (including a shared love of the land and of farming) and that the apartheid-era separation of people according to racial categories is beginning to break down. At the same time, however, the play suggests that some of the consequences of apartheid may take longer to disappear. The coloured characters in the play refer to 'The Author' as 'Master', and when he eventually acquires the farm he will become the 'master' of the coloured family who have lived and worked on the farm for generations. The use of role doubling in *Valley Song*, then, contributes to the play's exploration of the complexities of social, economic, interpersonal and inter-racial issues in post-apartheid South Africa. Yet, although role doubling is written into the dramatic text – in stage directions such as '*In the course of the song* ['The Author'] *moves into the character of* Buks' – its effects can only be fully experienced by an audience. While a reader of the dramatic text will tend to think of 'The Author' and Buks as two entirely different characters, the audience is constantly reminded of the fact that there is a significant connection between them through witnessing the actor repeatedly switching from role to role.

25.6.3 Cross-dressing

Another device that serves to disassociate actors from characters is 'cross-dressing' – i.e. the practice of having male actors play female roles, or female actors playing male roles. As we have seen, cross-dressing was inevitable prior to 1660 when women were not allowed to appear on the stage. Since the early part of the twentieth century, however, cross-dressing has become another alienation device written into dramatic texts in order to highlight the issues that the play is exploring. A pioneering example is Brecht's specifying that the female actor who plays the prostitute Shen Teh in *The Good Person of Setzuan* should also play her (invented) male cousin, Shui Ta. Like role doubling, cross-dressing is a device that can be read in the dramatic text, but whose effect can only be fully experienced by watching the play in performance.

25.6.4 Directly addressing the audience

In realist and naturalist drama the pretence is that the audience is looking through a transparent fourth wall into the private lives of the characters. If a character were directly to address the audience, that pretence would be shattered. Thus, if a character soliloquizes, he or she is thought to be thinking aloud rather than addressing the audience. However, in the plays (and films) of the twentieth century that seek to shatter the realist illusion, the direct address to the audience (or camera) is often written into the text. Good examples of this can be seen in Fugard's *Valley Song*.

ACTIVITY 25.1

Caryl Churchill's *Cloud Nine* (1979; published 1996) is divided into two acts, the first of which 'takes place in a British colony in Africa in Victorian times', while the second 'takes place in London in 1979. But for the characters it is twenty-five years later'. Role doubling occurs through having actors play different parts in Acts I and II. The list of characters for Act I specifies the use of cross-dressing:

> CLIVE, a colonial administrator
> BETTY, his wife, played by a man
> JOSHUA, his black servant, played by a white
> EDWARD, his son, played by a woman
> VICTORIA, his daughter, a dummy
> MAUD, his mother-in-law
> ELLEN, Edward's governess
> HARRY BAGLEY, an explorer
> MRS SAUNDERS, a widow

The first scene of Act One opens as follows:

> *Low bright sun. Verandah. Flagpole with union jack. The Family –*
> CLIVE, BETTY, EDWARD, VICTORIA, MAUD, ELLEN, JOSHUA

> ALL [*sing*] Come gather, sons of England, come gather in your pride.
>   Now meet the world united, now face it side by side;
>   Ye who the earth's wide corners, from veldt to prairie, roam.
>   From bush and jungle muster all who call old England 'home'.
>   Then gather round for England,
>   Rally to the flag,
>   From North and South and East and West
>   Come one and all for England!
> CLIVE: This is my family. Though far from home
>   We serve the Queen wherever we may roam
>   I am a father to the natives here,
>   And father to my family so dear.
> [*He presents* BETTY. *She is played by a man.*]
>   My wife is all I dreamt a wife should be,
>   And everything she is she owes to me.
> BETTY: I live for Clive. The whole aim of my life
>   Is to be what he looks for in a wife.
>   I am a man's creation as you see,
>   And what men want is what I want to be.
> [CLIVE *presents* JOSHUA. *He is played by a white.*]
> CLIVE: My boy's a jewel. Really has the knack.
>   You'd hardly notice that the fellow's black.
> JOSHUA: My skin is black but oh my soul is white.
>   I hate my tribe. My master is my light.

I only live for him. As you can see,

What white men want is what I want to be.

[CLIVE *presents* EDWARD. *He is played by a woman.*]

CLIVE: My son is young. I'm doing all I can

To teach him to grow up to be a man.

EDWARD: What father wants I'd dearly like to be.

I find it rather hard as you can see.

[CLIVE *presents* VICTORIA, *who is a dummy*, MAUD, *and* ELLEN.]

CLIVE: No need for any speeches by the rest.

My daughter, mother-in-law, and governess.

ALL [*sing*] O'er countless numbers she, our Queen,

Victoria reigns supreme;

O'er Afric's sunny plains, and o'er

Canadian frozen stream;

The forge of war shall weld the chains of brotherhood secure;

So to all time in ev'ry clime our Empire shall endure.

Then gather round for England,

Rally to the flag,

From North and South and East and West

Come one and all for England!

[*All go except* BETTY. CLIVE *comes.*]

BETTY: Clive?

CLIVE: Betty. Joshua!

[JOSHUA *comes with a drink for* CLIVE]

BETTY: I thought you would never come. The day's so long without
you.

CLIVE: Long ride in the bush.

BETTY: Is anything wrong? I heard drums.

CLIVE: Nothing serious. Beauty is a damned good mare. I must get
some new boots sent from home. These ones have never been
right. I have a blister.

BETTY: My poor dear foot.

CLIVE: It's nothing.

BETTY: Oh but it's sore.

CLIVE: We are not in this country to enjoy ourselves. Must have ridden
fifty miles. Spoke to three different headmen who would all gladly
chop off each other's heads and wear them round their waists.

BETTY: Clive!

CLIVE: Don't be squeamish, Betty, let me have my joke. And what has
my little dove done today?

BETTY: I've read a little.

CLIVE: Good. Is it good?

BETTY: It's poetry.

CLIVE: You're so delicate and sensitive.

1   What dramatic functions do the opening song and the embedded introduction of the characters perform? Do any of the following terms apply:
prologue; chorus; narrative exposition; dramatic irony; realism; alienation
effect?

   1.1   What do the opening song and introduction of characters imply
about (a) the colonial situation; and (b) the colonial family?

   1.2   What are the implications or effects in the song and introduction of
characters of the fact that (a) Betty is played by a man; (b) Joshua
is played by a white; (c) Edward is played by a woman; and (d)
Victoria is 'played' by a dummy?

2   What does the opening of the prose section – from '*All go except* BETTY'
to 'You're so delicate and sensitive' – imply about (a) the colonial situation; and (b) gender relations in the colonial family?

   2.1   What are the implications or effects in the prose section of the fact
that Betty is played by a man?

3   Which of the effects identified in your answers to questions 1 and 2 can
be discerned from reading the dramatic text (as we have given it), and
which could only be discerned from seeing the play performed?

4   What relationship is there, if any, between the play's use of theatrical
devices (including cross-dressing) and the play's representation of British
colonialism?

Reading

Abrams, M.H. (1993) *A Glossary of Literary Terms*, 6th edn, New York and London:
Harcourt Brace Jovanovich.
Aristotle (1965) *On the Art of Poetry*, in T.S. Dorsh (ed.) *Aristotle, Horace, Longinus:
Classical Literary Criticism*, Harmondsworth and New York: Penguin.
Lennard, John and Luckhurst, Mary (2002) *The Drama Handbook: A Guide to Reading
Plays*, Oxford: Oxford University Press.
Pickering, Kenneth (2003) *Studying Modern Drama*, London: Palgrave Macmillan.
Preminger, Alex and Brogan, T.V.F. (eds) (1993) *The New Princeton Encyclopedia of
Poetry and Poetics*, Princeton, NJ: Princeton University Press.
Wallis, Mick and Shepherd, Simon (1998) *Studying Plays*, London: Arnold; New York:
Oxford University Press.
Worthen, W.B. (2000) *The Harcourt Brace Anthology of Drama*, 3rd edn, Boston, MA:
Heinle.

Unit 26

Literature in performance

Ask almost anyone what the main kinds of literature are and they will say novels, poems . . . and plays (see **Unit 4, Genre**). For many people involved in theatre, however, plays are not literature – or rather, they are more than literature. Plays, they suggest, combine all the conventional literary qualities with something more: the performance, spectacle and pleasures of social occasion associated with theatre.

Discussion of the slightly odd place of drama in our notions of literature tends to develop in two main directions. In one direction, printed versions of plays are viewed as merely notation for the fuller experience of theatre; this way of viewing drama is discussed in **Unit 25, Ways of reading drama**. In the other direction, drama serves as the exemplary case of a broader issue: the relationship, in general, between *all* literature, viewed as a set of books, and literature thought of as something different and less tangible. That different and less tangible something may be stored in books but its essence would be found elsewhere: perhaps in a set of values, or in an attitude of mind, or in particular ways of reading.

This second direction in debates over drama is the topic of this unit. Among the issues it raises are how far what we consider to be literature can exist in forms or media other than on the printed page, and how relevant or applicable the ways of reading we develop for literature are when we engage with other kinds of text.

26.1 Medium and performance

One important consideration here is 'medium': the distinction, for example, between writing and speech. Most literary works are fixed as printed (written) text, yet one of our deepest habits in reading is to imagine a sort of speaking inner voice. Until relatively recently, in historical terms, people did in fact mostly read out loud, to children, family and friends – and also to themselves. (Remember, too, that not all adults can read even today – **literacy** rates vary significantly from country to country and community to community.) Many people still do read aloud to children, and books are serialized and read aloud on radio, as well as being available to buy as audio-books. Even considering literature narrowly as a set of books requires us to take into account its inter-action with the spoken and performed.

26.1.1 Oral literature

Literature that is spoken is not new. In many oral societies (that is, societies that do not employ writing as a system of representation), stories and lyricism are presented in memorized and extensively improvised spoken performances. Such **standardized oral forms** are collectively known as **oral literature**, a term that can at first seem paradoxical: the word 'oral' means to do with the spoken; yet the etymology of 'literature' in 'litterae' (Latin: 'letters') suggests a central preoccupation with, or existence in, the written form.

Composition of oral literature in oral societies often occurs as a communal practice of improvisation. It is only with a transition to a substantially literate society – especially one that develops institutions of print literacy – that the modern category of the author emerges (see **Unit 14, Authorship and intention**).

The classical Greek culture of Homer, around the eighth century BC, represents an especially significant historical moment, being often considered the beginning of the development of Western, writing-based literature (see Ong, 2002). The elaborate patterning of poetic language found in Homer's epics, the *Iliad* and the *Odyssey*, appears to have developed cumulatively over many generations, the result of a combination of tradition and improvisation. Writing was not commonly used at the time for literary purposes, so bards recited without the aid of a written text. Instead of composing and memorizing fixed works, they used a large stock of verbal formulae that enabled them, by altering and recombining elements to suit the context, to perform long poems more or less spontaneously. The poems now attributed to Homer may in fact be substantially a written record – a transcript – of earlier, oral production.

Traditions of oral composition and performance are neither historically or geographically remote. Nor do they exist only in cultures without writing systems. Oral traditions can be found in industrialized, especially multicultural, societies where they flourish alongside written literatures. In Britain, some poets (especially poets with Caribbean origins or links, such as Grace Nichols or John Agard) recite in ways that foreground oral tradition and performance, as well as publishing collections of their poetry. Oral storytelling traditions from Africa, the Indian sub-continent and among Native Americans exist in a flex-ible relation with published, printed texts. Several generations of performed 'pop' poetry have existed in Britain: Liverpool poets (alongside Merseybeat

pop music in the 1960s); Punk poets during the 1970s; and recently impro-
visatory poetry performance events, known as **poetry slams** (or sometimes as
poetry jams), on both sides of the Atlantic.

26.1.2 Public readings

Poetry slams now form part of a literary performance scene that also includes
more formal readings by the authors of published novels and poetry collections
in bookshops and at literary festivals. Possibly the most celebrated example of
a novelist giving public readings, however, comes much earlier in the history:
that of Charles Dickens (1812–70).

Dickens had a lifelong enthusiasm for amateur theatricals, and began to
read to friends as an extension of his involvement in dramatic entertainment,
before going on to read in public for charity. Gradually, he developed public
reading into a lucrative business, despite initially sharing the reservation of
many of his contemporaries that paid public speaking undermines the dignity
of literature. Even relatively early in his reading career, Dickens performed to
audiences of nearly four thousand and went on tours of between fifty and a
hundred readings (eighty-eight readings in ninety days in 1858). When he
started his farewell tour in 1869, on one occasion at least a thousand people
had to be turned away because the auditorium was full.

This example of Dickens's public readings makes clear, in respect of
fiction, what is evident already in the example of drama: the stereotypically
lonely creative experience of an author writing is interwoven with more
social institutions of performance and reception; there is no historically fixed
or impermeable boundary between literary writing and various kinds of
performance.

26.1.3 Literature, lyrics and music

Interconnection between literature and performance can also be seen in the
cluster of literary concepts involving lyrics and **lyricism**. The word 'lyric', for
instance, may now evoke particular poetic qualities (e.g. individual contemplation of experience); but the term originally meant to do with the lyre, the
musical instrument on which Classical Greek poetry was conventionally accompanied. (The Muses of Classical Greece were each thought to preside over a
verbal art that would be accompanied by a specific type of music: flute music,
choral songs and dance, and music on the lyre.) In medieval France, lyric
forms such as the canzone and rondeau were developed by troubadours and
trouvères for singing; and in Germany the early singing lyricists were called
Minnesingers. During the sixteenth and seventeenth centuries in Britain, the
term 'lyric' also applied to verse that was sung (as in madrigals or the songs
of poet-singers and composers like Thomas Campion or John Dowland),
though increasingly the term was also used of verse that was not sung. In some

cases we may now find ourselves, without being aware of it, reading a poem on the page that was actually composed as a song and originally performed with musical accompaniment.

In the contemporary period, lyricism also combines with forms of accompaniment, most notably in popular music. Emerging from traditions of toasters and DJs, rap forms involving highly accentuated speech based on rhyming couplets have come to prominence in mainstream media. Connecting this popular tradition with high-cultural literary expectations, some recognized poets have performed from published works but with backing bands (as Linton Kwesi Johnson and Benjamin Zephaniah have done); and some singer-songwriters first successful in the music field have represented themselves as poets (Bob Dylan, Leonard Cohen, Suzanne Vega, etc.). Such performers evidently blur boundaries between high and popular culture; but they also blur traditional boundaries between verbal and other (audio and audio-visual) arts centred on performance.

26.2 How does performance affect reading literature?

The two illustrations above – of oral literature and lyricism – suggest that our notion of literature and the literary cannot easily be separated off from formal and historical links with performance. But how do such interconnections affect the process we call 'reading'?

If you 'read' a novel or poem in audio-book form, you are likely to be highly sensitive to its sound properties: the text performed *is* the text. Equally, if you go to a public reading, you may be struck by how differently phrases and sentences are grouped together, or particular words given emphasis, as compared with your own mental representation of the printed page. Speech on the public platform or on tape not only combines with extra, visual cues given by facial expression, gesture and posture; it also performs aspects of language that are only reflected in very simplified form in writing.

Alongside accent (see **Unit 6, Language and place**), features of tempo, voice quality, pauses and intonation – collectively, language's **prosodic and paralinguistic systems** – add emphasis and signal a speaker's attitudes towards what is being said. **Intonation** in particular negotiates nuances of meaning that may remain unspecified on the printed page. The linguist Roman Jakobson reports how, for example, the Russian theatre director Konstantin Stanislavsky (1863–1938) developed verbal subtlety through intensive training, and is said once to have required an actor at audition to depict forty distinct situations just by saying the Russian words for 'This evening' (Jakobson, 1987, p. 67).

With theatre evolving as a social institution over many centuries, some aspects of performed speech have become codified or stylized. Voices in stage drama have to fill a large auditorium, and so specialized, theatrical styles of projected speech have developed: speech that is often declamatory or ritual-istic (and which employs some techniques whose seriousness, in an era of modern media, can now be difficult to maintain, such as the stage whisper).

In different periods of theatre, how far play scripts mirror conversational styles has varied, with arguably a gradual, long-term shift taking place from declaimed, public rhetoric towards close-up representation of face-to-face inter-action. However, even where written dialogue seeks to simulate speech closely – as many contemporary stage and film scripts do – such written speech never precisely matches naturally occurring spoken discourse; it is always a selective, conventionalized representation. (You can check this by comparing pauses, repetitions and local incoherence in real conversation with dramatic dialogue on the page; for discussion of differences between conversation and written dialogue, see also **Unit 22, Speech and narration**.)

As written stage dialogue is realized in a performing voice, performance extends what is said on the written page, by adding features of sound that were not notated in the written form. It also narrows it down, by tracing a specific, spoken path between multiple possibilities that can co-exist in silent reading (see **Unit 25, Ways of reading drama**).

26.3 The influence of medium

As well as interpreting – both extending and narrowing – what is said on the page, the process of turning writing into performed speech also has an effect of unsettling conventional notions of literary achievement and value, because of differences between the two media in which literature then exists.

A written text performed as speech problematizes, for instance, where we draw the boundary between the work, anchored on the page, and variable performances of it. A public reading of a printed poem may be a performance; but if that performance is then made available in recorded form, it is a text again – though now with an added audio or audio-visual dimension. The awkwardness of such distinctions is one reason why many people prefer simply to view all kinds of language performance as texts. We could then say that there is no need to fix any particular boundary between literary text and performance, since we already recognize that texts come in many versions (such as different editions), and performance simply gives us parallel versions of texts in different media.

Definition matters, however, if you feel that the core objects of literary enquiry need to be distinguished from related but arguably secondary texts and contextual material that surround them. Few people doubt that a TV or film serialization of *Pride and Prejudice* can be an enjoyable and worthwhile version of Jane Austen's novel (1813). But there continues to be vigorous argument about whether such an adaptation should be read as on an equal footing with the novel it is an adaptation of; whether it is a useful supplement to reading the novel but of secondary importance to it; or whether the two texts should be treated as for all practical purposes different works. Alternatively, cutting through such distinctions, we might say that we can now only see Jane Austen's 'original' novel through the lens of all these other, performed versions that we have heard or seen. If so, then these other versions are no longer merely incidental, later performances but instead an addition to the literary work itself. (Think of all the films and TV drama serializations you know that have either a direct, an indirect or a remote link to a particular literary work if you think there is a clear-cut answer to these questions; and for further discussion, see **Unit 13, Intertextuality and allusion** and **Unit 24, Film and prose fiction.**)

26.3.1 Competing myths of print and live speech

A further consideration makes defining a boundary between literary work and performance more than a question of placing textual versions relative to a historical original. In matters of textual circulation and influence, written and spoken are not treated as equals: the medium of a text itself affects that text's perceived value, because of potentially confusing myths – or sets of unexamined cultural beliefs – that attach to print and to live speech as modes of representation.

What might be called a 'myth of print' is created, for instance, when a piece of language is considered disproportionately important, authoritative, or final and non-negotiable, simply because that utterance appears in print. Such mythical attributes arise as a result of both the technological and social history of literacy. Until the advent of sound recording, there was no means of replicating spoken performance permanently; and without a permanent record speech was often viewed as inconsequential or even unreliable, with reports of speech mere hearsay. In contrast with the fleeting or ephemeral nature of speech, anything in a book came to be seen as more serious; and written and printed texts came in many cases to be revered documents, enjoying far higher cultural status than the same words in speech would have done. Special authority has been conventionally attached, in many cultures, to religious and legal documents within the broader range of religious and legal practices; and something of the authority associated with religious books in particular is claimed for literature when traditions of literary work are referred to as a **canon**, or specified set of holy books.

Much in the cultural history of Western literary traditions is connected with this special status of print. Literary institutions have been closely involved with book production and preservation, as well as with 'battles of the books'; and conventional literary scholarship and hermeneutics, or efforts to understand written texts from earlier cultural moments, are in many respects a **bibliophile**, or book-loving, activity – an aspect of literature that is reflected in the closeness between two historically influential senses of being 'literate': being able to read, and being well read.

The 'myth of print' collides, however, with an equally pervasive cluster of beliefs that surround use of speech. A competing 'myth of orality' is created when special value is placed on the presumed power of speech (and, with it, live performance in general) to offer direct or immediate expression of physically lived experience. When that speaking self addresses others, a further valued effect is thought to be created: that of closeness or communion between speaker and hearer(s) – even, paradoxically, if they are shouting at each other.

The myth of orality underpins the high value often placed on performance. It encourages us to see the uniqueness and 'unrepeatability' of a live, performed event as inherently worthwhile and desirable, rather than as an inevitable, practical consequence of performance as a real-time event (as it had to be, before audio and audio-visual recording). It also drives our wish to hear an author read, even if we already know the book, because in presenting in person an author will give us what we then see as a more personally authentic version of it. Performance in this sense embodies or breathes life into a literary work (note the vocabulary here of closeness between oral performance, the human body and claimed vitality).

There is also a cultural dimension to the myth of orality. Oral expression is sometimes treated as if it is the essential channel, or lifeblood, of any organic or fundamentally united community, in which people would talk directly with one another rather than communicating at a distance. Many modern poets have aspired, as would-be bards from an oral society, to this promise of the spoken, as compared with the isolated garret and presumed disempowerment associated with writing.

26.4 Reading between the myths

Literature in performance is made a sensitive issue in the modern period by the scale of shifts in our textual environment. Over the last hundred years public communication has moved from an environment dominated by the authority of print media to one in which relayed and reproduced forms of speech, as well as images, so-called 'live' documents and interactive web materials all play an increasingly important part.

Interestingly, despite the divergence between the myths of print and performance illustrated above, the act of reading a page itself shows in microcosm the properties of both: the printed words are a sort of notation, to be realized in a performed interpretation; the act of reading has a specific duration, like a performance, in that reading is a time-based activity; and reading a page varies between different performers and occasions, as different readings are produced.

Understanding present relations between literature and performance involves building towards general arguments about our textual environment on the basis of specific analyses (such as analysis of the act of reading a page, or making sense of a radio programme or multimedia text), rather than leaping to general claims about orality, literacy, print or performance.

26.4.1 Does literature have a future?

If people nowadays, especially young people, consume narrative and drama more in films and on television than in books or on the stage, and lyricism more in pop lyrics than in collections of poetry, does it then follow that literature is dying?

Many of the examples introduced in this unit suggest that literature has always involved a performance dimension. In this respect, the recent technological extension of modes of performance into new media represents a stage of growth and change in the general process of interaction between written and spoken, rather than a fundamental transformation of mode of representation. If this is so, then warnings of the death of literature because of its co-existence with other media discourse types are unnecessary.

Predicting what mix of texts will be read in fifty or a hundred years' time is risky: how much print; how much on-screen text; how much audio and audio-visual material; how much hypertext, interactive and streamed material – and how much text in forms and formats not yet envisaged? It is not particularly future text types or delivery systems that will determine whether the insights and pleasures associated with literary reading have a future, however. What will be more important is to relate changing media properties and capabilities to the working of creativity at other levels, including choice of topic, reproduction of and experimentation with form, and engagement with new issues and audiences.

ACTIVITY 26.1 _____

1   Identify, in each of the five extracts below, any evidence you find in the form of the extract that the text it comes from has been specially composed for performance. At this stage, ignore whatever you know about any of the texts. In looking for signs of being 'written for performance', consider four types of performance:

   • reading aloud (e.g. in a public reading);
   • musical performance (with the text used as words of a song or other musical composition);
   • audio representation (e.g. as a radio drama, audio-book or CD);
   • dramatic representation (including in the theatre, on television, or video/DVD).

Look for any kind of evidence you consider relevant, but pay particular attention to the following possible markers: layout, for instance division into lines; repetition of phrases, as in a musical chorus; implied identity of a specific speaker or narrator; and naming of various speakers as a cast or list of dramatis personae.

2   Are there features in any of the extracts that would make the text difficult, or even impossible, to perform in any of the four ways listed above?

[Tasks continue after the five extracts]

Text A

Can I not sing but 'hoy'
When the jolly shepherd made so much joy?

The shepherd upon a hill he sat;
He had on him his tabard and his hat,
His tar-box, his pipe and his flagat*;
His name was called Jolly, Jolly Wat,
    For he was a good herdsboy.
      With hoy!
For in his pipe he made so much joy.

[* = flask]

Text B

'Bill, Bill, for dear God's sake, for your own, for mine, stop before you spill my blood! I have been true to you, upon my guilty soul I have!'

The man struggled violently to release his arms; but those of the girl were clasped round his, and tear her as he would, he could not tear them away.

'Bill,' cried the girl, striving to lay her head upon his breast, 'the gentleman and that dear lady, told me to-night of a home in some foreign country where I could end my days in solitude and peace. Let me see them again, and beg them, on my knees, to show the same mercy and goodness to you; and this dreadful place, and far apart lead better lives, and forget how we have lived, except in prayers, and never see each other more. It is never too late to repent. They told me so – I feel it now – but we must have time – a little, little time!'

The housebreaker freed one arm, and grasped his pistol. The certainty of immediate detection if he fired, flashed across his mind even in the midst of his fury; and he beat it twice with all the force he could summon, upon the upturned face that almost touched his own.

She staggered and fell: nearly blinded with the blood that rained down from a deep gash in her forehead; but raising herself, with difficulty, on her knees, drew from her bosom a white handkerchief – Rose Maylie's own – and holding it up, in her folded hands, as high towards Heaven as her feeble strength would allow, breathed one prayer for mercy to her Maker.

It was a ghastly figure to look upon. The murderer staggering backward to the wall, and shutting out the sight with his hand, seized a heavy club and struck her down.

Text C

FIRST VOICE
Blind Captain Cat climbs into his bunk. Like a cat, he sees in the dark. Through the voyages of his tears he sails to see the dead.

CAPTAIN CAT
Dancing Williams!

FIRST DROWNED
Still dancing.

CAPTAIN CAT
Jonah Jarvis.

THIRD DROWNED
Still.

FIRST DROWNED
Curly Bevan's skull.

ROSIE PROBERT
Rosie, with God. She has forgotten dying.

FIRST VOICE
The dead come out in their Sunday best.

SECOND VOICE
Listen to the night breaking.

FIRST VOICE
Organ Morgan goes to chapel to play the organ. He sees Bach lying on a tombstone.

ORGAN MORGAN
Johann Sebastian!

CHERRY OWEN (*Drunkenly*)
Who?

ORGAN MORGAN
Johann Sebastian mighty Bach. Oh, Bach fach.

Text D

         FIRST VOICE
'But tell me, tell me! speak again,
Thy soft response renewing—
What makes that ship drive on so fast?
What is the ocean doing?'

         SECOND VOICE
'Still as a slave before his lord,
The ocean hath no blast;
His great bright eye most silently
Up to the Moon is cast—

If he may know which way to go;
For she guides him smooth or grim.
See, brother, see! how graciously
She looketh down on him.'

         FIRST VOICE
'But why drives on that ship so fast,
Without or wave or wind?'

         SECOND VOICE
'The air is cut away before,
And closes from behind.

Fly, brother, fly! more high, more high!
Or we shall be belated:
For slow and slow that ship will go,
When the Mariner's trance is abated.'

Text E

And did those feet in ancient time
Walk upon England's mountains green?
And was the holy Lamb of God
On England's pleasant pastures seen?

And did the Countenance Divine
Shine forth upon our clouded hills?
And was Jerusalem builded here
Among these dark Satanic Mills?

Bring me my Bow of burning gold!
Bring me my Arrows of desire!
Bring me my spear! O clouds, unfold!
Bring me my Chariot of fire!

> I will not cease from Mental Fight,
> Nor shall my Sword sleep in my hand,
> Till we have built Jerusalem
> In England's green and pleasant land.

3   When you have listed all the evidence you can find in the form of the extracts, consider the following extra information:

Text A: First stanza of an anonymous Medieval poem or song; evidence about whether this text was sung rather than recited or read is conjectural, based on what we know and assume about how texts circulated during the period.

Text B: The final passage of Chapter 47 in Charles Dickens's *Oliver Twist* (1837–8), the chapter in which Nancy is murdered by her companion in crime, Bill Sykes; see activity in **Unit 3** (pp. 38–9) for context. Dickens started to prepare for public reading of this passage (which he read from earlier in the chapter than the extract reproduced here) in 1863, but only began performing it, to massive public acclaim, in 1868. So sensational was Dickens's rendering of the passage considered to be that, during his farewell tour in 1869–70, the author included a special reading of the Nancy episode for an assembled audience of professional actors.

Text C: From towards the end of Dylan Thomas's *Under Milk Wood: A Play for Voices*. This work was first broadcast by the BBC, January 1954, then presented on stage at the Edinburgh Festival and in London in 1956, with extracts also shown on television. A film of the play was released in 1972, and it has been produced in many different versions since.

Text D: The beginning of Part VI of Samuel Taylor Coleridge's 'The Rime of the Ancient Mariner', a poem written in a combination of narrative and dramatic modes and included in *Lyrical Ballads* (1798). During the Romantic period, some poets wrote extensively in dramatic dialogue, or in mixed dramatic and non-dramatic modes, even where a work was not intended for the stage.

Text E: The poem 'Jerusalem', from the Preface to William Blake's *Milton: A Poem* (1804–8). This poem is more widely known as a hymn, with music composed in 1916 by Sir Charles Herbert Parry. Together, the words and music serve as the anthem of both the British Women's Institute (since the 1920s) and also more recently of the far-right British National Party. The musical, hymn version has been released in cover versions by Emerson, Lake and Palmer, Iron Maiden vocalist Bruce Dickinson, The Fall, Billy Bragg and the Pet Shop Boys, as well as in instrumental versions including that by the Grimethorpe Colliery Brass Band.

4   How much does the form in which you have encountered a text before, or what you know about it, affect your view of its suitability for performance?

5   Finally, a version of each extract can probably be imagined in a multi-media environment combining still and moving images, written text, speech, sound effects and music. How would such adaptation of the texts presented here affect their literariness? How much of their quality as literature would you say is carried over into the new form of representation?

Reading

Finnegan, R. (2002) *Communicating: The Multiple Modes of Human Interconnection*, London: Routledge.

Jakobson, R. (1987) *Language in Literature*, Cambridge, MA: Belknap Press.

Ong, W. (2002) *Orality and Literacy: The Technologizing of the Word*, London: Routledge.

Thompson, J.B. (1995) *The Media and Modernity: A Social Theory of the Media*, Cambridge: Polity Press.

Appendix: notes on activities

Unit 1 Asking questions as a way into reading

The author, Ee Tiang Hong, is a Malaysian writer, who was born in Malacca in 1933 and educated at Tranquerah English School and High School, Malacca. Until his death in the early 1990s, he lived mostly in Australia.

Tranquerah Road: the road is an extension of Heeren Street, in Malacca.

Kampong Serani: 'Portuguese Village', in the suburb of Ujong Pasir.

Limbongan: a suburb adjacent to Tranquerah. The Dutch used to moor their vessels off the coast here.

Kimigayo: the Japanese national anthem.

Nihon Seishin: 'Japanese Soul'.

Greater East Asia Co-Prosperity Sphere: the Japanese scheme to unify Asia, during the Second World War.

Meliora hic sequamur: the motto of the Malacca High School ('Here let us do better things').

Merdeka: 'Independence'.

Negara-ku: 'My Country'; the Malayan, and then Malaysian, national anthem.

pontianak: a succubus, or evil spirit.

jinn: genie; evil spirit.

Omitohood: a Buddhist benediction ('Om Mane Pudmi Hum'), in the Hokkien Chinese dialect.

Unit 3 Analysing units of structure

The first sentence should read:

Following Nancy's death Sikes tries to escape the hue and cry.

The order of the sentences in the published companion is:

15, 11, 3, 8, 9, 2, 6, 12, 4, 7, 1, 14, 5, 10, 13.

Glossary

Accent Distinctive pattern of pronunciation associated with a place, region or group; in other contexts, the term 'accent' means an additional stress that accentuates a syllable by making it relatively prominent.

Address Means by which a text seems to be 'talking' to the reader or to the text's addressee. See also **Direct address**, **Indirect address** and **Mode of address**.

Addressee Designated or implied recipient of an utterance. The addressee may overlap with the reader of a text but the two do not always coincide. Poems, for instance, have been addressed to a 'tyger' (Blake) or a skylark (Shelley) or a Grecian urn (Keats) without these being likely readers of the poems in question. In each case, however, these specific entities are defined by the poem as the projected addressee.

Aesthetics Systematic study of the abstract properties of beauty. In philosophy, a branch of study dealing with what appeals to the senses. In the study of literature, aesthetics is particularly concerned with kinds of formal patterning, such as rhyme, rhythm and alliteration, that help to define its distinctive appeal.

Affective fallacy Error or failing in interpreting a text that results from over-attention to our own personal responses at the expense of what the words of the text actually say. The term was first used by two American critics, W.K. Wimsatt and M.C. Beardsley, in 1946. (See also **intentional fallacy**.)

Agent Person (or animal or similar) who makes something happen.

Alienation effect Effect produced in drama when the theatrical illusion is broken in ways that make the audience perceive the drama as a product of theatrical techniques rather than something 'real'. The technique was

342

initially developed by Bertolt Brecht, whose purpose was to 'estrange' realist theatrical conventions and the bourgeois ideology he believed such conventions support. The term is also used to describe the equivalent effect in other literary forms.

Allegory   (From the Greek for 'speaking otherwise'.) A narrative fiction in which characters and actions, and sometimes the setting, can be seen as referring to a parallel (often political, religious or moral) story.

Alliteration   Type of sound pattern in which nearby words begin with similar sounds (or have their most strongly stressed syllables beginning with similar sounds).

Allusion   Moment when one text makes an implicit or explicit reference to another text, either by directly quoting the second text or by modifying the second text in order to suit the new context.

Ambiguity   When a phrase or statement can be interpreted in more than one way. The capability of being understood in two or more ways sometimes arises from different meanings of a given word, and sometimes from unclear grammatical relationships between words in a sentence. Ambiguity is an inevitable feature of language use and can be accidental or deliberate, but in literary forms of expression (especially poetry) it is assumed to be deliberate and may be used to keep more than one meaning in play or to suggest connections between different possible meanings.

Anglophone   English-speaking. Many countries around the world formerly colonized by Britain have significant Anglophone populations and Anglo-phone features within the national culture, such as books written in English or cinema produced in English.

Anti-language   In sociolinguistics and literary stylistics, a mode of expression or linguistic variety adopted by a group of people to mark off their way of speaking or writing from dominant traditions they wish to reject. Anti-language may consist of private words ('jargon', 'cant', 'argot'), or a more extended code of specialized idioms.

Apostrophe   Rhetorical figure in which a speaker addresses either someone who is not there, or even dead, or something that is not normally thought of as able to understand language or reply (e.g. an animal or an object).

Archaism   Language that seems as if it is more commonly found in earlier periods and whose usage seems unusual or marked in a contemporary context.

Archetypal genres   Four selected genres (comedy, romance, tragedy and satire), which, according to the literary critic Northrop Frye (in *Anatomy* *of Criticism: Four Essays*, 1957), correspond emotionally to the four seasons and may be linked to a rich cultural reservoir of myth (for instance, surrounding perceived stages in human life). These genres may be considered 'archetypal' in the sense of not being just conventional styles but possibly expressions of something collective and more profound about us as human beings.

Attitude   See **propositional attitude**.

Author   Person credited with composing the literary work. This person is not necessarily the same as the **implied author**, who is a presence inferred by the reader as the guiding personality behind the work. One and the same actual author may compose texts featuring different implied authors.

Background knowledge   Information that it is assumed a reader will self-evidently know or agree to. (See also **schema**.)

Ballad   Simple poem, usually in short and formulaic stanzas, in which a popular story is narrated. Ballads were often originally accompanied by music and danced to, but the form evolved in two different directions: continuing folk ballads, performed out loud in spoken form, and urban **broadside ballads**.

Bibliophile   Book-loving. Sometimes the word is used to describe not just the characteristic or quality of loving books but a person who shows a strong taste for or devotion to them.

Binary opposition   Two-way choice, or dichotomy, between mutually exclusive, alternative options. The two terms need not be simply neutral: one may have a positive, the other a negative value (as in the pairs good/evil, life/death, hero/villain). Such oppositions – of particular interest in **structuralism** – provide a simple, pervasive mechanism for organizing thought and experience, but have important cultural consequences in the way they distribute value.

Bricolage   In art, a technique (characteristic of **postmodernism**) in which works are constructed from various materials available or to hand. In cultural studies, the term describes the processes by which people assemble objects from across social divisions and use them to project new cultural identities.

Broadside ballads   **Ballads** circulated in printed form on large, single sheets of paper ('broadsheets'), or in chapbooks. Such ballads typically present popular songs, romantic tales and sensational or topical stories, often celebrating or attacking particular people or institutions.

Canon   Body of literary works traditionally regarded as the most important, significant, long-lasting and worthy of study: the literary classics. Earlier, 'canon' was used to describe the collection of books of the Bible accepted by the Christian Church as genuine and divinely inspired. The term was then applied to other sacred books and later extended to writings of a secular **author** accepted as being authentic or genuine; in this enlarged context, 'canonical' means accepted, authoritative or standard.

Catharsis   Purification of emotions brought about by watching rather than having an experience, especially when we watch a play. In Aristotle's *Poetics*, catharsis achieves this purging or purification by means of feelings of pity and fear aroused in the audience by the dramatic spectacle involved in tragedy.

Chiasmus   Type of **parallelism** where the order of elements in the first part is reversed in the second part.

Chorus   Originally consisted of twelve to fifteen men who sang odes and delivered speeches in the tragic drama of classical Greece. This classical chorus typically represented the conservative views of society and so served to contrast with the tragic hero and his society. The chorus fell out of favour after the classical period, but is occasionally used – usually as a single character rather than as a group – in plays from the Renaissance to the early twentieth century. In contemporary drama choruses feature mostly to create an **alienation effect**.

Chronicle play   Play that presents a historical narrative and topics. A number of Elizabethan plays (including some by Shakespeare) were based on the sixteenth-century historian Ralph Holinshed's chronicles or stories from English history.

Classic realism   Form of **realism** employed especially by nineteenth-century writers such as George Eliot; seen as the standard mode of realist writing.

Clause   In linguistics, a full or partial sentence contained inside another sentence. Usually contains a verb but may be missing some of the components of a full sentence such as a subject or tense.

Code-switching   Behaviour consisting of (sometimes repeated) changes between different varieties of language, for example, between styles addressed to different audiences or matched to different situations, or between a standard variety and a dialect. (See also **register** and **dialect**.)

Coherence/coherent   How parts of a discourse hold together in an intelligible fashion. This may depend as much on the ability of readers to supply connections between parts of the discourse as upon explicit connections within the discourse itself. (See also **schema** and **inference**.)

Collage   Composition formed when different pieces of text, or styles, or genres are placed alongside one another. Juxtaposition forces us to consider the two (or more) things side-by-side; we either unify the contrasting materials into some new, compound form, or else see in them some form of implied comparison. (See also **bricolage**.)

Comedy   A term used primarily to categorize plays and novels that are designed to amuse the audience/reader. Although the characters encounter problems and crises, we expect that the main characters will achieve happiness at the end, often through love and marriage, while the unsympathetic characters will receive their punishment.

Concordance   List of all the words used in a particular text (or collection of texts, often those of a particular author) usually arranged alphabetically. The list shows where the words are used, and often quotes some surrounding context. (See also **corpus**.)

Conjunction   Term from **grammar** used to describe words whose major function is to signal a relationship between one sentence and a previous sentence or sentences. Examples of conjunctions are *and*, *but*, *so*, *then*. In speech these are usually found at the beginning of a new sentence. In writing, equivalent terms are *moreover*, *however*, *therefore*, *afterwards*.

Constituent element   Some identified part, or component, of a larger whole that is important in giving it its overall form; an element that organizes something or makes it what it is (see **form**). If a sentence must contain a noun phrase, for example, then 'noun phrase' is a constituent element of a sentence; or, if rolling final credits are found in films, though presented in different films in different styles, then 'final credits' might be considered a constituent element of a film.

Content   The propositions that a text communicates.

Corpus   Body or collection of writings; the whole body of written material on a given subject. Also commonly used to mean the body of written or spoken data, collected either from particular texts or from language use more generally, on which a linguistic analysis is based. Such corpora are mostly electronically stored and searchable, making it possible to find all examples of a particular word (a 'key word in context', or KWIC).

Cross-dressing   Practice of having male actors play female roles, or female actors playing male roles.

Cultural code   Statements that the reader can understand because they share the same cultural values as the writer of the text.

Death of the author   Theoretical and rhetorical claim made by the French post-structuralist critic Roland Barthes in order to undermine the habit in traditional criticism of invoking authorial intention in order to control interpretation.

Decorum   Convention or rule, important in the history of **rhetoric** and literary composition, that **style** should be appropriate – or, more judgmentally, seemly or befitting – to subject matter and situation. Following classical authors such as Horace, styles were often categorized as 'grand', 'middle' or 'plain', with each style judged suitable for a different literary genre (e.g. 'grand' style for epic composition). In more recent literary work, such fixed style expectations are less important, and mixed styles are far more common, along with deliberate experiments in style-switching.

Demonstrative   In linguistics, words whose prime function is to point to something in the immediate context of speaker and hearer. Examples of demonstratives are *this*, *that*, *here* or *there.*

Dénouement   French term meaning 'unknotting', often used to describe the conclusion of a novel, film or play in which the problems that have driven the action are resolved, either comically or tragically.

Dialect   Regional (as well as social class and occupational) variations in grammar, vocabulary and **accent**. Common dialect contrasts include those between urban and rural, or between different rural areas; between classes; or between different social roles and jobs. The term 'dialect' carries no necessary implication that one dialect is better than another, though some speakers use the word in that way. In many literary texts, regional varieties have been used, especially in dialogue, for comic effect, despite the resulting effect of stereotyping.

Dialect map   Map based on linguistic field work showing the different areas where dialect features such as particular words or forms of pronunciation are used.

Dialogism   English version of a term developed by Russian critic Mikhail Bakhtin to refer to the way novels in particular are inhabited by a multiplicity of different and perhaps competing voices – those of narrators and characters, but also potentially including all the voices or registers (of philosophy, of horticulture, etc.) that are available at the time of writing. (See also **hierarchy of voices**.)

Dialogue   Conventional way of presenting, in writing, the conversational interaction that takes place between people (not necessarily two people, since any number of people can take part). 'Dialogue' is conventional because many features of real-life verbal interaction (e.g. overlap between speakers, pauses, repetition) are either excluded altogether or extensively tidied up or simplified.

Direct address   Way of addressing the reader by name, by using questions or commands (such as 'Could you be mortgage-free faster?' or 'Stop smoking'), or by using 'you' or 'we'.

Discourse   In linguistics, stretches of language in use whose units of description project beyond the sentence. Also used in related disciplines to mean something like a unified field of statements that construct domains of reality in a particular way – e.g. 'legal discourse', 'the discourse of empire', 'neo-conservative discourse'. In narrative theory the term refers to the various devices available for rendering or transmitting the basic storyline and embraces issues of point of view, temporal presentation and ordering, choice of medium and so on.

Dominant reading   Reading that seems self-evidently to make sense of the text, but that does so by drawing on stereotypes and ideologies circulating within society.

Dramatic irony   When a character on stage and involved in a dramatic action has a specific belief that the audience knows to be false. Typically, that incorrect belief will be about some crucial component of the plot, and hence the dramatic irony functions as a narrative mechanism.

Elegy   Conventional poem or song lamenting someone's death; a funeral poem. Historically such elegies were associated with a particular metre, so sometimes 'elegy' is used as the term for all poetry written in such 'elegiac' metre, including **pastoral** poems delivered in the voice of shepherds that are not concerned with the death of any particular person.

Enigma   Literally 'a puzzle'. The term is important in the study of narrative since in many cases narratives are driven by a quest to solve a puzzle – or resolve an enigma. Crime or detective fiction is often organized in this way.

Epigraph   Inscription or quotation at the beginning of a literary work or document (or a section of one), setting out or highlighting a theme.

Epilogue   Speech, often in verse, addressed to the audience at the end of a play.

Epithalamium   Wedding song or poem declaimed in praise of a bride and bridegroom, and praying for their prosperity; more generally, a poem written for and proclaimed at a public occasion, for example, to celebrate a victorious person such as an athlete or general.

Estuary English   Name given, by reference to the estuary of the River Thames, to a regional accent currently spreading out from London into the southeast of England, and containing features of both **Received Pronunciation** and regional London accents such as Cockney (associated with the city's East End).

Eventuality   Event (something happens), or an action (something is made to happen by an agent), or a state of affairs. Eventualities occur in the (real or fictional) world and are represented by sentences.

Exposition Passage or passages in a literary text or play, often early on in the plot, in which a **narrator** or characters provide the **reader**/audience with necessary information about events that have led up to the events presented in the text or on stage.

Feminine rhyme Rhyme between two words in which the final syllable is not stressed.

Figurative language General term for a number of non-literal uses of language.

Focalizer In narrative theory, a term for describing who or what witnesses the events of the **narrative**. There may be more than one focalizer in the course of a narrative.

Foot Group of two or three **syllables**, one (called the 'head of the foot') being more prominent than the others. The four main types of foot in English are: iambic, anapaestic, trochaic and dactylic.

Form When we look specifically at the form of a text we look at its construction from a collection of characteristic components. The components can be used in other texts, and include linguistic components such as sounds and words, metrical components such as feet, and narrative components such as 'donor' or 'orientation'. Aspects of form include the division of the text into sections (such as lines, or narrative episodes, or chapters), and relationships that arise between components or between sections (such as sound patterning or **parallelism**).

Formalism Concern with how the components of language, or of a particular text, fit and work together (see **form**). As a branch of linguistics, an emphasis on grammatical structures and the meaning of sentences largely in isolation from their communicative function or the context in which they are set. Formalism is also the name given to a linguistic and literary movement of the early twentieth century (now most commonly associated with the work of the linguist Roman Jakobson) concerned with analysis of form and technique.

Formalist theories In historical linguistics, forms of analysis that concentrate on formal features of language such as change in the pronunciation of vowels and that see these changes as occurring because of fairly autonomous processes intrinsic to language itself.

Free indirect speech Term used in **stylistics** to describe a kind of **indirect speech** or reported speech in which the words spoken by (or thoughts entertained by) a particular character and the voice of the reporting narrator are blended, normally with no reporting clause indicated. Free indirect speech (or thought) appears more vivid than indirect speech (or thought), in that a particular character's own words and point of view come through into the reporting voice. This produces a sense of being inside the character's mind while being told things by the narrator.

Free verse   Verse whose lines do not have their length and rhythm regulated.

Functionalist theories   In historical linguistics, forms of analysis that see language change as due to, or reflecting, social or political processes.

Gatekeepers of language   Institutions, and people working within them, who must authorize a change in language if it is to be widely adopted.

Gender specific   Applied to terms that can only be used for either women or men: for example, 'actress' is only used to refer to women.

Generic noun   A noun, like 'police officer', that refers to both men and women, but that may often be used as if it is referring primarily to men.

Generic pronoun   Use of the pronoun 'he' to stand for people in general, including both men and women.

Grammar   Rules of selection and combination that govern possible relationships between words in a language. Relatedly, systematic description of a language as we find it in a sample of speech or writing, or by eliciting examples from native speakers. Sometimes 'grammar' is used to refer only to features of structural organization (principally sentence structure) that can be studied independently of sound or meaning; sometimes the term is used more widely, to include all aspects of how language is organized.

Great Vowel Shift   Interrelated changes in pronunciation that occurred across a range of vowels in English during the fifteenth to eighteenth centuries.

Haiku   A short poem (imitating a Japanese form), constructed in three lines of five, seven and five syllables respectively, intended to capture a moment of spiritual insight and designed to elicit an emotional response in the reader.

Hermeneutics   General art or science of interpretation, involving efforts to understand how understanding can be achieved, what rules it should follow, and what its limits are, especially when the text we are trying to understand comes from an earlier period, or from a different culture, or is for some other reason resistant to understanding. (See also **reader**; **reading**.)

Hierarchy of voices   The relationship between the various different voices and perspectives of a complex, layered text such as a novel (which may contain one or more narrators, as well as possibly a large number of major and minor characters). In interpreting such a text, we distinguish what any given character says from what the work as a whole says; in this process, a different status is accorded to each of the various different voices that make up the text.

Iambic pentameter   Metre that requires the line to have ten **syllables**, divided into five feet; in each **foot** (pair of syllables), the second syllable is more strongly stressed than the first.

Iconic   Refers to a type of sign where there is close resemblance between the material used to convey meaning and the meaning itself.

Implied author   Critical term developed to distinguish between the real author and the impression produced by some texts (especially novels) that there is a designing consciousness or voice within the text itself.

Implied reader   Position that the text constructs and that it is assumed the text is addressing.

Indirect address   When a text addresses its readers by presenting them with information or opinions with which they are assumed to agree. If a text is not using **direct address**, then it is addressing the reader indirectly.

Indirect speech   Way of reporting the words someone uses without directly quoting them. Instead, those words are made subordinate to a verb of saying and introduced with the word 'that' (e.g. 'Tess replied that she already knew' compared with 'Tess replied, "I already know"'); sometimes also called reported speech. (See also **free indirect speech**.)

Inference   Drawing a logical or reasonable conclusion from statements or evidence.

Inferencing   Interpretive process that is based on the reader's or hearer's assumption that a piece of language is a meaningful communication and that proceeds by making inferences about the author's likely intentions by examining the text and its context.

Intentional fallacy   Error or failing in interpreting a text that results from an unwarranted shift from what the words appear to mean to what we imagine the author meant by using them. The term was first used by two American critics, W.K. Wimsatt and M.C. Beardsley in 1946. (See also **affective fallacy**.)

Intertextuality   Term used to describe the variety of ways that texts interact with other texts; in particular, the notion of intertextuality stresses the idea that texts are not unique, isolated objects but are made out of the recycled voices and registers of other literary texts and the general culture they exist in.

Intonation   Melodic patterning of the voice, combining upward or downward pitch movements with contrasts achieved by placing the principal stress in different places in any given group of words. Intonation conveys information, feeling or attitude that go beyond the meanings of the actual words. Apart from occasional italics or capitals, written texts do not notate intonation; readers of words on a page assign different, imagined intonational patterns to what they read.

Irony   Use of language in which the speaker or writer covertly indicates disagreement with what is directly expressed by the words. (See also **verbal irony**, **situational irony**, **dramatic irony** and **structural irony**.)

Literacy   Skill in using a code of communication, especially ability to read and write. Historically the term has mostly applied – and is still most often used – of written communication, and can be used to describe either individuals, social groups or whole populations. Sometimes the term is also applied to other, non-written forms of communication, as in 'media literacy' and 'computer literacy'.

Lyric poem   Usually short and devoted to the expression or exploration of emotion (grief, love, pity, admiration) embodied in a single voice (not necessarily that of the poet). The term derives from the Classical Greek word for a stringed instrument (the 'lyre' – similar to a harp), which was used to accompany song and recitation.

Lyricism   Expression of poetic qualities, including contemplation and aesthetically pleasing arrangement or musicality. (See also **lyric poem**.)

Masque   Form of courtly dramatic entertainment popular in the sixteenth and seventeenth centuries and containing music, disguise and dancing. Costumes and stage machinery were elaborate, and members of the audience, which was generally aristocratic, were invited to contribute to the action or dancing.

Medium (pl. media)   Means by which something is communicated. Typically used to refer to the modern electronic media of radio, television and the Internet, but also includes film, telegraph, print and other forms of transmission and inscription. In media studies the plural term also includes those agencies and institutions associated with particular means of transmission.

Metalanguage   Specialized language we use to talk about language itself; includes expressions like 'noun', 'sentence' and 'figurative'.

Metaphor   Figure of speech in which one thing or idea or event is spoken of as if it were another (revealingly similar) thing, idea or event.

Metonymy   Figure of speech in which one thing or idea or event is referred to as if it were another thing, idea or event with which it is normally associated.

Metre   Pattern regulating the length and, to some extent, the rhythm of a line. Metres are often named in terms of the type of **foot** they consist of and how many of those feet there are; e.g. **iambic pentameter**.

Mimesis   Universalized or generalized vision of life, from contemplating which the reader can learn something about universal truths and values.

Mode of address   How a text invokes its audience, whether directly or indirectly; includes features such as honorifics (e.g. 'thou'/'you', 'madam'/'sir'), choice of register and markers of politeness. Together such features signal attitude towards – or how we wish to relate to – the person or people we are communicating with.

Modernism   Literary movement most commonly understood as exemplified by writers – such as James Joyce, Gertrude Stein, T.S. Eliot and Ezra Pound – writing for the most part in the first half of the twentieth century, between the First and Second World Wars. Such writers are generally considered to have been committed to radical experimentation with form and language.

Montage   In film editing, juxtaposition of seemingly unrelated shots or scenes, which, when combined in sequence, produce a meaning that goes beyond what is contained simply in the isolated shots.

Motif   Recurrent thematic element in a literary text or group of texts.

Narrative   Something that tells a story; an account of a series of events, usually given in order and with connections established between them.

Narrator   The voice that tells the story. Not all narratives have narrators. Film and theatre, for instance, depict stories but do so often without a narrator. Other genres and media, however, depend upon them. The novel as a genre has been particularly inventive in drawing on different types of narrator, ranging from a character within the story to an impersonal, anonymous voice speaking from outside the events of the tale. In the latter case it is important not to identify the narrator too directly with the author. (See also **implied author**.)

Naturalism   Dramatic and literary genre of the late nineteenth century that aimed at representation of 'real life', focusing on the factors (society, history, personality and so on) that determine characters' actions.

Network Standard   Standard American variety of English, sometimes called network English, modelled on and maintained in the United States by network television announcers; roughly analogous to the idea of BBC English.

New Criticism   Critical theory and practice promoted by a group of critics who taught in British and American universities from the 1940s onwards. New

Criticism promoted the idea that students of literature should focus on literary texts rather than background material, and argued that the goal of literary criticism is to discover, through close analysis, an organic unity between a text's **form** and **content**. (See also **organic form**.)

Non-realist texts   Texts that may draw on some elements of realist style but subvert that style in some way.

Non-self-reflexive language   Language that seems to be simply delivering information; language that is not literary or poetic in any way.

OED   *Oxford English Dictionary*, which gives not only the definition of words, but also the meanings of words at particular historical moments, with extensive illustrative quotation.

Oral literature   Forms of poetry, storytelling and drama in a tradition or culture in which the spoken word is the chief form of communication. Works of oral literature are memorized and improvised, and handed down from generation to generation.

Organic form   Idea, first developed in literary criticism by the poet Samuel Taylor Coleridge but extended and adapted subsequently, that the form of a literary work occurs or grows of itself, with its various parts coordinated into a unified whole like a living organism, rather than made according to a human or social design.

Paradox   Originally a statement that goes against received opinion or what we generally believe to be the case, now more usually an absurd or self-contradictory statement that may, when we investigate it, turn out to be well founded.

Parallelism   Similarity in sound sequence, or sentence structure, or word meaning between two close or adjacent sections of the text.

Parts of speech   Types of word, classified on the basis of how they behave, where they can come in a well-formed (grammatical) string of words, or what other words they can be replaced with. Common parts of speech include nouns, verbs, adjectives, adverbs, articles and prepositions. (See also **grammar**.)

Pastiche   Literary or artistic composition that incorporates different **styles** or parts drawn from a variety of sources, usually so that it appears to be a kind of copy. Pastiche often exaggerates or makes fun of a particular style by clearly signalling its element of imitation, typically merging conventions from one genre with subject matter from another in a way that is obviously incongruous.

Pastoral   Style of literary composition, or resulting literary work, that portrays rural life or the life of shepherds, especially in an idealized or romantic form. Pastoral writing celebrates country life in depictions of simple rural and idyllic scenes, but tends also to have a reflective or nostalgic dimension.

Pathetic fallacy Error or failing in interpreting a text (first formulated by John Ruskin as a weakness of particular painters and writers, rather than a problem in reading) that results from ascribing emotions and feelings to inanimate objects and then assuming those feelings to exist outside us, in the world.

Patient Object or person (or animal, etc.) to whom something is done.

Persona Invented character or voice deliberately assumed by an author in a novel, poem or other work. The effect is as if the writer is writing as a different person, or as a particular dramatic character; the views or values of the persona character cannot be read off as those of the author. (See also **implied author**.)

Personification Figure of speech in which a thing or idea or event is spoken of as if it were a human being or had human characteristics. (See also **pathetic fallacy**.)

Picaresque A kind of novel that tells the story of a roguish hero or antihero living by his wits in a corrupt society, exemplified in English by Henry Fielding's *Tom Jones* or *Joseph Andrews*.

Plot Events that make up a story in the order in which they are supposed to have occurred.

Poetic speaker The 'speaker' of a poem, on the assumption that a distinction is drawn between the creator of a poem and its fictional speaker (since the fictional speaker is a poetic device or effect). (See also **persona**.)

Poetry slam (sometimes also **poetry jam**) Type of poetry performance event, originating in US clubs during the 1980s as a variation on 'open mike' sessions, often with a competition format and involving audience participation.

Postmodernism Philosophical and cultural response to cultural conditions believed characteristic of the contemporary period in industrialized societies. So much of our experience is held to consist of exposure to communication and **media**, by comparison with 'real' or actual personal experience, that any act of communication requires a high degree of self-awareness about conventional genres in which it usually takes place. Straightforward communication, without irony or some reference to the formulae by means of which a particular topic is usually represented, is considered less and less possible or credible. (See also **non-self-reflexive language**.)

Prologue Prefatory speech by a **narrator**, **chorus** or character introducing a play, or part of a play; also used to refer to the character who delivers such a prefatory speech.

Propositional attitude A proposition is a statement about the real world or about some fictional world; attached to each proposition is an attitude, which expresses the speaker's or writer's relation to that proposition.

Prosodic and paralinguistic systems Features of the sound structure of language that go beyond individual sound segments and concern such things as **intonation**, tempo, loudness, **rhythm**, pauses and voice quality. Prosodic and paralinguistic systems create meanings by superimposing additional contrasts onto the flow of sound segments.

Protagonist Chief character in a literary text, especially in a play; also used in the plural (since there may be two or more protagonists).

Reader In its most basic sense, whoever decodes a piece of writing. In literary studies, an ideal or **implied reader** who will take the literary work, or the text, on the terms in which it is offered. (See also **resisting reader**.)

Readership Idealized group of typical **readers** for a text or group of texts.

Reading Process of decoding a written text. When used in literary studies as a count noun ('a reading'), it can also refer to the interpretive outcome of decoding. A text may yield alternative readings and may be designed to do so. (See also **hermeneutics**; **implied reader**; **ambiguity**.)

Realism Conventions that allow a text to appear to be written in a realist style and so create and depict a credible world, or the effect created by such a style; in the nineteenth-century novel the use of a **hierarchy of voices** graded in terms of their reliability, with the omniscient **narrator** considered the most reliable. The use of **forms** that enable a text to give the impression that it represents real **eventualities**.

Reality effect Creation, by means of a set of conventions, of the appearance of something as being real.

Received Pronunciation Often known as RP, the least regional form of British English pronunciation, traditionally considered the most accepted form. RP emerged during the nineteenth century as a non-regional prestige form, but continues to change, including in social status.

Register In linguistics and literary criticism, how the kind of language we use is affected by the context in which we use it, so that certain kinds of usage become conventionally associated with particular situations.

Repertoire As regards language use generally, range of styles a speaker is able to speak or write in, or **accents** he or she habitually uses. In dramatic performance and music, the stock of pieces that a performer or company is able to perform.

Representation   Act of making something present to an audience through description, portrayal, symbolization or other form of embodiment or enactment.

Resisting reader   Someone who chooses not to agree with statements made by the text and who produces an alternative reading strategy for the text.

Rhetoric   Study of the arts of persuasion. A rhetorical device is a way of using language or communication for the purpose of persuasion. Advertising as a persuasive discourse is full of rhetorical devices.

Rhyme scheme   Pattern of line-final rhymes in verse, such as AxAx to indicate that first and third lines rhyme but second and fourth do not, or ABABCC to indicate that first and third, second and fourth, and fifth and sixth lines rhyme.

Rhythm   Performed sequence of relatively strongly and relatively weakly stressed syllables. Rhythms are periodic when the pattern is regularly repeated.

Role doubling   Practice of using one actor to play two or more parts in a drama.

Schema   Structured set of assumptions in our minds about how things are done (laying the table, telling a story). Schemas are largely unconscious but nevertheless order our expectations and **inferences** when we interpret situations, events and texts. In jokes, literary composition and some kinds of behaviour, schemas are disrupted to draw attention to and possibly criticize them, or to create absurdity and humour.

Semantic field   Pair or larger set of words that belong to the same general area of meaning. For example, 'uncle, aunt, cousin, son, daughter' belong to the semantic field of 'kinship', while 'rain, drizzle, hail, snow, sleet' belong to the semantic field of 'precipitation'.

Shot   Minimal unit in film analysis traditionally consisting of a continuous strip of motion picture film, made up of a series of frames, that runs for an uninterrupted period of time. Shots may be classified in terms of degrees of closeness to the subject: close, medium or long. When a human figure is involved, a close shot will give head and shoulders, a medium shot will frame the figure from the waist upwards and a long shot will place the whole figure against a background.

Simile   Figure of speech in which one thing or idea or event is said to be similar to, or like, another thing, idea or event.

Situational irony   A **plot** device whose main feature is that the audience/reader knows more than the characters who are the victims of the irony; the irony is produced when the characters speak or act in a way that is contrary to how they would do if they knew what the audience/reader knows; the ironic situation may either be comic or tragic, depending on the circumstances, the outcome and our feelings towards the characters. (See also **dramatic irony**; **irony, structural irony**.)

Soliloquy   Speech by a character who is usually alone onstage and who speaks to him- or herself and/or to the audience.

Sonnet   **Lyric poem** of fourteen lines that conforms to a specific pattern of rhyme and metre. Typical **rhyme schemes** for the sonnet are abba abba cde cde (known as Italian or Petrarchan) or abab cdcd efef gg (known as English or Shakespearean); sometimes there is variation from these two patterns. The rhythm is typically **iambic pentameter**.

Sound symbolism   The meanings communicated by sounds. In general such meanings seem to be associated with specific sounds by convention or because of context. In the first case many examples of sound symbolism seem to be conventional associations of particular meanings with particular sounds. In the second case, where a specific sound or type of sound is very noticeable in a text, there is also an occasional tendency to associate the sound with the meaning of the text.

Speech event   Unit of analysis in investigating connections between verbal behaviour and its social setting. Beyond the form of the utterance itself, we can specify what kind of speaker is making the utterance, who to, when, where and for what purpose.

Speech situation   A text's speech situation may be worked out by asking 'who is speaking to whom?' The speech situation is characteristically different in different genres. In drama, characters speak to one another or, in soliloquy, to themselves and/or the audience. In **narrative**, characters speak to each other, but their speech is reported by a **narrator** (who addresses an **implied reader**). In lyric poetry, a poet or poetic speaker speaks to him- or herself or to a silent or absent person (or even an animal or object) who is part of the fictional situation represented in the poem. In Shelley's 'To a Skylark' (1820), for example, the speech situation consists of the poet (or a poetic speaker) addressing a skylark. The person or thing spoken to is called the **addressee** (the addressee is therefore distinguished from the **reader**, except in poems in which the speaker directly addresses the reader). Working out the speech situation is often the key to understanding a **lyric poem**.

Standardized Oral Form   Term used in anthropology (e.g. in the work of Jack Goody) to describe stories and lyrics presented in memorized and extensively improvised spoken performances, especially in societies where writing does not exist and so cannot be used to produce a script or text. (See also **oral literature**.)

Structuralism   Literary and cultural theory that emerged in France in the 1950s and 1960s, based on Ferdinand de Saussure's linguistics. Individual literary texts were held to be made possible and meaningful by a pre-existing literary system consisting of conventional techniques and devices, such as the conventions of genre and the general symbolic codes of a culture. The goal of **reading** was taken to be not so much to interpret an individual text as to study the literary system.

Structural or situational irony   Irony produced when a speaker or character says something sincerely but which is made ironic by the situation, usually because he or she lacks a vital piece of knowledge (available to the reader or audience) which would allow him or her to realize that what he or she has said is not a true view of the situation. This creates a structure in which the reader or audience sees the irony, while the character or speaker does not. (See also **situational irony**.)

Style   In literary studies, distinctive patterning of language associated with an **author**, movement or period amounting to a 'verbal fingerprint' or 'verbal trademark'.

Stylistics   Branch of linguistics devoted to the study of **style**. A set of techniques for analysing how language is used for expressive purposes (mainly in literary works, but also in adverts, jokes and other verbal forms).

Surrealism   Typified in visual arts by the work of Salvador Dali and René Magritte, surrealism strips ordinary objects of their normal significance by juxtaposing them in startling ways to create a new image that cuts across ordinary formal organization. Surrealist work often has a dream-like quality and is sometimes seen as an attack on conventional notions of reality.

Syllable   Group of sounds around a single salient sound such as a vowel or diphthong. The most salient sound is called the nucleus; the sounds before the nucleus are the onset, and the sounds after the nucleus are the coda.

Synecdoche   Figure of speech in which one thing or idea or event is spoken of by referring to a part of that thing, idea or event.

Tense   Grammatical distinction in linguistics used to indicate the potential of verb forms to signal the relative time of an action (e.g. 'she *smiles*' versus 'she *smiled*').

Tragedy   Literary or dramatic genre that represents actions that typically result in the death of the main **protagonist** or protagonists. From Classical

Greece up to the eighteenth century, the tragic protagonist was normally a man (sometimes a woman) of high birth in a situation of conflict (with him- or herself, with society, or with God or the gods); the outcome of the tragedy was the protagonist's fall and had serious consequences for the state. From roughly the eighteenth century onwards, more bourgeois or domestic tragedies emerged that focused on the tragic fate of middle-class characters. Since the mid-twentieth century, plays such as Arthur Miller's *The Death of a Salesman* (1949) have explored tragic possibilities in characters from 'ordinary' life.

Transitivity   Generally investigating transitivity involves analysis of who does what to whom. It is the analysis of who acts in a clause and who is acted upon by others. The analysis of these choices about how to represent an event can be extended throughout a text so that generalizations can be made about, for example, literary characters or about political actors in newspapers.

Verb   Traditionally understood as a part of speech that encodes action or predication; instances are italicized in the following example: She *was* happy. She *smiled*. Then she *turned* and *left*. A verb can have its shape altered to encode time (i.e. it can carry **tense**).

Verbal irony   Use of language where we do not literally mean what we say; instead we imply an attitude of disbelief towards the content of our utterance or writing. (See also **irony**; **situational irony**; **dramatic irony**.)

Verse   Text divided into sections (called 'lines') that have one or more of the following features: (1) there is rhyme at the end of the line; (2) there is a pause, or major syntactic break at the end of the line; (3) the line is structurally parallel to an adjacent line; (4) the line is of a certain length, counting **syllables** or stressed syllables (in which case it is metrical); and (5) when printed on the page, the line does not necessarily reach from one side of the page to the other, and may be followed by blank space. (See also **rhyme scheme**; **rhythm**; **accent**.)

References

Abrams, M.H. (1993) *A Glossary of Literary Terms*, 6th edn, New York and London: Harcourt Brace Jovanovich.

Aitchison, J. (2003) *Teach Yourself Linguistics*, Teach Yourself Series, London: Hodder.

Aristotle (1965) 'On the Art of Poetry', in T.S. Dorsh (ed.) *Aristotle, Horace, Longinus: Classical Literary Criticism*, Harmondsworth and New York: Penguin.

Aristotle (1996 [*c.*400 BC]) *Poetics*, trans. Malcolm Heath, Harmondsworth: Penguin.

Attridge, D. (1995) *Poetic Rhythm: An Introduction*, Cambridge: Cambridge University Press.

Auerbach, E. (1953) *Mimesis: The Representation of Reality in Western Literature*, Princeton, NJ: Princeton University Press.

Baker, N.L. and Huling, N. (2001) *A Research Guide for Undergraduate Students*, 5th edn, New York: MLA Publications.

Bakhtin, Mikhail (1981) 'Discourse in the Novel', trans. Caryl Emerson and Michael Holquist, in Vincent B. Leitch (ed.) (2001) *The Norton Anthology of Theory and Criticism*, London and New York: Norton.

Bal, M. (1985) *Narratology: Introduction to the Theory of Narrative*, Toronto: Toronto University Press.

Barber, C. (1976) *Early Modern English*, London: André Deutsch.

Barthes, R. (1968) 'The Death of the Author', in Vincent B. Leitch (ed.) (2001) *The Norton Anthology of Theory and Criticism*, New York and London: Norton.

Barthes, R. (1971) 'From Work to Text', in Vincent B. Leitch (ed.) (2001) *The Norton Anthology of Theory and Criticism*, New York and London: Norton.

Barthes, R. (1986) *The Rustle of Language*, Oxford: Blackwell.

Bate, J. (1970) *The Burden of the Past and the English Poet*, London: Chatto & Windus.

Berger, P. and Luckman, T. (1966) *The Social Construction of Reality*, Harmondsworth: Penguin.

Bergvall, V., Bing, J. and Fried, A. (eds) (1996) *Rethinking Language and Gender Research: Theory and Practice*, London: Longman.

Bloom, H. (1973) *The Anxiety of Influence*, Oxford: Oxford University Press.

Booth, W. (1961) *The Rhetoric of Fiction*, Chicago, IL: University of Chicago Press.

Bordwell, D. (1985) *Narration in the Fiction Film*, London: Methuen.

Branigan, E. (1984) *Point of View in the Cinema*, New York: Mouton.

Brecht, B. (1977) 'Against Georg Lukács', in T. Adorno, W. Benjamin, E. Bloch, B. Brecht and G. Lukács (eds) *Aesthetics and Politics*, London: New Left Books.

Briggs, K. (1970) *A Dictionary of British Folk Tales in the English Language*, London: Routledge and Kegan Paul.

Burgin, V. (1976) 'Art, Common Sense and Photography', in S. Hall and G. Evans (eds) (1999) *Visual Culture: The Reader*, London: Sage/Open University, pp. 41–50.

Burke, S. (ed.) (1995) *Authorship: From Plato to the Postmodern: A Reader*, Edinburgh: Edinburgh University Press.

Burke, S. (1998 [1992]) *The Death and Return of the Author: Criticism and Subjectivity in Barthes, Foucault and Derrida*, 2nd edn, Edinburgh: Edinburgh University Press.

Burton, D. (1982) 'Through Glass Darkly: Through Dark Glasses', in R. Carter (ed.) *Language and Literature: An Introductory Reader in Stylistics,* London: George Allen & Unwin, pp. 195–214.

Cameron, D. (1985) *Feminism and Linguistic Theory*, London: Macmillan.

Cameron, D. (1994) 'Words, Words, Words: The Power of Language', in S. Dunant (ed.) *The War of the Words: The Political Correctness Debate*, London: Virago, pp. 15–35.

Cameron, D. (1995) *Verbal Hygiene*, London: Routledge.

Caughie, J. (ed.) (1981) *Theories of Authorship: A Reader*, London: Routledge & Kegan Paul/British Film Institute.

Chatman, S.B. (1978) *Story and Discourse: Narrative Structure in Film and Prose Fiction*, Ithaca, NY and London: Cornell University Press.

Coward, R. (1986) 'This Novel Changes Lives: Are Women's Novels Feminist Novels?', in M. Eagleton (ed.) *Feminist Literary Theory: A Reader*, Oxford: Blackwell, pp. 155–60.

Coward, R. and Black, M. (1981) 'Linguistic, Social and Sexual Relations: A Review of Dale Spender's Man Made Language', in D. Cameron (ed.) (1990) *The Feminist Critique of Language*, London: Routledge.

Crowther, B. and Leith, D. (1995) 'Feminism, Language and the Rhetoric of Television Wildlife Programmes', in S. Mills (ed.) *Language and Gender: Interdisciplinary Perspectives*, London: Longman, pp. 207–26.

Crystal, D. (2005) *The Stories of English*, Harmondsworth: Penguin.

Culler, J. (1983) 'Reading as a Woman', in J. Culler, *On Deconstruction*, London: Routledge & Kegan Paul.

Culler, J. (2002) *Structuralist Poetics: Structuralism, Linguistics and the Study of Literature*, London: Routledge.

Culpeper, J. (1997) *History of English*, London, Routledge.

Duff, D. (ed.) (2000) *Modern Genre Theory*, London: Longman.

Dunant, S. (ed.) (1994) *The War of the Words: The Political Correctness Debate*, London: Virago.

Durant, A. and Fabb, N. (1990) *Literary Studies in Action*, London: Routledge.

Eisenstein, S. (1979a) 'The Cinematographic Principle and the Ideogram', in G. Mast and M. Cohen (eds) (1979) *Film Theory and Criticism,* Oxford: Oxford University Press, pp. 85–100.

Eisenstein, S. (1979b) 'A Dialectic Approach to Film Form', in G. Mast and M. Cohen (eds) *Film Theory and Criticism*, Oxford: Oxford University Press, pp. 101–22.

Eliot, T.S. (1919) 'Tradition and the Individual Talent', in Vincent B. Leitch (ed.) (2001) *The Norton Anthology of Theory and Criticism*, New York and London: Norton.

Eliot, T.S. (1922) '*The Waste Land*', in T.S. Eliot (2005) *Complete Poems and Plays*, London: Faber & Faber.

Erlich, V. (1969) *Russian Formalism: History – Doctrine*, The Hague: Mouton.

Fabb, N. (1997) *Linguistics and Literature*, Oxford: Blackwell.

Fabb, N. (2002) *Language and Literary Structure*, Cambridge: Cambridge University Press.

Fabb, N. (2005) *Sentence Structure*, 2nd edn, London: Routledge.

Fabb, N. and Durant, A. (2005) *How to Write Essays and Dissertations: A Guide for English Literature Students*, Harlow: Pearson.

Fabb, N. and Halle, M. (2007) *The Meter of a Poem*, Cambridge: Cambridge University Press.

Fairclough, N. (1989) *Language and Power*, Harlow: Longman.

Fairclough, N. (1992) *Discourse and Social Change*, London: Polity Press.

Fetterley, J. (1981) *The Resisting Reader: A Feminist Approach to American Fiction*, Bloomington, IN: Indiana University Press.

Finnegan, R. (1992) *Oral Traditions and the Verbal Arts: A Guide to Research Practices*, London: Routledge.

Finnegan, R. (2002) *Communicating: The Multiple Modes of Human Interconnection*, London: Routledge.

Foucault, M. (1970) *The Order of Things: An Archaeology of the Human Sciences*, London: Tavistock.

Foucault, M. (1978) *The History of Sexuality*, vol. 1, Harmondsworth: Penguin.

Foucault, M. (1989) *The Archaeology of Knowledge*, London: Routledge.

Fowler, R. (1986) *Linguistic Criticism*, Oxford: Oxford University Press.

Fox, J.J. (ed.) (1988) *To Speak in Pairs: Essays on the Ritual Languages of Eastern Indonesia*, Cambridge: Cambridge University Press.

Frye, N. (1957) *Anatomy of Criticism*, Princeton, NJ: Princeton University Press.

Fuller, J. (1972) *The Sonnet*, London: Methuen.

Furniss, T.E. and Bath, M. (2006) *Reading Poetry: An Introduction*, 2nd edn, London: Longman.

Fussell, P. (1979) *Poetic Meter and Poetic Form*, New York: McGraw-Hill.

Garvin, P. (ed. and trans.) (1964) *A Prague School Reader in Aesthetics, Literary Structure and Style*, Washington, DC: Georgetown University Press.

Giddings, R., Selby, K. and Wensley, C. (1990) *Screening the Novel: The Theory and Practice of Literary Dramatization*, London: Macmillan.

Gifford, T. (1999) *The Pastoral,* New Critical Idiom Series, London: Routledge.

Gilbert, S. and Gubar, S. (1979) *The Madwoman in the Attic*, New Haven, CT: Yale University Press.

Glucksberg, Sam (with Matthew S. McGlone) (2001) *Understanding Figurative Language: From Metaphors to Idioms*, Oxford and New York: Oxford University Press.

Hall, S. (1973) 'Encoding/Decoding', reprinted in S. Hall, D. Hobson, A. Lowe and P. Willis (eds) *Culture, Media, Language*, London: Hutchinson.

Halliday, M.A.K. (1978) *Language as Social Semiotic: The Social Interpretation of Language and Meaning*, London: Arnold.

Halliday, M.A.K. and Hasan, R. (1976) *Cohesion in English*, London: Longman.

Harner, J.L. (2002) *Literary Research Guide: An Annotated Listing of Reference Sources in English Literary Studies*, 4th edn, New York: MLA Publications.

Harrison, S. (2005) *Adaptations: From Short Story to Big Screen: 35 Great Stories That Have Inspired Great Films*, New York: Random House/Three Rivers Press.

Hobby, E. and White, C. (eds) (1991) *What Lesbians Do in Books*, London: Women's Press.

Holmes, J. and Meyerhoff, M. (eds) (2003) *Handbook of Language and Gender*, London: Blackwell.

Hutchinson, P. (1983) *Games Authors Play*, London: Methuen.

Irwin, William (ed.) (2002) *The Death and Resurrection of the Author?*, Westport, CT and London: Greenwood Press.

Jakobson, R. (1987) *Language in Literature*, Cambridge, MA: Belknap Press.

Jakobson, R. (1988) 'Linguistics and Poetics', in D. Lodge (ed.) *Modern Criticism and Theory: A Reader*, London: Longman, pp. 32–57.

Jeffers, R. and Lehiste, I. (1979) *Principles and Methods for Historical Linguistics*, Cambridge, MA: MIT Press.

Kachru, B. (ed.) (1982) *The Other Tongue: English Across Cultures*, Oxford: Pergamon.

Kaplan, C. (1986) 'Keeping the Color in *The Color Purple*', in *Sea Changes: Culture and Feminism*, London: Verso, pp. 176–87.

Kidd, V. (1971) 'A Study of the Images Produced Through the Use of the Male Pronoun as Generic', *Moments in Contemporary Rhetoric and Communication* 1: 25–30.

Kirkham, S. (1989) *How to Find Information in the Humanities*, London: Library Association.

Kövecses, Zoltán (2002) *Metaphor: A Practical Introduction*, Oxford and New York: Oxford University Press.

Lakoff, G. and Johnson, M. (1980) *Metaphors We Live By*, Chicago, IL: University of Chicago Press.

Lakoff, R. (1975) *Language and Woman's Place*, New York: Harper Colophon.

Laws, S. (1990) *Issues of Blood: The Politics of Menstruation*, Basingstoke: Macmillan.

Leech, G. (1969) *A Linguistic Guide to English Poetry*, London: Longman.

Leech, G. and Short, M. (1981) *Style in Fiction*, London: Longman.

Leitch, Vincent B. (ed.) (2001) *The Norton Anthology of Theory and Criticism*, New York and London: Norton.

Leith, D. (1983) *A Social History of English*, London: Routledge & Kegan Paul.

Leith, D. and Myerson, G. (1989) *The Power of Address*, London: Routledge.

Lemon, L.T. and Reis, M.J. (eds) (1965) *Russian Formalist Criticism: Four Essays*, Lincoln, NE: University of Nebraska Press.

Lennard, John and Luckhurst, Mary (2002) *The Drama Handbook: A Guide to Reading Plays*, Oxford: Oxford University Press.

Lodge, D. (1977) *The Modes of Modern Writing*, London: Edward Arnold.

Lodge, D. (1992) *The Art of Fiction*, Harmondsworth: Penguin.

Lukács, G. (1962) *The Historical Novel*, London: Merlin.

MacCabe, C. (1979) *James Joyce and the Revolution of the Word*, London: Macmillan.

MacCabe, C. (1981) 'Realism and the Cinema: Notes on Some Brechtian Theses', in T. Bennet, S. Boyd-Bowman, C. Mercer and J. Woollacott (eds) *Popular Television and Film*, London: Open University Press and BFI, pp. 216–35.

McCrum, R., Cran, W., and McNeil, R. (2002) *The Story of English*, London: Faber.

McFarlane, B. (1996) *Novel to Film*, Oxford: Oxford University Press.

Martin, E. (1997) 'The Egg and the Sperm: How Science has Constructed a Romance Based on Stereotypical Male–Female Roles', in L. Lamphere, H. Ragone and P. Zavella (eds) *Situated Lives: Gender and Culture in Everyday Life*, London: Routledge, pp. 85–99.

Miller, C. and Swift, K. (1979) *Words and Women*, Harmondsworth: Penguin.

Mills, J. (1989) *Womanwords*, London: Longman.

Mills, S. (1987) 'The Male Sentence', *Language and Communication* 7: 189–98.

Mills, S. (ed.) (1994) *Gendering the Reader*, Hemel Hempstead: Harvester Wheatsheaf.

Mills, S. (1996) *Feminist Stylistics*, London: Routledge.

Mills, S. and Pearce, L. (1996) *Feminist Readings/Feminists Reading*, 2nd edn, Hemel Hempstead: Harvester.

Montgomery, M. (1995) *An Introduction to Language and Society*, 2nd edn, London: Routledge.

Muecke, D.C. (1970) *Irony and the Ironic*, London: Methuen.

Mulvey, L. (1975) 'Visual Pleasure and Narrative Cinema', *Screen*, 16(3): 6–18. Reprinted in L. Mulvey (1989), *Visual and Other Pleasures*, Bloomington, IN: Indiana University Press.

Mulvey, L. (1981) 'Visual Pleasure and Narrative Cinema', in T. Bennett, S. Boyd-Bowman, C. Mercer and J. Woollacott (eds) *Popular Television and Film*, London: Open University/BFI, pp. 206–16.

Murray, J.H. (1997) *Hamlet on the Holodeck: The Future of Narrative in Cyberspace*, Cambridge, MA: MIT Press.

Newton-de Molina, D. (ed.) (1976) *On Literary Intention*, Edinburgh: Edinburgh University Press.

O'Barr, W.F. and Atkins, B.K. (1982) 'Women's Speech or Powerless Speech', in S. McConnell-Ginet, R. Borker and N. Furman (eds) *Women and Language in Literature and Society*, New York: Praeger.

Onega Jaén, S. and Garcia Landa, J.A. (eds) (1996) *Narratology: An Introduction*, London: Longman.

Ong, W.J (2002) *Orality and Literacy: The Technologizing of the Word*, London: Routledge.

Opie, I. and Opie, P. (1951) *The Oxford Dictionary of Nursery Rhymes*, Oxford: Oxford University Press.

Pauwels, A. (1998) *Women Changing Language*, London: Longman.

Pickering, Kenneth (2003) *Studying Modern Drama*, Palgrave Macmillan.

Preminger, Alex and Brogan, T.V.F. (eds) (1993) *The New Princeton Encyclopedia of Poetry and Poetics*, Princeton, NJ: Princeton University Press.

Propp, Vladimir (1968) *The Morphology of the Folktale*, Austin, TX: University of Texas Press.

Renza, L.A. (1990) 'Influence', in F. Lentricchia and T. McLaughlin (eds) *Critical Terms for Literary Study*, Chicago, IL: Chicago University Press, pp. 186–202.

Richards, I.A. (1936) *Philosophy of Rhetoric*, Oxford: Oxford University Press.

Rifkin, B. (1994) *Semiotics of Narration in Film and Prose Fiction*, New York: Peter Lang.

Rimmon-Kenan, S. (1983) *Narrative Fiction: Contemporary Poetics*, London: Methuen.

Sacks, S. (ed.) (1979) *On Metaphor*, Chicago, IL: University of Chicago Press.

Said, E. (1993) 'Jane Austen and Empire', in E. Said, *Culture and Imperialism*, London: Chatto & Windus, pp. 95–115.

Scholes, R. (1982) *Semiotics and Interpretation*, New Haven, CT: Yale University Press.

Shklovsky, V. (1917) 'Art as Technique', in D. Lodge (ed.) (1988) *Modern Criticism and Theory: A Reader*, London: Longman, pp. 16–30.

Shklovsky, V. (1921) 'Sterne's *Tristram Shandy*: Stylistic Commentary', in L.T. Lemon and M.J. Reis (eds) (1965) *Russian Formalist Criticism: Four Essays*, Lincoln, NE: University of Nebraska Press.

Shohat, E. and Stam, R. (1994) *Unthinking Eurocentrism: Multiculturalism and the Media*, London: Routledge.

Showalter, E. (1977) *A Literature of Their Own*, Princeton, NJ: Princeton University Press.

Simpson, P. (1993) *Language, Ideology and Point of View*, London: Routledge.

Simpson, P. (1997) *Language Through Literature: An Introduction*, London: Routledge.

Simpson, P. (2003) *On the Discourse of Satire*, Amsterdam: John Benjamins.

Simpson, P. (2004) *Stylistics*, London: Routledge.

Spender, D. (1980) *Man Made Language*, London: Routledge & Kegan Paul.

Sperber, D. and Wilson, D. (1995) *Relevance: Communication and Cognition*, 2nd edn, Oxford: Blackwell.

Spiegel, A. (1976) *Fiction and the Camera Eye: Visual Consciousness in Film and the Modern Novel*, Charlottesville, VA: University Press of Virginia.

Stacey, J. (1994) *Star Gazing: Hollywood Cinema and Female Spectatorship*, London: Routledge.

St John Butler, Lance (1999) *Registering the Difference: Reading Literature Through Register*, Manchester: Manchester University Press; New York: St Martin's Press.

Tannen, D. (1991) *You Just Don't Understand: Women and Men in Conversation*, London: Virago.

Thompson, J.B. (1995) *The Media and Modernity: A Social Theory of the Media*, London: Polity Press.

Toolan, M. (2001) *Narrative: A Critical Linguistic Introduction*, 2nd edn, London: Routledge.

Uspensky, B. (1973) *A Poetics of Composition,* Berkeley, CA: University of California Press.

Van Zoonan, L. (1994) *Feminist Media Studies*, London: Sage.

Voloshinov, V. (1973) *Marxism and the Philosophy of Language*, New York: Seminar Press.

Wagner, Geoffrey (1975) *The Novel and the Cinema*, Rutherford, NJ: Fairleigh Dickinson University Press.

Wallis, Mick and Shepherd, Simon (1998) *Studying Plays*, London: Arnold; New York: Oxford University Press.

Watt, I. (1972) *The Rise of the Novel*, Harmondsworth: Penguin.

Widdowson, H. (1975) *Stylistics and the Teaching of Literature*, London: Longman.

Widdowson, H. (1992) *Practical Stylistics: An Approach to Poetry*, Oxford: Oxford University Press.

Williams, R. (1966) *Modern Tragedy*, London: Chatto & Windus.

Williams, R. (1985) *The Country and the City*, London: The Hogarth Press.

Williams, R. (1988) *Keywords: A Vocabulary of Culture and Society*, London: Collins.

Wimsatt, W.K. and Beardsley, M.C. (1946) 'The Intentional Fallacy', in D. Lodge (ed.) (1972) *Twentieth Century Literary Criticism*, Harlow: Longman, pp. 334–44.

Wimsatt, W.K. and Beardsley, M.C. (1949) 'The Affective Fallacy', in D. Lodge (ed.) (1972) *20th Century Criticism*, Harlow: Longman, pp. 334–44.

Woolf, V. (1979) 'Women and Writing', in D. Cameron (ed.) (1990) *The Feminist Critique of Language*, London: Routledge.

Worthen, W.B. (2000) *The Harcourt Brace Anthology of Drama*, 3rd edn, Boston, MA: Heinle.

Subject index

Italic entries indicate a cross-reference to indexed names and texts discussed. **Bold** numbers indicate entry in Glossary.

Index of names and texts discussed

Italic cross-references refer to subject index. **Bold** numbers indicate entry in Glossary.

eBooks – at www.eBookstore.tandf.co.uk

A library at your fingertips!

eBooks are electronic versions of printed books. You can store them on your PC/laptop or browse them online.

They have advantages for anyone needing rapid access to a wide variety of published, copyright information.

eBooks can help your research by enabling you to bookmark chapters, annotate text and use instant searches to find specific words or phrases. Several eBook files would fit on even a small laptop or PDA.

NEW: Save money by eSubscribing: cheap, online access to any eBook for as long as you need it.

Annual subscription packages

We now offer special low-cost bulk subscriptions to packages of eBooks in certain subject areas. These are available to libraries or to individuals.

For more information please contact webmaster.ebooks@tandf.co.uk

We're continually developing the eBook concept, so keep up to date by visiting the website.

www.eBookstore.tandf.co.uk